Advances in Spatial Science

Springer

Berlin
Heidelberg
New York
Barcelona
Hong Kong
London
Milan
Paris
Tokyo

Titles in the Series

Zoltan J. Acs · Henri L.F. de Groot
Peter Nijkamp

Editors

The Emergence
of the Knowledge
Economy

A Regional Perspective

With 52 Figures
and 86 Tables

 Springer

Prof. Dr. Zoltan J. Acs
University of Baltimore
Merrick School of Business
1420 North Charles Street
Baltimore, MD 21201, USA

Dr. Henri L. F. de Groot
Prof. Dr. Peter Nijkamp

Free University Amsterdam
Department of Spatial Economics
De Boelelaan 1105
1081HV Amsterdam, The Netherlands

ISBN 3-540-43722-3 Springer-Verlag Berlin Heidelberg New York

Library of Congress Cataloging-in-Publication Data applied for
Die Deutsche Bibliothek – CIP-Einheitsaufnahme
The Emergence of the Knowledge Economy: A Regional Perspective;
with 86 Tables / Zoltan J. Acs ... Ed. – Berlin; Heidelberg; New York; Barcelona; Hong Kong;
London; Milan; Paris; Tokyo: Springer, 2002
    (Advances in Spatial Science)
    ISBN 3-540-43722-3

Springer-Verlag Berlin Heidelberg New York
a member of BertelsmannSpringer Science + Business Media GmbH

http://www.springer.de

© Springer-Verlag Berlin Heidelberg 2002
Printed in Germany

The use of general descriptive names, registered names, trademarks, etc. in this publication does not imply, even in the absence of a specific statement, that such names are exempt from the relevant protective laws and regulations and therefore free for general use.

Cover design: Erich Kirchner, Heidelberg

SPIN 10881539   42/2202-5 4 3 2 1 0 – Printed on acid-free paper

Preface

Modern economic development is to an important extent determined and driven by the emergence of the knowledge economy. Knowledge has in recent years become a key driver for growth of regions and nations. Access to knowledge is generally recognised as a key condition for innovative activities in our modern space-economy. Consequently, also the creation and dissemination of new knowledge may act as a critical success factor for regional and national development. Knowledge has, however, important characteristics of a fluid good, which gets easily obsolete. It also has various features of both public and private goods. These characteristics of knowledge prompt a wide range of questions regarding knowledge research and knowledge policy. This is therefore a timely period to take stock of the importance of knowledge in regional development.

This book resulted from a series of conferences in the last few years organised by the Regional Science Association. It illustrates some of the most recent developments in the research fields of knowledge, innovation, and regional development. This research field addresses the fundamental question why some regions grow fast while others stagnate. All papers have in common that they aim at combining insights from various fields of research that have so far largely been developed in isolation, namely the new growth theory, the new economic geography and the new innovation theory. The papers aim at empirically operationalising the rich concepts developed in these theories.

We are grateful to Frans Boekema, Maarten Cornet, Marina van Geenhuizen, Geoffrey Hewings, Heli Koski, Ed Malecki, Richard Nahuis, Jacques Poot, and several contibutors to this book for thoroughly reviewing the papers included in the book. Their useful suggestions and remarks have substantially improved the individual papers as well as their mutual coherence.

In editing a book like this one, editors heavily rely on co-operation of the authors as well as the professional guidance by the publisher. We are grateful to the authors for both their patience as well as their co-operation in finalising this book. The people at Springer have also been very co-operative and helpful in preparing the final version of this book and provided useful and detailed comments on the manuscript, which significantly improved the quality.

Zoltan Acs, Henri de Groot and Peter Nijkamp
Baltimore and Amsterdam, April 2002

Contents

1 Knowledge, Innovation and Regional Development

Zoltan J. Acs[1], Henri L.F. de Groot[2] and Peter Nijkamp[2]

[1] University of Baltimore, Baltimore, MD, USA; [2] Free University, Amsterdam, The Netherlands

1.1 Introduction

For the past three decades the world has been fascinated by developments in "Silicon Valley." The developments we have in mind are the ubiquitous creation of new product innovations in this part of the world. The valley has had an unprecedented record of success in the introduction of computers, software, semiconductors, telecommunications equipment and a host of other innovations that have come to dominate modern information technology. While this is not the only region of the world that has experienced an outflow of innovations, the truth of the matter is that regions that are innovative appear to grow faster (Suarez-Villa 2000). There is a growing consensus that innovation is the key driving force behind regional economic growth, standards of living, and international competitiveness (Acs 2002).

Modern information technology – The Information Age – begins with the invention of the transistor, a semiconductor device that acts as an electrical switch and encodes information in binary form. The first transistor was constructed at Bell labs in 1947 and won the Nobel Prize in Physics in 1956. The next major milestone in information technology was the co-invention of the integrated circuit by Jack Kirby of Texas Instruments in 1958 and Robert Noyce of Fairchild Semiconductor in 1959. The introduction of the Personal Computer (PC) by IBM in 1981 was a watershed event in the development of information technologies. The sale of Intel's 8086-8088 microprocessor to IBM in 1978 for incorporation into the PC was a major business breakthrough for Intel. In 1981, IBM licensed the MS-DOS operating system from Microsoft Corporation founded by Bill Gates. Semiconductors are also an important input into telecommunications and communications technology and are crucial for the rapid development and diffusion of the Internet.

Since 1995, capital investment in the United States has significantly increased, and investment in information technologies has accounted for at least half of this investment. According to Jorgenson (2001, p. 2), "The development and deployment of information technology is the foundation of the American Growth resurgence. A mantra of the 'new economy' – *faster, better, cheaper* – captures the speed of technological change and product improvement in semiconductors and the precipitous and continuous fall in semiconductor prices. The price decline has been transmitted to the prices of products that rely heavily on semiconductor technology like computers and telecommunications equipment." The investment in information technologies provided a surge to productivity increases and economic growth. Investment in telecommunications infrastructure, computers and software can lead to economic growth in two ways. First, investing in information technology goods does itself lead to growth because its products lead to increases in demand for the goods and services used in their production. These products appear in Gross Domestic Product as investments. Second, Gross Domestic Product also includes the services of information technology products consumed by households and governments. For example, as the telecommunications infrastructure improves, the cost of doing business falls and output will increase for individual firms, sectors and regions. There is a significant positive causal link between telecommunications infrastructure and economic growth for 21 OECD countries over 20 years, especially when a critical mass of telecommunications infrastructure is present (Roller and Waverman 2001).

The title of this book, and others like it, seems to imply that there is something new about growth being based on knowledge, as if knowledge is more important today than in the past. This may be true but the idea may be misleading as well.[1] It has long been the consensus among economists who have studied the problem that long-term growth is always based on the growth of technical and organisational capabilities (Chandler 2000). Every era of rapid sustained growth has been one in which new knowledge transformed peoples' lives. The information revolution we are now living through is dramatically raising the premium on particular kinds of knowledge and skill, while rendering others obsolete (Hobijn and Jovanovic 2001).[2]

According to Howitt (1996), what is new about knowledge, from the economist's point of view, is that we are now beginning to incorporate it into our

---

[1] It is worth noting that high-technology industry accounts for nearly 22% of value of world trade in manufacturing, rising at a rate of 10% between 1991 and 1997 (Archibugi and Coco 2001). If to this we add knowledge-intensive services, a further 50% of value for 1997 is explained (Dunning 2000). Thus, knowledge-intensive goods account for at least 70% of the value of world trade, and this is overwhelmingly situated in cities.

[2] Each of the last three industrial revolutions was characterised by a revolution that made the transportation of both raw material and finished goods to the market cheaper. During the first industrial revolution (1780–1830), a system of canals in England made possible the transportation of goods at a fraction of previous cost. During the second industrial revolution (1830–1850), the railways provided cheap continent wide transportation in England, Germany and the United States. During the third industrial revolution (1920–1940), the automobile, truck and aeroplane made transportation of goods and people inexpensive. The fourth industrial revolution now under way also has as one of its integral parts a transportation revolution. However, it is a revolution not in the transportation of goods, but of information.

framework of analysis. Even more important we are doing this not as an extraneous outside influence, but as one of the main unknowns whose evolution we seek to explain as the outcome of economic forces. Although many of the ideas of the new growth theory go back to writers such as Schumpeter, it is only with the work of Romer (1986) and Lucas (1988) that economists were able to incorporate these ideas into simple dynamic, stochastic, general equilibrium models.

One of the hallmarks of the new growth theory is that it allows a broader discussion of regional issues. While the Kaldorian approach to growth, also pointed to a need for regional economic policies, the new endogenous growth theories suggest that such policies would need to be more supply-oriented, focusing on innovation, infrastructure and ecological sustainability, rather then the traditional tools of demand stimuli through lower interest rates and subsidies (Nijkamp and Poot 1987). While the endogenous growth theories give us new insights into the role of knowledge in economic growth, they only hint at how knowledge creates innovations.

1.2 Theoretical Background

Recently several books have appeared that try to identify the underlying processes and interconnections that govern regional innovation (Braczyk et al. 1998; de la Mothe and Pacquet 1999; Ratti et al. 1997; Debresson et al. 1996; Acs 2000). While these books take different approaches, rely on different methodologies, use different data, and define the unit of analysis differently, they all suggest that there is something fundamental at work at the regional level. While these works are all interesting, illuminating pieces of the regional innovation puzzle, none of them – neither singularly, nor in concert – answers the bigger question of why some regions are more innovative than others.

If we are to understand why some regions grow and others stagnate there are three fundamental questions that need to be answered.[3] First, "Why and when does economic activity become concentrated in a few regions leaving others relatively underdeveloped?" Second, "What role does technological change plays in regional economic growth?" Third, "How does technological advance occur, and what are the key processes and institutions involved?" Answers to these questions can be found in: The New Economic Geography (e.g., Krugman 1991), The New Growth Theory (initiated by Romer 1986; Lucas 1988), and The New Economics of Innovation (e.g., Nelson 1993).

The *new economic geography* answers the question why economic activity concentrates in certain regions but not others, but leaves out innovation and economic growth (see, e.g., Krugman 1999; Fujita et al. 1999). The contribution of Krugman's theory on economic concentration is not in its elements, but in the way the system was put together. It had already been well known in economic geography and regional economics that decreasing transportation costs, economies of

---

[3] This section draws heavily on Acs and Varga (2002b).

scale or increasing demand favour agglomeration. However, the way Krugman put these elements together in a general equilibrium model is novel. The model provides a case for the treatments of spatial issues in the way economists are accustomed to. The model provides a technique to analyse geographical concentration of economic activities as being induced by some initial combinations of basic parameters. However, the model in its current form does not seem to be suitable for modelling technology-led regional economic growth for at least two reasons. First, Krugman's definite insistence on avoiding modelling the role of technological externalities in regional economic growth prevents the model from being applicable in innovation-led regional development since spillovers and innovation networks are in the core of this type of development as exemplified in the literature on innovation systems. Second, while the model is very strong in working out the characterisation of specific initial combinations of parameters favouring geographical concentration, it is weak in actually modelling the growth process.

The *new growth theory* explains the causes of economic growth or – more precisely – technological progress. We refer to, for example, Grossman and Helpman (1991), Barro and Sala-i-Martin (1995) and Aghion and Howitt (1998) for extensive surveys of what has been achieved in this field. A principal assumption in the early theories of endogenous growth is that for creating new sets of technological knowledge the total stock of knowledge is freely accessible for anyone engaged in research. However, it is increasingly recognised that new technological knowledge (the most valuable type of knowledge in innovation) has important elements of tacitness and firm specificity (see, for example, Dosi, 1988). Furthermore, it has convincingly been shown that the accessibility of knowledge is bounded by geographic proximity in the growing literature of geographic knowledge spillovers (Jaffe 1989; Acs et al. 1994; Anselin et al. 1997; Varga 1998, 2000) and innovation systems (Saxenian 1994; Braczyk et al. 1998; Sternberg 1999; Acs 2000). The relevance of these phenomena is increasingly recognised in recent endogenous growth theories that address the relevance of tacit knowledge (e.g., Smulders and van de Klundert 1995; de Groot and Nahuis 2002), conditional knowledge spillovers (e.g., Benhabib and Spiegel 1994), and understanding the process of technology adoption instead of technology development (e.g., Jovanovic 1997).

Similar to the case of relaxing the neoclassical assumption of equal availability of technological opportunities in all countries of the world, a relaxation of the assumption that knowledge is evenly distributed across space *within* countries seems also to be necessary (Acs and Varga 2002b). The non-excludable part of the total stock of knowledge seems to be correctly classified. It is assumed to have two portions: a perfectly accessible part consisting of already established knowledge elements (obtainable via scientific publications, patent applications etc.) and a novel, tacit element, accessible by interactions among actors in the innovation system (Dosi 1988). While the first part is available without restrictions, accessibility of the second one is bounded by the nature of interactions among actors in a "system of innovation" (Oinas and Malecki 1999).

The *new economics of innovation* while explaining the institutional arrangements in the innovation process leaves out regional issues and economic growth. The systems of innovation approach provides a conceptual framework that many scholars and policymakers consider useful for the analysis of innovation. Although the systems of innovation approach is not considered to be a formal and established theory, its development has been influenced by different theories of innovation such as interactive learning theories and evolutionary theories. In recent years, efforts have been made to percolate general theoretical and empirical observations from this literature up into a conceptual framework capable of guiding policy. This framework has loosely been organised around the idea of a "national system of innovation."

The concept of a "national" innovation system may be problematic. Krugman has suggested that as economies become less constrained by national frontiers, (as globalisation spreads) they become more geographically specialised. Important elements of the process of innovation tend to become regional rather than national. Some of the largest corporations are weakening their ties to their home country and are spreading their innovation activities to source different regional systems of innovation. Regional networks of firms are creating new forms of learning and production. These changes are important and challenge the traditional role of "national systems of innovation" (see Fuchs, Chap. 14 of this volume).

According to Acs and Varga (2002b) each one of the above three approaches has its strengths and weaknesses that can be integrated to develop an appropriate model of technology-led regional economic development by channelling the systems of innovation literature into a more general regional economic growth problem. A specific combination of the Krugmanian theory of initial conditions for spatial concentration of economic activities with the Romerian theory of endogenous economic growth complemented with a systematic representation of interactions among the actors of Nelson's innovation system could be a way of developing an appropriate model of technology-led regional economic development. The central element of the model could be the "regional knowledge production equation" distilled from the predominantly empirical literature of innovation networks as presented in the literature of the new economics of innovation (Varga 1998).

In the traditional model of the knowledge production function firms exogenously exist and then engage in the pursuit of new economic knowledge as an input into the process of generating innovative activity. However, the knowledge production function has been found to hold most strongly at broader levels of aggregation. Where the relationship becomes less compelling is at the desegregated microeconomic level of enterprises, establishments, or even lines of business. For example, while Acs and Audretsch (1990) found that the simple correlation between R&D inputs and innovative output was 0.84 for four-digit standard industrial classification manufacturing industries in the United States, it was only about 0.40 among the largest U.S. corporations.

The model of the knowledge production function becomes even less compelling in view of the evidence by Acs and Audretsch (1988) that entrepreneurial firms are the engine of innovative activity in some high-technology industries, which raises the question, "Where do new and small firms get the innovation-producing inputs, that is, the knowledge?" One answer proposed by Audretsch (1995) is that, although the model of the knowledge production function may still be valid, the implicitly assumed unit of observation – at the level of the firm –

may be less valid. The reason why the knowledge production function holds more closely for more aggregated degrees of observation may be that investment in R&D and other sources of new knowledge spills over for economic exploitation by third-party firms.

The issue of knowledge spillovers has led to a large literature on what has become known as the *appropriability problem*. The underlying issue revolves around how firms that invest in the creation of new economic knowledge can best appropriate the economic returns from that knowledge (Arrow 1962). Audretsch proposed shifting the unit of observation away from exogenously assumed firms to individuals – agents with endowments of new economic knowledge. When the lens is shifted away from focusing upon the firm as the relevant unit of observation to individual entrepreneurs, the question becomes, "How can economic agents with a given endowment of new knowledge best appropriate the returns from that knowledge?" As Audretsch himself suggested (1995, p. 48) we "...propose shifting the unit of observation away from exogenously assumed firms to individuals – agents confronted with new knowledge and the decision whether and how to act upon that new knowledge." This question is at the heart of modern entrepreneurship research (Shane and Venkataraman 2000). Acs and Armington (2002) find evidence that regions that have more entrepreneurial activity are more competitive and grow faster.

Many of the chapters in this book employ modern spatial econometric analysis. This development reflects some really significant advances over often purely descriptive work. Using state of the art estimation techniques, this volume empirically investigates the emergence of the knowledge economy in the late 20th Century. New knowledge and the knowledge base are both inputs into the process of endogenous technological change. The chapters in this volume examine aspects of the relationship between knowledge inputs and innovative outputs in the information, computer and telecommunications sector (ICT) of the economy. The importance of the ICT sector is that it has created prime conditions for entrepreneurial discovery, the pursuit of opportunity and innovation. Innovations in the ICT sector made the information age possible by enabling major reductions in transaction costs across most processes in society. This sector is composed of a wide range of products and service technologies. In a fundamental sense, the global economy includes the fusion of these ICT components into a local, regional, national and global infrastructure. This book examines the impact of innovation in the information technology sector at the regional level.

1.3 Concepts and Measurement

The papers come in four groups. The first group deals with the problem that arises from the lack of a theoretical background for understanding the knowledge economy at the regional level. The issues focus on innovation, entrepreneurship and measurement. While these papers do not resolve the fundamental problems involved in dealing with knowledge they help to identify important avenues for further research, which are to some extent picked up in subsequent contributions in this book.

The first paper by Camagni and Capello presents a review of the literature on the concept of the milieu innovateur, and "translates" some theoretical concepts into testable propositions. The major contribution of the authors is an attempt to measure milieu effects in a quantitative way, through the help of econometric and statistical techniques. Up to now, in fact, empirical analyses witnessing the existence of milieu effects have been of a qualitative nature. Among all milieu effects underlined by the GREMI theory (Ratti et al. 1997) the paper focuses the attention on the concept of collective learning. The paper provides evidence that collective learning is a way of increasing factor productivity and of supporting product innovation in small firms, which are spatially clustered.

The next paper by Masurel, van Montfort and Nijkamp presents new empirical results from a study on critical success factors in the entrepreneurial innovation process. Based on an extensive literature survey, a taxonomy of 14 success factors is identified. In a survey questionnaire among Dutch SMEs a total of 50 features of these critical success factors is investigated. The resulting multivariate data set is analyzed by means of a separate factor analysis per critical success factor. The results appear to be illuminating in that entrepreneurship is perceived as the most prominent crucial success factor in the SME innovation process. This result turns out to be rather robust after a sensitivity analysis by distinguishing various segmentations in their sample: manufacturing vs. service firms, entrepreneurs vs. managers, real vs. less innovative firms, and smaller vs. larger firms.

The paper by Suarez-Villa provides a broad, macro-level perspective on the relationship between network structure, inter-firm alliances and the development of research linkages. As innovation becomes increasingly important for survival, many firms find it essential to engage in alliances and networks to obtain or benefit from new knowledge. Indications are that alliances can be most effective when they occur within networks that can support research unit-to-research unit linkages where new knowledge can be exchanged, or ideas are cross-fertilised to produce innovations. Networked alliances and research unit-to-research unit linkages can therefore become important vehicles for internalising or integrating innovation in research-intensive firms. Such alliances are becoming more important as firms try to meet the challenges posed by rapid technological change and global competition.

Next Ridder, van Montfort and Kleinknecht estimate the fixed costs of the introduction of new products. They examine two indicators of innovative output, (1) sales of products 'new to the firm' and (2) sales of products 'new to the industry'. They estimate fixed cost thresholds using data from the Dutch part of the Community Innovation Survey (CIS) from 1992. The outcomes inform us about factors that impede or promote innovation. Growth of demand has a positive impact on sales of imitative and innovative products. The most important factor to decrease the fixed costs of introduction of new products is R&D collaboration, pointing at the relevance of organisational factors for understanding innovative behaviour.

The paper by Lever focuses on the challenge faced by urban regions of the developed word from increasing globalisation. The patterns of production and trade in manufacturing goods have shifted towards a new international division of labour in which multinational enterprises have sought low-wage manual workers. Against this background the developed nations have been required to identify in which sectors or clusters of activities they retain a competitive advantage, and how this competitive advantage can be sustained through knowledge policies.

Building on the previous paper, the final paper in this section, by Huovari, Kangasharju and Alanen, constructs an index to measure regional variations in competitiveness. Regional competitiveness is defined as an ability of regions to perpetuate and attract mobile production factors. The index contains available statistical indicators that approximate regional variations in human capital, innovative potential, agglomeration and accessibility. They find that the index is highly correlated with traditional long-term indicators of economic well being, such as per capita GDP and personal income. However, the association between the index and short-term outcome indicators, such as change in production, employment and population is clearly lower than that in the long-term indicators.

1.4 Knowledge Spillovers and University Research

Knowledge spillovers have been traditionally identified with those aspects of research and development externalities in which ideas discovered within any given research project affect the productivity of other projects. The basic idea is that the creation of new knowledge by one firm has positive external effects on the knowledge production activities of other firms, either because knowledge cannot be kept secret or because patents do not guarantee full protection from imitation. A second type of knowledge spillovers originates from production activities. The character of the externality stems from the fact that the protection of proprietary knowledge is incomplete. This is clearly the case with university research.

The paper by Fischer and Varga sheds some light on the issue of geographically mediated knowledge spillovers from university research activities in high-tech industries in Austria. Knowledge spillovers occur because knowledge created by a university is typically not contained within that institution, and thereby creates value for others. It is assumed that knowledge production in the high-technology sectors essentially depends on two major sources of knowledge: the university research that represents the potential pool of knowledge spillovers and R&D performed by the high-tech sectors themselves. Using district-level data and employing spatial econometric tools, evidence is found of university research spillovers that transcend the geographic scale of the political district in Austria. It is shown that geographic boundedness of the spillovers is linked to a decay effect.

The next paper by Acs, FitzRoy and Smith uses data from 37 American cities and 6 high-technology groupings to present estimates of University R&D spillovers on employment while controlling for sample selection bias, wages, prior innovations and state fixed effects. Wages and employment are strongly positively related, which can be explained in various ways. In particular these results are consistent with increasing returns to scale and long-run growth. Consistent with studies showing R&D spillover effects on innovation at the city level, we find robust evidence that university R&D is a statistically significant determinant of city high technology employment and some evidence for employment effect of innovation. Surprisingly we find no support for the relevance of human capital on high technology employment.

The final paper in this section, by Fromhold and Schartinger, specifically looks at the issue of regional relevance on sub-national levels of analysis. It examines the question, "How can the role of universities as agents of technology transfer to nearby firms adequately be assessed, relating to the common quest of local politicians to render resident academic institutions major contributors to regional innovation systems?" First, a general methodological framework is presented which elucidates the set of indicators that is necessary for appraising the knowledge-intensive interaction of universities with regional firms. It emphasises that, in addition to data on collaboration projects themselves, certain structural aspects determining the provision of suitable academic know-how and the regional economic receptiveness for those transfers ought to be included.

1.5 The ICT Sector and Regional Development

The third group of chapters deals with the sector of the economy that is particularly central to knowledge-based growth, namely information, computers and telecommunications. This sector, as pointed out in Sect. 1.1, undertakes a sizeable fraction of all R&D spending in the economy. The resulting innovations affect the efficiency of the entire economy, since communication is vital for linking the whole economy together. Communication networks are, of course, rife with externalities and spillovers characteristic of the growth process. Moreover, the telecommunication sector is at the heart of the information communication revolution that underlies technological change.

The first chapter in this section by Stough and Kulkarni examines the knowledge needs of entrepreneurs in a regional context with particular emphasis on the information, computers and telecommunications sector. The chapter begins by clarifying the basic concepts. This is followed by the introduction of the entrepreneurial fountain as a model of the entrepreneurial milieu and as a framework for examining the factors that influence the expansion and contraction of knowledge and entrepreneurial activity. The role that knowledge plays in entrepreneurial discovery and the exploitation of opportunity is examined, and the implications of this are presented.

The next chapter by Norton looks back on the innovations introduced by a handful of entrepreneurs, typically from the South and West, as factors eroding AT&T's monopoly position, both before and after the formal 1984 break-up of the Bell System. Parallels and contrasts are drawn between the decentralising effects of innovations in telecommunications and in the computer industry. As symbolised by Supreme Court rulings on the same day in 1982, IBM's decline occurred without formal governmental action, while AT&T's reflected both anti-trust rulings and competition from younger firms in the South and West. In each industry, the prodigious patent performance of the two established giants proved inadequate to the task of delivering radical innovation. A further comparison may be made with Europe, where Ericsson and Nokia have proved more innovative than the former chartered monopolies of larger countries in the region.

The chapter by Karlsson and Klaesson deals with the development of the Information and Communication Technologies sector in Sweden during the 1990s. They examine what characterises this sector and, in particular, investigate the spatial development of the sector. The question posed in this paper is, "What factors determine the spatial dynamics of the ICT sector?" In doing so a division into two sub sectors are made, i.e., the ICT manufacturing sub-sector and the ICT services sub-sector. They analyse such features as employment, industrial organisation, and share of university graduates employed. These features entail such factors as the spatial distribution of the well-educated workforce, accessibility to transport infrastructure, and economies of agglomeration.

The final chapter in this section, by Fuchs, argues that a successful medium- and long-term development of regional economic areas is dependent on a combination of regional and global ties. The specific combination of both kinds of ties is crucial. The paper develops an intermediary position between the supporters of a regionalisation and a globalisation thesis. The paper first recapitulates the regionalisation and globalisation thesis and characterises the strengths and weaknesses of regional and global ties. Then the different kinds of regional and global ties and their meaning for the development of economic areas in general and especially for multimedia clusters are discussed.

1.6 Regional Case Studies

In recent years, efforts have been made to percolate general theoretical and empirical observations from systems of innovation literature up into a conceptual framework capable of guiding policy and loosely organised around the idea of a "national system of innovation". The concept of a "national" innovation system may be problematic. As economies become less constrained by national frontiers, (as globalisation spreads) they become more geographically specialised. As pointed out above, important elements of the process of innovation tend to become regional rather than national. Some of the largest corporations are weakening their ties to their home country and are spreading their innovation activities to source different regional systems of innovation. Regional networks of firms are creating new forms of learning and production. These changes are important and challenge the traditional role of "national systems of innovation". The chapters in this section focus on regional innovation issues.

The first chapter in this section, by Ceh, uses small key-technology firms in Canada to better understand the major characteristics of these firms, the spatial distribution of their patented inventions, and to determine if their spatial adaptation follows patterns of agglomeration, dispersion, and/or specialisation. These firms in the core region of the Quebec City-Windsor corridor were found to operate in a wider set of industries compared to their counterparts in the periphery. Surprisingly, many of the corridor's small key-technology firms were founded earlier then expected, which is necessary for them to have acquired the resources needed to be knowledge firms. Geographically, small key-technology firms locate close to larger technology firms and exhibit patterns of concentration, dispersion, and specialisation.

According to Arita and McCann much of the current literature on high-technology developments within the electronics industry tends to focus on the spatial and organisational arrangements evident in innovative clusters such as Silicon Valley. There are many different forms of spatial organisation that engender innovations within the semiconductor industry, and these variations depend on the particular sub-sector of the semiconductor industry. They discuss the case of Japanese vertically integrated semiconductor producers. The paper analyses data from over one hundred Japanese semiconductor plants located within Japan and develops a series of regressors which relate various measures of production technology and innovation to firm, plant and location characteristics at a prefecture level. Their results indicate that the spatial arrangements in Japan are very different from those evident in the US or Europe.

The next chapter, by Aslesen, presents an analysis of the Oslo area, the capital region of Norway, with respect to firms' innovation activity. It examines the question: "To what extent does city location have an effect on firms taking part in innovation activity?" The main finding is that geographical proximity is a necessary but not sufficient condition for firms' interaction with the scientific community. Important barriers are shown to exist between SMEs and the scientific community that are difficult to overcome by proximity. SMEs' difficulty in using the scientific community for innovation purposes is rooted in both a competence mismatch, and a "cultural" mismatch. The paper explores ways in which barriers for innovation collaboration can be overcome, and potentially raise the innovation performance of the Oslo region.

The final chapter, by Pérez and Sánchez, analyses the spatial distribution of the results of the technological process (patents granted) in the Spanish medical equipment industry. The paper reveals a polarisation towards the two large urban agglomerations of Barcelona and Madrid. At the province level, the analysis shows that the use of information technologies and the proximity to medical facilities are more important for patenting than the concentration of technological activities. This suggests that small 'hi-tech' medical equipment firms may develop and locate in peripheral provinces.

1.7 Conclusion

This book contains a rich set of papers exemplifying some of the recent advances in the research field of knowledge, innovation, and regional development. This research field addresses the fundamental question why some regions grow quickly while others stagnate. All papers have in common that they aim at combining insights from various fields of research that have so far largely been developed in isolation, namely the new growth theory, the new economic geography and the new innovation theory. The papers aim at empirically operationalising the rich concepts developed in these theories, oftentimes using state of the art spatial econometric analysis.

Although these papers add to our knowledge, several important questions remain for future research. At a theoretical level, further integrating the insights from the new growth theory, the new economic geography and the new economics of innovation can be fruitful in that it can yield insights into the potentially relevant interactions among the key relationships analysed in these theories. Also further rigorous empirical testing of these theories – though admittedly difficult – is relevant in order to get beyond the useful and interesting but also highly specific case studies that are prevalent in the literature. These empirical analyses will lead to results and insights that can be generalised. For the latter, there is a strong need for new datasets at a very detailed level. All in all, there is a highly challenging task ahead of use, consisting of the development and use of rich and detailed datasets and the revelation of the fundamental microeconomic factors behind the complex processes of regional development, innovation and knowledge creation and diffusion.

References

Acs Z (ed) (2000) Regional innovation, knowledge and global change. Pinter, London

Acs Z (2002) Innovation and the growth of cities. Edward Elgar, Cheltenham UK

Acs Z, Audretsch DB (1990) Innovation in large and small firms. MIT Press, Cambridge MA

Acs Z, Varga A (eds) (2002a) Special Issue: Regional innovation systems. International Regional Science Review 25: 3–148

Acs Z, Varga A (2002b) Geography, endogenous growth and innovation. International Regional Science Review 25: 132–148

Acs Z, Audretsch DB, Feldman M (1994) R&D spillovers and recipient firm size. Review of Economics and Statistics 76: 336–340

Aghion P, Howitt P (1998) Endogenous growth theory. MIT Press, Cambridge MA

Anselin L, Varga A, Acs Z (1997) Local geographic spillovers between university research and high technology innovations. Journal of Urban Economics 42: 422–448

Archibugi D, Coco A (2001) The technological performance of Europe in a global setting. Industry and Innovation 8: 245–266

Arrow K (1962) The economic implications of learning by doing. Review of Economic Studies 29: 155–173

Audretsch DB (1995) Innovation and industry evolution. MIT Press, Cambridge MA

Barro RJ, Sala-i-Martin (1995) Economic growth. McGraw-Hill, New York

Benhabib J, Spiegel MM (1994) The role of human capital in economic development: Evidence from aggregate cross-country data. Journal of Monetary Economics 34: 143–173

Braczyk H-J, Cooke P, Heidenreich M (eds) (1998) Regional innovation systems. The role of governance in a globalized world. UCL Press, London

Chandler A Jr. (2000) The information age in hisorical perspective. In: Chandler AD, Cortada JW (eds) A nation transformed by information: How information has shaped the United States from colonial times to the present. Oxford University Press, Oxford, pp 3–38

Debresson C (1996) Economic interdependence and innovative activity. Edward Elgar, Cheltenham UK

De la Mothe J, Paquet G (eds) (1998) Local and regional systems of innovation. Kluwer Academic Publishers, Boston

Dosi G (1988) Sources, procedures, and microeconomic effects of innovation. Journal of Economic Literature 26: 1120–1171

Dunning J (2002) Regions, globalization, and the knowledge-based economy. Oxford University Press, Oxford

Fujita M, Krugman P, Venables AJ (1999) The spatial economy. MIT Press, Cambridge MA

Groot HLF de, Nahuis R (2002) Optimal Product Variety and Economic Growth. Journal of Economics, forthcoming

Grossman G, Helpman E (1991) Innovation and growth in the global economy. MIT Press, Cambridge MA

Jorgenson D (2001) Information technology and the U.S. economy. American Economic Review 91: 1–32

Hobijn B, Jovanovic B (2001) The information-technology revolution and the stock market: evidence. American Economic Review 91: 1203–1220

Howitt P. (ed) The implications of knowledge-based growth for micro-economic policies. Calgary University Press, Calgary, Alberta

Jaffe A (1989) Real effects of academic research. American Economic Review 79: 957–970

Jovanovic B (1997) Learning and growth. In: Kreps DM, Wallis KF (eds) Advances in economics and econometrics: Theory and applications. Cambridge University Press, Cambridge

Krugman P (1991) Geography and trade. MIT Press, Cambridge MA

Krugman P (1999) The role of geography in development. International Regional Science Review 22: 142–161

Lucas R (1988) On the mechanics of economic development. Journal of Monetary Economics 22: 3–42

Martin R (1999) The new "geographical turn" in economics: some critical reflections. Cambridge Journal of Economics 23: 65–91

Nelson RR (ed.) (1993) National innovation systems. Oxford University Press, New York

Nijkamp P, Poot J (1997) Endogenous technological change, long run growth and spatial interdependence: a survey. In: Bertuglia C, Lombardo S, Nijkamp P (eds) Innovative Behavior in time and space. Springer, Heidelberg, pp 213–238

Oinas P, Malecki EJ (1999) Spatial innovation systems. In: Malecki EJ, Oinas P (eds) Making connections. Technological learning and regional economic change. Ashgate, Aldershot UK, pp 261–275

Ratti R, Bramanti A, Gordon R (1997) The dynamics of innovative regions. Ashgate, Aldershot UK

Roller L, Waverman L (2001) Telecommunications infrastructure and economic development: A simultaneous approach. American Economic Review 91: 909–923

Romer P (1986) Increasing returns and long-run growth. Journal of Political Economy 94: 1002–1037

Romer P (1990) Endogenous technological change. Journal of Political Economy 98: S71–S102

Romer P (1994) The origins of endogenous growth. Journal of Economic Perspectives 8: 3–22

Saxenian A (1994) Regional advantage: culture and competition in Silicon Valley and Route 128. Harvard University Press, Cambridge MA

Shane S, Venkataraman A (2000) The promise of entrepreneurship as a field of research. Academy of Management Review 25: 217–226

Smulders S, Klundert TCMJ van de (1995) Imperfect competition, concentration and growth with firm-specific R&D. European Economic Review 39: 139–160

Sternberg R (1999) Innovative linkages and proximity: empirical results from recent surveys of small and medium sized firms in German regions. Regional Studies 33: 529–540

Suarez-Villa L (2000) Invention and the rise of technocapitalism. Rowman & Littlefield, New York

Varga A (1998) University research and regional innovation: A spatial econometric analysis of academic knowledge transfer. Kluwer Academic Publishers, Boston

Varga A (2000) Local academic knowledge spillovers and the concentration of economic activity. Journal of Regional Science 40: 289–309

2 Milieux Innovateurs and Collective Learning: From Concepts to Measurement

Roberto Camagni and Roberta Capello

Department of Management, Economics and Industrial Engineering, Politecnico di Milano, Milan, Italy

2.1 Introduction[1]

Since the middle eighties a new theoretical approach to the study of local innovative behaviour has been developed, centred upon the concept of the innovative milieu;[2] in this approach, economic space is defined as a "relational space", the field of social interactions, interpersonal synergies and social collective actions that determine the innovative capability and the economic success of specific local areas.

The approach in terms of *milieux* differentiates itself from other similar or parallel approaches to local development – viz. those centred on the notions of the marshallian district, organisational proximity, untraded interdependencies, local "context", etc. – thanks to many peculiarities. First of all, this theory puts a particular emphasis on innovation processes: since the beginning, the GREMI approach was characterised by the inspection of innovation factors, in a dynamic perspective, rather than by the analysis of the locational advantages of single territories or the definition of those elements that, in a static perspective, are able to enhance the competitive advantage of systems of small firms vis-à-vis the big firms.

A second peculiarity of the theory of the milieu innovateur is the conceptualisation of the innovative capability of the *milieux* in terms of economic theory, and in particular of the evolutionary theory of technical change (Nelson and Winter 1977; Dosi 1982; Dosi et al. 1988); the rationale for, and the strategic role of, the innovative *milieu* is found in the reduction of uncertainty, the reduction of co-ordination costs, the supply of the durable substrate for (collective) learning processes.

---

[1] Though the paper is the result of common research work, Roberto Camagni has written Sects. 2.1 and 2.2.1, while the remaining Sects. have been written by Roberta Capello.

[2] For the "milieu innovateur" theory, see Aydalot (1986), Aydalot and Keeble (1988), Camagni (1991b), Maillat et al. (1993), Ratti et al. (1997), and RERU (1999).

A third peculiarity which characterises this theory is an evolution of the theorisation of the *milieux* in time: from the early analyses of the synergetic elements that link the different local actors, to the coupling of internal and external networking, to the theorisation of collective learning processes.

Moreover, this approach is characterised by the exploitation of the same abstract concepts for the interpretation of apparently different empirical realities, like the local systems of SMEs and the city (as a territorial archetype). This element is the most recent one, where some theoretical and empirical reflections have been put forward,[3] but where some work still needs to be done.

Although the theory has already been developed for some years, the empirical analyses have always been of a qualitative nature. To a certain extent, this is inherent to a theory based on largely unmeasurable facts, such as collective learning, dynamic synergies, and dynamic externalities. However, no attempt has so far been made to formulate these concepts in such a way that may be amenable to quantitative measurement. This paper presents a first attempt in this direction.

The aims of the present paper are therefore the following:

- to present a review of the literature on the milieu innovateur, with the aim to stress the theoretical propositions that have to be measured empirically in order to support the theory;

- to measure in quantitative terms the milieu effects in areas with a high concentration of high-tech firms.

The chapter is structured as follows. In Sect. 2.2 a review of the milieu theory is presented, and an overview of testable hypotheses underlined. Sect. 2.3 provides insights into the database and methodologies. Sects. 2.4–2.6 present the empirical findings on the milieu effects. Sect. 2.7 presents some concluding remarks concerning the policy implications of the findings.

2.2 The Theory of the Milieu Innovateur: a Review and an Overview of Testable Propositions

2.2.1 A Review of the Theory

An innovative milieu has been defined as a set of relationships happening on a limited territory, encompassing in a coherent way a production system, different economic and social actors, a specific culture and a representation system, and generating a dynamic process of collective learning (Camagni 1991a).

---

[3] See in this respect Camagni (1999) and Capello (2001), respectively, for the theoretical and empirical reflections.

The conceptualisation of the innovative milieu is forcedly abstract; the milieu itself has to be considered as an economic and territorial archetype more than an empirical reality. Its conceptualisation in economic terms supplies us with the possibility of generalising some new empirical findings, showing the importance of relational assets in the success of some special territories and finding an economic rationale for them in the support of innovation processes. The characteristics of the innovative *milieux* are never perfectly and totally realised in real territorial systems; the relationship between the presence of these characteristics and the innovation outcome is tested in some empirical cases, and is above all theoretically justified, but may never be considered as a deterministic one. In a sense, the presence of these characteristics in real territories may be considered as a precondition, neither necessary nor sufficient, for innovation; only an element increasing the probability of an innovative outcome.[4]

The milieu innovateur functions like a microcosm in which all those elements which are traditionally considered as the genetic sources of development and economic change operate as if they were *in vitro*, thanks to the high density of SMEs interactions, highlighted and enhanced by spatial proximity and by those economic and cultural homogeneities which allow the milieu itself to exist. Smithian processes of division of labour among units belonging to the same productive cycle; processes of learning-by-doing and learning-by-using *à la* Arrow, amplified beyond each enterprise by the high mobility of the specialised labour force inside the local area; Marshallian or Allyn Young-type externalities, generated by a common industrial culture and intense input-output interactions; the formation of Schumpeterian entrepreneurship, facilitated by specific historical competencies, sectorial specialisation and ample possibilities of imitation; cross-fertilisation processes *à la* Freeman, which generate systems of integrated and incremental innovations – all these are essential components of the milieu innovateur.

Two kinds of synergetic processes involve (and in a sense create) the milieu:

- a set of mainly informal, "un-traded" relationships – among customers and suppliers, among private and public actors – and a set of tacit transfers of knowledge taking place through the individual chains of professional mobility and inter-firm imitation processes;

- more formalised, mainly trans-territorial co-operation agreements – among firms, among collective agents, among public institutions – in the field of technological development, vocational and on-the-job training, infrastructure and services provision.

---

[4] Therefore, we cannot accept the criticism, made recently by Storper (1995), about the risk of circular reasoning in the concept of innovative milieu ("innovation occurs because of a milieu, and a milieu is what exists in regions where there is innovation"): the milieu is a concept, referring to some economic conditions and processes that, on the basis of economic theorisation, make innovation easier and more likely. Furthermore, as far as the forecast of the innovativeness of territories is concerned, both in time and in space, no conceptualisation can assure it, *et pour cause!*

The former kind of relationships is in fact the "glue" that creates a "milieu" effect; it is complemented by the latter, more formalised kind of relationships, which can be interpreted as "network relations" proper. Both sets of relationships may be regarded as tools or "operators" that help the (small) firm in its competitive struggle, enhancing the potential of the single firm's creativeness and reducing the dynamic uncertainty intrinsically embedded in innovation processes.

In trans-territorial networks, partners are single, selected economic units: enterprises, banks, research centres, training institutions, or local authorities, in which the location element is, roughly, only one co-ordinate among many serving to identify the unit itself. At a first glance, therefore, these networks only link together different economic actors, with no necessary relation with space. But when the location of a unit takes on a significant meaning, inasmuch as it reveals a set of relations which generate territorial development and identity (e.g., Apple at Cupertino, Silicon Valley) and when these network relations start to multiply, they do become territorial. When carefully observed, the identity of the local *milieu* often prevails over the identity of the individual partner, stressing the importance of the territory: the strategic importance of links with a company in Silicon Valley resides more in the opening of a "technological window" in Silicon Valley than in access to that specific company's know-how.

In terms of economic theory, the function of the local *milieu* is threefold:

- it reduces the elements of uncertainty which are particularly present in innovative processes, at the same time minimising obstacles to change.[5] In the case of large companies, the functions of information collection, its assessment and transcoding, selection of decision-making routines – all working towards reducing static or dynamic uncertainty – are generally undertaken by R&D units, or by strategic planning units; in the case of the milieu innovateur, they are undertaken in a collective and socialised way by the milieu itself, through rapid circulation of information and processes of imitation and co-operation (Camagni 1991a). Particularly relevant in the field of innovative processes is the transcoding of information function, as it channels relevant information towards an economic use by the firm;

- it reduces the ex-ante co-ordination costs between single decision-making units, as long as they engage in collective action (addressed to the provision of co-operative or collective goods or to the simple integration of private investment decisions). Generally this co-ordination suffers from limited and costly information, and from the equally costly risk of opportunistic and free-riding behaviours: the existence of the milieu reduces these costs, as it allows easier information circulation, possibilities for co-ordinating decisions thanks to proximity and opportunities offered by any social event (a process also men-

---

[5] Different sources of uncertainty may be kept under control through the milieu: imperfect and costly information, presence of hidden characteristics, imperfect information processing ability, imperfect assessment of decision outcomes, and imperfect control on other actors' decisions. For the way in which the milieu acts on these uncertainty channels, see Camagni (1991a).

tioned by Adam Smith, referring to agreements on prices reached by entrepreneurs meeting for weddings or Sunday mass), reduction of opportunistic behaviours as a consequence of trust and social sanctioning. This last social/psychological element is crucial: it derives from the sharing of common values, behavioural codes and representation systems, and acts, on the positive side, developing loyalty and trust, and on the negative side, developing fast processes of isolation and punishment of free-riding behaviours (Camagni and Rabellotti 1997), which are all elements that make ex-ante co-ordination easier. This mechanism is reinforced through public-private co-operation when private costs of collective actions are greater than the benefits for single actors: local public institutions become not only tools for regulating individual behaviour, but also instruments for the planning of public goods and specific resources, necessary to the innovative processes (Arrighetti and Seravalli 1999);

• the milieu innovateur plays a further, crucial function within the innovative process, that of supplying the durable substrate for learning mechanisms, guaranteeing the circulation, appropriation and continuous regeneration of know-how and non-codified, non-material assets among enterprises. In large enterprises, these functions are ensured by the presence of large-scale R&D and engineering departments and by their interaction, and can take place thanks to the fact that the enterprises themselves are long-term structures, developing their own internal culture. On the contrary, in small-enterprise districts, in which the life-cycle of single productive units is characteristically short and turbulent, these functions take place in a socialised way outside each enterprise and find their element of continuity and embeddedness in the labour market and in the local productive culture, the style of local institutions, the density of interpersonal and inter-generational links (Camagni 1995).

These three functions of the milieu are shown in Table 2.1, where they are referred to the two main and genetic characteristics of the local milieu, namely:

• geographical proximity, and

• what we may call "relational proximity", encompassing the linkages that happen thanks to economic integration of firms, socio-cultural homogeneity of local population and dense public/private co-operation and partnership.

The fundamental characteristic of the processes that happens thanks to geographical and relational proximity in the functioning of the milieu is that they are "collective" rather than explicitly co-operative. They are elements that occur inside an atmosphere of competition (often of outstanding individualism), set apart from a conscious co-operative will by the single actors. This co-operative attitude may of course exist or develop, accentuating the efficiency of collective processes. The commercial signals conveyed by a specialised district or milieu are independent from the existence of explicit territorial marketing; the process of learning and accumulation of specific competencies is embedded in the local labour market, independently of the co-operative decisions of enterprises regarding possible training programmes; and the same imitative processes mainly occur against the will of the first innovators.

Table 2.1. Functions of the Local Milieu

CONDITIONS

		Geographical proximity	Relational proximity
FUNCTIONS	Reduction of uncertainty	• Information collection/selection • Vertical integration within "filierès" • Local signalling (collective marketing)	• Information transcoding • Selection of decision routines • Risk sharing among partners
	Reduction of coordination costs	• Information collection • Reduction of transaction costs (à la Williamson) • Ex-ante co-ordination of day-to-day decisions (à la Marshall)	• Reduction of control costs through trust and loyalty • Social sanction of opportunistic behaviours • Ex-ante co-ordination in strategic decision-making
	Durable substrate for collective learning	• Labour turnover inside the milieu • Imitation of innovation practices	• Co-operation in industrial projects • Tacit transfer of knowledge • Public/private partnership in complex development schemes

In the theory of the milieu innovateur, collective learning is the territorial counterpart of learning processes happening inside the firm; it is thought of as the vehicle for knowledge transmission, both in a temporal and in a spatial dimension. In the former dimension, the transfer of knowledge takes place through an element of continuity; in the latter by the interaction among agents (Table 2.2).

The local labour market plays an important role within the local production system, as the high internal turnover of specialised labour and the low external mobility guarantee cross-fertilisation processes for firms and professional upgrading for individuals; a local know-how grows through a collective and socialised process, subject, and this is the other side of the coin, to risks of isolation and locking-in, unless external energy is also captured through selected external co-operation linkages.

Table 2.2. Preconditions and Channels for Learning Processes in Innovative Milieux

Preconditions Context	Continuity	Dynamic synergies	
Firms	R&D functions	Functional interaction Tacit transfer of knowledge	INTERNAL LEARNING
Territory	Low mobility of the labour force outside the milieu	High mobility of the labour force within the milieu	
			COLLECTIVE LEARNING
	Stable linkages with suppliers and cus-tomers	Co-operation for innovation with suppliers and customers Local spin-off	
Networking	Stability as a conse-quence of the com-plexity of strategic alliances	Transfer of knowledge via co-operation	LEARNING THROUGH NETWORKING

If the labour market constitutes the main element of continuity, a second element may be envisaged in the stable linkages between suppliers and customers: stable input-output relationships generate a codified and tacit transfer of knowledge between suppliers and customers, which cumulates over time and defines patterns of incremental innovation which feed a specific technological trajectory. Also in this case, the comparison with the firms' technological trajectory is straightforward. As Aydalot (1986) suggested, the innovation process in a territorial entity like the milieu is a process of "rupture/filiation" (break and continuity): if an innovation is a break with a pre-existing situation, economic creativity and innovation potential have their seeds exactly in the local cumulated knowledge and know-how acquired over time.

However, the existence of an element of continuity is not sufficient to produce learning, and collective learning. A second element is required in both firms and districts, to assure the transfer of cumulated knowledge, an element that may be interpreted as dynamic synergies.

In large enterprises, information collection and knowledge is transferred through functional interaction, among R&D, production, marketing and organisation departments. In the milieu and in territorial systems of small firms this function of transferring information and know-how within the boundaries of the milieu is played by the high internal mobility of the labour force, as said before, by intense innovative interactions with suppliers and customers and by mechanisms of local spin-off.

Theoretically, a spin-off is defined as a new indipendent firm fulfilling two criteria (Perhankangas and Kauranen 1996): a) the start up of a new business by an agent previously belonging to another local firm, and b) the derivation of the new business idea from the previous employment of the founder. Local milieux provide both the social and the market preconditions for this phenomenon to take place: from the social point of view, high trust and a common sense of belonging to the same cultural society make this process acceptable.[6] Local market conditions, like stable interactions with suppliers known in the previous job, a receptive local demand of particular products developed in the previous job, and the presence of external economies, assure locational advantages, guarantee the achievement of profits and thus give rise to chances for survival on the local market.

As in the case of learning processes, preconditions exist at the spatial level which guarantee the development of dynamic and creative synergies. These preconditions are embedded in the capability of local firms to co-operate, not only on technical elements, but also on managerial and organisational ones, thanks to their organisational and cultural proximity. As the French proximity school underlines, organisational proximity overcomes the economic separation among actors by generating common interpretations of the reality, used on their turn for the formulation of personal strategies and economic choices (Bellet et al. 1993; Rallet 1993; Dupuy and Gilly 1995).

As said before, the mechanisms of collective learning and transfer of knowledge take place in a socialised way, a creative knowledge cumulating outside the single firm as a sort of club good: no (or low) rivalry in its use by agents belonging to the club, and very limited excludability of external agents from taking advantage of it. In this sense, collective learning supplies typical "club goods" à la Buchanan (1965) from which club externalities may be exploited.

In this perspective, collective learning may be defined as a dynamic and cumulative process of knowledge production, transfer and appropriation, taking place thanks to the interactive mechanisms which are typical of the local milieu.

However, "intra-firm" and "collective" learning processes do not exhaust all possible learning channels available to firms. In fact, a third category exists, which may be labelled "learning through networking". Through strategic alliances, non-equity agreements and technological co-operation, firms are able to capture some of the necessary assets from outside, overcoming the costs of internal development. This model is in a sense intermediate between internal and collective learning, in that it opens the firm to the general context, but maintains it in a set of selected and targeted relationships.[7] In this sense, the continuity element is generated by the relative complexity of the process of setting the terms of the co-operation contract, the clauses and sections for excluding opportunistic behaviour, all elements that push towards a long term horizon and a relative stability of these agreements. On the other hand, the knowledge transfer element is generally seen as fast and powerful, as a consequence of the complementarity of the different partners in the co-operation network.

---

[6] On the social homogeneity of local districts a vast literature exists. See, among others, Bagnasco and Trigilia (1984), Becattini (1979, 1990). An overall synthesis of local district theories is contained in Rabellotti (1997) and in Bramanti and Maggioni (1997).

[7] On the concept of "firms' networking", see, among others, Chesnais (1989), Gordon (1991), and Scott (1993).

2.2.2 An Overview of Testable Propositions

From the review presented before, some testable propositions can be highlighted in order to prove some theoretical underpinnings of the theory of the milieu innovateur.

An important element that constitutes a milieu is the presence of collective learning mechanisms, as channels for knowledge acquisition. These channels for knowledge acquisition can be used by firms according to their interests and strategies and our interest is to test whether the willingness to grasp these opportunities depends on: a) the type of innovation to develop; b) the firm size.

Collective learning embeds all historical knowledge cumulated in the local labour market over time, which is the pre-requisite for a jump on a new technological trajectory in respect with the technological trajectories typical of the single firm. Radical product innovations are mainly based on new technologically creative knowledge and on new scientific resources, those resources that stem from a historical process of cumulative know-how. Once an agent is willing to achieve a radical innovation, it is more inclined to grasp the opportunity to exploit the local labour market, where these creative resources have been cumulated over time. It is also in this respect that, once a local actor exploits collective learning, he participates, even against his will, in the process of creation of new resources, which will be in the long run embedded in the local market. On the contrary, in front of process innovations that require incremental innovation and feed themselves of cumulated knowledge within each firm, the choice of local actors will be more oriented towards the exploitation of internal knowledge. In the same logic, the size of the firm is another determining element in the decision to exploit collective learning. A large firm is more oriented towards the exploitation of internal creative resources even for breakthrough innovations: by definition, a large firm has more resources to devote to knowledge creation, is less willing to grasp and to participate unconsciously in the socialisation process of creative knowledge. A small firm is for the opposite reasons more inclined to grasp collective learning, once this externality is present in the area.

It becomes interesting to prove these hypotheses empirically, by testing:

a. whether it is true that different learning behaviours exist within a milieu among which collective learning represents one of them;
b. whether the smallest and most innovative firms are the ones exploiting collective learning more.

Another important aspect which is at the basis of the theory of the milieu innovateur is that collective learning provides local firms with positive external effects on factor productivity. In particular, the knowledge capital of firms, in the form of patents, R&D expenditures, and expenses for R&D activity in general, is influenced by the know-how present locally, which cumulates locally thanks to a cross fertilisation process of innovative ideas, and by an external know-how, which prevents the local area from being locked-in its know-how. In fact, as has been underlined in the literature (Bianchi 1989; Camagni and Rabellotti 1997), a high degree of personal cohesion may translate into regressive coalition. Local firms' capacity to innovate relies thus on both internal and external know-how, the latter being achieved by developing national and international networking with firms located outside the local area (Camagni 1991a; Maillat et al. 1993). If this is the case, scientific capital productivity in the form of cumulated knowledge should then be influenced by a know-how both internal and external to the milieu.

Moreover, structural characteristics of the local labour market are expected to influence labour productivity, since they are channels for knowledge acquisition: a high internal turnover of the labour force accompanied by a high stability of labour force within the boundaries of the milieu is in fact underlined by the milieu theory as a way of cumulating knowledge and expertise within the milieu.

In this sense, the interest of our empirical analysis is to test:

- whether factor productivity is influenced by the degree of exploitation of collective learning channels. More specifically, this means to test whether capital productivity in firms located in the milieu depends on know-how cumulated over time in the milieu, and whether labour productivity in firms located in the milieu is influenced by the stability of the labour market and by the dynamic synergy effects which take place in the labour market of the milieu;

- whether different learning behaviours exist and whether the collective learning behaviour is linked to the most innovative firms (proposition a) (Sect. 2.4);

- whether collective learning is more appreciated by the smallest and most innovative firms (proposition b) (Sect. 2.5);

- whether collective learning channels influence firms' productivity (proposition c) (Sect. 2.6).

Before presenting the results, the next section presents the database and the methodologies applied to the analyses.

2.3 Database and Methodologies

In order to test the theoretical issues presented above, a database has been built on firms located in three high-tech milieux areas in Italy, namely Pisa, Piacenza and the North-Eastern part of Milan, where high-tech firms are geographically clustered.[8] 63 firms in the three milieux are interviewed in these areas in a period of a month. Firms are equally distributed among the three milieux: 20 firms in Pisa and Piacenza respectively and 23 in Milan. The same database is applied to all the empirical analyses presented hereafter.[9] The sample, randomly chosen, covers both small (1–49 employees) and medium (50–199) firms. The former represent 81%

---

[8] The following sectors have been included as high-tech sectors: telecommunications instruments (ISTAT code 32), computer science (ISTAT code 30), and optical and medical instruments (ISTAT code 33).

[9] In the case of the estimate of the production function, only 55 interviews were suitable for the analysis.

of the sample, the latter 19%. The distribution of firms in favour of small rather than medium size is representative of the universe of firms. The average number of employees is 16 for the first group, and 123 for the second group. The sample firms show a certain dynamic capacity. The overall turnover has in fact increased over the last 5 years for 80% of the firms interviewed, while the number of employees has increased in 70% of our firms, during the same period. In general, the interviewed firms are innovative firms: all firms in fact have developed product innovation during the last 5 years; 60% of them put in place process innovations. Moreover, if we split the product innovation into breakthrough and upgrading innovation, 60% of our sample developed breakthrough innovations and the others upgrading innovations.

Face-to-face interviews have been run, which contained direct questions covering different themes, including: a) the characteristics of firms, in terms of size and innovative capacity (see Table 2A.1 in the Appendix); b) the different channels for know-how acquisition, and the characteristics of the local labour market, in terms of quality of the labour force, formal and informal channels for labour acquisition, the turnover within the firm, stability of the labour market (see Table 2A.2 in Appendix); c) district locational advantages, like industrial atmosphere, stable labour market, cultural proximity with the labour force (see Table 2A.3 in the Appendix). The information obtained were mainly qualitative, discrete and redundant; in order to obtain synthetic and quantitative indicators, a factor analysis has been run on the two groups of characteristics. Factor analysis allows us to identify for each group of qualitative characteristics a smaller number of "derived" quantitative variables. The main results of this statistical exercise are summarised in Table 2A in the Appendix to this paper. In statistical terms, the results are quite satisfactory: all factor analyses run on the two groups of characteristics presented above explain a large share of total sample variance, and summarise a high number of questions. Also in economic terms, the results of the factor analysis are interesting; the economic interpretation leads in fact to the definition of factors representing the stability of the labour market, the local spin-off phenomenon, the know-how of the milieu, and the know-how external to the area, which are necessary for our empirical analysis.

The methodologies used to reply to the above mentioned theoretical issues are of a statistical nature. In particular, in order to describe learning behaviour for innovative activities among our firm sample a cluster analysis is used. With the aim of identifying the structural characteristics of the innovation behaviour shared by each group, cluster analysis groups firms according to the degree of statistical vicinity among the variables we think can influence the behaviour of firms in their innovation activities. In our case, a wide spectrum of possible variables explaining the innovative behaviour of firms, aggregated through a factor analysis, was used in the cluster analysis: type of innovation, learning channels, and degree of cooperation with local suppliers and customers. The analysis was able to group firms according to the structural characteristics of their innovation behaviour.

The second proposition is estimated through a linear regression model: this allows us to measure the degree to which innovative activities are influenced by collective learning elements. The variables inserted in the regression are again obtained via the factor analysis. In these regression analyses the interesting aspect to test is the sign of the relationship between innovative activities and learning channels, more than the significance of the model as a whole. In other words, the statistical exercise is made to test the sign and significance of some variables (t-student), and not the significance of the whole model (R^2).

For what concerns the third proposition, the methodology applied to estimate the effects of collective learning on factor productivity is similar to the one used during the seventies to estimate agglomeration economies at an urban aggregate level[10] (urbanisation economies) or sectoral[11] (localisation economies). In general, these models apply a Cobb-Douglas production function, which allows the simple least-square method for the estimate of its parameters. These studies are able to estimate the effects of urban size on factor productivity, and thus agglomeration advantages obtained from large-scale cities.

A similar methodology is applied to this study, with the exception that we choose a Transcendental Logarithmic function (Translog), which, contrary to the Cobb-Douglas production function, allows us to estimate second order variables and cross-variable effects[12] (Christensen et al. 1973).

The following indicators have been useful in the estimate of the production function model:

- an indicator of labour, easily obtainable with the number of employees in each firm;

---

[10] See, among others, Henderson (1974), Marelli (1981), Segal (1976), and Sveikauskas (1975).

[11] Sectoral analyses are contained in Kawashima (1975) and Shefer (1973).

[12] A large debate exists around the necessity to impose restrictions on parameters of production functions, so that they are able to approximate the stylised facts of economic behaviour that neoclassical economists generally agree characterise the real world (Chambers 1988). On the production function, these restrictions regard:
- monotonicity (and strict monotonicity) of the production function;
- quasi-concavity (and concavity) of the production function;
- weak essentiality (strict essentiality);
- closed and non-empty input requirement set for all outputs;
- the production function is finite, non-negative, real valued for all non-negative and finite inputs;
- the production function is everywhere twice-continuously differentiable.

It has been underlined, however, that these restrictions have generally been rejected in econometric analyses (Evans and Heckman 1984). The choice to impose these restrictions even if they have been rejected by empirical data, as is often the case, is not required by any direct comparison between our analysis and other studies where the restrictions have been imposed. Moreover, in our particular case the economic reasoning behind these analytical restrictions is difficult to accept a priori. Our production function is in fact a quasi-production function (where inputs are more than the conventional capital and labour inputs), representing an aggregate economic behaviour which may not immediately follow the same economic rules imposed by the neoclassical individual firm's behaviour.

- an indicator of the physical capital stock, as the result of the monetary assessment of plants, machines, industrial instruments, and in general all machines used within the firm (like computers), obtained from the official balance sheets available from the Chamber of Commerce;[13]
- an indicator of the non-material capital stock of firms, measured by the value of R&D expenses, licences, industrial awards and patents of each firm, available from the balance sheets;
- an indicator of local know-how, obtained from the first factor analysis (Table 2A.2 in Appendix), indicating the degree of importance attributed to the local labour market in providing the high quality labour force necessary for the firm;
- an indicator of know-how external to the milieu, represented by another factor (Table 2A.2 in Appendix), indicating the number of scientists and technicians coming from outside the local market employed by local firms;
- an indicator of the spin-off mechanisms, obtained from the factor analysis as factor 4 (Table 2A.2), representing the importance attributed to the informal knowledge accumulated by technicians and scientists before spin-off took place;
- an indicator of the stability of the labour market, obtained as factor 3 in the factor analysis run on the location advantage characteristics (Table 2A.2 in Appendix), which measures the degree of importance of a stability of the labour market for choosing local labour force.

Once the indicators have been built, other methodological problems have been faced. In particular, for the cross-section estimate of the production function all variables need to be standardised for a scale element, in order to:

- eliminate the collinearity between capital and labour;
- eliminate the size effects due to the presence of variables in absolute terms.

In general, the variable chosen for such an exercise is labour. In our case, we decided to standardise all variables by the physical capital stock indicator, which represented, as expected, a high correlation with labour,[14] and thus could easily be interpreted as a firm size variable. With such a choice, we were able to keep both non-material capital stock and labour as independent variables, and measure the effects of collective learning on both production factors. In the next Section the results of our empirical exercise are presented.

2.4 Learning and Innovative Behaviours in Milieux

The first theoretical element to test empirically was the existence and importance of a "milieu" effect, in particular in terms of learning processes. In SMEs areas we

---

[13] The author is grateful to the Chamber of Commerce in Milan for providing access to the official balance of sheets registered in 1996.

[14] The Pearson correlation coefficient between the two variables assumes a value of 0.85.

expect heterogeneous learning behaviours of local firms, according to their size and to the intensity of their innovative activity. In particular, we expect collective learning behaviours to be put in place by smaller firms and by firms which have more breakthrough innovation.

The cluster analysis, run on the basis of a factor analysis, has produced a three-fold typology of learning behaviour (Table 2.3):[15]

- a first cluster depicts a condition where district economies and networking behaviour prevail: in this group of firms learning is based primarily on know-how external to the local area. This cluster is in fact characterised by dynamic and innovative firms, by traditional local district advantages (like industrial atmosphere and cultural proximity with the labour force) and by the acquisition of know-how from outside the district: it is probably in these external linkages that the innovative roots of these firms feed themselves;
- a second cluster shows a sub-system of autonomous firms: learning is in fact based on firms' internal competencies. Firms belonging to this cluster are specialised in process innovation: for these firms, as expected, the main channels of learning are a) learning within the firm; b) technological proximity with customers and suppliers;
- a third cluster depicts a pure "milieu" behaviour where learning stems from socialised mechanisms of spatial transfer of knowledge: i.e., from collective learning. The smallest and most innovative firms in terms of radical product innovation feed their innovative activities through collective learning mechanisms: local spin-off, a stable market over time associated with a high turnover of the labour force, high dynamic synergies with local suppliers and organisational and industrial proximity with them, and informal contracts with customers are all characteristics of this cluster, and represent all channels through which the innovative breakthrough activity of these firms probably feeds itself.

---

[15] The cluster analysis method used here is the hierarchical cluster, which provides evidence of the stability of a cluster.

Table 2.3. Typologies of Learning Behaviour in Three Italian High-Tech Districts: Results of the Cluster Analysis

Factors	Cluster 1 (networking)	Cluster 2 (autonomous)	Cluster 3 (collective learning)
Dynamic and innovative firms	0.127	−1.32	−0.24
Industrial atmosphere	0.047	−0.33	−0.48
Cultural proximity	0.010	−0.039	−0.20
Learning external to the area	0.02	−0.19	−0.18
Process innovative firms	−0.01	0.25	−0.103
Proximity to the mother firm	0.009	0.08	−0.46
Learning internal to the firm	−0.04	0.55	−0.18
Presence of local innovative customers	−0.05	0.51	0.28
Technological proximity with customers	0.039	0.17	−1.53
Technological proximity with suppliers	0.009	0.15	−0.64
Smallest and most innovative firms	−0.0009	−0.35	0.89
Labour Market stability	0.014	−0.30	0.33
High labour force turnover	0.0021	−0.18	0.41
Spin-off	0.0027	−0.039	0.02
Standard contracts with customers	0.02	−0.52	0.63
Institutional and organisational proximity with customers	−0.05	0.29	0.68
Presence of local innovative suppliers	−0.059	0.42	0.61
Institutional and organisational proximity with suppliers	−0.03	0.18	0.47

Source: Capello (1999a)

These results support our theoretical expectations. Learning mechanisms are rather differentiated, and seem to be correlated with two main elements: a) the kind of innovative activity a firm has to face and b) firm size. Collective learning is, as expected, more linked with small size and with radical innovation processes. Process innovation, on the contrary, seems to require mostly internal knowledge, cumulated by the firm, and some technological proximity with suppliers and customers.

Other important aspects of our conceptual framework are underlined in these empirical results. Collective learning plays a crucial role when both the continuity element and the dynamic synergy element are present: a stable local market is associated with a high turnover of the labour force. The dynamic synergies among suppliers and customers, empirically measured as the importance of the local suppliers and customers in the innovative process of the firm, are associated with the institutional and organisational proximities, what we called the local preconditions for the constitution of a milieu.

An interesting and meaningful result is the distribution of firms sample among the three statistical clusters obtained: more than 85% of our sample firms belong to the first cluster, 13% to the second, and the remaining 2% to the third. In these local systems, the prevailing spatial behaviour is one coping district economies (specialised labour force, cultural homogeneity and industrial atmosphere) and external networking. Collective learning, though significant, is fully exploited and appreciated by a minority of firms. Other firms rely on other channels for knowledge acquisition, and in particular, as shown in Table 2.3, through internal and networking learning processes.

2.5 Milieux Effects and Innovative Activities

Another important theoretical element in the theory of the milieux innovateurs is the role played by collective learning in the innovative activities of firms. In fact, if it is true that collective learning is the way of achieving new creative resources for SMEs in local areas, we would expect product innovation and breakthrough innovation to be positively correlated with collective learning.

Linear regression analyses have been run to test this hypothesis among the factors identified above. In particular, the three factors explaining structural and innovative characteristics of the sample firms have entered the model as dependent variables, and regressed on the other factors representing learning channels and/or preconditions for exploiting collective learning mechanisms.

The factors representing the innovative capacity of firms were regressed on factors which represent the learning channels, and the results obtain suggest the following considerations.

Table 2.4. Results from Regression Analyses

Dependent variables:	SMIN	PROCIN	DININ
Independent variables			
Turnover	0.666	–0.19	
	(2.33)	(–2.025)	
Cultural proximity			0.465
			(2.339)
Spin-off	0.655		
	(3.219)		
R^2	0.18	0.13	0.10

Note: t-student is reported in parentheses. Source: Capello (1999a)

The first model of Table 2.4 shows that the radical innovation activity of the smallest firms (variable SMIN) deeply depends on both the turnover of the labour force within the district, and spin-off mechanisms; they both describe channels for collective learning processes. This result witnesses that in the areas analysed, the radical innovative activity of the smallest firms is strictly linked to the exploitation of collective learning channels. The relationships between the variables is in fact significant from a statistical point of view (significant t-students), and have the expected negative sign.

The second model deals with process innovation activity; interestingly enough, this variable is negatively and significantly correlated with the turnover; it thus seems that collective learning channels do not support, and even damage, process innovation activity.

The third model deals with product innovation activities (especially incremental); the degree to which the sample firms develop product innovation is strictly linked to the degree of cultural proximity between firms. The latter expresses one of the traditional locational advantages typical of local districts, and exploited also by the theory of the milieu innovateur as a precondition for the implementation of collective learning.

The results of this section stress the relationship existing at the empirical level between the firms' innovation activity and collective learning channels. In particular, the results show that, as conceptually expected, the positive and statistically significant sign exists between radical innovation of smallest firms and the exploitation of collective learning channels. On the contrary, this is not the case for process innovative activities and for incremental activities. Especially the former do not take advantage of collective learning, while the latter seem to appreciate a good and common cultural spirit.

2.6 Milieux Effects on Local Competitiveness

2.6.1 The Model: A Spatial Expansion Method

In this Section we provide empirical evidence of the role of "milieu" effects on local competitiveness, by measuring factor productivity of SMEs with respect to different levels of exploitation of collective learning processes. We expect that those firms exploiting collective learning more are also the ones showing the greatest factor productivity.

As mentioned above, the methodology consists of the estimation of a production function at the firm level, where capital and labour parameters also depend on collective learning elements and local know-how. For this reason, the method applied consists of a spatial expansion method. This method is defined as a model that involves widening the scope of a "simpler model" by redefining its parameters into functions of "expansion" variables that index a substantially relevant "context" of the model (Casetti 1972; Casetti 1997; Casetti and Tanaka 1992). In our case, the parameters of the "traditional production function model" are redefined into functions that relate the efficiency of the production factors to the exploitation of collective learning channels. In particular, the expansion model relates labour productivity to two indicators representing the cumulative and the interactive elements in the labour market: the stability of the local labour market and the spin-off. For what concerns capital, the expansion model relates nonmaterial capital, i.e., the internal knowledge of the firm, expressed in terms of R&D expenses and patents, to knowledge cumulated in general in the local labour market and/or through linkages with external firms.

As the terminal model consists of a large number of product variables, it generally suffers from multicollinearity, even though it is not present in the initial model (Lauridsen 1996). In the present paper, the problem of multicollinearity in the terminal model is handled by using the principal component, or factor analysis to derive the product variables; the way in which the product variables are built guarantees their mutual independence. Another statistical problem arises when the observations are from a cross-section, since they may give rise to spatial dependence in the initial as well as in the terminal model. In our case, this problem is partially handled by analysing cross-section observations obtained in three different spatial milieux.

The terminal model includes space in the analysis, which is not the case in the initial production function model. In fact, the parameters of the production function model are redefined with variables indicating the degree of exploitation of collective learning channels, which are definitely of a spatial nature; these variables are then replaced into the initial production function model, so that the terminal model obtained involves space.

In the case of a firm, a technology production function reads as (Griliches 1979; Antonelli 1995):

$$Y = AK^a L^b \tag{2.1}$$

where Y is the output of the firm, K is the capital, L the labour, A represents the general efficiency parameter and a and b the partial efficiency parameters of, respectively, capital and labour. Technological change influences the parameters A, a and b, since it generates increasing general and partial efficiency, i.e., higher factor productivity.

If the firm is located in a milieu, factor productivity is influenced by collective learning, put in place by cumulative and self-reinforcing elements, stable over time and space. However, the firm can get knowledge inputs also outside the milieu via network linkages with firms located outside the milieu; these theoretical assumptions may be formalised as follows:

$$a = a_0 + a_1 KH + a_2 EL \tag{2.2}$$

where a is the capital efficiency parameter which may depend on the know-how the firm can find within the milieu, cumulated over time (KH), and a know-how obtained from the firm outside the area (EL), as claimed above. As far as labour is concerned, its efficiency parameter reads as:

$$b = b_0 + b_1 SMK + b_2 SP \tag{2.3}$$

where SMK represents the stability in the labour market and SP the spin-off effects, which represent the continuity elements, respectively over time and space. In this way, both the stability and synergy elements, emphasised in Table 2.1 above, are present.

Our production function thus becomes:

$$\ln Y = \ln \eta + a \ln K + b \ln L + c \frac{1}{2} \ln K^2 + d \frac{1}{2} \ln L^2 + f \ln K \ln L \qquad (2.4)$$

where Y is the firms' outcome, K and L are respectively capital and labour. If we substitute equations (2.2) and (2.3) into equation (2.4), we obtain:[16]

$$\ln Y = \ln \eta + a_0 \ln K + a_1 KH \ln K + a_2 EL \ln K + b_0 \ln L +$$
$$b_1 SMK \ln L + b_2 SP \ln L + c \frac{1}{2} \ln K^2 + + d \frac{1}{2} \ln L^2 + f \ln L \ln K \qquad (2.5)$$

This kind of function allows the direct estimate of outcome elasticity with respect to all input variables, capital and labour, that is the percentage outcome changes due to a 1 percent change of a specific determinant, other things being equal. In order to test whether the change in the capital has increased or decreased firms' outcome (*ceteris paribus*) it is enough to calculate the following expression and to test the sign of e_K:

$$e_K = a_0 + a_1 KH + a_2 EL + c \ln K + f \ln L \qquad (2.6)$$

where e_K represents the outcome elasticity with respect to capital. At the same time, outcome elasticity with respect to labour is easy to obtain, by calculating the following expression and testing the sign of e_L:

$$e_L = b_0 + b_1 SMK + b_2 SP + d \ln L + f \ln K \qquad (2.7)$$

Moreover, thanks to equation (2.6), we can estimate how outcome elasticity with respect to capital changes when the know-how of the milieu changes, by simply calculating:

$$e_{KKH} = a_1 \qquad (2.8)$$

and how outcome elasticity with respect to capital changes when the level of learning obtained from outside the area changes, by calculating:

$$e_{KEL} = a_2 \qquad (2.9)$$

The same reasoning can be applied to outcome elasticity with respect to labour, by measuring how it changes, for different levels of labour market stability and spin-off effects, by calculating respectively:

$$e_{LSMK} = b_1 \qquad (2.10)$$

$$e_{LSP} = b_2 \qquad (2.11)$$

---

[16] The same methodology has been applied to test the importance of co-operation with innovative customers and suppliers on factor productivity (Camagni and Capello 2000).

2.6.2 The Results: Collective Learning and Factor Productivity

The results obtained from the estimate of the production function model are satis-factory first of all from a statistical point of view. No restrictions were made on the parameters, and the good fitness of the estimate is witnessed by an R^2 equal to 0.66[17] (Table 2.5).

Table 2.5. Results of the Econometric Estimation

	Coefficient	t-student
Labour productivity		
– in firms having an average level of labour	0.99	6.01
– in firms having the highest level of labour	0.99	2.19
– in firms having the lowest level of labour	0.98	1.66
– in firms exploiting labour market stability the most	1.13	4.84
– in firms exploiting labour market stability the least	0.69	2.93
– in firms attributing a high importance to the informal knowledge accumulated by technicians and scientists be-fore spin-off took place	1.05	5.44
– in firms attributing a low importance to the informal knowledge accumulated by technicians and scientists be-fore spin-off took place	0.66	1.08
Non-material capital productivity		
– in firms having an average level of non-material capital	–0.09	–0.70
– in firms having the highest level of non-material capital	0.01	0.05
– in firms having the lowest level of non-material capital	–0.34	–1.06
– in firms exploiting the local know-how the most	0.15	0.53
– in firms exploiting the know-how the least	–0.26	–1.24
– in firms exploiting external know-how the most	–0.48	–1.18
– in firms exploiting external know-how the least	–0.01	–0.08

Source: Capello (1999b)

Also from an interpretative point of view, the results are rather interesting, and support the theoretical hypotheses. Fig. 2.1 contains the results of the analysis.

In the first model, labour shows an increasing marginal productivity in the sample firms: as Fig. 2.1a demonstrates, labour productivity[18] is higher in those firms where, ceteris paribus, labour is higher. However, labour productivity in-creases at very low rates.

---

[17] All the results, as well as the programme, are available from the author.

[18] Outcome elasticity with respect to labour represents labour productivity when the latter is measured as a percentage. The same holds for the elasticity of outcome with respect to capital, which measures capital productivity.

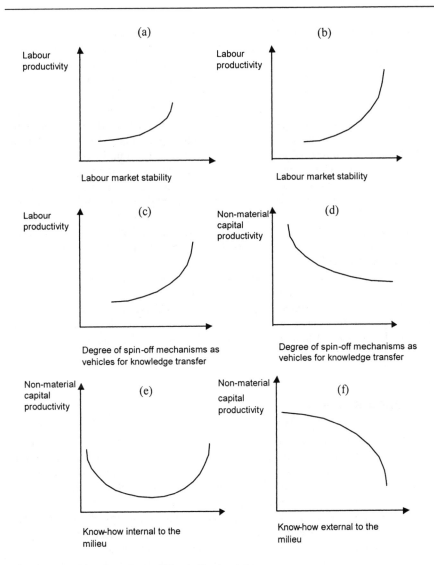

Fig. 2.1. Collective Learning and Factor Productivity

The results change if labour productivity is measured taking into account the different degrees to which firms in the districts appreciate the stability of the labour market. As Fig. 2.1b shows, labour productivity increases drastically in those firms that demonstrate to attribute a high importance to the stability of the local labour market.

A similar result is achieved if labour productivity is measured for different levels of importance attributed to spin-off effects as vehicles for generating a cumulative knowledge among technicians and scientists. In those firms attributing a high importance to spin-off mechanisms, labour productivity is higher than in firms where the importance attributed to spin-offs is very low (see Fig. 2.1c).

These results support the theoretical expectations: collective learning mechanisms, in the form of elements guaranteeing both a cumulative process of knowledge over time and dynamic synergies over space, increase labour productivity.

Fig. 2.1 also shows the results for non-material capital productivity.[19] Non-material capital productivity decreases, witnessing that a critical mass of knowledge is necessary in order to turn innovative knowledge into business results. In fact, after a certain threshold level, capital productivity turns upwards (Fig. 2.1d).

Fig. 2.1e shows what happens to non-material capital productivity if firms exploit the know-how present locally with different intensity. In firms that exploit the local know-how with very low intensity, capital productivity is negative (–0.26), while it achieves a much higher level in firms exploiting the local know-how with a high intensity (0.15). In other words, the local know-how helps local firms to achieve a critical mass of knowledge, which is important to achieve the expected positive results.

An interesting result is the one achieved while non-material capital productivity is measured for different levels of exploitation of know-how coming from outside the milieu. As Fig. 2.1f shows, capital productivity decreases in those firms exploiting external know-how in a more intense way. This result supports the idea that cumulated external knowledge does not lead to a higher labour productivity than local knowledge does.

2.7 Conclusions

The theorisation of innovative processes through the milieu paradigm represents in our opinion a relevant contribution to the wider (or collective) reflection about the relevance of spatial, relational assets in economic evolution. Similarities with parallel theorisations and cross fertilisations were important in the structuring of the paradigm, which nevertheless maintains its specificity.

This paper provides a review of the theoretical underpinnings of the milieu approach and translates some theoretical elements into testable propositions. Up to some years ago, the milieu paradigm has found empirical support in qualitative analyses, which, mainly through case-study methodologies, were able to describe the milieu phenomenon.

In this paper, the efforts made in terms of quantitative analyses have been presented. Different methodologies have been applied to the sample of high-tech clustered SMEs firms and were able to demonstrate that:

- the cluster analysis run to describe the learning behaviours of firms depicts different groups of firms, according to their innovative activity and size. Different learning channels exist in milieux; the collective learning channels are ex-

---

[19] As mentioned before, the "non-material capital" is measured in terms of R&D expenditures and patent values.

ploited by the smallest and most innovative firms, which take advantage of spatial and territorial assets and use them to overcome the limits of their size. For large firms, mainly dealing with process innovation, a profile of learning internal to the firm is more typical;

- regression analyses demonstrate that a positive and significant correlation exists between collective learning and radical innovation activities of small firms: in this respect, the main idea that collective learning enhances the innovative capability of small firms turns out to be proved;
- factor productivity of firms depends on collective learning mechanisms. Ceteris paribus, a firm has higher labour and capital productivity, the higher the exploitation of collective learning.

These kinds of statistical and econometric methodologies have never been applied to this research field and provide an insight into measurement issues, which in the field of innovative local systems are unfortunately widely overlooked. Further research directions exist in this area, which is worth mentioning. Especially from the methodological point of view, the search for other quantitative indicators is necessary, in order to measure other "unmeasurable facts". The indicators used here in fact are obtained from discrete information, which is transformed into continuous variables through statistical analyses: it is worth mentioning that, while these techniques are efficient in the results achieved, they inevitably generate a loss of variance (and thus of information); for this reason the availability of continuous indicators would be of great help. To go towards this direction, from the theoretical point of view, new insights are necessary in generating theoretical definitions that can be turned into measurable concepts.

The suggested effort to develop further econometric analysis is extremely important for two kinds of reasons. First of all, a solid empirical analysis reinforces theory, as it is always the case. Secondly, the theory becomes much more useful for supporting the development of local policies oriented towards the implementation of local synergy elements.

References

Antonelli C (1995) The economics of localised technological change and industrial dynamics. Kluwer Academic Publisher, London

Arrighetti A and Seravalli G. (eds) (1999) Istituzioni intermedie e sviluppo locale. Donzelli, Roma

Aydalot Ph (ed) (1986) Milieux innovateurs en Europe. GREMI, Paris

Aydalot Ph, Keeble D (eds) (1988) High technology industry and innovative environment. Routledge, London

Bagnasco A, Trigilia C (1984) Società e Politica nelle Aree di Piccola Impresa: Il Caso di Bassano. Arsenale, Venezia

Becattini G (1979) Dal settore industriale al distretto industriale: alcune considerazioni sull'unità di indagine della politica industriale. Economia e Politica Industriale 1: 1–79

Becattini G (1990) The Marshallian industrial district as a socio-economic notion. In: Pyke F, Becattini G, Sengenberger W (eds) Industrial districts and inter-firm cooperation in Italy. ILO, Geneva

Bellet M, Colletis G, Lung Y (eds) (1993) Economies de Proximités. Special issue of the Revue d'Economie Régionale et Urbaine 3

Bianchi P (1989) Concorrenza dinamica, distretti industriali e interventi locali. In: Gobbo F (ed.) Distretti e sistemi produttivi alle soglie degli anni novanta. Franco Angeli Editore, Milan, pp 47–60

Bramanti A, Maggioni M (eds) (1997) La dinamica dei sistemi produttivi territoriali: Teorie, tecniche, politiche. Franco Angeli Editore, Milan

Buchanan J (1965) An economic theory of clubs. Economica 32: 1–14

Camagni R (1991a) Local "milieu", uncertainty and innovation networks: towards a new dynamic theory of economic space. In: Camagni R, Innovation Networks: Spatial Perspectives. Belhaven-Pinter, London, pp 121–144

Camagni R (1995) Global network and local milieux: Towards a theory of economic space. In: Conti S, Malecki E, Oinas P (eds) The industrial enterprise and its environment: Spatial perspective. Avebury, Aldershot, pp 195–216

Camagni R (1996) I milieux di alta tecnologia e nuove riflessioni sul concetto di milieu innovateur. Mimeo

Camagni R (1999) The city as a milieu: Applying the gremi approach to urban evolution. Révue d'Economie Régionale et Urbaine 3: 591–606

Camagni R (ed.) (1991b) Innovation networks: Spatial perspectives. Belhaven-Pinter, London

Camagni R, Capello R (2000) The role of inter SMEs networking and links in innovative high-tech milieux. In: Keeble D, Wilkinson F (eds) High-technology clusters, networking and collective learning in Europe. Ashgate Publisher, Avebury, pp 118–155

Camagni R, Rabellotti R (1997) Footwear production systems in Italy: A dynamic comparative analysis. In: Ratti R, Bramanti A, Gordon R (eds) The dynamics of innovative regions. Ashgate, Aldershot, pp 139–164

Capello R (1999a) Spatial transfer of knowledge in high-tech milieux: Learning vs. collective learning processes. Regional Studies 3: 353–366

Capello R (1999b) A measurement of collective learning effects in Italian high-tech milieux. Révue d'Economie Régionale et Urbaine 3: 449–468

Capello R (2001) Urban innovation and collective learning: Theory and evidence from five metropolitan cities in Europe. In Fischer MM, Froehlich J (eds) Knowledge, complexity and innovation systems. Springer, Heidelberg, pp 181–208

Casetti E (1972) Generating models by the expansion method: Applications to geographical research. Geographical Analysis 4: 81–91

Casetti E (1997) The expansion method, mathematical modelling and spatial econometrics. International Regional Science Review 20: 9–33

Casetti E,Tanaka K (1992) The spatial dynamics of Japanese manufacturing productivity: An empirical analysis of expanded Verdoorn equations. Papers in Regional Science 71: 1–13

Chambers RG (1988) Applied production analysis. Cambridge University Press, Cambridge

Chesnais F (1988) Technical cooperation agreements among firms. STI Review 4, OECD, Paris

Christensen L, Jorgenson D, Lau L (1973) Transcendental logarithmic production frontiers. Review of Economics and Statistics 55: 28–45

Dosi G (1982) Technological paradigms and technological trajectories: A suggested interpretation of the determinants and directions of technical change. Research Policy 11: 147–162

Dosi G, Freeman C, Nelson R, Silverberg G, Soete L (eds) (1988) Technical change and economic theory. Pinter Publisher, London

Dupuy C, Gilly J-P (1995) Dynamiques industrielles, dynamiques territoriales. Paper presented at the International Conference of ASRLF, held in Toulouse, August 30–September 1

Evans D, Heckman J (1984) A test of subadditivity of the cost function with application to the Bell System. American Economic Review 74: 615–623

Gordon R (1991) Innovation, industrial networks and high-technology regions. In: Camagni R (ed) Innovation networks: Spatial perspectives. Belhaven-Pinter, London, pp 174–195

Griliches Z (1979) Issues in assessing the contribution of research and development to productivity growth. Bell Journal of Economics 10: 92–116

Henderson JV (1974) The sizes and types of cities. American Economic Review 64: 640–656

Kawashima T (1975) Urban agglomeration economies in manufacturing industry. Papers of the Regional Science Association 34

Lauridsen J (1996) Multicollinearity and spatial effects in expanded linear models. In: Kristensen G (ed) Symposium on the expansion focus on parametric variation. Odense University, pp 121–163

Maillat D, Quévit M, Senn L (1993) Réseaux d'innovation et milieux innovateurs: Un pari pour le développement régional. EDES, Neuchâtel

Marelli E (1981) Optimal city size, the productivity of cities and urban production functions. Sistemi Urbani 1/2: 149–163

Marshall A (1919) Industry and trade. Macmillan, London

Nelson R, Winter S (1977) In search of a useful theory of innovation. Research Policy 6: 36–76

Perhankangas A, Kauranen I (1996) Spin-offs from established corporations – A systematic classification of spin-off firms and a study of their contribution to industry growth. Paper presented at the European Network Meeting on Networks, Collective Learning and Research and Technology Development in Regionally Clustered High-Technology SMEs, held in Nice, September 27–28

Rabellotti R (1997) External economies and cooperation in industrial districts: A comparison of Italy and Mexico. Macmillan, London

Rabellotti R, Schimtz H (1999) The internal heterogeneity of industrial districts in Italy, Brazil and Mexico. Regional Studies 33: 97–108

Rallet A (1993) Choix de proximité et processus d'innovation technologique. In: Revue d'Economie Régionale et Urbaine 3: 365–386

Ratti R, Bramanti A, Gordon R (eds) (1997) The dynamics of innovative regions. Ashgate, Aldershot

RERU (1999) Le paradigme de milieu innovateur dans l'économie contemporaine. Revue d'Economie Régionale et Urbaine 3

Scott AJ (1993) Technopolis, high-technology industry and regional development in Southern California. University of California Press, Berkley

Segal D (1976) Are there returns to scale in city size? Review of Economics and Statistics 53: 339–350

Shefer D (1973) Localisation economies in SMSA'A: A production function analysis. Journal of Regional Science 13: 55–64

Storper M (1995) La géographie des conventions: Proximité territoriale, interdépendences hors marché et dévelopement economique. In: Rallait A, Torre A (eds) Économie industriale et économie spatiale. Economica, Paris, pp 111–127

Sveikauskas L (1975) The productivity of cities. Quarterly Journal of Economics 89: 393–413

Williamson O (1985) The economics of institutions of capitalism. The Free Press, New York

Appendix 2A.1 Results of the Factor Analysis

The methodology used to describe learning behaviour for innovative activities among our firm sample is a cluster analysis. However, before entering the behavioural analysis, factor analysis is run, with the primary goal of simplifying the description of local systems and of their innovative and learning behaviour. Factor analysis allows the identification of a relatively small number of underlying principal elements of "factors" that explain the correlation among a set of variables; in other words, it summarises a large number of variables with a smaller number of "derived" variables.[20] In fact, from our questionnaire, many variables could be used to describe:

a) firms' characteristics, in terms of:

• growth, size, and innovative activity;
• relationships with suppliers, in terms of role played by suppliers in the innovative activity of the firm, and whether organisational and institutional proximity matters;
• relationships with customers, as in the case of suppliers;

b) the local area characteristics, in terms of:

• district locational advantages, like industrial atmosphere, stable labour market, cultural proximity with the labour force;
• local labour market, especially in terms of mechanisms associated with the learning of the local labour force, either internal or external to the firm, and in this latter case, either within or outside the district.

Factor analysis has been run in order to identify for each group of characteristics mentioned above, which could be represented by many explanatory variables of our questionnaire, a smaller number of "derived" variables. In statistical terms,

---

[20] The use of factor and cluster analysis to local districts theory is not new: see, in this perspective, Rabellotti (1997), and Rabellotti and Schmitz (1997).

the results are quite satisfactory: all factor analyses run in each of the above mentioned groups of characteristics explain a large share of total sample variance.

For what concerns firms characteristics (Table 2A.1), three main principal factors have been found to be significant and meaningful, explaining 67% of total sample variance, and being simple to interpret from an economic point of view. A first factor, labelled DININ, represents firms with increasing turnover, highly innovative. A second factor, labelled SMIN, can be interpreted as a size and product innovation factor: firms of small size with breakthrough innovation. A third factor in this area, labelled PROCIN, represents firms characterised by high process innovation.

The area of traditional local district advantages provides interesting statistical and economic results (Table 2A.2). Four main factors are identified, explaining 67% of the total sample variance: cultural proximity with the labour force, proximity to the original firm, stable local labour market, and industrial atmosphere. Also in these results, the economic interpretation is simple: the main industrial districts locational efficiency, (reduction of transaction costs due to labour market cultural proximity) and external economies (industrial atmosphere) are clearly represented in the factors while more traditional locational advantages, related to a traditional accessibility element (geographical proximity to important motorways or airports contained in question a91), do not emerge as important.

The area of learning incorporates all possible variables representing possible channels for learning. In our conceptual framework learning is a process of cumulative knowledge embedded in the labour force: for this reason, all questions related to the training channels of the local labour force are part of this factor analysis. Again, also in this case the results are quite satisfactory at both the statistical and economic level: four factors are achieved (Table 2A.3). A first factor represents learning external to the district: scientists and technicians coming from other firms in the area and informal mechanisms of hiring. The second factor represents a learning internal to the firm being composed by an emerging variable representing the number of technicians and scientists that have trained in local firms. The third factor deals with the turnover of the labour force, merging a high percentage of both employees that joined and left the firm in the last five years. The fourth factor represents the spin-off mechanism.

Table 2A.1 Factor Analysis on the Structural Characteristics of Firms

Variables	Factor 1 Product innovative firms DININ	Factor 2 Smallest and most innovative firms SMIN	Factor 3 Process innovative firms PROCIN
Turnover over the sample average	0.51	–0.74	0.01
Increasing turnover	0.74	0.04	0.18
75% of the turnover depending on innovation	0.35	0.84	–0.04
Significant product innovation developed over the last 5 years	0.45	0.08	–0.61
Breakthrough product innovation developed over the last 5 years	0.64	0.012	–0.15
Significant process innovation developed over the last 5 years	0.19	0.009	0.84
Explained variance by each factor (in %)	26	21	19
Share of total explained variance	67%		

Table 2A.2 Results of the Factor Analysis on Possible Learning Channels

	Factor 1 Internal learning to the firm	Factor 2 Learning external to the milieu	Factor 3 Turnover of the labour force
The firm is the result of a spin-off	−0.49	−0.38	−0.21
Degree of importance for the firm of scientific and technical expertise before the spin-off	−0.06	0.24	0.13
Share of scientists and technicians recruited in firms outside the milieu	−0.18	0.67	−0.29
Share of scientists and technicians recruited in firms within the milieu	−0.44	−0.73	−0.14
Share of scientists and technicians recruited in research centre in the milieu	0.33	0.09	0.11
Share of scientists and technicians recruited in research centre outside the milieu	0.12	0.40	−0.04
Training of scientists and technicians within the firm	0.85	0.17	−0.07
Training of scientists and technicians in other firms	−0.81	0.08	−0.20
Degree of importance of the local labour market to provide the right expertise	−0.0003	−0.0001	−0.14
Share of employees who have been recruited by the firm	0.25	−0.031	0.81
Share of employees who have left the firm	−0.10	−0.038	0.85
Degree of importance of informal channels for the recruitment of technicians via local associations	0.19	0.20	0.003
Degree of importance of informal channels for the recruitment of scientists via local associations	0.10	0.57	0.09
Degree of variance explained by each factor	20.9%	13.8%	11.6%

Table 2A.2 (cont.)

	Factor 4 Spin-off	Factor 5 Know-how internal to the milieu	Factor 6 Informal recruitment
The firm is the result of a spin-off	0.67	-0.15	0.07
Degree of importance for the firm of scientific and technical expertise before the spin-off	0.72	0.03	0.004
Share of scientists and technicians recruited in firms outside the milieu	0.03	−0.11	0.0
Share of scientists and technicians recruited in firms within the milieu	−0.07	−0.10	0.02
Share of scientists and technicians recruited in research centre in the milieu	0.51	0.53	−0.05
Share of scientists and technicians recruited in research centre outside the milieu	−0.27	−0.04	−0.50
Training of scientists and technicians within the firm	0.05	−0.09	0.06
Training of scientists and technicians in other firms	0.005	−0.22	−0.09
Degree of importance of the local labour market to provide the right expertise	−0.10	0.86	−0.003
Share of employees who have been recruited by the firm	0.20	0.09	0.07
Share of employees who have left the firm	−0.12	−0.20	−0.02
Degree of importance of informal channels for the recruitment of technicians via local associations	−0.07	−0.02	0.84
Degree of importance of informal channels for the recruitment of scientists via local associations	0.09	0.44	0.35
Degree of variance explained by each factor	9.4%	8.2%	7.5%
Share of total sample variance explained	71.4%		

Table 2A.3 Results of the Factor Analysis on Location Advantages

	Factor 1 Common cultural back-ground	Factor 2 Proximity to the original firm	Factor 3 Stability of the labour market	Factor 4 Industrial atmosphere
Proximity to motorways	−0.02	−0.62	0.26	0.06
Existence of an industrial atmos-phere	0.28	0.29	−0.05	0.84
A low labour cost	−0.14	0.29	−0.71	−0.04
A similar culture among the labour force	0.81	0.011	0.18	−0.08
Similar technical background of the labour force	0.84	0.05	−0.20	0.22
Stable labour market	−0.11	0.13	0.82	−0.05
Proximity to the residential place	0.33	0.49	−0.07	−0.64
Proximity to the original firm	0.01	0.82	0.16	0.17
Share of variance explained by each factor	24%	17.8%	15.5%	14.2%
Share of total sample variance ex-plained	71.5%			

3 Entrepreneurship and Innovation in the SME Sector[1]

Enno Masurel, Kees van Montfort and Peter Nijkamp

Faculty of Economics and Business Administration, Free University, Amsterdam

3.1 Setting the Scene

Entrepreneurship has become a topical research issue in recent years. In particular, the role of the entrepreneur in innovation processes has received much attention, as is witnessed in the seminal review of Malecki (1997). Many studies in this field appear to refer to Schumpeter (1934) as an important stepping stone. Schumpeter views the entrepreneur as the key actor in the innovation process. In his view, the entrepreneur is a change actor who is permanently seeking new opportunities (see for a review also Nijkamp 2002). The wealth of empirical research in the past decades has clearly demonstrated that the 'entrepreneurial attitude' as an 'animal spirit' is a complex and ambiguous concept that can only properly be studied by thorough empirical research.

Many findings in recent decades have revealed a multitude of drivers for the innovation process. Several authors have suggested that small and medium-sized enterprises (SMEs) play a central role in the innovation process (both product and process innovations). The question whether SMEs exhibit a high degree of innovativeness has recently extensively been studied in the literature. The findings are not always conclusive, and future research is no doubt warranted. In the present paper we will examine the innovation perceptions and attitudes of entrepreneurs and managers in SMEs from the following perspective: which factors do they perceive as critical for success in the innovation process? This exploratory research question can only be answered by solid empirical research on the drivers of innovation behaviour. In this paper, innovations refer to entirely new products (or services), to improved versions of an existing product (or service) or to a new market for an existing product (or service).

The research approach in our study is as follows. Based on an extensive literature survey, we will identify a systematic classification of 14 possible important drivers of innovative behaviour in the SME sector. These factors will act as a test frame for our empirical research on entrepreneurial attitudes regarding innovation.

---

[1] The authors thank Pascal van der Hart for his role in the data collection process and Ramon Lentink for his statistical assistance.

Then the design and findings of an extensive survey questionnaire among SMEs in the Netherlands will be discussed. The empirical results will be derived from a multivariate statistical analysis (i.e., factor analysis) of the empirical data. The paper will be concluded with some retrospective conclusions on innovative behaviour of SMEs.

3.2 An Exploratory Literature Review

There is an avalanche of literature on the motives and socioeconomic implications of entrepreneurship in the SME sector (see for recent contributions inter alia Marsili 2000; Peneder 2000).

Although SMEs provide an engine of innovative activity (Thurik 1996), there is only sparse empirical knowledge on the specific success factors of SME innovation, in contrast to innovative behaviour in large corporate organisations. Nooteboom (1994) speaks of dynamic complementarity in innovation between SMEs and large firms. SMES are usually strong in applications of basic technologies, in generating inventions, in implementing promising results, and in conquering market niches and residual markets. Their talents and qualities are clearly related to their core characteristics: independence and flexibility, inevitably associated with the personality of the entrepreneur ('entrepreneurial spirit'). Yap and Souder (1994) argue that the small entrepreneurial high-technology firms have to adopt competitive strategies that are very different from the ones used by large corporate organisations, in order to maximise their chances of success with the introduction of new products or services. Large firms are more skilled in exploiting findings from fundamental research and in adopting efficient production methods, thereby benefiting from scale economies. Thus, the performance of small and large firms may differ. We will raise here the question which specific factors can be identified that provide a significant explanation as critical success conditions for innovative behaviour in the SME sector.

In the economic literature seeking to explain the competitive benefits of innovative behaviour a great variety of economic, social, institutional, geographic and technological drivers is normally mentioned (see, e.g., Kleinknecht 1986; Davelaar 1992; Bertuglia et al. 1997). The identification of a systematic list of drivers of innovative attitudes and behaviour in the SME sector – in terms of technogenesis and adoption of new findings – is not easy, as the SME sector is extremely diverse. Economic research has not yet been able to design a generally applicable framework for SME innovation. Consequently, in our analysis we will deploy a rich variety of scientific studies as a source for the selection of indicators that may potentially explain innovation in the SME sector. The validity of this exploratory approach has to be tested by means of empirical fieldwork on SME firms. On the basis of an extensive literature search we were able to extract by way of a systematic classification 14 drivers of SME innovations. And these will successively now be described. This classification was inferred from reading the extensive literature by way of an inductive approach and was not based on a prior defined and specified theoretical construct.

3.2.1 Unique Product Advantages

On the literature on SME innovation, a prominent place is assumed by unique product advantages, in terms of product quality, product functions, quality/price ratio and product design. So the specificity of a product is not only related to its internal features, but also to its position in the market. The customer should be provided with real value, that is superior to competitive products, so that his needs are optimally satisfied. We refer inter alia to Song and Parry (1997), Atuahene-Gima (1996), Montoya-Weiss and Calantone (1994), Edgett, Shipley and Forbes (1992), Zirger and Maidique (1990), Cooper (1990), Cooper and Kleinschmidt (1987) and Rothwell et al. (1974) for further exposition on the importance of this factor for innovative entrepreneurial attitudes.

3.2.2 Human Resources Management

A second important success factor for the innovation process in the SME sector is human resources management, in terms of technological knowledge, marketing knowledge, customer orientation, and training and development of skills. Investment in human resources and in labour quality is essential here. All these elements play a key role in the innovation process, as people are one of the major success factors. These findings are substantiated in many studies, amongst others by Heracleous (1998), Huiban and Bouhsina (1998), Hatch and Mowery (1998), Coopey et al. (1998), Atuahene-Gima (1996), Craig and Hart (1992), Dwyer and Mellor (1991) and Cooper (1990).

3.2.3 Marketing Activities

The proficiency of marketing activities comes at the third place. Many authors, for instance, Song and Parry (1997), Calantone et al. (1996), Montoya-Weiss and Calantone (1994), Song and Parry (1994), Edgett et al. (1992), Maidique and Zirger (1984) and Rothwell et al. (1974) have stressed the importance of the right market entrance, inter alia with the help of communication and efficient market intelligence. Based on this literature survey, marketing activities can be operationalised and distinguished into testing of prototypes, provision of additional services, strength of distribution channels, advertising and promotion, and the presence of a sales department. This requires of course detailed information on the firm's marketing strategy.

3.2.4 Project Definition

Innovative behaviour is not generic in nature, but addresses specific opportunities. Thus, before the implementation of an innovation, a sharp project definition is needed. Consequently, an important critical success factor for the innovation process concerns the specification of the target group, the positioning of the product, the development of the product functions and the technical product specifications; for details we refer to Song and Parry (1994), Craig and Hart (1992), Cooper (1990), Cooper and Kleinschmidt (1987), Maidique and Zirger (1984) and Rothwell et al. (1974). A project definition can also be described in terms of a protocol consisting of a clear definition of the target market prior to the product development stage. Clearly, this factor cannot be seen in isolation from the above described success factors comprising product advantages, human resources management and marketing activities.

3.2.5 Market

Effective demand is a sine qua non for a successful innovation. This holds in particular for the SME sector which has only limited possibilities to influence or control the market or to cope with unexpected failures. And therefore, the presence of a sufficient market (in terms of size and growth potential) is a success factor in the innovation process of SME firms. According to Calantone et al. (1996), Song and Parry (1994), Yap and Souder (1994), and Zirger and Maidique (1990), the market as such contributes significantly to the success of new products. It goes without saying that this factor is not independent of the above mentioned success factor of marketing activities.

3.2.6 Product-Company Fit

The product identity of a firm is essential for its position in a competitive market. Consequently, the importance of a proper product-company fit (i.e., complementarity) has often been emphasised in the literature, amongst others by Song and Parry (1994), Yap and Souder (1994), Zirger and Maidique (1990), and Maidique and Zirger (1984). In operational terms, the product-company fit refers in particular to the integration with the current product assortment (portfolio), with the group of current clients and with the current technological knowledge of the firm.

3.2.7 Pre-Development

The introduction of a new product or service on the market incorporates a high risk for the firm concerned. Since 'forewarned is forearmed', an important key success condition is the execution of feasibility studies in the form of pre-development research, in particular in terms of assessment of client wishes and demands, analysis of the competition, and technical and financial feasibility in an early stage. This early orientation is mentioned in several studies, e.g., by Cooper and Kleinschmidt (1987), Dwyer and Mellor (1991) and Cooper (1990). Such a pro-active strategy may also be necessary to acquire venture capital.

3.2.8 Technological Activities

New technologies are not 'manna from heaven', but require dedicated actions and an entrepreneurial profile seeking new technological opportunities. In the literature we find several authors who emphasise the importance of a technological orientation, for instance Calantone, Schmidt and Song (1996) and Montoya-Weiss and Calantone (1994). These authors indicate that greater proficiency in technological activities increases the likelihood of success for new products. Such technological activities can be translated into assembling technological knowledge, flexible development, internal testing of a prototype, and organisation of the production process.

3.2.9 Competition

Entrepreneurship in the SME sector is normally characterised by many potential competitors. The development of a competitive course requires insight into the motives and actions of other competitors, so as to position a new product properly, in terms of degree of market appeal, novelty of the new product and the possibility for patents. Calantone, Schmidt and Song (1996), for instance, mention the strategic importance of collecting and assessing information on the competition in the market. Competitive product advantage is also mentioned as a key determinant for new product success (see Song and Parry 1997).

3.2.10 Entrepreneur

The entrepreneur is characterised by a series of creative qualifications (see, e.g., Nijkamp 2002). It is striking that the entrepreneur as such is hardly mentioned as a success factor in the innovation process. Heunks (1998) shows that a certain combination of order, flexibility and creativity fosters innovation; these are typical entrepreneurial aspects. It is noteworthy that Quinn (1985) mentions that large firms stay innovative by behaving like small entrepreneurial ventures. The entrepreneurial style may be interpreted in terms of commitment and determination, persistence in problem solving, creativity and team spirit, and motivational capacities.

3.2.11 Project Approach

The introduction of a new product requires a broad range of activities; careful planning prior to the production is a prerequisite for success. Zirger and Maidique (1990) have revealed that new product development tends to be more successful if the process is professionally planned and well implemented (i.e., project definition). In operational terms, this factor depends on the project leader's strength, thorough planning and organisation, careful monitoring of progress, and multidisciplinary composition of the project team.

3.2.12 Innovation Culture

It is well known that innovative behaviour needs proper seedbeds through which creativity can flourish. This is well documented in the incubation theory (see Davelaar 1992, for a review). Pickard (1996) has shown the importance of an innovative culture and open environment in which people feel empowered to take risks. In this situation freedom, support for ideas, time for experimentation, flexibility, trust, and dynamism are very important. In reality, such factors can be assessed in terms of opportunity to air innovative opinions, space to elaborate innovative ideas and support for these innovative ideas as operationalisations.

3.2.13 Financial Means

Each new product or production process requires investment in human resources and in physical equipment. Sometimes this can be very costly for a small firm. And therefore, a balance between costs and revenues in the short term is necessary. In this context, Maidique and Zirger (1984) mention the contribution margin of the new product as being important for a new product's success. In operational terms, we may interpret this success condition by means of the internal and external availability of financial means.

3.2.14 Collaboration

Innovative firms tend to operate in industrial networks (including knowledge networks). Exchange of information but also outsourcing may be a strategic move. In general, inter-firm collaboration may be seen as a critical success factor in the innovation process. Many recent studies have highlighted the importance of collaboration for business success of SMEs from various perspectives. We refer here inter alia to Stern et al. (1996) and Galbraith (1980).

After this broad exposition on the various performance conditions for creative SME entrepreneurship, it is necessary to substantiate the above designed multidimensional framework for innovative behaviour by means of real-world facts. And therefore the remainder of this paper is devoted to a statistical application.

3.3 Data Collection

Based on the above literature review, we were able to identify systematically 14 critical success factors for the (SME) innovation process. This taxonomy of 14 success conditions has to be operationalised for further empirical research; they may essentially be conceived of as latent variables which have to be measured by observable indicators. In our fieldwork we were able to translate these 14 factors into 50 variables (see Table 3.1). Clearly, such a classification is never unambiguous, since most items are not mutually exclusive. In fact, many factors in this multi-dimensional table are interrelated. The information on these 50 operational indications was obtained from survey questionnaires sent to SME respondents. To test the meaning of the 50 items, the respondents were also asked whether they agreed that this operationalisation was crucial in the innovation process as perceived by the respondent. All the fieldwork was done in postal form.

Apart from the direct questions on the 50 items, some other background questions were formulated concerning, e.g., the involvement in either the manufacturing sector or the service sector, the person filling out the questionnaire (entrepreneur or manager), the number of innovations in a given year, and the size of the firm.

The field survey was held among Dutch firms in the SME sector. In total, 960 firms were asked to fill out a postal questionnaire. 638 of them were randomly selected from the Dutch MarktSelect CD-Rom (which comprises over 800,000 organisations). The sole selection criterion applied by us was being a SME (i.e., according to the official Dutch standard: fewer than 100 employees). The selection consisted of 388 service firms and 250 manufacturing firms. To increase this sample, in a later stage, 322 more firms were selected from other databases (magazines and personal networks). These latter firms were already known for their involvement in innovations, although no information was available on their size or the sector they belonged to. Clearly, the selection procedure as a whole exhibits some potential bias as a consequence of random and selective sampling, but as a whole the dispersion of returned questionnaires was rather balanced, so that some confidence in the representativeness is warranted.

The response rate for the postal questionnaire was more or less normal for Dutch standards. 167 firms (17.4%) returned the completed questionnaire on time. 47.3% of the respondents belonged to the manufacturing sector, 27.5% to the service sector, and 25.2% to other sectors. 68.3% of the questionnaires were filled out by the entrepreneurs themselves; the rest were filled out by others (usually managers). It is noteworthy that 26.8% of the SMEs considered had ten or more successful innovations; they may be seen as the real successful innovators in our sample. It is also interesting that 43.8% of the responding firms did not employ more than seven employees (6.9% of the firms appeared to employ in the meantime more than 100 people). The number of seven employees was chosen here because this is, according to the standard management literature, the virtual maximum number that an individual superior can usually manage (in terms of span of control).

Table 3.1. Critical Success Factors in the Innovation Process: Operationalisation

1	Unique Product Advantages	Product Quality
		Product Functions
		Quality/Price Relation
		Design
2	Human Resource Management	Technological Knowledge
		Marketing
		Knowledge
		Customer Orientation
		Training and Development
3	Marketing Activities	Testing Prototype
		Provision of Additional Services
		Strength of Distribution Channels
		Advertising and Promotion
		Sales Department
4	Project Definition	Specification of Target Group
		Positioning Product
		Product Functions
		Technical Product Specifications
5	Market	Size
		Growth Potential
6	Product-Company Fit	Relation with Current Assortment
		Relation with Current Clients
		Relation with Current Technological Knowledge
7	Pre-Development	Determination Client Wishes and Demands
		Competition Analysis
		Technical Feasibility
		Financial Feasibility
8	Technological Activities	Assembling Technological Knowledge
		Development Prototype
		Internal Testing Prototype
		Organization Production Process
9	Competition	Degree
		Novelty of the New Product
		Possibility for Patents
10	Entrepreneur	Commitment and Determination
		Persistence in Problem Solving
		Creativity
		Team Spirit and Motivational Capacities
11	Project Approach	Strength of Project Leader
		Planning and Organisation
		Progress Checking
		Multidisciplinary Composition of Project Team
12	Innovation Culture	Opportunity to Air Innovative Opinions
		Space to Elaborate Innovative Ideas
		Support for Innovative Ideas
13	Financial Means	Internal Disposability
		External Disposability
14	Collaboration	With Other Companies
		With Knowledge Centres
		Involvement of Consultants

Regarding the statistical information collected, it should be mentioned that the opinions of the respondents on the 50 critical success factors were all measured on a five-point Lickert scale. This seems to be meaningful, as the reliability of answers to the question on backgrounds of the success of a new product or service appears to depend strongly on simple operational exercises. The choice of options for the answers was: fully disagree, disagree, no opinion, agree, and fully agree. In the next sections we will describe and interpret the results of our empirical analysis.

3.4 Data Analysis

As mentioned above, all 14 critical success factors described in Sect. 3.2 were operationalised by means of 50 observable indicators. In order to compare the relative importance of the different critical success factors, we decided to summarise for each critical success factor the corresponding measurable attributes into a few aggregate indicators (preferably one), by using multivariate statistical methods. Therefore, for each success factor a separate factor analysis model was deployed in order to obtain a summary measure for the observable attributes (see Lewis-Beck, 1994). Such a model assumes that the measured operational attributes can be represented by just one unobserved common variable known as a factor (or a limited number of factors). As is well known, such a data transformation may contain a margin of error. Thus, the factor model is basically a measurement model for the unobserved common factors (i.e., the newly defined critical success factors).

In our numerical exercise, standard SPSS software was used to obtain Maximum Likelihood estimates of the unknown coefficients in the factor analysis model. The percentage variances (R^2 values) of the operational features, explained by the unobserved common factors, provided a good indication of the quality of the factor analysis model used here. Apparently, the model gives a good fit, as all R^2 values fall between 60% and 100%, as is witnessed in Table 3.2. This means that each unobserved common factor (i.e., critical success factor) is a reasonable representation of the corresponding group of operational attributes.

Table 3.2. Results of the Factor Analysis Models

Critical success factor	R^2 value of the Factor Analysis Model of the critical success factors
Unique Product Advantages	0.681
Human Resource Management	0.732
Marketing Activities	0.628
Project Definition	0.816
Market	0.948
Product-Company Fit	0.906
Pre-Development	0.806
Technological Activities	0.948
Competition	0.965
Entrepreneur	0.755
Project Approach	0.771
Innovation Culture	0.887
Financial Means	0.910
Collaboration	0.940

In the second step of our analysis, the estimates for the unknown coefficients of the 14 factor analysis model and the factor scores of all operational features enabled us to estimate the individual firm's scores for each of the unobserved common factors of the 14 separate factor analysis model (see Lewis-Beck 1994). These estimates of the unobserved common factors appear to be all satisfactory indicators of the values of the underlying latent critical success factors.

Next, we used the values of the different critical success factors for each firm, in order to compute the means of the various critical success factors and to compare these means. Of course, it is also possible to compute the correlations between the different critical success factors. From Table 3.3 it follows that all pairs of critical success factors are positively correlated (between 0.07 and 0.56). This means that if a firm has a high (low) value for one specific critical factor, the firm also tends to have high (low) values for the other critical factors.

Table 3.3. Correlations Between Critical Success Factors

	V1	V2	V3	V4	V5	V6	V7	V8	V9	V10	V11	V12	V13	V14
V1	1													
V2	0.12	1												
V3	0.55	0.33	1											
V4	0.48	0.20	0.43	1										
V5	0.17	0.37	0.33	0.07	1									
V6	0.40	0.18	0.48	0.38	0.13	1								
V7	0.46	0.27	0.56	0.48	0.17	0.40	1							
V8	0.39	0.28	0.17	0.29	0.39	0.18	0.22	1						
V9	0.12	0.30	0.22	0.42	0.25	0.20	0.18	0.30	1					
V10	0.38	0.16	0.49	0.39	0.19	0.42	0.33	0.17	0.21	1				
V11	0.21	0.27	0.36	0.50	0.38	0.17	0.21	0.28	0.26	0.30	1			
V12	0.49	0.18	0.47	0.36	0.17	0.46	0.36	0.13	0.20	0.44	0.18	1		
V13	0.18	0.13	0.13	0.26	0.30	0.28	0.19	0.22	0.15	0.18	0.30	0.19	1	
V14	0.29	0.16	0.27	0.18	0.16	0.41	0.47	0.14	0.29	0.31	0.14	0.40	0.21	1

Note: V1=Unique Product Advantages; V2=Human Resource Management; V3=Marketing Activities; V4=Project Definition; V5=Market; V6=Product-Company Fit; V7=Pre-Development; V8=Technological Activities; V9=Competition; V10=Entrepreneur; V11=Project approach; V12=Innovation Culture; V13=Financial Means; V14=Collaboration

Now the main interest of this paper is to compare the means of the different success factors. Table 3.4 depicts these mean values. The critical factors were ranked in decreasing order of importance, from the highest mean to the lowest mean. To show intersectoral differences, Table 3.5 presents the separate mean scores for the manufacturing sector and the service sector, respectively. Table 3.6 contains analogous mean scores for personal qualifications, viz. entrepreneurs and managers. Furthermore, Table 3.7 presents the mean scores for the real innovative firms (ten or more innovations) and the less innovative firms. Finally, Table 3.8 quotes the mean scores for different firm sizes.

Table 3.4. Determinants of Innovation Success

Critical Success Factor	mean score	t-value for difference between current and next mean in row	probability level for difference between current and next mean in row
Entrepreneur	4.34	4.59	0.000*
Unique Product Advantages	4.11	0.36	0.722
Innovation Culture	4.09	0.89	0.375
Project Approach	4.05	1.48	0.140
Technological Activities	3.99	0.12	0.907
Human Resource Management	3.99	0.80	0.424
Marketing Activities	3.95	0.25	0.800
Project Definition	3.94	0.05	0.962
Pre-Development	3.93	1.68	0.096**
Market	3.82	1.43	0.153
Financial Means	3.71	3.53	0.001*
Competition	3.46	0.87	0.386
Product-Company Fit	3.38	1.30	0.197
Collaboration	3.30	–	–

Note: * significant at a 0.05 level; ** significant at a 0.10 level

Table 3.5. Determinants of Innovation Success: Manufacturing Sector vs. Service Sector

Critical Success Factor	mean score manufacturing sector	mean score service sector	t-value for difference between sectors	probability level for difference between sectors
Entrepreneur	4.33	4.35	−0.20	0.839
Unique Product Advantages	4.19	4.00	2.26	0.025*
Innovation Culture	4.13	4.01	1.05	0.296
Project Approach	4.05	4.05	0.03	0.980
Technological Activities	4.04	3.88	1.39	0.167
Human Resource Management	3.99	3.98	0.11	0.917
Marketing Activities	4.05	3.53	2.21	0.029*
Project Definition	3.99	3.84	1.51	0.134
Pre-Development	4.02	3.72	3.16	0.002*
Market	3.84	3.77	0.53	0.594
Financial Means	3.74	3.60	1.10	0.274
Competition	3.54	3.25	2.15	0.033*
Product-Company Fit	3.41	3.38	0.26	0.794
Collaboration	3.38	3.08	2.22	0.028*

Note: * significant at a 0.05 level

Table 3.6. Determinants of Innovation Success: Entrepreneurs vs. Managers

Critical Success Factor	mean score entrepreneurs	mean score managers	t-value for difference between respondents	probability level for difference between respondents
Entrepreneur	4.35	4.30	0.56	0.577
Unique Product Advantages	4.12	4.13	−0.99	0.922
Innovation Culture	4.11	4.13	−0.24	0.812
Project Approach	4.01	4.01	−0.28	0.777
Technological Activities	4.05	3.94	0.93	0.355
Human Resource Management	4.00	4.00	−0.05	0.963
Marketing Activities	3.93	4.07	−1.73	0.086*
Project Definition	3.97	3.95	0.20	0.841
Pre-Development	3.91	4.02	−1.18	0.241
Market	3.84	3.75	0.68	0.499
Financial Means	3.73	3.62	0.90	0.369
Competition	3.43	3.57	−1.05	0.294
Product-Company Fit	3.46	3.27	1.50	0.137
Collaboration	3.29	3.33	−0.321	0.749

Note: * significant at a 0.05 level

Table 3.7. Determinants of Innovation Success: Real Innovative vs. Less Innovative Firms

Critical Success Factor	mean score real innovative companies	mean score less innovative companies	t-value for difference between real and less companies	probability level for difference
Entrepreneur	4.34	4.34	0.10	0.493
Unique Product Advantages	4.14	4.08	1.20	0.186
Innovation Culture	4.08	4.10	−0.44	0.563
Project Approach	4.06	4.04	1.00	0.210
Technological Activities	3.99	4.00	−0.25	0.537
Human Resource Management	3.99	3.99	0.07	0.497
Marketing Activities	4.10	3.91	2.30	0.039*
Project Definition	3.94	3.95	−0.87	0.593
Pre-Development	4.08	3.88	2.80	0.027*
Market	3.84	3.80	0.93	0.364
Financial Means	3.71	3.72	−0.55	0.584
Competition	3.46	3.46	0.27	0.463
Product-Company Fit	3.37	3.39	−0.97	0.693
Collaboration	3.30	3.30	−0.12	0.505

Note: * significant at a 0.05 level

Table 3.8. Determinants of Innovation Success: Large vs. Small Firms

Critical Success Factor	mean score large companies	mean score small companies	t-value for difference between large and small companies	probability level for difference
Entrepreneur	4.31	4.38	−0.83	0.407
Unique Product Advantages	4.07	4.10	−0.37	0.711
Innovation Culture	3.99	4.24	−2.58	0.011*
Project Approach	4.04	4.00	0.48	0.631
Technological Activities	3.99	4.02	−0.25	0.803
Human Resource Management	4.02	3.91	1.32	0.189
Marketing Activities	3.85	4.14	−3.31	0.001*
Project Definition	3.99	3.89	1.11	0.269
Pre-Development	3.91	3.91	0.02	0.983
Market	3.81	3.75	0.43	0.665
Financial Means	3.75	3.68	0.55	0.582
Competition	3.48	3.41	0.52	0.602
Product-Company Fit	3.52	3.24	2.03	0.021*
Collaboration	3.23	3.37	−1.12	0.266

Note: * significant at a 0.05 level

3.5 Interpretation and Results

In this section we will first take a look at the results for the complete set of data (Table 3.4). Using a t-test for paired samples (see Moore and McCabe 1993), we investigated whether the mean scores for any two critical success factors differed significantly. The last column of the table shows which different critical success factors do statistically indeed have different mean scores at a 10 or even 5 percent significance level.

It is noteworthy that our findings differ considerably from the general views expressed in the literature, where for example, entrepreneurship is not so frequently mentioned as a key driver. But from the perspective of the respondents, the entrepreneur is the most essential factor in the innovation process in the SME sector. Next, a closely interwoven cluster of mainly internal factors follows the entrepreneurial factor (viz. unique product advantages, innovation culture, project approach, technological activities, human resource management, marketing activities, project definition and pre-development). The next clusters of explanatory factors comprise mainly external aspects such as market, financial means, competition, product/company match and collaboration. It should be noted however that financial means entail both internal and external aspects. Thus a main finding is that a Schumpeterian type of entrepreneurship – in the sense of a change manager – is an essential success condition for innovative behaviour in the SME sector.

In the next step of our empirical analysis we compared the results for the manu-facturing sector and service sector (Table 3.5). Running the t-test for independent samples reveals that unique product advantages, marketing activities, pre-development strategy, competition and collaboration offer statistically higher scores in the manufacturing sector than in the service sector, while nowhere in the service sector was a critical success factor score higher than those in the manu-facturing sector found. The question of intangibility of services might be crucial in this respect. A new service must be considered more carefully and communicated more thoroughly to the potential client than a new product. In the latter case a more objective factor like unique product advantages or visibility might play a more prominent role. The internal factors related to pre-development strategy and marketing activities, and the external factors related to competition and collabora-tion, underline once more the importance of these advantages.

An interesting finding is also that perceptions and views of entrepreneurs and managers hardly differ, as can be seen from Table 3.6. This phenomenon may be explained by the fact that the management in SMEs is in general very close to the entrepreneur. In both subgroups (i.e., entrepreneurs and managers) the entrepre-neur is mentioned as the most critical success factor. The only significant differ-ence is that the managers depend less on marketing activities than entrepreneurs do. As mentioned, several SMEs are very innovative. Table 3.7 presents the re-sults for the real innovators and the less innovative firms. It appears that marketing activities and pre-development strategies are more important for the real innova-tive firms than for the other firms. These factors appear to offer ultimately the real explanations for successful innovation in the SME field. This seems to be plausi-ble, as both a market coverage and professional preparation are of eminent im-portance for firm behaviour in the SME sector.

Finally, the data set was subdivided into small and large firms (Table 3.8), in order to test for firm size effects. Innovation culture and marketing activities ap-pear to be more crucial for small firms than for large ones. The lesser importance of marketing for the entrepreneurs might be attributable to self-confidence or firm-blindness (myopic behaviour). Economies of scale and bureaucracy might be ex-planatory factors for the differences between large and small firms. Positioning the innovation culture opposite the product-company fit as a driving force to success, brings us back to the earlier mentioned difference between SMEs and large firms: SMEs tend to be strong in applications, whereas large firms tend to profit more from scale economies. Marketing activities might be a specific obstacle for the successful commercialisation of research projects in SMEs.

3.6 Conclusions

The entrepreneur is the crucial success factor in the SME innovation process, ac-cording to the opinion of the respondents in our Dutch survey questionnaire. This is an interesting result, as in many cases either institutional impediment or geographical/infrastructural factors are mentioned as critical success conditions for successful business. Apparently, the human factor prevails.

Although hardly mentioned in the literature, the entrepreneur is also mentioned as a number one factor by the various subgroups: manufacturing and service firms, entrepreneurs and managers, real and less innovative firms, small and large firms. After entrepreneurship, a cluster of controllable internal success factors appear to follow: unique product advantages, innovation culture, project approach, technological activities, human resource management, marketing activities, project definition and pre-development. External aspects (by definition non-controllable) such as market, financial means, competition, product/company match and collaboration appear to show up only in subsequent low-order clusters. So the SMEs involved in our research appear to place entrepreneurship and internal factors – controllable by themselves – on top. This attitude obviously entails a considerable risk of over-estimation of their own role and competence.

Although all subgroups discussed here regard the entrepreneur as the number one factor in the innovation process, some differences appear to occur in the perceived importance of other success factors. Unique product advantages, marketing activities, pre-development, competition and collaboration are more important for the manufacturing sector than for the service sector. Tangibility of products (as opposed to intangibility of services) might be the explanation for these differences. The expressed opinions of entrepreneurs and managers do hardly differ, probably due to the fact that the management in SMEs is in general very close to the entrepreneurial tasks. Marketing activities and pre-development strategies are more important for the real innovative firms than for the less innovative firms. And finally, innovation culture and marketing activities are more crucial for small firms than for large ones.

This study has aimed to shed new light on the innovation process of SMEs, especially on the way the SMEs themselves perceive the innovation process. It is striking that non-controllable factors only end up in the rear of explanatory factors. These findings deserve to be investigated more thoroughly by means of other studies. If a verification based on a larger study and in other countries would lead to similar results, such new aspects would have to be incorporated in public and private policy towards SME innovation.

References

Atuahene-Gima K (1996) Differential potency of factors affecting innovation performance in manufacturing and services firms in Australia. Journal of Product Innovation Management 13: 35–52

Bertuglia C, Lombardo S, Nijkamp P (eds) (1997) Innovative behavior in space and time. Springer-Verlag, Berlin

Calantone RJ, Schmidt JB, Song XM (1996) Controllable factors of new product success: A cross-national comparison. Marketing Science 15: 341–358

Cooper RG, Kleinschmidt EJ (1987) New products: What separates winners from losers. Journal of Product Innovation Management 4: 169–184

Cooper RG (1990) New products: What distinguishes the winners? Research and Technology Management 33: 27–31

Coopey J, Keegan O, Emler N (1998) Managers' innovations and the structuration of organization. Journal of Management Studies 35: 263–284

Craig A, Hart S (1992) Where to now in new product development research. European Journal of Marketing 26: 1–47

Davelaar EJ (1992) Regional economic analysis of innovation and incubation. Ashgate, Aldershot

Dwyer L, Mellor R (1991) Organizational environment, new product process activities, and project outcomes. Journal of Product Innovation Management 8: 39–48

Edgett S, Shipley D, Forbes G (1992) Japanese and British companies compared: Contributing factors to success and failure in NPD. Journal of Product Innovation Management 9: 3–10

Galbraith JK (1980) American capitalism. M.E. Sharpe, White Plains

Hatch NW, Mowery DC (1998) Process innovation and learning by doing in semiconductor manufacturing. Management Science 44: 1461–1477

Heracleous L (1998) Better than the rest: Making Europe the leader in the next wave of innovation and performance. Long Range Planning 31: 154–158

Heunks FJ (1998) Innovation, creativity and success. Small Business Economics 10: 263–272

Huiban JP, Bouhsina Z (1998) Innovation and the quality of labour factor: An empirical investigation in the French food industry. Small Business Economics 10: 389–400

Kleinknecht A (1986) Crisis and prosperity in Schumpeterian innovation patterns. MacMillan, London

Lewis-Beck MS (ed) (1994) Factor analysis and related techniques. SAGE Publications, London

Maidique MA, Zirger BJ (1984) A study of success and failure in product innovation: The case of the U.S. electronics industry. IEEE Transaction Engineering Management 31: 192–203

Malecki EJ (1997) Entrepreneurs, networks, and economic development. Advances in Entrepreneurship, Firm Emerge and Growth 3: 57–118

Marsili O (2000) The anatomy and evaluation of industries. Edward Elgar, Cheltenham

Montoya MM, Calantone R (1994) Determinants of new product performance. Journal of Product Innovation Management 11: 397–417

Moore DS, McCabe GP (1993) Introduction to the practice of statistics (second edition). Freeman and Company, New York

Nijkamp P (2002) Entrepreneurship in a modern network economy. Regional Studies (forthcoming)

Nooteboom B (1994) Innovation and diffusion in small firms: Theory and evidence. Small Business Economics 6: 327–347

Peneder M (2001) Entrepreneurial competition and industrial organization. Edward Elgar, Cheltenham

Pickard J (1996) A Fertile Grounding. People Management 24: 28–35

Rothwell R, Freeman C, Horlsey A, Jervis VTP, Robertson AB, Townsend J (1974) SAPHO updated – project SAPHO phase II. Research Policy 3: 259–291

Quinn JB (1985) Managing innovation: Controlled chaos. Harvard Business Review May-June: 73–84

Schumpeter JA (1912) Theorie der wirtschaftlichen Entwicklung. Duncker und Humbolt, Leipzig

Schumpeter J (1934) The theory of economic development. Harvard University Press, Cambridge, MA

Song XM, Parry ME (1994) The dimensions of industrial new product success and failure in state enterprises in the People's Republic of China. Journal of Product Innovation Management 11: 105–118

Song XM, Parry ME (1997) The determinants of Japanese new product successes. Journal of Marketing Research 34: 64–76

Stern LW, El-Ansary AI, Coughlan AT (1996) Marketing channels. Prentice Hall International, Englewood Cliffs

Thurik AR (1996) Introduction: Innovation and small business. Small Business Economics 8: 175–176

Yap CM, Souder WE (1994) Factors influencing new product success and failure in small entrepreneurial high-technology electronic firm. Journal of Product Innovation Management 11: 418–432

Zirger BJ, Maidique MA (1990) A model of new product development: An empirical test. Management Science 36: 867–883

4 Networked Alliances and Innovation

Luis Suarez-Villa

School of Social Ecology, University of California at Irvine, Irvine, California, USA

4.1 Introduction

Innovation and research are becoming increasingly important components of most production and service activities. The pressures introduced by global competition and rapid technological change have made it essential for many firms and organisations to engage in continuous innovation, where research and development (R&D) units are expected to successively come up with new knowledge and discoveries at a very rapid pace. In many advanced technology sectors and activities, research units have therefore taken up a central role in firm survival and in the formulation of company strategy.

Very often, however, firms and organisations do not internally possess all the resources required to create the expected new knowledge or discoveries. Thus, firms are finding it increasingly necessary to co-operate and form alliances with other organisations in order to gain access to external creativity and new knowledge. Indications are that exchanges of new knowledge or ideas can be optimised when such alliances occur within networks. How networks are structured and the patterns of control and linkage that develop in them have therefore become important in determining how successful any inter-firm alliance will become.

Research unit-to-research unit (R2R) linkages between firms engaged in networked alliances (alliances that occur within networks) can become an important vehicle to exchange knowledge or cross-fertilise ideas that can lead to innovations. The new knowledge that R2R linkages can provide can also serve as a transformational tool to internalise and integrate innovation within firms. Possibly, the greatest benefit of such linkages can be found in advanced technology sectors and activities, such as biotechnology, advanced electronics, or software design. Firms involved in these activities are typically very research-intensive and must depend greatly on new knowledge and discoveries for survival.

The term *transformational integration* will be used in this contribution to represent the internal changes and benefits that can occur in research-intensive firms when they join a networked alliance where R2R linkages proliferate. Clearly, transformation in this context implies benefits that could only be obtained by becoming a member of an alliance in which collaboration and interaction with other research-intensive firms occurs. As will be discussed later on, transformation through R2R integration in a networked alliance can confer three major kinds of benefits related to: (i) the incubation of new firms or technologies, (ii) increased value related to research capabilities and output, and (iii) enhanced returns to scale, which a firm could not otherwise obtain on its own.

The transformational integration of innovation in organisations occurs by assimilating new knowledge through alliances, whereby such knowledge can then be turned into innovations for products and services. Such integration into a networked alliance can result in substantial advantages that may ensure an organisation's or firm's survival and development. Integrating into a networked alliance can therefore become a means to transform an organisation's innovative capabilities and resources. Such transformations would occur by developing R2R linkages within a network, whereby R&D units develop interrelationships through shared interests, trust and mutually beneficial projects.

This contribution will provide, first, an overview of the significance of networked alliances for innovation. Such alliances are becoming particularly important for firms in research-intensive sectors or activities that must meet the challenges posed by rapid technological change and global competition. A second component will then explore the main types of network structures that can embed inter-firm alliances and R2R linkages. Such aspects as internal control, the development of hierarchies, and disparities of influence and empowerment will be considered as each type of network architecture is discussed. The final section will then consider three major benefits that R2R linkages can obtain through networks their relationship with network structure, and their implications for integrating innovation in linked firms. Emphasis will be placed on providing a broad or macro-level perspective, rather than considering micro-analytical details.

4.2 Alliances in Networks

Strategic alliances between organisations can serve as the basic building block for transformational integration in organisations, involving such aspects as product innovation, design, or the development of existing products (see, for example, Bleeke and Ernst 1993; Limerick and Cunnington 1993; Gerybadze 1995; Yoshino and Rangan 1995). These are the kinds of activities that are typically found in research and development (R&D) units. Organisations typically have limited knowledge, and joining a network and alliance can provide greater resources for R&D, particularly when capital is scarce and the future is uncertain. Many new advanced technology firms, for example, lack all the research knowledge they need and have no established markets from which they can draw a dependable source of revenue to come up with new discoveries. Thus, joining an alliance can provide the kind of knowledge-intensive resources that will support their most important requirement for survival: innovation.

In R&D activities, for example, joining an alliance that links a firm with a research institution, such as a university or a major laboratory, can increase the value of participants through all the new knowledge that can be obtained on the latest techniques or discoveries (see, for example, Vassallo 1999; Cross and Borgatti 2000). When the alliance occurs in a network of firms or organisations linking their R&D units, their value can be compounded (see Davenport et al. 1996; Bayles 1998; Gattiker et al. 2000; Pauleen and Yoong 2001; Wellman 1999, 2001). Accelerating innovation diffusion would be a likely result of R&D alliances that occur in networks, and it would likely be much more effective than through isolated, bilateral inter-organisational agreements. Thus, linking up with alliances that occur in networks (or networked alliances) can provide the sort of cross-fertilisation of ideas and discoveries that only the cumulative and specialised knowledge of the various firms in the network can provide (see Suarez-Villa 1998).

Much of the knowledge needed to perform and maintain effective innovative capabilities today tends to be cumulative, providing a substantial advantage to organisations or firms that can co-operatively apply their research memories toward a given R&D objective (see Barley et al. 1992; Forrest and Martin 1992; Grabowski and Vernon 1994; Henderson 1994; Rosenfeld 1996; Suarez-Villa 1998; Orsenigo et al. 2001). The inter-firm research linkages involved can therefore serve as diffusion channels for new discoveries, enhancing the value and the resources of the organisations that become partners in the networked alliance. Such linkages can become vehicles for the transformational integration of innovation in those firms, depending on the kinds of network structures that develop. At the international level, for example, joining a networked research alliance can make it easier for a firm to introduce innovations in new markets or deal more effectively with government regulation. Such arrangements may well be the most effective vehicle to establish market niches for new products and services. Network alliances with international links may, for example, help secure patenting in various nations by sharing research memories and findings.

Better access to capital markets may also benefit the firms that join a networked alliance, whenever such participation leads to more dynamic research performances. The stock markets, for example, seem to value more the firms that join research alliances, particularly when firms are small but very innovative. Such is the typical case for many small biotechnology firms when they join an alliance with larger firms that can provide more support for research or fund new R&D activities. Also, when many of the firms in a networked research alliance are geographically concentrated, the alliance and its networks can provide a "critical mass" that can help attract more research resources and venture capital investment to a locality. Firms engaged in networked alliances in Silicon Valley, for example, have helped the local economy considerably, by attracting venture capitalists to the area who then finance new research in start-up firms (see, for example, Hanson 1982; Rogers and Larsen 1984; Malone 1985; Saxenian 1994). In contrast, similarly innovative start-up firms located in other places tend to find it much more difficult to obtain venture capital financing. Thus, a networked alliance's links with larger firms and its geographical concentration can affect significantly the innovative capabilities and the kind of transformational integration experienced by the organisations that compose the network (see, for example, Suarez-Villa and Walrod 1997; Suarez-Villa 2002).

In sum, establishing research alliances in networks can be an important vehicle to enhance both value-added and the transformational integration of research activities within organisations. A networked alliance can ensure the integration of research activities to provide greater synergy and focus between and within the participating organisations. Through such alliances, firms may be able to optimise their strongest capabilities in a way that produces greater value for themselves and, at the same time, for the other networked firms. Alliances in networks may be particularly important for nurturing new and very innovative firms in high technology sectors, such as biotechnology or advanced electronics, which are typically small and lack the resources to survive on their own.

4.3 Network Structures

The structure of a research network influences how firms participate and relate to one another. Network structures can also influence how firms join a research alliance and to what extent they benefit from it (see Suarez-Villa 1998). The internal *division of functions* within a networked research alliance is largely a product of network structure. Such divisions of functions help determine the role that each participating organisation's research unit will play, and the level of commitment that each deploys toward co-operation within the network. Trust, which is a fundamental component of such relationships, is also very much influenced by network structure and the alliances that develop within it (see, for example, Cook and Emerson 1978; Luhmann 1979; Gambetta 1988; Hansen 1992; Misztal 1996).

Thus, for example, firms that take up a "nodal" research function within a network are bound to play important roles in how co-operation is co-ordinated, the way resources are deployed or allocated to each participating member, how "gate-keeping" is operated to provide access to the network and its embedded alliances, and how conflict resolution is managed when any disputes arise between participating firms. Network architectures, and the internal division of functions they structure, also help determine the disparities that occur within a network, such as those resulting from access to the internal research resources of the alliance, or the external links that can benefit some participating firms more than others.

Commitment to a research alliance is also a by-product of network structure (see, for example, Cook and Emerson 1978; Ghemawat 1991; Lorange and Roos 1991; Alter and Hage 1992; Bramanti 1992; Pisano and Mang 1993; Arora and Gambardella 1994; Powell et al. 1996). Commitment can be provided broadly or narrowly, based on the research needs of the various firms involved. It can, for example, be deployed in a broad way by engaging in multiple relationships that can encompass various projects, or in an open, long-term engagement to co-operate in any area of expertise. Commitment can also be deployed in a narrow way, for example, by limiting co-operation to specific projects of a limited scope and duration. Network structures and the level of commitment they elicit may also be an important determinant of the "embeddedness" of firms in a networked alliance. Such embeddedness, for example, helps determine how strongly integrated firms eventually become within the network and how intensively they participate in nurturing the common values and interests of the entire network. Embeddedness can also help "anchor" participating firms to a research alliance and a specific locality, by providing advantages that may be difficult to match by other competing alliances, areas or nations. The commitment or embeddedness of firms in a networked research alliance can also go a long way toward developing a local culture for research and innovation, which can provide resilience in times of stress, or enlist governmental support to attract badly needed resources.

Network structure can also influence how participating firms support innovation. Support for research projects involving continuous innovation may depend greatly on the nodal or co-ordinating role that some of the participant firms play, involving such aspects as the sharing of R&D secrets or new discoveries. Trust and reciprocity are fundamental ingredients of such co-operation, particularly between small firms with very limited resources. The level of trust deployed in such co-operation may also be a function of the commitment that participating firms have to an alliance, their embeddedness within the network, and the expectation of benefits to come.

There are three main structural typologies that can be related to networked research alliances, particularly between R&D units in advanced technology firms. The circuit non-nodal network structure tends to occur more between the research units of small, independent firms (see Fig. 4.1). There is a lack of hierarchy associated with this structural type, leading to very fluid relationships. In many cases, the circuit non-nodal structure provides a relatively open network architecture, where additional participants can be quickly accommodated. Co-operation in such structures tends to occur as needs arise, being less formal than in the other structural types. Reciprocity and trust tend to be tacit prerequisites for co-operation. In the circuit non-nodal structure, for example, "two-way" outsourcing of R&D may occur, through which some firms outsource (or subcontract) some of their research within the networked alliance while they, at the same time, allow themselves to be subcontracted for specific research tasks by other participating firms. Such "two-way" relationships may be particularly helpful during very stressful times, if there is much unutilised research capacity in some firms while others experience shortfalls due to high levels of activity (see, for example, Suarez-Villa and Walrod 1997; Suarez-Villa and Karlsson 1996; Suarez-Villa and Rama 1996; Suarez-Villa and Fischer 1995).

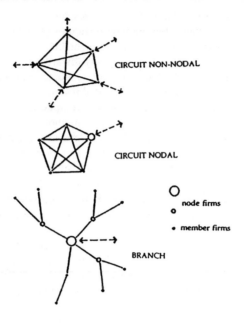

Fig. 4.1. Network Structures

The circuit nodal network structure develops when the research units of some firms take up a coordinating or "gate-keeping" function within the network (see Fig. 4.1). The empowerment of such firms to develop a decision-making function (as "nodes") within the network may be granted or accepted for specific projects, or for definite periods of time, and can be a result of the need to specialise or to manage a complex project more efficiently. A tacit sort of acceptance of such empowerment may also result from seniority, when older firms are present or were the initiators of the network or an alliance. The division of labour introduced by the circuit nodal structure can raise concerns about disparities within the network, regarding decision-making prerogatives, access to research resources or favouritism toward any of the participating firms. A result of such concerns could be reduced trust, and more limited co-operation or embeddeness within a networked alliance. Thus, a trade-off between greater efficiency within the networked alliance and co-operation may develop, leading to greater inter-firm tensions and a more limited level of commitment.

The development of network nodes may become inevitable, as the possibility of realising more gains more rapidly becomes a major priority for some firms. Such possibilities can be particularly important for firms with very limited knowledge or resources. A nodal firm can, for example, become a sort of clearinghouse, to select and manage new knowledge or the R&D resources needed for a specific project. The need for some firms to take up an outreach function may also become necessary, if there is a need to find additional partners or seek new research arrangements to complete a project. Such nodal functions can become very important when the network's member firms are very specialised and cannot undertake outreach on their own. Greater specialisation is therefore an important outcome of the circuit nodal network, leading to the establishment of a hierarchy that may confer more power on some firms at the expense of greater equity and trust.

The branch network structure is potentially the most hierarchical of all, leading to greater specialisation and disparities than in the circuit form (see Fig. 4.1). Nodal firms or organisations are an integral or inseparable part of the branch network architecture, and are typically empowered to control flows and serve as gatekeepers to a much greater extent than in the previous type. Major disparities in access to knowledge and resources may likely occur, even when some forms of participatory governance are present. In many cases, therefore, some or all of the non-nodal firms in the network may be subsidiaries or spin-offs of the nodal firms. In high technology sectors, for example, branch networks occur when very large firms subdivide themselves or create new units to serve specialised research functions. Computer hardware manufacturer IBM, for example, not long ago split itself into eighteen different units to deal with research and production more effectively. As it subdivided itself, it created a branch network where each of the units was highly dependent on the parent firm, with the latter controlling pretty much the flows of resources.

Disparities can become stronger in the branch network as the division of functions deepens and the hierarchy develops levels. Such levels also introduce differential empowerments, to control certain parts or branches of the network. Thus, for example, in a three-level branch hierarchy the general control of the network may remain with the central nodal firm, while secondary nodes are developed to taking up less important gate-keeping functions. The firms at the lowest level of such a hierarchy then become very dependent on the secondary nodes that control their access and flows. In this kind of hierarchy and network structure, therefore, co-operation is more likely to be "programmed" or organised by the central nodal firm and the secondary nodal organisations, and the interests of the lowest firms in the hierarchy will be subordinated to those of the higher levels.

The hierarchical dependence of the branch network structure may also make it more difficult for some participating firms to exit, because of their specialised function and "fit" within the network. Such dependency may lead to a sort of compulsory participation, where a firm finds itself with little choice but to remain in the network or alliance, since the costs of breaking away on its own or joining another network can be prohibitive. Such compulsory participation can therefore become a sort of "no-choices" commitment that can last until a firm finds a viable way to exit the network. Commitment may thus depend greatly on the lack of external opportunities rather on any substantial willingness to be a pro-active member of a research network or alliance. As soon as such opportunities become present, firms caught in the hierarchy of the branch structure may decide to bolt the network and gain independence or join a more advantageous network or alliance.

Such is the case, for example, with small biotechnology firms engaged in research alliances with large pharmaceutical firms, who decide to leave for a more advantageous relationship with another company that can provide more R&D support (see, for example, Suarez-Villa and Walrod 2003).

It is important to understand the different characteristics of these research network structures and the kinds of relationships they condition between participating organisations. All too often, the literature refers to networks as if they were all of one kind, without reference to the different structural types or the substantial qualitative effects they have on inter-firm linkages and relations. Each of these structures can have a remarkably different effect on the transformational integration of R&D functions within the organisations that form a networked alliance.

4.4 Transformational Integration and R2R Linkages

The most effective transformational integration of research occurs when research alliances develop within networks of firms. Such networked research alliances are the most effective vehicles to establish research unit-to-research unit (R2R) linkages between firms. R2R linkages are possibly the most difficult and sensitive of all business-to-business (B2B) relationships, since they often involve access to private research knowledge that can guarantee the survival of a firm or organisation, particularly for those engaged in highly competitive product markets.

R2R linkages can diffuse very private research knowledge, for example, that can then pre-empt a firm's potential first-mover (or proprietary) advantage for any given invention. In such situations, the firm receiving the new knowledge can develop a second-mover advantage that can substantially cut into the originating firm's market advantage for a new product. R2R linkages, therefore, must involve a great deal of trust if they are to work effectively. When trust breaks down, a R2R linkage or even an entire networked research alliance can be severely damaged, as each participating firm reduces its commitment and limits access to its own resources and discoveries.

R2Rs within networked research alliances become most important for small firms engaged in expensive research requiring substantial resources and lengthy testing delays for government approval. Such is the case, for example, for many biotechnology firms who attempt to find new medications (see Orsenigo 1989; Arora and Gambardella 1994; Henderson 1994; McKelvey 1995; Liebeskind et al. 1996; Acharya 1999; Orsenigo et al. 2001). Years can pass before a new discovery can gain government approval, through extensive clinical trials and detailed scrutiny. In the meantime, and until a discovery can be certified and marketed, such firms have few or no sources of independent financial support and must rely on their R2R linkages with large pharmaceutical companies, their allies or subsidiaries. Those R2R alliances can provide much needed income for the biotech firms, through the testing of pharmaceutical products or the modification of existing ones. At the same time their advanced or unique research knowledge can attract subcontracts from other large pharmaceutical companies or from medical equipment firms that seek to develop existing products.

Networked R2R alliances have also become fundamental for some aerospace and advanced electronics firms engaged in defence or new weapons contracting. Typically, many private firms participate in such projects, since no single organisation has all the required knowledge or expertise to complete a contract. The research involved in such R2R alliances is highly secretive and requires much coordination, as well as extensive safeguards to prevent disclosure or diffusion outside or even within the networked alliance. Thus, for example, the research required to produce a new type of military aircraft may require a high level of fragmentation of functions (or finely detailed division of labour) within the networked alliance, in order to keep all but one of the participating firms from gaining an overall, comprehensive understanding or knowledge of the project. Thus, R2R linkages within the networked alliance may be carefully parcelled out in a way that circumscribes knowledge to very specific aspects or components of the project. The assembly of all components may then become the main task of a central co-ordinating member of the networked alliance, who then puts all the various research products together to produce a prototype of the new aircraft. Such a networked research alliance probably best exemplifies the research and development that went into the first prototype of the so-called "stealth" bomber in the United States, where one of the alliance members (Northrop Corp.) held the central co-ordinating role.

R2R exchanges typically involve the exchange of new ideas for potential projects, or of results of tests and experiments. Such exchanges can occur between R&D units engaged in projects targeted to produce complementary rather than competing products. Or they can involve R&D units engaged in the sequential development of an innovation, where one or several firms take responsibility for a stage of innovation and then others take up the subsequent stages until all the R&D work is completed (see, for example, Vassallo 1999; Cross and Borgatti 2000; Schwartz et al. 2000). R2R exchanges can also involve feedbacks on performance once an innovation is marketed. In some cases, R2R exchanges can involve parallel testing of an innovation or a new discovery, as a means to cut the testing time and establish more quickly a proprietary (or first-mover) claim to a new discovery. In such cases, all of the firms co-operating in the R2R exchange may share proprietary claims to the discovery, or compensation agreements may instead arranged if the new discovery happens to succeed after it is marketed. Such parallel R2R testing arrangements have become more common in the biotechnology sector, where substantial testing and approval delays often jeopardise firm survival.

Every R2R exchange typically involves highly talented individuals, on whose expertise and knowledge often rides the future of an entire firm. Today, many R&D-intensive firms in such sectors as biotechnology and advanced electronics are fully or partly owned by their R&D personnel. Such "inventor-firms" have become a common feature of the high technology landscape in various nations (see Suarez-Villa 2000, pp. 65–70). When R2R exchanges are carried out by non-owners, however, questions of trust and loyalty come to the fore, as firms try to maintain some control over their most private research knowledge. It can happen, therefore, that when such R&D personnel leave a firm, it may be in a firm's best interest for them to find employment in any firm within the networked alliance, as a way to prevent competitors from gaining their research knowledge. Even when some competition occurs within the firms of a networked research alliance, the organisation that loses an individual to an allied firm may feel less apprehensive that its secrets may eventually be put to use by a competitor outside the alliance. Many firms in Silicon Valley, for example, tend to encourage allied firms to hire departing employees as a means to limit the diffusion of their research knowledge to competitors. Firms within a networked research alliance may therefore end up exchanging R&D employees frequently, as a sort of mutually protective measure.

4.4.1 Incubation

There are three basic aspects of R2R linkages between firms in networked research alliances that are crucial for transformational integration. Most of the benefits that may eventually be derived from transformational integration within a networked alliance may ride on how well such aspects are understood and adjusted for. The first aspect may be called incubation. Transformational integration within networked research alliances very often involves a process of incubation of new firms with very fluid research agendas and a very uncertain future. Such incubation can involve a great deal of internal transformation, as the new firm attempts to find its way by determining its research priorities in concert with the resources available within the networked alliance. The more expensive and resource-intensive its research is, the more likely it is that the firm will rely on the resources provided by the networked alliance. Such reliance (or dependence) on the alliance can accelerate the process of transformational integration, since the firm will not be able to subsist on its own, and will have to become integrated with the networked alliance to the extent that its research interests require. In some sectors, such as biotechnology, for example, such integration can be both rapid and very intense, given the very expensive resources that are needed and the long waiting times that must be endured before a firm can reap the rewards of its research.

Incubation typically produces small gains and little growth. In some sectors, such as biotechnology, incubation can be long and stressful for the firms involved, requiring much support from other firms in a networked research alliance. However, if a firm's research efforts are successful, then a period of exponential growth may follow. The "tipping point" beyond which such growth begins may require a very long wait, but the period of rapid growth that follows typically brings substantial wealth and resources to the firms that experience it and, indirectly, to many of the firms engaged in a networked research alliance. It is crucial, however, that the opportunity to "embed" a new firm's R2R linkages in incubation not be lost. Once the "tipping point" is reached and rapid growth begins, it will be very difficult to capture or embed a firm that has not been incubated within a networked research alliance. After rapid growth begins, a firm that has not been incubated within a networked research alliance will need the support of the alliance less than ever before. For that reason, incubation of new firms' R2R linkages must be seen opportunistically, with a view toward the substantial rewards that may be reaped if incubation and R2R linking are successful in leading to the marketing of new products or services.

An outline of the potential relationships between the basic R2R aspects, network structure and transformational integration is provided in Table 4.1. Incubation of new firms' R2R linkages possibly fits in best with the circuit non-nodal network structure, where integration within a networked research alliance is most likely to be open-ended and non-hierarchical. The flexibility provided by the circuit non-nodal structure may be very important in benefiting the R2R linkages of start-up firms with no known or established markets, high research resource requirements, and no significant financing of their own that can support them over a long incubation period. Such firms would indeed live precariously if they were on their own, and their probability for surviving independently is usually very low. This is precisely why developing strong R2R linkages within a networked alliance is so important for these firms. And it is during incubation that their most intense transformational integration can occur, as they internalise new knowledge and adjust their research agenda to the resources available within the networked alliance.

Table 4.1. R2R Benefits, Network Structure and Integration

	R2R benefits			
Network structure	Incubation	Value	Returns to scale	Integration characteristics
Circuit non-nodal	High	Low	Moderate	Open-ended, non-hierarchical
Circuit nodal	Moderate	Moderate	High	Node specialisation
Branch	Low	Moderate	Low	Hierarchical, controlled

4.4.2 Value

The second aspect of R2R linkages between firms in networked research alliances is *value*. Transformational integration must necessarily create value when R2R linkages are developed, if they are to be sustained at all. Generating value from R2R linkages is a daunting task for most firms, since research projects often give no clear indication of where they will lead or what they will accomplish after they are completed. In many cases, the R2R linkages that are developed may only create new knowledge value, rather than market value. For very innovative projects, such as those involving biotechnology products, for example, it is usually very difficult (if not impossible) to anticipate what the eventual market value of a discovery will be. Nevertheless, the knowledge value from such research can be quite substantial, even from knowing which experiments will not work.

The uncertainty involved, which pervades most every research activity, even when it only includes simple development of existing products or services, makes it difficult to determine which kind of network structure may provide the highest market value to R2R linkages (see Table 4.1). It seems, however, that the circuit non-nodal structure may benefit R2R linkages with relatively lower market value than the other types, if much incubation activity is involved. Its more fluid and open-ended character may make it more difficult to capture market value. The sort of market value derived by deepening the commercial applications of products and services, differentiating products to capture greater revenue, or promoting the spread of applications may be less attractive to highly innovative firms that are relatively new and value research much more than marketing or distribution. An example of a research product fitting this context may be open-ended, freely available software which can be rich in new knowledge value but relatively poor in generating market value.

In many ways, however, the circuit non-nodal network structure is likely to generate R2R linkages with high knowledge value if the firms it comprises are very innovative organisations. Capturing market value, on the other hand, is possibly more likely to occur in network structures that have some hierarchy and specialisation (such as the circuit nodal or the branch structures) within the networked alliance. Therefore, relatively more closed hierarchical structures with a significant degree of specialisation among the participating firms may end capturing more market value for R2R linkages and their research products, even though the new knowledge value generated through those linkages may be substantially less. In a way, it seems unfortunate or unfair that highly innovative firms with strong R2R linkages may be unable to generate the kind of market value they deserve, but it must be remembered that some of the best knowledge generated throughout human history very often brought little in the form of market rewards to its discoverers. Others, perhaps less creative but better organised to follow up on the tedious and routine sort of work required to make a research product a market success, have often ended up with the largest material rewards.

4.4.3 Returns to Scale

The third aspect of R2R linkages in networked research alliances is *returns to scale*. As networks of R2R linkages expand, they tend to incur increasing returns to scale, since adding new member firms and their R2R links will increase the benefits to each member of the network. Such benefits often increase exponentially when a network's scale expands significantly. This basic characteristic is diametrically opposed to the standard economic principle that assumes greater scarcity to be the source of increasing returns or higher market value. Networks, and particularly those involving R2R linkages, in contrast, incur greater benefits as access and membership increase. The process is further compounded as more members join a networked research alliance and new knowledge that can be channelled into R2R linkages increases. Thus, in this respect, the standard economic principle of scarcity is turned on its head. For R2R linkages and the generation of new knowledge in networked alliances, this ages-old principle underpinning conventional economic theory seems to be totally irrelevant.

Possibly, the most beneficial returns to scale for R2R linkages are to be found in circuit nodal network structures (see Table 4.1). Because of their internal organisation, which involves a more finely detailed division of functions and specialisation, and the possibility of developing multiple nodes accommodating a greater diversity of firms and research knowledge, the circuit nodal network structure may be able to expand its scale more rapidly than the other structures. As this network type expands, the opportunities and choices to expand R2R linkages can increase exponentially. Such expansion in scale can generate a richer and deeper variety of research knowledge that will benefit the participating firms.

In contrast, the branch network structure may be the least likely one to increase scale rapidly, mainly because its characteristically high level of centralised or hierarchical control can be a limiting, if not discouraging, factor for entry. Typically, the branch networks are controlled by very large firms, which tend to dictate or at least exercise a significant amount of control over the research agendas and R2R links of the firms within the networked alliance. Such control, and the large inter-firm disparities in power and influence it usually generates, can discourage independent and highly innovative small or medium-size firms from joining such networks. Unless the benefits of joining are so important that they cannot be matched by any other networked alliance, many firms are likely to shy away from linking up their R&D units with firms involved in such networks. Sometimes, the branch network structures can become a form of "club" that can limit membership and impose very selective criteria for member firms and their R2R links. Thus, the branch structure's possibilities for expanding its scale (and, eventually, its higher returns) are likely to be the lowest of the three network structures.

The quality and strength of R2R linkages are therefore a function of the network architecture in which a networked alliance is embedded. The integration of innovations in firms and organisations in each of those structures is likely to vary substantially, and will be affected by differences in returns to scale, incubation possibilities, and value. How integration unfolds with respect to R2R linkages will be largely affected by how links are structured, and the many intangibles that will come into play as flows occur and develop. Such intangibles will involve not only the quality and uniqueness of knowledge in the linkages, but also the relations of empowerment, control and flexibility that are a part of a networked alliance's culture of co-operation. Unfortunately, these considerations are seldom taken into account when R&D strategies are mapped out, even in firms whose very survival and development depend on the R2R linkages they develop with other firms.

4.5 Conclusion

This paper has provided an overview of the relationship between the structures of networked research alliances and research unit-to-research unit (*R2R*) linkages. The twenty-first century is very likely to be the century of the knowledge society, with continuous innovation and discovery becoming the centrepiece of its most important firms and the main driving force behind its economy. Networks and alliances are bound to play a very important role in its economy, since firms will have to rely more than ever on externally generated knowledge and creativity to survive.

It is precisely through those networks and alliances that the transformation and integration of firms in the knowledge society and its economy will occur. R2R linkages will be the vehicles of such transformation, since they will provide the channels through which new research knowledge will flow. R2R linkages will become as important to firm survival in this new century as B2B (business-to-business) linkages for production and marketing are now becoming for productivity and growth. How far individual firms get in the new economy of the knowledge society may well depend on how they structure their R2R linkages to support their own research and development (R&D) activities.

The forces behind our intensifying global competition are unleashing a global technology race that will require a continuous and more rapid pace of innovation in many firms. In this new "winners-take-all" global technology race, the firms that are able to develop strong R2R linkages in order to generate and internalise innovations and transform themselves are likely to emerge as the main actors of the new global economy. Managing research relationships, projects and transactions along R2R linkages is bound to become an important prerequisite to increase the internal pace of innovation and, in turn, strengthen value-adding activities, productivity, customer relationships, and market share. Unfortunately, the importance of research activities has largely escaped the attention of most of the literature on new management concepts and methods. It is hoped that this contribution will provide a window of awareness on the importance that R2R linkages and R&D activities are likely to have in the firms of the new century.

References

Acharya R (1999) The emergence and growth of biotechnology. Edward Elgar, Northampton MA

Alter C, Hage J (1992) Organizations working together: Coordination in interorganizational networks. Sage, Newbury Park CA

Arora A, Gambardella A (1994) Evaluating technological information and utilizing it: Scientific knowledge, technological capability, and external linkages in biotechnology. Journal of Economic Behavior and Organization 24: 91–114

Barley SR, Freeman J, Hybels RC (1992) Strategic alliances in commercial biotechnology. In: Nohria N, Eccles RG (eds) Networks and organizations. Harvard Business School Press, Boston

Bayles D (1998) Extranets: Building the business-to-business web. Prentice-Hall, Englewood Cliffs

Bleeke J, Ernst D (1993) Collaborating to compete: Using strategic alliances and acquisitions in the global marketplace. John Wiley, New York

Bramanti A (1992) The spread of cooperative attitudes among small firms with different territorial backgrounds: The case of Northern Italy. Canadian Journal of Regional Science 15: 289–302

Cook K, Emerson R (1978) Power, equity and commitment in exchange relationships. American Sociological Review 43: 721–739

Cross R, Borgatti S (2000) The ties that share: Relational characteristics that facilitate knowledge transfer and organizational learning. Working Paper. Carroll School of Management, Boston College, Boston

Davenport T, Jarvenpaa S, Beers M (1996) Improving knowledge work processes. Sloan Management Review 37: 53–65

Forrest JE, Martin MJC (1992) Strategic alliances between large and small research intensive organizations: Experiences in the biotechnology industry. R&D Management 22: 41–53

Gambetta D (ed) (1988) Trust: Making and breaking co-operative relations. Basil Blackwell, Oxford

Gattiker UE, Perlusz S, Bohmann K (2000) Using the internet for B2B activities: A review and future directions for research. Internet Research 10: 126–140

Gerybadze A (1995) Strategic alliances and process redesign: Effective management and restructuring of cooperative projects and networks. Walter de Gruyter, Berlin

Ghemawat J (1991) Commitment: The Dynamics of Strategy. Free Press, New York

Grabowski H, Vernon J (1994) Innovation and structural change in pharmaceuticals and biotechnology. Industrial and Corporate Change 4: 435–449

Hansen NM (1992) Competition, trust and reciprocity in the development of innovative Regional Milieux. Papers in Regional Science 71: 95–106

Hanson D (1982) The new alchemists: Silicon Valley and the microelectronics revolution. Little, Brown, Boston

Henderson R (1994) The evolution of integrative capabilities: Innovation in cardiovascular drug discovery. Industrial and Corporate Change 3: 607–630

Liebeskind J, Oliver A, Zucker L, Brewer M (1996) Social networks, learning, and flexibility: Sourcing scientific knowledge in new biotechnology firms. Organization Science 3: 783–831

Limerick D, Cunnington B (1993) Managing the new organization: A blueprint for networks and strategic alliances. Jossey-Bass, San Francisco

Lorange P, Roos J (1991) Why some strategic alliances succeed and others fail. Journal of Business Strategy 12: 25–30

Luhmann N (1979) Trust and power. John Wiley, New York

Malone MS (1985) The big score: The billion dollar story of Silicon Valley. Doubleday, New York

McKelvey M (1995) Evolutionary innovation: The business of biotechnology. Oxford University Press, Oxford

Misztal BA (1996) Trust in modern societies. Polity, Oxford

Orsenigo L (1989) The emergence of biotechnology. St. Martin's, New York

Orsenigo L, Pammolli F, Riccaboni M (2001) Technological change and network dynamics: Lessons from the pharmaceutical industry. Research Policy 30: 485–508

Pauleen DJ, Yoong P (2001) Facilitating virtual team relationships via Internet and conventional communication channels. Internet Research 11: 190–202

Pisano GP, Mang PY (1993) Collaborative product development and the market for know-how: Strategies and structures in the biotechnology industry. In: Burgelman RA, Rosenbloom RS (eds) Research on technological innovation, management and policy, Volume 5. JAI Press, Greenwich CT

Powell WW, Doput KW, Smith-Doerr L (1996) Interorganizational collaboration and the locus of innovation: Networks of learning in biotechnology. Administrative Science Quarterly 41: 116–145

Rogers EM, Larsen JK (1984) Silicon Valley fever: Growth of high technology culture. Basic Books, New York

Rosenfeld S (1996) Does cooperation enhance competitiveness? Assessing the impacts of inter-firm collaboration. Research Policy 25: 247–263

Saxenian A (1994) Regional advantage. Harvard University Press, Cambridge, MA

Schwartz D, Divitini M, Brasethvik T (2000) Knowledge management in the Internet age. In: Schwartz D, Divitini M, Brasethvik T (eds) Internet-based knowledge management and organizational memory. Idea Group Publishing, London

Suarez-Villa L (1998) The structures of cooperation: Downscaling, outsourcing and the networked alliance. Small Business Economics 10: 5–16

Suarez-Villa L (2000) Invention and the rise of technocapitalism. Rowman & Littlefield, New York

Suarez-Villa L (2002) High technology clustering in a polycentric metropolis: A view from the Los Angeles metropolitan region. International Journal of Technology Management 25, in press

Suarez-Villa L, Fischer MM (1995) Technology, organization and export-driven research and development in Austria's electronics industry. Regional Studies 29: 19–42

Suarez-Villa L, Karlsson C (1996) The development of Sweden's R&D-intensive electronics industries: Exports, outsourcing and territorial distribution. Environment and Planning A 28: 783–818

Suarez-Villa L, Rama R (1996) Outsourcing, R&D and the pattern of intra-metropolitan location: The electronics industries of Madrid. Urban Studies 33: 1155–1197

Suarez-Villa L, Walrod W (1997) Operational strategy, R&D, and intra-metropolitan clustering in a polycentric structure: The advanced electronics industries of the Los Angeles basin. Urban Studies 34: 1343–1380

Suarez-Villa L, Walrod W (2003) The collaborative economy of biotechnology: Alliances, outsourcing, and R&D. International Journal of Technology Management 26, forthcoming

Vassallo P (1999) The knowledge continuum: Organizing for research and scholarly communication. Internet Research 9: 232–242

Wellman B (ed) (1999) Networks in the global village. Westview Press, Boulder

Wellman B (2001) Computer networks as social networks. Science 293 (14 September): 2031–2034

Yoshino MY, Rangan US (1995) Strategic alliances: An entrepreneurial approach to globalization. Harvard Business School Press, Boston

5 The Innovation Decision and Fixed Costs

Kees van Montfort[1], Geert Ridder[2] and Alfred Kleinknecht[3]

[1] Free University Amsterdam, The Netherlands; [2] University of Southern California, Los Angeles, USA; [3] Delft University of Technology, The Netherlands

5.1 Introduction

In this study we analyse two new indicators of a firm's innovative output, i.e., sales per employee of products that are 'new to the firm' and sales per employee of products that are 'new to the firm's industry'. These indicators were first analysed in Brouwer and Kleinknecht (1996). They noted that, during the observation year, many firms had no sales in either of these two categories and proposed an *ad hoc* model to deal with the observations with zero sales. A drawback of their procedure is that the parameter estimates do not have a clear interpretation.

In this study we start from the assumption that, in order to introduce a product innovation, the firm must incur fixed costs. When considering a new product introduction, the firm will compare fixed costs with expected (net) revenues during the economic lifetime of the product. Of course, only if expected revenues exceed costs will the firm introduce the product. We show that this simple theoretical model leads to a specific censored regression model, the stochastic threshold model. Moreover, from theoretical considerations one can argue that variables that affect fixed costs do not have a direct effect on the level of sales. This suffices to identify the parameters of the threshold model. Although, without further assumptions, we cannot estimate fixed costs directly because of lack of adequate data, we can identify determinants of the threshold and of the sales of innovative products. This is an improvement on the estimates obtained in Brouwer and Kleinknecht (1996) who did not distinguish between these two equations. Their estimates are reduced-form estimates, while we present structural estimates that correspond to a structural economic model, and allow for an interpretation in the context of that model.

Our paper is organised as follows. In Sect. 5.2 we introduce the theoretical model and describe the corresponding econometric model. Sect. 5.3 discusses our data. Sect. 5.4 presents our hypotheses. In Sect. 5.5 we present and discuss the outcomes of our estimates. Sect. 5.6 describes some simulations and conclusions are drawn in Sect. 5.7.

5.2 Sales of Innovative Products with Fixed Costs of Introduction

Some investments have the character of irreversible sunk costs, which explains the observation that the resale or scrap value of certain investments (e.g., some specialised pieces of machinery) is much lower than the purchasing price. The introduction of an innovative product that is new to the firm or new to the industry is also imperfectly reversible and involves fixed costs. Such fixed costs can be related to investment in specific knowledge, acquisition of patent rights, training, market research, advertising, or purchase of specialised equipment. In this section we develop a theoretical model that takes into account these fixed costs of introduction. This model implies that the innovative product is introduced if (expected) sales exceed a certain threshold. We then specify a statistical model that corresponds to this economic model, and we show that the restrictions that can be derived from the economic model are sufficient to identify this threshold, which we assume to be firm specific.

5.2.1 The Theoretical Model

Besides fixed costs of introduction, there may be other reasons of why an R&D performing firm does not have sales of innovative products in a particular year. The product may be still under development or the firm may have realised only *process* innovations that were asked for in a yes/no question (without assessing sales related to it). In our analysis, we concentrate on firms that engage *permanently* (other than occasionally) in R&D and that have been developing new products in the recent past. Wider definitions of sample firms have also tentatively been used in our estimates but will not be documented in detail, since these analyses did not lead to substantially different outcomes. We assume that our R&D performing firms must decide in any year whether to introduce some innovative product.

First, we introduce the variables used in the model.

s = R&D spending;
y = annual sales of the innovative product;
μ = expected annual sales of the innovative product;
c = fixed cost of introduction of the innovative product;
T = economic life of the innovative product;
r = discount rate;
γ = mark-up of the price over variable cost per unit.

Without loss of generality we assume that all R&D spending is done at time 0, just before the introduction decision. At that time the expected discounted return from the investment s is

$$\int_0^T \gamma\mu(s)e^{-rt}\,dt - s - c \tag{5.1}$$

We assume that R&D spending s has a positive effect on the expected sales of the innovative product. The first-order condition for a profit maximum is

$$\frac{\gamma}{r}(1-e^{-rT})\mu'(s) = 1 \tag{5.2}$$

If we assume that $\mu''(s) < 0$ and $\mu'(s) > 0$, then the first-order equation has a finite solution which may be 0. We denote this optimal R&D investment by s^{opt}. The optimal level of R&D spending is independent of the fixed cost of introduction c. Furthermore, R&D spending rises with γ, which is an index of competition. The stronger competition, the lower the optimal R&D spending. The optimal level rises also with T, and it falls with r. The longer the economic life of an innovative product the higher R&D spending.

Note that $\mu(s)$ is the expected sales at the time that the level of R&D spending is determined. At the moment that the decision whether to introduce the innovative product is taken, the expected sales differ from their previously expected value by a prediction error v and are equal to

$$y = \mu(s^{opt}) + v \tag{5.3}$$

The innovation is introduced if and only if the expected discounted return exceeds the fixed cost of introduction

$$\frac{\gamma(\mu(s^{opt}) + v)(1-e^{-r.T})}{r} > c \tag{5.4}$$

Eq. (5.3) and inequality (5.4) specify a threshold regression model: if the expected revenues exceed the threshold costs (in inequality (5.4)) then sales are given in Eq. (5.3).

The simple theoretical model implies that the optimal level of R&D spending and hence, the expected sales of the new product, is independent of the cost of introduction. This does not mean that the R&D effort is independent of the costs of introduction. If the expected costs of introduction are high, the project may be unprofitable, i.e., the expected discounted return in Eq. (5.1) may be negative, and the project will not be implemented. However, given that a project is profitable, the optimal spending is independent of the fixed costs of introduction. This result is important for the specification of the threshold model, because it justifies the exclusion of variables that affect the fixed cost of introduction from the sales equation. It should be stressed that in our empirical model R&D effort is an explanatory and not a dependent variable, i.e., we model sales of innovative products given (past) R&D effort.

5.2.2 The Econometric Model

For the specification of the econometric model that corresponds to Eqs. (5.3) and (5.4), it is convenient to introduce some further notation:

y	=	observed annual sales of innovative products;
y^*	=	latent annual sales of innovative products;
c^*	=	latent fixed threshold;
x	=	exogenous variables that influence the sales of innovative products;
z	=	exogenous variables that influence the threshold of sales of innovative products;
β	=	vector of regression coefficients of variables x;
α	=	vector of regression coefficients of variables z;
ε	=	error term of sales equation;
η	=	error term of threshold equation;
σ_ε	=	standard deviation of ε;
σ_η	=	standard deviation of η;
ρ	=	correlation coefficient of ε and η.

We do not attempt to estimate the structural model in (5.3) and (5.4) directly. From Eq. (5.4) we see that the threshold is

$$c^* = \frac{cr}{\gamma(1-e^{-rT})} \tag{5.5}$$

Without further assumptions we cannot recover the cost c. Instead, we express c^* in Eq. (5.5) and $\mu(s^{opt})$ in Eq. (5.3) as a function of exogenous variables z and x, respectively. In the sequel, we use the exclusion restrictions of the economic model. In other words, variables that affect the threshold through the fixed cost c do not enter the sales Eq. (5.3). Hence we obtain the latent regression equations

$$c^* = z\alpha + \eta \tag{5.6}$$

$$y^* = x\beta + \varepsilon \tag{5.7}$$

$$\begin{pmatrix} \varepsilon \\ \eta \end{pmatrix} \sim N\left(\begin{pmatrix} 0 \\ 0 \end{pmatrix}, \begin{pmatrix} \sigma_\varepsilon^2 & \cdot \cdot \\ \rho\sigma_\varepsilon\sigma_\eta & \sigma_\eta^2 \end{pmatrix} \right) \tag{5.8}$$

Firms will have sales of new products if and only if the (expected) sales of the new product exceed the threshold c^*. Hence, the latent and observed variables are related by

$$I = I\left(y^* > c^*\right) \tag{5.9}$$

$$y = \begin{bmatrix} 0 & if & I = 0 \\ y^* & if & I = 1 \end{bmatrix} \tag{5.10}$$

The probability of positive sales of a new product is

$$\Pr(I = 1) = \Pr\left(y^* > c^*\right) = \Phi\left(\frac{x\beta - z\alpha}{\sqrt{\sigma_{\eta^*}^2}}\right) \tag{5.11}$$

where $\sigma_{\eta^*}^2 = \sigma_\eta^2 + \sigma_\varepsilon^2 - 2\rho\sigma_\varepsilon\sigma_\eta$, and Φ is the cumulative distribution function of the standard normal distribution. The expected sales of the innovative product, conditional on the event that they are positive, are

$$E(y \mid I = 1) = x\beta + \frac{\sigma_\varepsilon^2}{\sigma_{\eta^*}^2} \cdot \frac{\varphi\left(\dfrac{x\beta - z\alpha}{\sqrt{\sigma_{\eta^*}^2}}\right)}{\Phi\left(\dfrac{x\beta - z\alpha}{\sqrt{\sigma_{\eta^*}^2}}\right)} \tag{5.12}$$

where φ is the density function of the standard normal distribution.

The likelihood function of the threshold model is derived from the joint distribution of the observed variables (y, I)

$$F_{y,I}(I = 0) = \Pr\left(y^* < c^*\right) = 1 - \Phi\left(\frac{x\beta - z\alpha}{\sigma_{\eta^*}}\right) \tag{5.13}$$

$$F_{y,I}(y, I = 1) = \Pr\left(c^* < y^*, y^* = y\right) = \Pr\left(c^* < y^* \mid y^* = y\right)\Pr\left(y^* = y\right) =$$

$$\Phi\left(\frac{(y - z\alpha) - \rho.\sigma_\eta\left(\dfrac{y - x\beta}{\sigma_\varepsilon}\right)}{\sigma_\eta\sqrt{1 - \rho^2}}\right) \cdot \frac{\varphi\left(\dfrac{y - x\beta}{\sigma_\varepsilon}\right)}{\sigma_\varepsilon} \tag{5.14}$$

Hence the loglikelihood is:

$$
LogL_i = \sum_{i=1}^{N}
\left\{
\begin{array}{l}
(1 - I_i).Log\left[1 - \Phi\left(\dfrac{x_i\beta - z_i\alpha}{\sigma_{\eta^*}}\right)\right] + I_i.Log\left[\dfrac{\varphi\left(\dfrac{y_i - x_i\beta}{\sigma_\varepsilon}\right)}{\sigma_\varepsilon}\right] \\[4ex]
+ I_i.Log\left[\Phi\left(\dfrac{(y_i - z_i\alpha) - \rho.\sigma_\eta\left(\dfrac{y_i - x_i\beta}{\sigma_\varepsilon}\right)}{\sigma_\eta\sqrt{1 - \rho^2}}\right)\right]
\end{array}
\right\}
\tag{5.15}
$$

It is also possible to estimate the model by a two-stage estimation method (see Maddala (1983, pp. 228–230)). We used the estimates of the two-stage method as starting values for the maximum likelihood estimation.

Nelson (1977, p. 315) and Maddala (1983, p. 229) discuss the identification of the parameters of the threshold model. A sufficient condition for identification is that the sales equation contains at least one exogenous variable that is not in the threshold equation. As noted before, variables that affect the threshold through the cost of introduction can be excluded from the sales equation, so that this condition can be easily satisfied.

5.3 The Data

5.3.1 Source and Background

We use data from the Dutch part of the *Community Innovation Survey* (CIS) for the year 1992. This survey was conducted by Kleinknecht and Brouwer with financial assistance by the Dutch Ministry of Economic Affairs and by Directorate General 13 of the European Commission. The data collection in 1992 was the pilot round of the CIS.

The population covers all firms with 10 and more employees in all branches of Dutch manufacturing and services. The sample size was about 8,000 firms with a response rate of 50.8%. The available information on the non-responding firms (among which outcomes of a brief survey among non-respondents) indicate that they do not differ systematically from the respondents (for a detailed documentation, see Brouwer and Kleinknecht 1994).

The questionnaire consisted of two parts. In the first part, firms were asked to report basic information on the firm, such as the branch of principal activity, sales, exports, employment, etc. The second part contained questions on R&D, innovation and related issues. Only firms that answered at least one of the following three questions in the affirmative were asked to complete the second part of the questionnaire:

- Did your firm develop any technologically changed products during 1990–92?
- Did your firm develop any technologically changed processes during 1990–92?
- Does your firm plan to develop any technologically changed products or processes in the years 1993–95?

In the survey, a distinction is made between three types of product: (1) essentially unchanged products, (2) incrementally improved products and (3) radically changed or totally new products. In this paper, we shall join the latter two categories into one category: 'innovative products'. In the survey a further distinction is made between:

- Products 'new to the firm' (i.e., already known in the industry);
- Products 'new to the industry' (i.e., not introduced earlier by a competitor).

While products in the second category can be interpreted as 'true' innovations, the first category will often include imitations of innovations introduced earlier by competitors. In other words, the sales of innovative products 'new to the firm' are an indicator of imitation and technology diffusion rather than of 'true' innovation.

5.3.2 Descriptive Statistics

The sample consists of 4094 firms. After exclusion of firms with missing values on essential variables, and of firms with highly implausible answers (for instance, implausibly large sales per employee) we are left with a data set of 2887 firms (data set 1). For our empirical analysis we will distinguish two other data sets. By further omitting firms from the sample that reported that they had *no* innovative activity (i.e., no product or process innovation and no plans for future innovations) during 1990–92 we obtain data set 2 (1593 firms). Moreover, when omitting firms that have only occasional (other than permanent) R&D efforts, we obtain data set 3 (622 firms).

Initially, we restrict attention to the firms in the third data set because these (permanently R&D performing) firms are most likely to have developed new products in their laboratories and they have to decide whether to engage in their commercial market introduction. The descriptive statistics for the third data set are given in Table 5.1, while App. 5A contains the descriptive statistics of the other two data sets. All the variables concern the year 1992, except for sales growth between 1990 and 1992. Table 5.1 also covers statistics for firms that have positive sales of products 'new to the *firm*' and products 'new to the *industry*'.

The latter two are obtained by multiplying the total sales of the firm by the share of sales derived from innovative products introduced during 1990–92. In order to correct for firm size differences we divide the sales of new products by the number of employees.

The average of annual sales of products 'new to the firm' and 'new to the industry' respectively is about f 104,000 and f 11,000 (Dutch guilders).[1] The standard deviations are quite large because there are a few large (multinational) companies in the sample with high labour productivity and high sales of new products.[2]

The growth of sales between 1990 and 1992 is relatively high, i.e., about 12% in a period in which GDP growth was only seven percent in current prices. A plausible explanation for this difference is that our selection is confined to innovators that are supposed to grow more rapidly. There is evidence in the literature of a positive correlation between exports and innovation (Hughes 1986, Brouwer and Kleinknecht 1993), which explains that the average export share in our subsample is high (around 43%), compared to the national average (around 25%).

The sales threshold in Eq. (5.5) depends on the fixed costs of introduction. A possible proxy for these fixed costs is the minimum efficient scale (MES) that is often used as an indicator of the cost structure of enterprises. In our empirical work we follow Sutton (1991, p. 96), and estimate the MES by the median plant size in an industry. We try to improve on this by not using the median firm size, but the median number of employees engaged in R&D. There are at least four problems with this proxy of fixed costs. In the first place, the proxy is a very crude way of approximating fixed costs. Secondly, the proxy does not vary between firms within one industry, and, thirdly, some firms belong to more than one industry. Fourth, the economic model of Sect. 5.2 refers to the fixed costs of market introduction.

---

[1] One US dollar was approximately f 1.6 in 1992.

[2] We have estimated the model also without the large multinationals. The estimates were not sensitive to this omission.

Table 5.1. Descriptive Statistics of the Variables Used in the Model

Variables	total sample		firms which had in 1992 some sales of products new to the *firm*		firms which had in 1992 some sales of products new to the *industry*	
Background variables	Mean	SD	Mean	SD	Mean	SD
total sales 1992 (million guilders)	243.42	1291.33	255.59	1346.60	273.04	1599.68
% sales of products new to the firm	36.09	26.52	39.32	25.28	34.74	23.16
% sales of products new to the industry	4.00	10.27	3.92	9.58	10.10	14.32
Endogenous variables						
logarithm of average sales per employee of products new to the firm	10.40	3.20	11.33	0.80	10.75	2.56
logarithm of average sales per employee of products new to the industry	3.83	4.78	3.95	4.79	9.64	1.19
Exogenous variables						
product-R&D intensity in %	3.55	5.02	3.62	5.12	4.22	6.10
sales growth in % between 1990 and 1992	12.09	25.09	11.79	24.95	13.02	23.09
export share in sales in %	43.10	34.54	44.24	34.12	42.56	35.14
number of employees in f.t.e.	790.65	4210.11	832.54	4390.31	916.85	5448.51
proxy for MES: median of R&D man-years in an industry	4.57	4.83	4.55	4.90	4.91	4.48
average length of life cycle in an industry (years)	10.58	1.91	10.58	1.87	10.72	1.77
small business presence (fraction of firms with less than 50 employees in a firm's sector of principal activity)	72.05	10.97	72.60	8.81	70.91	11.33
firm belongs to high technological opportunity sectors	0.57		0.58		0.59	
firm belongs to the service sector	0.22		0.20		0.23	
firm is located in a central region	0.71		0.71		0.72	
firm is strongly dependent on mother company	0.15		0.14		0.11	
firm consulted an Innovation Advice Centre	0.28		0.29		0.31	
firm engaged in R&D co-operation	0.53		0.54		0.62	
firm acquired external technological knowledge	0.66		0.66		0.72	
number of observations	622		570 (92%)		246 (44%	

The descriptive statistics of the variables for data set 1, 2 and 3 are almost the same, except for the following variables: number of employees, shares in total sales of products new to the firm and new to the industry, product-R&D intensity (i.e., R&D budgets related to new product development as a percentage of total sales), sales growth between 1990 and 1992, export share in sales, and fixed costs

(MES). Data set 1 has the lowest values and data set 3 the highest values for these variables (see App. 5A).

Fig. 5.1 shows non-parametric kernel estimates of the density functions of (the logarithm of) average sales per employee of products 'new to the firm' and 'new to the industry'.[3] As expected, the mode of the distribution of average sales per employee of products new to the firm is larger than that of the distribution of average sales per employee of products new to the industry, namely f 100,000 and f 25,000 respectively. The dispersion is greater for average sales per employee of products new to the industry. The logarithmic transformation makes both (unconditional) distributions symmetric around the mode, and a log normal distribution seems to be appropriate, although the distribution for products new to the firm is rather peaked.

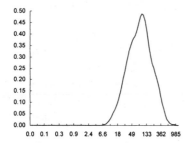 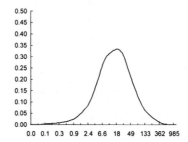

Fig. 5.1. Density Functions of Logarithm of Average Annual Sales (thousands of guilders; logarithmic scale) per Employee of Products New to the Firm (left panel) and of Products New to the Industry (right panel): non-parametric kernel estimates

5.4 Hypotheses

Before we present the results we formulate the hypotheses to be tested with our model. This allows us to identify variables that can be included or excluded from either the threshold equation or sales equation.

H1: Product related R&D increases sales of new products.

Since R&D is a major input into the innovation process, we expect a firm's R&D intensity and, in particular, R&D connected to product development, to be related directly to its 'output' of product innovations.

H2: R&D co-operation lowers the threshold of sales of new products

---

[3] See Silverman (1986, pp. 15 and 43). We use the bandwidth suggested by Silverman.

The sharing of knowledge and risks through R&D co-operation agreements decreases the fixed cost of introduction of new products, besides enhancing future innovation benefits by internalising positive external effects.

H3: Demand growth stimulates the prospect for successful sales of innovative products

Schmookler (1966) suggested that demand is crucial to innovation efforts. Recent empirical investigations provided support for this hypothesis (Scherer 1982; Walsh 1984; Kleinknecht and Verspagen 1990; Geroski and Walters 1995).

H4: Firms located in urban agglomerations benefit from externalities and knowledge spillovers and because of that have a lower threshold for introduction of new products.

A firm's environment may be more or less conducive to innovation (see Gottmann 1961, p. 577). It has often been argued that firms in dense urban agglomerations may benefit from regional spillovers since direct contacts with business partners facilitate the exchange of information and networking. Using a recently developed agglomeration index by Manshanden (1996) for the Netherlands, we can test this hypothesis.

H5: The longer the life cycle of the innovative product the lower the sales threshold

This follows directly from Eq. (5.5). A long economic life implies that the cost of introduction per unit of product sold is relatively low. We use as a proxy the average length of the life cycle of innovative products in an industry. This information has been collected at the firm level. However, due to the substantial item non-response we were forced to transform this information into an average sectoral variable.

H6: The stronger the presence of small innovators in an industry, the lower the threshold for introduction of new products

To test the hypothesis we include the variable 'small business presence' in the threshold equation This is the fraction of innovating firms with less than 50 employees in a firm's sector of principal activity.

H7: Consultation of regional Innovation Advice Centres reduce the costs of sales of new products and hence the sales threshold

During our observation period, the Dutch government established 18 regional Innovation Advice Centres. The intention is that these centres are intermediaries in the market of technological knowledge. They advise small and medium-sized firms to find their way in the regional and national R&D infrastructure. We shall test whether consultation of an Innovation Advise Centre reduces the costs of market introduction and hence the threshold of sales of new products.

In addition to these factors, we include other variables that obviously should have some influence on innovation performance, e.g., acquisition of external technology. Also the proxy for MES should have a positive effect on the costs of innovation.

5.5 Results

The estimates of the threshold model for data set 3 are summarised in Table 5.2 for products new to the firm and in Table 5.3 for products new to the industry. A positive coefficient in the threshold equation means that the corresponding variable is positively related to the sales threshold. In other words, it increases the threshold. If the coefficient of a variable that appears in the threshold equation *and* in the sales equation is positive and if it is larger in the sales equation than in the threshold equation, then the variable increases the probability that the firm innovates (see Eq. 5.11). The same is true if the coefficient in the sales equation is negative and smaller than in the threshold equation.

Even though the threshold is not observed, the parameters of the threshold equation and those of the sales equation are identified by exclusion restrictions. The theoretical model of Sect. 5.2.1 implies that variables that affect the fixed costs can be excluded from the sales equation. For that reason a variable such as R&D collaboration does not enter the sales equation. This variable as well as the dummy for service firms is significant in the threshold equation, both for products new to the firm and new to the industry. Although the exclusion of the service sector dummy from the sales equation is more questionable, the results are not sensitive to the inclusion of this variable in the sales equation. We do allow for correlation between the error terms in the threshold and sales equations. This correlation captures common firm-specific variables that have been omitted from both equations. Next, we discuss the parameter estimates in Tables 5.2 and 5.3.

Table 5.2a. Estimates for Products 'New to the *Firm*'. Threshold Equation

Exogenous variables:	coefficients	standard errors
Intercept	11.181[**]	2.809
average length of life cycle in an industry	0.034	0.147
proxy for fixed costs, median of R&D man-years by industry	−0.046	0.070
small business presence in % (fraction of firms with less than 50 employees in a firm's sector of principal activity)	−0.064[**]	0.022
Dummy variables		
firm consulted an Innovation Advice Centre	−1.046	0.651
firm engaged in R&D collaboration	−0.904[*]	0.535
firm acquired external technological knowledge	0.349	0.549
firm is located in a central region	−0.111	0.568
firm belongs to high technological opportunity sector	−0.173	0.670
firm belongs to the service sector	2.029[**]	0.748
firm is strongly dependent on mother company	1.147	0.790

Note: see Table 5.2b

Table 5.2b. Sales-per-Employee Equation (log) of Products 'New to the *Firm*'. The dependent variable is the log of the average annual sales-per-employee of products "new to the firm" in thousands of guilders (logarithmic scale).

Exogenous variables:	coefficients	standard errors
Intercept	10.897[**]	0.158
log of numbers of employees	0.041[*]	0.025
product-R&D intensity (product related R&D man-years as a percentage of a firm's total employment)	0.036[**]	0.006
firm's sales growth 1990–92	0.004[**]	0.001
export share in sales	0.503[**]	0.100
Dummy variables		
firm belongs to high technological opportunity sectors	−0.271[**]	0.082
firm belongs to the service sector	−0.111	0.112

Notes: [*] = coefficient is significant at 90% level; [**] = coefficient is significant at 95% level; Standard deviation of OLS estimate: 0.751 (significant); Standard deviation of THRESHOLD estimate: 3.139 (not significant); correlation coefficient of ε and η: 0.154 (not significant); loglikelihood −803.4; number of firms: 622; R^2 (only OLS-part): 0.12

- R&D intensity. Both for products that are 'new to the firm' and for products 'new to the industry', a higher R&D intensity results in higher sales of new products per employee. This is consistent with the economic model of Sect. 5.2 and hypothesis 1 above.
- R&D collaboration. R&D collaboration reduces the sales threshold considerably, both for products new to the industry and for products new to the firm. In both cases, the effect is statistically significant. This is a new result because

Brouwer and Kleinknecht (1996) were not able to include R&D collaboration in the equation explaining the decision to introduce innovative products.[4] One could, of course, argue that R&D collaboration also has an influence on sales of new products, since such collaboration may strengthen the competitive position of the participants, which will result in higher sales of new products. However, tentative inclusion of the R&D collaboration variables in our earlier estimates suggested that this was not the case (see Brouwer and Kleinknecht 1996). A possible explanation for not finding a positive effect of collaboration on sales of innovative products is that R&D collaborators not only share costs and risks, but also have to share later innovative benefits with their partners. They will therefore only engage in collaboration if they need to do so. For example, if they lack specific competencies, if they cannot bear the risk alone or if they fear losing too much time with respect to competitors. In other words, the dummy for R&D collaborators may tend to capture weaker innovators. The fact that this group did not have a negative sign in the estimates by Brouwer and Kleinknecht (1996) may illustrate that R&D collaboration still has considerable benefits.

Table 5.3a. Estimation Results for Products 'New to the *Industry*': Threshold equation

Exogenous variables:	Coefficients	standard errors
Intercept	12.037**	2.855
average length of life cycle in an industry	−0.124	0.142
proxy for fixed costs, median of R&D man-years by industry	−0.013	0.055
fraction of innovators with less than 50 employees in a firm's sector of principal activity	0.025	0.025
Dummy variables		
firm consulted an Innovation Advice Centre	−0.711	0.554
firm engaged in R&D collaboration	−1.361**	0.532
firm acquired external technological knowledge	−0.763	0.553
firm is located in a central region	−0.164	0.548
firm belongs to high technological opportunity sectors	−0.563	0.653
firm belongs to the service sector	−1.333	0.764
firm is strongly dependent on mother company	1.733	0.751

Notes: see Table 5.3b

---

[4] This was not possible, since questions about R&D collaboration were only asked to innovating firms.

Table 5.3b. Sales-per-Employees Equation (log). The dependent variable is the log of the average annual sales-per-employee of products "new to the industry" in thousands of guilders (logarithmic scale).

Exogenous variables:	Coefficients	standard errors
Intercept	9.428[**]	0.578
log of numbers of employees	−0.047	0.060
product-R&D intensity (product related R&D man-years as a percentage of a firm's total employment)	0.029[**]	0.013
firm's sales growth 1990–92	0.007[**]	0.003
export share in sales	0.365	0.235
Dummy variables		
firm belongs to high technological opportunity sectors	−0.198	0.213
firm belongs to the service sector	−0.533[**]	0.235

Notes: [*] = coefficient is significant at 90% level; [**] = coefficient is significant at 95% level; Standard deviation of OLS estimate: 1.173 (significant); Standard deviation of THRESHOLD estimate: 4.505 (not significant); correlation coefficient of ε and η: −0.057 (not significant); loglikelihood −785.6; number of firms: 622; R^2 (only OLS-part): 0.09

- Sales growth. The growth of a firm's sales over the 1990–92 period has a small but significantly positive effect on sales of products 'new to the firm' and 'new to the industry'. Adherents of Schmookler's 'demand-pull' hypothesis will take this as a confirmation that demand enhances innovation, while others may argue that the opposite causation can also hold: firms that innovate successfully grow more rapidly. Against this it can be argued that a recent Granger causality test of the demand-pull hypothesis by Geroski and Walters (1995), using aggregate time series, confirmed that the causal link runs from demand to innovation. Moreover, we tested whether the demand variable was endogenous, using a simple version of the Hausman test (Greene 1991, p. 303). If demand were endogenous, we would need to develop an instrumental variable. It turned out that this was not the case.
- Location. The location of a firm has the expected negative sign but fails to have a statistically significant effect on the sales threshold. It should be noted that Brouwer, Budil-Nadvornikova and Kleinknecht (1999) did find indications of regional spillovers in the Netherlands: with a given R&D intensity (and other firm characteristics being kept constant), firms in more centralised regions have a higher innovation output. However, while a firm's location in a central agglomeration may enhance its innovative output due to externalities, central locations also have higher factor costs that may drive up costs of market introduction.
- Life cycle of products. The average length of the life cycle does not influence sales of innovative products. Hence we reject hypothesis 5. As a qualification, we should note that the life cycle variable had to be aggregated due to a high item non-response in the survey. Moreover, the de-

scriptive data in Table 5.1 show that this variable does not show very much variance.

- Competition from small innovators. Using small business presence as a measure of competition in a firm's sector of principal activity, we accept hypothesis 6 for products new to the firm and reject hypothesis 6 for products new to the industry. Of course, the proxy is an indirect measure of the mark-up of the price over variable cost per unit that plays a role in the economic model. Moreover, the causality may also run the other way around, i.e., from the size of the threshold to competition. If the threshold is low, many entrepreneurs see profits, if competition is fierce, only innovations with low cost of introduction will be brought to the market.

- Regional Innovation Advice Centres. For Dutch policy-makers it is encouraging that firms which consulted one of the regional Innovation Advice Centres have a lower threshold and hence, a higher probability that an innovation is introduced. As a qualification, it should be noted that the coefficients for innovative products are relatively large but not significant. Sceptics may argue that causality is running opposite to what is assumed in our model, i.e., that Innovation Advice Centres attract innovating firms. This is not convincing, however, since we only selected firms with permanent R&D activities.

- Other factors. We included a dummy variable for manufacturing firms that belong to high-technological opportunity sectors. This dummy is defined as in Pavitt's (1984) 'taxonomy' of innovating sectors.[5] Against our expectations, the coefficients tend to be negative. Probably by including R&D collaboration and product R&D intensity in the model, the high-technological opportunity sectors lost explanatory power. Another possibility is that the years 1990–92 were dramatic years for electronics in the Netherlands. We also included a dummy for service firms. It appears that service firms have a significantly smaller probability of having any sales of innovative products. Furthermore, sales of products 'new to the industry' (per employee) generated by service firms are less than those sales of manufacturing firms.

To test whether firm size is relevant for the sales (per employee) of new products we included the logarithm of the number of employees in the sales equation. We found that sales per employees of products new to the firm increase with the number of employees. The effect is not significant for products new to the industry. It should be added here that, in our initial estimates on sales of innovative products, the differences between larger and smaller firms were more pronounced

---

[5] High-technological opportunity sectors include chemicals and plastics, the pharmaceutical industry, the electro-technical and electronic industry, transportation equipment (motor vehicles and aircraft), mechanical engineering, instrument and optical industries. These sectors coincide with what Pavitt (1984) called 'science-based', 'scale intensive' and 'specialised suppliers' industries, as opposed to 'supplier-dominated' industries, which we count as 'low-technological opportunity' industries.

than those documented here. This can be explained by our repair work for a possible measurement bias in the survey. The CIS questionnaire asked for products 'new to the industry'. It is conceivable that larger firms with considerable international operations may interpret the term 'new to the industry' more restrictively as they tend to compare themselves to their major competitors in international markets. Small firms are often oriented to regional and national markets and may therefore perceive more of their new products as 'not previously introduced by a competitor'. In other words, larger firms may interpret the notion of 'new to the industry' more narrowly, because of a difference in perspective.

We corrected for this measurement bias by including as an exogenous variable the firm's export-intensity (that is, the percentage share of exports in total sales). If there were no measurement bias, one would expect export-intensive firms to be more innovative, because of a positive relationship between innovation and export (Hughes 1986; Brouwer and Kleinknecht 1993). It appears that the coefficient of export-intensity is only positively significant for sales of products new to the firm (as expected). It is *not* significant for sales of products new to the industry. The latter can be explained by two counteracting influences: on the one hand, a positive influence of export-intensity on innovation, and, on the other hand, the aforementioned bias which causes internationally oriented firms to interpret the notion of 'new to the industry' more restrictively.

Innovative Firms Versus Non-innovative Firms

In the above analysis we dealt with only those companies that had innovative activities during 1990–92 *and* that also performed permanent (other than occasional) R&D activities (data set 3). We repeated the analysis for a larger data set, including those firms that had innovative activities during 1990–2 but did not necessarily have permanent R&D activities (data set 2). Moreover, we repeated our analysis for the most extensive data set containing *all* the firms, i.e., innovators and non-innovators and permanent and occasional R&D performers (data set 1). It turned out that the results for the initial analysis and the two additional analyses did not differ that much (see App. 5.B and 5.C). The most notable outcomes of our sensitivity analysis were the following.

The significant variables of the threshold equations of data set 3 were also significant in the threshold equations of data set 1 and 2. Moreover, the threshold equations on sales of products new to the industry also contained the significant dummy variable on "acquisition of external technological knowledge" (negative) and "firm is located in a central region" (negative). On the other hand, the variable "average length of life cycle in an industry" (negative) is only significant for data set 1 (as it was in the analyses by Brouwer and Kleinknecht 1996). The equation explaining the sales-per-employee of innovative products showed one major deviation between the three data sets: in the case of sales 'new to the industry' the variable "log of number of employees" (negative) is significant in data set 1 and 2, but not in data set 3.

The relative insensitivity of the estimation results to the sample selection is re-assuring. It indicates that differences in R&D intensity are the main difference between the firms in the three data sets.

Specification Tests for the Threshold Models

This paper assumes a threshold model for the relation between sales per employee and some exogenous variables. Brouwer and Kleinknecht (1996) deal with a more restrictive model, i.e., a tobit model. If we set the correlation between the errors ε and η equal to zero, the tobit model is nested in our threshold model. To compare our six threshold models with the six corresponding tobit models we use a lo-glikelihood ratio test. The loglikelihood ratio test statistic is equal to twice the lo-glikelihood of the threshold model (assuming that the correlation between ε and η is equal to zero) minus twice the loglikelihood of the tobit model. These six test statistics are distributed chi-squared with 12 degrees of freedom under the null hy-pothesis that the regression coefficients in the threshold equation and the variances of the error terms η are equal to zero.

For the sales of innovative products 'new to the firm' data set 1, 2 and 3 get the test statistic values 34.1, 27.0 and 23.0 with corresponding probability levels 0.002, 0.009 and 0.030. The test statistics for sales of products 'new to the indus-try' are equal to 32.6, 25.3 and 22.8 (probability levels 0.003, 0.014 and 0.035). These results may give confidence that our six threshold models can give useful additional information.

5.6 Simulations

To improve our understanding of the implications of the estimates, we performed some simulations. For that purpose we define a reference firm that resembles the average firm in our sample. The notes of Table 5.4 report its characteristics that turned out to be significant in the previous section. In the simulations we change one exogenous variable at a time and consider its effect on the sales threshold, the sales per employee of innovative products, and the probability that an innovative product is introduced. The results for the significant variables are reported in Ta-ble 5.4. Note that Table 5.4 is based on Eqs. (5.6), (5.7) and (5.11). The values of the parameters are fixed at the estimated values. The first three columns refer to products new to the firm and the last three to products new to the industry. All amounts in this table are in thousands of guilders and are rounded to the nearest f 100.

The reference firm has sales per employee of products new to the firm of f 105,000 and a sales threshold of only f 500 per employee (note that the reference firm has about 800 employees). This suggests that the threshold is rather low. The probability of introduction is 96%, which is close to the proportion reported in Ta-ble 5.1 (570 out of 621 firms; 92%). For products new to the industry the results are dramatically different. The expected sales threshold is larger than the expected sales per employee of products new to the industry, ƒ 27,000 and ƒ 13,000 respectively. The probability of introduction is 44%, which is close to the fraction in Table 5.1 (246 firms out of 621 firms; 40%). We conclude that for the 'average' firm the fixed cost of introducing products 'new to the *firm*' are relatively unimportant, while their effect on the decision to introduce products 'new to the *industry*' is considerable.

Table 5.4. Effects of Variables on the Sales Threshold per Employee for New Products, the Sales per Employee of New Products, and the Probability of the Introduction of a New Product.

	value	Products new to the firm			Products new to the industry		
		Threshold (thousand guilders)	Sales (thousand guilders)	Prob. of introduction	Threshold (thousand guilders)	Sales (thousand guilders)	Prob. of introduction
Reference firm (see notes)		0.5	105.4	95.9%	26.7	12.8	43.8%
Continuous variables							
Product-R&D intensity	5%	0.5	109.3	96.0%	26.7	13.2	44.0%
Firm's sales growth	6%	0.5	102.9	95.8%	26.7	12.3	43.5%
(1990–92)							
Export share in sales	60%	0.5	110.8	96.1%	26.7	13.3	44.1%
Small business presence	50%	1.7	105.4	90.8%	16.2	12.8	48.0%
Number of employees	900	0.5	105.9	95.9%	26.7	12.7	43.8%
Dummy variables							
Firm did not engage in R&D collaboration		1.2	105.4	92.7%	104.3	12.8	32.8%
Firm belongs to high technological opportunity sectors		0.4	80.4	95.6%	15.2	10.5	46.9%
Firm belongs to the Service sector		3.5	94.3	85.4%	7.1	7.5	50.5%

Notes: The reference firm has a product R&D intensity of 4%, a sales growth of 12%, 800 employees, an export share in sales of 50% and a small business presence of 70%. The firm is engaged in R&D collaboration, does not belong to the high technological opportunity sectors and does not belong to the service sector.

We restrict the discussion of Table 5.4 to products new to the industry. The interpretation for products new to the firm is analogous. An increase of the product-R&D intensity level by 1 percent point increases the average sales per employee of new products by ƒ 400. The probability of introduction increases by 0.2 percent point. The effect of a firm's sales growth is small, as is the effect of firm size. R&D co-operation is the most important determinant of the sales threshold of products new to the industry. The threshold increases by ƒ 78,000 if a firm has no R&D co-operation. Firms belonging to the high technological opportunity sectors or to the service sector have a lower sale threshold per employee and lower expected sales per employee than the reference firm.

5.7 Summary and Conclusions

Our summary has to begin with unavoidable caveats. The indicator of innovation output is a novel concept that was used for the first time in a survey on a European scale. Firms are not yet accustomed to answering questions regarding this indicator and their accounting procedures are not (yet) adapted to produce this type of information. As a consequence, many firms report 'rough estimates' rather than precise figures. Hence the data from this survey are not as reliable as will be the case in future routine surveys.

Another problem is that we have to reply on data from one survey only and can therefore hardly use time lags between exogenous and endogenous variables. A possible justification of not using lags is that many of our exogenous variables will not change dramatically in the course of time, i.e., we assume there to be some path dependency. But perhaps the biggest problem behind our estimate relates to data availability. Notable questions about R&D innovation costs (such as design, tooling-up, market research and specific investments in fixed assets related to innovation) have been badly reported. In future work, this type of data should be used for *directly* estimating the fixed (and sunk) costs of new product introduction, besides exploiting the panel data that will emerge from subsequent surveys.

This paper demonstrates a novel methodology. We propose an economic model to analyse the new indicator of innovation output. This model accounts for the fact that even among firms for which R&D is a permanent activity, a fraction of firms does not have sales of innovative products during a two-year observation period. The economic model implies some restrictions on the corresponding econometric model. The results of tests of these restrictions are mixed. Some cannot be rejected, e.g., the effect of R&D intensity on expected sales. However, we do find support for some of the other restrictions, such as the effects of the length of the product life cycle. So it seems too early to claim that we have a full understanding of the economic mechanism behind the indicator.

We do find a number of interesting results. A notable outcome is that R&D collaboration contributes to innovation by lowering the fixed costs of market introduction. We do not find that the regional environment has a significant impact on thresholds. However, we find a high but insignificant impact on threshold costs that comes from consultation of one of the regional Innovation Advice Centres.

References

Brouwer E, Kleinknecht AH (1993) Technology and a firm's export intensity: the need for adequate innovation measurement. Konjunkturpolitik 39: 315–325

Brouwer E, Kleinknecht AH (1994) Innovation in Dutch manufacturing and service industries (1992) (in Dutch), SEO Report to the Ministry of Economic Affairs, The Hague, Beleidsstudies Technologie Economie 27

Brouwer E, Kleinknecht AH (1996) Determinants of innovation: a micro econometric analysis of three alternative innovation output indicators. In: Kleinknecht AH (ed)

Determinants of innovation: The message from new indicators. Macmillan Press, London, pp 99–124

Brouwer E, Budil-Nadvornikova H, Kleinknecht AH (1999) Are urban agglomerations a better breeding place for product innovation? A firm-level analysis of new product announcements. Regional Studies 33: 541–549

Geroski PA, Walters CF (1995) Innovative activity over the business cycle. Economic Journal 105: 916–928

Gottmann J (1961) Megalopolis. The Twentieth Century Fund, New York

Greene WH (1991) Econometric analysis. Macmillan, New York

Hughes K (1986) Export and technology. Cambridge University Press, Cambridge

Kleinknecht AH (ed) (1996) Determinants of innovation: The message from new indicators. Macmillan Press, London

Kleinknecht AH, Verspagen B (1990) Demand and innovation: Schmookler re-examined. Research Policy 19: 387–394

Maddala GS (1983) Limited-dependent and qualitative variables in econometrics. Cambridge University Press, Cambridge

Manshanden W (1996) Zakelijke diensten en regionaal-economische ontwikkeling: de economie van nabijheid (in Dutch), Ph.D. Thesis University of Amsterdam, Amsterdam.

Nelson FD (1977) Censored regression models with unobserved, stochastic censoring thresholds. Journal of Econometrics 6: 309–327

Pavitt K (1984) Sectoral patterns of technological change: Towards a taxonomy and a theory. Research Policy 13: 343–373

Scherer FM (1982) Demand-pull and technological invention: Schmookler revisited. Journal of Industrial Economics 30: 225–237

Schmookler J (1966) Invention and economic growth. Harvard University Press, Cambridge

Silverman BW (1986) Density estimation for statistics and data analysis. Chapman and Hall, London

Sutton J (1991) Sunk costs and market structure: Price competition, advertising and the evolution of concentration. MIT press, Cambridge

Walsh V (1984) Invention and innovation in the chemical industry: Demand-pull or discovery-push? Research Policy 13: 211–234

Appendix 5.A Descriptive Statistics of the Variables Used in the Model

Variables	Data set 1 (whole sample)		Data set 2 (firms with innovative activities)	
	Mean	Std.Dev	Mean	Std.Dev
Background variables				
total sales 1992 (million guilders)	82.49	610.30	127.82	817.05
% sales of products new to the firm	16.00	24.79	28.99	27.14
% sales of products new to the industry	1.80	7.78	3.27	10.25
Endogenous variables				
logarithm of average sales per employee of products new to the firm	5.05	4.55	10.30	1.01
logarithm of average sales per employee of products new to the industry	1.51	3.54	3.01	4.5
Exogenous variables				
product-R&D intensity in %	0.98	0.40	1.76	0.53
sales growth in % between 1990 and 1992	8.45	9.66	10.85	18.63
export share in sales in %	21.49	30.64	29.27	33.18
number of employees in f.t.e.	681.54	2400.69	731.78	3612.01
proxy for MES: median of R&D man-years in sector	3.24	3.37	3.66	3.85
average length of life cycle in a sector (years)	10.45	2.05	10.34	2.15
small business presence (fraction of firms with less than 50 employees in a firm's sector of principal activity)	72.17	11.22	74.28	10.68
Dummy variables				
firm belongs to high technological opportunity sectors	0.35		0.45	
firm belongs to the service sector	0.43		0.31	
firm is located in a central region	0.75		0.74	
firm is strongly dependent on mother company	0.15		0.15	
firm consulted an Innovation Centre	0.13		0.21	
Firm engaged in R&D co-operation	0.17		0.31	
Firm acquired external technological knowledge	0.29		0.52	
Number of observations	2887		1593	

Appendix 5.B Threshold Equation and Sales Equation per Employee 'New to the *Firm*' for Data Set 1 and 2

Table 5.B.a Threshold Equation of Products 'New to the *Firm*' (data set 1)

Exogenous variables	coefficients	standard errors
Intercept	11.555**	2.798
average length of life cycle in a sector	0.183	0.271
proxy for fixed costs, median of R&D-man years by sector	−0.032	0.055
small business presence in % (fraction of firms with less than 50 employees in a firm's sector of principal activity)	−0.038**	0.017
Dummy variables		
firm consulted an innovation centre	−0.245	0.573
firm engaged in R&D collaboration	−0.332**	0.129
firm acquired external technological knowledge	−0.456	0.712
firm is located in a central region	−0.037	0.812
Firm belongs to high technological opportunity sector	−0.053	0.702
Firm belongs to the service sector	1.671**	0.648
Firm is strongly dependent on mother company	0.387	0.599

Notes: see Table 5.B.b

Table 5.B.b Sales-per-Employee Equation (log) of Products 'New to the *Firm*' (data set 1)

Exogenous variables	coefficients	standard errors
Intercept	10.67**	0.127
Log of numbers of employees	0.051**	0.023
Product-R&D intensity (product related R&D man years as a percentage of a firm's total employment)	0.031**	0.006
Firm's sales growth 1990-92	0.005*	0.003
Export share in sales	0.441**	0.091
Dummy variables		
Firm belongs to high technological opportunity sectors	−0.101**	0.049
Firm belongs to the service sector	0.038	0.082

Notes: * = coefficient is significant at 90% level; ** = coefficient is significant at 95% level; Standard deviation of OLS estimate: 0.986 (significant); Standard deviation of THRESHOLD estimate: 1.112 (significant); correlation coefficient of ε and η: 0.071 (not significant); loglikelihood −2745.1; number of firms: 2887; R^2 (only OLS-part): 0.16

Table 5.B.c Threshold Equation of Products 'New to the *Firm*' (data set 2)

Exogenous variables	coefficients	standard errors
Intercept	10.650**	1.901
Average length of life cycle in a sector	0.002	0.094
proxy for fixed costs, median of R&D-man years by sector	−0.039	0.073
small business presence in % (fraction of firms with less than 50 employees in a firm's sector of principal activity)	−0.601**	0.034
Dummy variables		
firm consulted an innovation centre	−0.138	0.157
firm engaged in R&D collaboration	−0.668**	0.258
firm acquired external technological knowledge	−0.065	1.810
firm is located in a central region	−0.043	0.277
firm belongs to high technological opportunity sector	−0.088	0.378
firm belongs to the service sector	2.003**	0.815
firm is strongly dependent on mother company	0.833	0.610

Notes: see Table 5.B.d

Table 5.B.d Sales-per-Employee Equation (log) of Products 'New to the *Firm*' (data set 2)

Exogenous variables	coefficients	standard errors
Intercept	10.650**	0.118
log of numbers of employees	0.054**	0.022
product-R&D intensity (product related R&D man years as a percentage of a firm's total employment)	0.024**	0.006
firm's sales growth 1990–92	0.025**	0.007
export share in sales	0.537**	0.089
Dummy variables		
firm belongs to high technological opportunity sectors	−0.165**	0.069
firm belongs to the service sector	0.039	0.081

Notes: * = coefficient is significant at 90% level; ** = coefficient is significant at 95% level; Standard deviation of OLS estimate: 1.494 (significant); Standard deviation of THRESHOLD estimate: 1.915 (significant); correlation coefficient of ε and η: 0.116 (not significant); loglikelihood −1403.9; number of firms: 1593; R^2 (only OLS-part): 0.15

Appendix 5.C Threshold Equation and Sales Equation per Employee 'New to the *Industry*' for Data Set 1 and 2

Table 5.C.a Threshold Equation of Products 'New to the *Industry*' (data set 1)

Exogenous variables	coefficients	standard errors
Intercept	11.87**	2.175
Average length of life cycle in a sector	−0.275**	0.123
Proxy for fixed costs, median of R&D-man years by sector	−0.065	0.070
Fraction of innovators with less than 50 employees in a firm's sector of principal activity	−0.071**	0.033
Dummy variables		
Firm consulted an innovation centre	−0.278	0.441
Firm engaged in R&D collaboration	−1.468**	0.606
Firm acquired external technological knowledge	−0.636**	0.212
Firm is located in a central region	−0.124**	0.064
Firm belongs to high technological opportunity sectors	−0.051	0.089
Firm belongs to the service sector	−1.351*	0.753
Firm is strongly dependent on mother company	1.232**	0.428

Notes: see Table 5.C.b

Table 5.C.b Sales-per-Employee Equation (log) of Products 'New to the *Industry*'(data set 1)

Exogenous variables	coefficients	standard errors
Intercept	10.101**	0.291
log of numbers of employees	0.960**	0.047
Product-R&D intensity (product related R&D man years as a percentage of a firm's total employment)	0.021**	0.010
firm's sales growth 1990-92	0.110**	0.044
Export share in sales	0.301	0.197
Dummy variables		
firm belongs to high technological opportunity sectors	−0.181	0.165
firm belongs to the service sector	−0.385**	0.175

Notes: * ○ coefficient is significant at 90% level; ** = coefficient is significant at 95% level; Standard deviation of OLS estimate: 1.271 (significant); Standard deviation of THRESHOLD estimate: 2.102 (significant); correlation coefficient of ε and η: −0.083 (not significant); loglikelihood −2499.1; number of firms: 2887; R^2 (only OLS-part): 0.19

Table 5.C.c Threshold Equation of Products 'New to the *Industry*' (data set 2)

Exogenous variables	coefficients	standard errors
Intercept	11.87**	2.588
Average length of life cycle in a sector	−0.012	0.070
Proxy for fixed costs, median of R&D-man years by sector	−0.041	0.069
Fraction of innovators with less than 50 employees in a firm's sector of principal activity	0.038	0.026
Dummy variables		
firm consulted an innovation centre	−0.073	0.447
firm engaged in R&D collaboration	−1.144**	0.499
firm acquired external technological knowledge	−0.636**	0.214
firm is located in a central region	−0.566**	0.223
firm belongs to high technological opportunity sectors	−0.079	0.672
firm belongs to the service sector	−1.453*	0.775
firm is strongly dependent on mother company	1.970**	0.749

Notes: see Table 5.C.d

Table 5.C.d Sales-per-Employee Equation (log) of Products 'New to the *Industry*' (data set 2)

Exogenous variables	coefficients	standard errors
Intercept	10.221**	0.324
log of numbers of employees	0.111**	0.047
product-R&D intensity (product related R&D man years as a percentage of a firm's total employment)	0.021**	0.011
firm's sales growth 1990–92	0.011**	0.005
export share in sales	0.478	0.391
Dummy variables		
firm belongs to high technological opportunity sectors	−0.183	0.169
firm belongs to the service sector	−0.397**	0.176

Notes: * = coefficient is significant at 90% level; ** = coefficient is significant at 95% level; Standard deviation of OLS estimate: 2.665 (significant); Standard deviation of THRESHOLD estimate: 2.135 (significant); correlation coefficient of ε and η: −0.061 (not significant); loglikelihood −1428.1; number of firms: 1593; R^2 (only OLS-part): 0.18

6 The Knowledge Base, Innovation and Urban Economic Growth

William F. Lever

Department of Urban Studies, University of Glasgow, Scotland, UK

6.1 Introduction

With the increasing globalisation of the world's economy the competitiveness of the urban regions of the developed world has increasingly been challenged firstly by the resource base and secondly by low cost labour in the developing world. The patterns of production and trade in manufactured goods have shifted towards a new international division of labour in which multinational enterprises have sought out low wage manual workers. From this industrial base these enterprises have developed new products and facilitated the growth of new indigenous enterprises (Daniels and Lever 1996). More recently, with the growth of the service sector, the new international division of labour has drawn investment in services to the developing world in search of low cost, but increasingly literate and numerate, workers in sectors such as data processing and global tourism (Coffey and Bailly 1992; Howland 1996). More recently still, concentrations of high skill service activities have developed in the Newly Industrialising Countries which threaten these specialisms in the United States and western Europe. An example would be the software writing concentration in Bangalore in India.

Against this background the developed nations, and especially their industrial urban regions, have been required to identify in which sectors or clusters of activities they retain a competitive advantage and how this competitive advantage can be sustained through policy initiatives. The answer generally has been that innovation, in products, services and processes is most likely to confer such competitive advantage and that such innovations are most likely to flow from the knowledge base. Typical of such initiatives is the United Kingdom's White Paper on *Our Competitive Future, Building the Knowledge Driven Economy* (Department of Trade and Industry 1998). Most initiatives are located in the context of national economies, but given that knowledge peaks are most likely to occur in urban areas, there is assumed to be a relationship between urban knowledge bases and the economic performance of the city (Kresl and Singh 1999; Lambooy 2000). Studies of urban competitiveness have stressed the importance of both the amount and the quality of different types of knowledge in generating innovation-led growth (Knight 1995). As society becomes increasingly knowledge-based, the nature of city development changes because activities in the knowledge sector are becoming more important and they require conditions and environments which are very different from those required by industry-based activities which are declining and which bring knowledge-based activities in expanding cities close to knowledge resources (Knight and Stanback 1970).

6.2 Theory

Theory links the development of the knowledge base with innovation and with economic growth. OECD (1999) pointed out that knowledge-based initiatives have been outpacing the overall rate of growth of GDP for many years in most member states. OECD identified the knowledge-base section as high and medium-high technology manufacturing industries and services such as finance, insurance and communications, now comprising more than 50 per cent of the total OECD economy, rising from 44 per cent in 1985. Within this total, knowledge-based services are now significantly more important than knowledge-based manufacturing industries.

The knowledge base is generated by investment in Research and Development, in software and in public-financed higher education, and currently represents eight per cent of OECD-wide investment, an amount similar to that in physical infrastructure. At the national level investment in knowledge generation is highest in the Nordic countries and France (10 per cent of GDP) and lowest in Italy and Japan (six per cent of GDP). To simplify the definition of the knowledge base, studies by OECD and others use two definitions. The first identifies the amount spent on Research and Development and, within this total, to distinguish between basic and nonbasic Research and Development with the former assumed to generate knowledge. At national levels, the amount of GDP committed to basic research is defined as that which is 'performed in the higher education sector and/or in government research laboratories' (p. 32). This it distinguishes from applied and experimental research. Basic research is 'experimental or theoretical work undertaken primarily to acquire new knowledge of the underlying foundation of phenomena and observable facts, without any particular application in view'. When there is a significant time lapse before the results of the basic research can be applied, this is considered long-term research, sometimes termed 'blue skies research' whose results are sometimes used at a much later date and for ends not foreseen by the initial researcher.

Knowledge in these reports can be of several types. There is technical knowledge which contributes to the innovation of products, services and processes. There is customer base knowledge which covers new markets, consumer choice and tastes and fashions. There is knowledge which relates to financial inputs to the production or service process. Lastly, there is knowledge as human capital in the form of skills and creativity. More importantly, however, there is a distinction between codified and tacit knowledge (Feldman 2000). Codified knowledge is widely available, amenable to telecommunications transmission and capable of sustaining economic growth. Tacit knowledge is more multidimensional, more limited in circulation, may often only be transmitted person-to-person (with better guarantees against ambiguity or falsification) and is much more likely to lead to innovation and associated economic growth.

Theoretically there is an assumed linear relationship between investment in Research and Development, the creation of knowledge, the generation of innovation and competitive advantage and subsequent economic success (Malecki 1997). If the level of Research and Development is increased, a corresponding increase in innovation and output should (eventually) follow. Carrying the argument one stage further, since it is basic research from which innovation ultimately flows, government science and industrial policy must include measures aimed at achieving the right balance between basic and applied research and in encouraging tacit as well as codified knowledge. The linear model is an outcome of the neo-classical framework which finds market failure in basic research (Smith 1995). The type of knowledge and innovation which flows from this type of policy intervention is characterised by high risk, indivisibilities (and often large minimum scale) and difficulties in appropriating (monopolising) the returns or benefits. Thus, governments must engage in, or subsidise, basic research and create property rights in the 'intellectual property' which results via systems of patents and other means to prevent the exploitation by others of what may be very expensively generated knowledge (May 2000).

The simple linear model linking Research and Development to general knowledge, from specific knowledge and innovation, however, has now been challenged. Myers and Robertson (1996) and Malecki (1997) have shown that far from knowledge being single linearly generated the process is characterised by an extensive range of feedback loops, circuits with dead ends and abandoned leads. Less than half the expenditure on Research and Development leads to commercially exploitable innovation and in some sectors such as pharmaceuticals the proportion may be significantly lower. The corporate logic of investment in Research and Development is not that each programme will generate a commercial profit but that a small number of innovations will be highly profitable and that these profits are then used to fund a subsequent round of research.

Whilst there is general acceptance of the relationship between the volume of Research and Development, knowledge generation, innovation and economic growth, the geography of these relationships is less clear. Most studies at the national level indicate that broad correlations exist between Research and Development and economic growth, although the relationships are likely to be reciprocal rather than one-way – Research and Development leads to economic growth, but economic growth and profit pay for further Research and Development. At subnational scales, however, the relationships are less clear. The existence of knowledge-based clusters is assumed to demonstrate the advantage that proximity confers through access to information. Despite the claimed ubiquity of telecommunications the importance of tacit rather than codified knowledge is thought to be demonstrated by the need for person-to-person contact. Examples of such knowledge-based clusters of innovation and creativity include Silicon Valley in California, middle Italy, Baden-Wurtemburg, the French technopoles of Toulouse and Montpellier and the Cambridge Science Cluster in East Anglia (Lever 2002).

The actual knowledge transfers within these clusters, however, are a matter of debate. In some cases they represent flows of goods usually through subcontracting work as in Baden-Wurtemburg focused on the automobile and electrical engineering sectors. In some cases shared creativity and design are represented in knowledge flows as in the clothing, footwear and furniture industry in middle Italy. In many clusters, however, there is little evidence that knowledge is shared. Having been gained expensively through investment in Research and Development, it is unlikely that findings or innovations will be shared with competitor firms. Simmie (2001), for example, found that the three high technology clusters in South East England rarely shared ideas or products but comprised firms who enjoyed shared external economies such as access to pools of skilled labour (often generated by universities), sympathetic local planning regimes, an active land and property market, and good access to transport infrastructure (Motorways, Heathrow Airport, etc).

Nevertheless there have been a number of attempts at the local, urban scale to link Research and Development with economic performance. One such attempt at the European scale was made by Cheshire and Carbonaro (1996). Several alternatively specified multiple regression models were developed to explain growth in the period 1979–90 for the 117 Functional Urban Regions (FURs) in western Europe. The independent variables were of several types including measures of population size and rate of growth, the impact of European integration on potential (i.e. access to markets), economic structural variables (agriculture, coalmining, port activities) linked to Objective 1 and 2 status, national dummies and significantly for the measurement of the knowledge base, the number of Research and Development establishments per million inhabitants. The dependent variable was rate of change of GDP per head, or per worker. In all models the Research and Development variable was found to be significant at the one per cent level of significance. There are, therefore, increasing returns to scale in the concentration of human capital employed in Research and Development. This suggests that localised knowledge spillovers and dynamic increasing returns to knowledge do, at least in part, 'explain' differentials in economic growth. The study, however, fails to establish an unambiguous causal link because of multiple colinearity between the variables. Research and Development may well be linked to the national dummies (high/positive in German cities; low/negative in Belgian cities) and to income changes and investment which act as intervening variables in GDP change.

A similar study of 24 cities in the United States (Kresl and Singh 1999) produces similar findings. Using the number of research centres per million workforce, the study is able to correlate research with competitive success measured by the relative growth of retail sales, manufacturing value added and business service receipts, in 1977–92. A second variable, the engineering and research component of the labour force is found to have a stronger relationship with competitiveness. The study instances Denver as a case of high competitiveness linked to both measures of research and knowledge followed by cities such as San Francisco, San Diego and Boston. At the other end of the scale come Milwaukee, Cleveland and St Louis.

An alternative approach to measuring the knowledge base in competitiveness across a number of cities was employed by Knight (1995) and by Drewett et al (1988) for the European Commission. The study pointed to the growing concentration of science-based techno-industrial activities in the core axis of western Europe, but, unlike the other studies, sought to distinguish between the various types of knowledge such as research and development, international finance, administrative headquarters of high level organisations, multinational corporations and non-governmental organisations. Other types of knowledge of a socio-cultural nature are less formalised and more widely dispersed. Twenty cities were asked to evaluate the relative importance of the various types of knowledge in city economic growth. The cities were also asked to indicate the importance of any elements which they felt to be lacking and needed to be added to the knowledge base for each type of knowledge resource. Recognition that elements of the intellectual infrastructure such as university programmes, libraries, research facilities, cultural institutions, were missing was acknowledged by at least half the cities surveyed.

6.3 Data

Most studies seeking to relate economic change to the knowledge base have used numbers of Research and Development establishments per million inhabitants or million workers. In this study we seek to develop a more multi-dimensional index of the scale of the knowledge base extending an earlier study of European cities (Lever 2001).We distinguish between three attributes of the knowledge base – tacit knowledge, codified knowledge and knowledge infrastructure.

Given that tacit knowledge almost certainly requires face-to-face contact for transmission the presence of major knowledge companies in a local urban economy facilitates dissemination. The Globalisation and World Cities Research Group have chosen to identify and rank world cities in terms of their knowledge base measured by the presence of 74 major advanced producer service firms. The initial study (Beaverstock et al. 1999) uses four service sectors engaged in knowledge transfer (accountancy, advertising, banking and finance, and law) to identify the leading cities in each sector. Only firms with offices in at least 15 cities worldwide are included in the study which scores cities between zero and three on each of the four sectors. The results for the European cities are unsurprising. London and Paris are identified as having the highest levels of knowledge services (along with New York and Tokyo) (Table 6.1). Milan, Zurich, Brussels and Madrid follow, Brussels because of the European Union presence, Zurich with its concentration of financial services and Madrid because it acts as the European hub for much of Latin America. More surprising is the speed with which the cities of Eastern Europe have risen in the hierarchy of European cities (Budapest, Moscow, Prague and Warsaw) and the relatively low ranking of Berlin part of whose provision has been claimed by Hamburg and the lack of important centres in southern

Mediterranean Europe. The subsequent study (Taylor and Walker 2001) goes on to use principal components analysis to identify distinctive knowledge clusters both sectorally and spatially.

Table 6.1. World Cities

	Score	Cities (Europe)
Alpha Cities	12	London, Paris
	10	Milan
Beta Cities	9	Zürich
	8	Brussels, Madrid
	7	Moscow
Gamma Cities	6	Amsterdam, Düsseldorf, Geneva, Prague
	5	Rome, Stockholm, Warsaw
	4	Barcelona, Berlin, Budapest, Copenhagen, Hamburg, Munich

Source: Taylor and Walker (1999)

A second way of measuring the level of accessibility to tacit knowledge is through the opportunities for travel and information exchange, as measured by airport connectivity and specific sectoral events such as fairs and exhibitions. A study by Buursink (1994) identified as 'Europoles' cities with consular offices and embassies and then measures the connectivity of their airport(s) to other airports by scheduled flights. He argues that

'the most indispensable attribute of a Eurocity is, without doubt, an airport which is an important node of international air traffic, in particular in intraEuropean traffic. A city, to enjoy economic growth at the European scale, cannot do without an airport offering frequent and fast air connections with other main centres in Europe' (p. 6)

Table 6.2 shows the pre-eminence of London's and Paris' airports in Europe. Two further trends can be identified – the impact of the opening up of eastern Europe on airports such as Frankfurt, Munich, Dusseldorf and Vienna as gateways to the east, and the growth of some very actively marketed hub airports such as Copenhagen and Milan.

Formal events for the exchange of commercial knowledge are also used as a measure of the knowledge base although the advantage accruing to the locations of such events is less clear. A study by Rubalcaba-Bermejo and Cuadrado-Rouba (1995) defines the economic advantage of holding fairs and exhibitions (FE): these include enhanced knowledge, increased competitive power, growth in trade and cultural exchange. The study develops an ambitious regression model to explain the level of FE activity (in terms of space, number of visitors and number of foreign visitors). High levels of activity are explained by local population size, rental levels, local per capita income, infrastructure, transition and even weather. The study develops a composite index of the scale of FE activity which generates a hierarchy of provision as shown in Table 6.3. The topmost cities are London and

Paris, cities with strong traditions of holding exhibitions and trade fairs such as Milan and Birmingham, and leading German cities such as Frankfurt and Cologne.

Table 6.2. European Airports and Their Connectivity

City	Connections	Change 1991–93
London	98	0
Paris	91	+1
Frankfurt	84	+14
Amsterdam	75	0
Zürich	70	+3
Brussels	65	+5
Copenhagen	64	+5
Munich	57	+11
Milan	47	+6
Düsseldorf	44	+6
Vienna	43	+5
Geneva	38	+3

Source: ABC World Airways Guide

Lastly within the category of tacit knowledge, we measure innovation from the rate of new enterprise formation, whilst recognising that many innovations take place within existing enterprises. More crucially, a large proportion of registered new businesses do not reflect innovation but are small wealth-absorbing consumer service outlets which confer no local economic advantage, except very marginally through enhancing quality-of-life (Keeble and Wever 1987). Some studies (e.g., Lever, McGregor and Paddison 1990) have used new firm formation rates per 10,000 population as a measure of economic innovation. There are substantial differences, for example, between Amsterdam (30), Milan (25) and Turin (23) with high rates and Lille (4), Bremen (4), Hamburg (5) and Lyons (5) with low rates, although national differences in registering new businesses may account for some of the difference.

Table 6.3. Major Exhibition Centres in Europe

Rank	City	Fairs	Visitors (*1000)
1	Paris	98	5230
2	London	136	2606
3	Milan	46	2972
4	Birmingham	80	1684
5	Frankfurt	22	1251
6	Cologne	22	1210
7	Hanover	17	1893
8	Bologna	15	1395
9	Munich	18	1333
10	Barcelona	36	1703
11	Madrid	42	1536
12	Düsseldorf	17	1358

Source: Feria Database

In seeking to measure the availability of codified knowledge we use two measures of access, both based upon research in local universities. A number of studies have simply used the number of students in the city's universities with the cities of southern Europe having the largest totals. Barcelona, Milan, Naples, Munich and Valencia, for example, all had in excess of 70,000 students in 1997. Such studies may be somewhat ambiguous because there is no guarantee that students will remain in the local economy on graduation. However, the use of student numbers does give a measure of the knowledge base available because of the assumed generation of pure new knowledge in universities which may find a commercial application or spin-off in the local science park or high technology small firm sectors in cities such as Cambridge, Montpellier and Barcelona.

A second measure of innovative knowledge derived from universities in European cities is provided by the volume of academic and scientific papers in refereed journals. The measures developed by Mathiessen and Schwarz (1999) and subsequently by Mathiessen and Anderson (2000) have the merit that the location of the research can be identified from authorship and the knowledge base can be divided into subsets such as engineering, natural sciences, medicine and computing science. However, it is only a measure of output and reflects local research but the benefit is widespread as, on publication, the knowledge passes into the public domain (David and Faray 1995). Table 6.4 shows the leading European research centres based on absolute numbers of articles for the period 1984–96 and in terms of the ratio between publications and local population. The large European capitals (London, Paris, Berlin, Moscow and the Randstad) figure prominently on the absolute measure, but on the relative measure smaller university cities (Oxford, Cambridge, Bristol, Geneva and Basel) head the rankings. In this study, we would argue that it is the absolute amount of published research, rather than its concentration which is the more important measure of innovative knowledge.

Table 6.4. Research Centres in Europe

Rank			Rank Papers per 1000		
1	London	64,742	1	Cambridge	81
2	Paris	45,752	2	Oxford-Reading	41
3	Moscow	39,903	3	Geneva	29
4	Randstad	36,158	4	Basel	20
5	Copenhagen	21,631	5	Bristol-Cardiff	15
6	Stockholm	20,195	6	Zürich	13
7	Berlin	19,872	7	Stockholm	12
8	Oxford-Reading	18,876	8	Helsinki	12
9	Edinburgh-Glasgow	18,688	9	Copenhagen	11
10	Manchester-Liverpool	17,764	10	Randstad	10
11	Cambridge	16,230	11	Munich	10
12	Madrid	15,947	12	Edinburgh-Glasgow	10

Lastly, given the importance of telecommunications in knowledge transmission, a measure of infrastructure is required. A recent study (Finnie 1998) ranks European cities (and world cities) in terms of the competitiveness of telecommunications provision in early 1998. The resultant rankings based upon technical definitions of the pricing of services, the choice of physical infrastructure available and the availability of the most advanced and sophisticated connections (broadband and 'darkfibre'). The best provision within Europe is to be found in London, Stockholm, Paris, Frankfurt, Amsterdam and Brussels (although these lag some way behind the best United States cities) followed by Milan, Zürich, Berlin and Madrid).

6.4 Analysis

To examine whether there is a relationship between the quality of the local knowledge base and economic growth, we have compiled a general index of the knowledge base using the rankings of European cities on seven measures comprising presence of corporate producer service companies in the knowledge sectors, the connectivity of the local airport, the hosting of commercial conferences and exhibitions, the rate of new enterprise formation, the size of the local universities (in student numbers), the absolute volume of academic research papers produced in 1994–96, and the quality of local telecommunications infrastructure. To qualify for inclusion cities had to score on at least four of the seven criteria: because of difficulties in measuring economic performance during the 1990s, the period of marketisation, the four qualifying cities of east and east central Europe (Prague, Budapest, Warsaw and Moscow) were omitted. The mean ranking on the knowledge variables was then calculated for the 19 remaining cities (Table 6.5).

The two genuine 'world cities' in Europe, London and Paris, are clearly far better provided with a knowledge base than the other cities, being ranked in the top three position in all but one variable (university size). Below the world city levels national capitals have, as expected, a good access to the knowledge base, including Stockholm, Amsterdam, Brussels, Madrid and Copenhagen. The presence of the world cities of London and Paris appears to have the effect of concentrating the knowledge base so that no other British or French cities occur in the list. This is in sharp contrast to the Federal Republic of Germany where several cities, Frankfurt, Cologne, Munich and Dusseldorf, have developed major knowledge bases because of the unusual position of Berlin, geographically and administratively. Peripherality appears to play a part in the ranking with Berlin and Vienna disadvantaged by their proximity to Eastern Europe and Rome significantly outranked by Milan and Bologna.

We use three measures of economic performance and success in Table 6.5. As the table shows on all three measures, annual employment change 1985–96, annual change in Gross Value Added per worker 1985–96, and the residual of the shift-share analysis 1978–96, the two world cities despite their excellent knowledge bases perform poorly. Both suffer declines in employment and below average rates of GVA growth. It would appear that the negative agglomeration economies of high rents, high wages, congestion and adverse social pathologies have been sufficient to offset the knowledge advantage of the two world cities. A third measure of economic performance, shift-share analysis is used as a more wide-ranging measure of competitiveness, using the residual value to standardise for economic structure. This shows an even greater disparity between the two world cities and the other cities (although Vienna and Brussels share the same poor performance).

Table 6.5. The Knowledge Base and Economic Performance

	Knowledge Base Mean Score	1985–96 Annual % Employment Change	1985–96 GVA Per Worker Change	1978–96 Shift-share Residual
London	2.8	−0.3	+2.0	−25.7
Paris	3.7	−0.1	+3.3	−11.8
Frankfurt	6.0	+0.2	+3.1	+6.5
Amsterdam	6.8	+2.5	+2.0	+21.0
Stockholm	7.0	+1.0	+3.5	+8.7
Milan	7.0	+0.1	+3.0	+4.7
Cologne	7.2	+0.3	+2.7	+4.8
Bologna	7.5	0.0	+2.9	+0.6
Zürich	8.0	+1.7	+3.3	+3.0
Brussels	8.3	−0.8	+2.8	−22.1
Madrid	10.0	+1.5	+4.1	+5.5
Munich	10.0	−0.1	+3.5	+10.6
Copenhagen	10.0	+0.2	+1.6	−7.1
Dusseldorf	10.3	+0.2	+2.5	+0.6
Barcelona	10.8	+1.6	+3.3	+1.6
Geneva	12.0	+1.7	+3.0	+1.0
Berlin	12.3	+1.7	+3.5	+1.2
Rome	13.3	+0.4	+2.9	+10.5
Vienna	14.5	+0.5	+2.3	−23.3

If the two world cities are excluded from the analysis and the remaining 17 cities are grouped into higher and lower knowledge scores the first two variables show little difference. The annual change in total employment is shown (Table 6.6) to vary little between high and low knowledge cities. This is probably because employment per se is not a good measure of economic performance unless it is taken in the context of changes in productivity and the possibilities for capital-labour substitution. There is slightly more difference between the rates of change of GVA per worker, suggesting that workers in cities with a higher knowledge base are increasing in productivity and income faster than those elsewhere. Most significant, however, is the differential between the employment shift share residual over the period 1978–86 where high knowledge cities, especially Frankfurt, Amsterdam and Stockholm have growth rates significantly above rates predicted on the basis of their original sectoral structure and European (not national) growth rates. There are exceptions to this relationship between high scores on the knowledge base and fast economic growth: Brussels does poorly despite good knowledge measures, Rome and Munich do well despite relatively poor knowledge measures. Lastly, it is worth stating that this is a very truncated urban size hierarchy concentrating as it does on the largest cities in Western Europe. Were these cities compared with smaller towns and cities (an exercise which lack of data prohibits) the comparative advantage of the assumed concentration of the knowledge base in the largest cities (excluding the two world cities) might be manifested, and the urban-rural transition in investment and employment be seen not to be a function of the knowledge base and access to tacit knowledge.

Table 6.6. High and Low Knowledge Scores

	1985–96	1985–96	1978–96
	Annual % Employm. Change	GVA Per Worker Change	Shift-share Residual
High Knowledge score cities	+0.7	+3.0	+3.7
Low Knowledge score cities	+0.8	+2.8	−0.6

6.5 Conclusion

Few studies have been able empirically to link the creation of new knowledge through Research and Development with innovation and economic growth. Those that have, have tended to use rather simple means of measuring the knowledge base in terms of numbers of Research and Development establishments. We have chosen a more multi-dimensional measure of the knowledge base and its ability to produce innovation and then related this measure to several measures of the relative economic performance of European cities. The most effective discriminant measure is the shift-share residual, rather than changes in total employment as GVA per worker. This does show some correlation between the knowledge base and growth rates above predicted levels, except that the two world cities in the group, London and Paris run counter to the trend with excellent knowledge bases but poor economic performances.

Governments will continue to relate competitiveness to the knowledge base, but remain less certain of the most appropriate forms of intervention. Tacit knowledge, in particular, is difficult to encourage. It is likely, therefore, that government policy initiatives will concentrate upon labour force training, especially at the post school level, upon the fiscal treatment of investment upon Research and Development, upon the installation of information infrastructure such as broadband systems, and upon increasing entrepreneurship and knowledge spin-offs.

References

Beaverstock JV, Smith AG, Taylor PJ (1999) A roster of world cities. Cities 16: 34–52

Buursink J (1994) Euroservices and Euroairports: The position of East European cities as Eurocities. Paper presented to the 'Cities on the Eve of the 21st Century' Conference, Lille

Cheshire PC, Carbonaro G (1996) Urban economic growth in Europe: Testing theory and policy prescription. Urban Studies 33: 1111–1128

Coffey WJ, Bailly AS (1982) Producer services and systems of flexible production. Urban Studies 29: 857–868

Daniels PW, Lever WF (1996) The global economy in transition. Addison, Wesley, Longman, Harlow

David FA (1995) Accessing and expanding the science and technology base. STI Review 16: 13–18

Department of Trade and Industry (1988) Our competitive future: Building and knowledge driven economy. Cmnd. 4176, London: DTI

Feldman MP (2000) Location and innovation: The new economic geography of innovation spillovers and agglomeration. In: Clark GR, Feldman MP, Gertler MS (eds) The Oxford handbook of economic geography. Oxford University Press, Oxford, pp 371–394

Finnie G (1998) Wired cities. Communications Week International, 18 May: 19–22

Howland M (1996) Producer services and competition from offshore: US data entry and banking. In: Daniels PW, Lever WF (eds) The Global Economy in Transition. Addison, Wesley, Longman, Harlow, pp 310–327

Keeble D, Wever E (1987) New firms and regional development in Europe. Croom Helm, London

Knight A, Stanback TM (1970) The metropolitan economy: The process of employment expansion. Columbia Free Press, New York

Knight RV (1995) Knowledge based development: Policy and planning implications for cities. Urban Studies 32: 225–260

Kresl PK, Singh B (1999) Competitiveness and the urban economy: Twentyfour Large US metropolitan areas. Urban Studies 36: 1017–1028

Lambooy JA (2000) Regional growth, knowledge and innovation. In: Kuklinski A, Orlowski WM (eds) The knowledge based economy: Global challenges for the 21st century. KBN, Warsaw, pp 100–113

Lever WF (2001) The geography of knowledge. In: Kuklinski A (ed) Economic challengers of the 21st century. KBN, Warsaw

Lever WF (2002) Measuring the knowledge base and competitive cities in Europe. In: Begg I (ed) Competitive Cities. Polity Press, London

Lever WF, McGregor A, Paddison R (1990) City audit: Comparative European urban performance data. CURR/TERU, University of Glasgow, Glasgow

Malecki E (1997) Technology and economic development: The dynamics of local, regional and national competitiveness. Addison, Wesley, Longman, Harlow

Matthiessen GW, Andersson AE (2000) Research gateways of the world. In: Andersson AE, Andersson DE (eds) Gateways to the global economy. Edward Elgar, Cheltenham, pp 17–31

Matthiessen GW, Schwarz AW (1999) Scientific centres in Europe. Urban Studies 36: 453–473

May C (2000) Foundation of weightlessness. The knowledge economy, the state and economic development. In: Kuklinski A, Orlowski WM (eds) The knowledge-based economy. KBN, Warsaw, pp 69–80

OECD (1999) OECD science, technology and industry scoreboard: Benchmarking knowledge based economies. OECD, Paris

Simmie J (2001) High technology clusters in South East England. In: Begg I (ed) Competitive cities. Polity Press, London

Smith K (1995) Interaction in knowledge systems: Foundations, policy implications and empirical methods. STI Review 16: 69–102

Taylor PJ, Walker DRF (2001) World cities: A first multivariable analysis of their service complexes. Urban Studies 38: 23–47

7 Constructing an Index for Regional Competitiveness[1]

Janne Huovari[1], Aki Kangasharju[2] and Aku Alanen[3]

[1] Pellervo Economic Research Institute, Helsinki, Finland; [2] Government Institute for Economic Research, Helsinki, Finland; [3] Statistics Finland, Helsinki, Finland

7.1 Introduction

Competitiveness receives a lot of attention. Commentators are often concerned about the loss of competitiveness, and policy actions are motivated by a desire to improve competitiveness. What is typically being referred to is the competitiveness of firms, nations or other geographic areas. The competitiveness of firms differs from that of geographic areas, however, and there is a need to clarify the difference between them.

Krugman (1995, 1996, 1997) is perhaps the best-known critic when it comes to using competitiveness with reference to nations. Krugman argues that using the term competitiveness is dangerous, as it can lead to protectionism and bad public policy. The term seems to imply that in the world economy, the benefit of one nation or region comes at the expense of another. Krugman argues that the concept of regional competitiveness is empty and refers to nothing other than the competitiveness of firms within regions.

Others have argued that competitiveness is also a useful concept in the context of national or regional units (Porter 1996; Begg 1999). For example, the concept can be used to indicate the relative economic fortune of regional units (countries or regions), as the level of economic activity and resource endowments vary between them. Siebert (2000) argues that the competitiveness of firms is simply a distinct concept from that of geographical areas. He states that competitiveness exists on at least three levels: firms, geographical areas and workers. Regions and countries compete against each other for mobile production factors in factor markets, while firms compete for market shares.

This study adopts the view that regional competitiveness is the ability of regions to build a production environment with high accessibility that perpetuates and attracts mobile production factors, and results in fostering the economy. These mobile factors include skilled labour, innovative entrepreneurs and footloose capital. Success in attracting these factors creates external economies, such as ag-

[1] This article is part of a project funded by the National Technology Agency, TEKES. We would like to thank the monitoring committee, Raija Volk and Vesa Vihriälä, for valuable comments.

glomeration and localisation benefits, that further enhance the economic fortune of a region.

The purpose of this study is to compare the competitiveness of 85 regional units that closely represent the labour market areas of Finland. In EU standards these units are called subregions and represent the NUTS–4 level. The objective is to collect a measurable set of attributes that describe the resources of population (potential labour force), (actual) labour force, firms, the level of agglomeration, and the accessibility of regions. These indicators are then used to construct a regionally comparable competitiveness index for each subregion.

In constructing the index we loosely follow the example given by comparisons of competitiveness across nations (World Economic Forum 2000; International Institute for Management Development 2000). International studies cannot be applied to a regional framework as such, however, since some of the indicators are unavailable or are meaningless at the regional level. These indicators include the efficiency of the public sector and finance, and barriers to foreign trade, as these variables do not vary within a country.

There have also been several regional studies on competitiveness (European Commission 1999; Department of Trade and Industry 1997; Kresl 1995; Mikkonen 1995). A common feature in all regional studies is that they tend to concentrate on a restricted number of aspects of competitiveness rather than providing an overall and coherent general index. Moreover, there have been only a few attempts at incorporating innovativeness as a part of regional competitiveness (Massachusetts Technology Collaborative 2000; Stern et al. 2000; Cambridge Econometrics 1998). Similarly, the role of agglomeration has received surprisingly little attention in competitiveness studies. The objective of the present paper is to at least partly address these shortages.

We have built an index that uses statistical indicators available at the labour market level and we have also measured the innovativeness and agglomeration of regions. Unfortunately, the use of currently available statistical indicators excludes some aspects of competitiveness that are extremely difficult to measure, including social capital.

Our results indicate that regional variations in competitiveness are closely related to those in several output variables, such as per capita GDP and personal income. We also find that the sub-indices of the total index tend to correlate with each other so that subregions with a high value for one sub-index also have high values for other sub-indices. This tends to show that a high level of competitiveness in one aspect helps to improve other aspects, a development which results in a high level of competitiveness overall.

However, the association between the index and short-term change in outcome indicators such as production, employment and population is lower than that in the long-term indicators. We conclude that our index, which captures various aspects of competitiveness, is essentially a long-term indicator.

The remainder of the paper is organised as follows. Sect. 7.2 develops a conceptual framework for an analysis of regional competitiveness. Sect. 7.3 describes the variables that are operationalised to measure various aspects of competitiveness and describes the construction of the index itself. Sect. 7.4 describes the constructed index and Sect. 7.5 provides the results. Finally, Sect. 7.6 concludes the paper.

7.2 A Conceptual Model of Competitiveness

Growth theory serves as a natural starting point for a conceptual model of competitiveness. In traditional growth models, production comes from the joining of labour and physical capital with a particular technology, the progress of which is assumed to be exogenous (Solow 1956; Swan 1956). New (endogenous) growth models stress that human capital is another essential production factor, as production processes have become more difficult, know-how a more important factor and technological progress more rapid (Aghion and Howitt 1998). Since within a country, and particularly in Finland, there are hardly any regional differences in the supply of physical capital, the role of human capital becomes even more critical. Geographic areas where highly educated labour is abundant are therefore more competitive than those where it is scarce.

Technological progress is another increasingly important source of growth. Endogenous growth models suggest that technological progress is not exogenous, but endogenously determined by research and development, learning-by-doing and other related processes. These lead to innovations that, in turn, are the channel through which technological progress takes place. In a regional context, R&D conducted in firms is not the only way of enhancing innovativeness. At the regional level, high innovativeness also requires a suitable environment, infrastructure, and co-operation within clusters of firms (Stern et al. 2000; Porter and Stern 1999). In this context, the presence of other sectors that support the innovativeness of one sector is important (Porter 1998).

In addition to human capital and innovativeness, the new economic geography provides us a third source of regional competitiveness. Urbanisation, agglomeration, localisation and other benefits accruing from external economies form one of the main channels that transform regional balance within nations (Fujita et al. 1999; Ottaviano and Puga 1998; Krugman 1991; Marshall 1920). The term agglomeration benefits can be seen to comprise both urbanisation and localisation benefits. Urbanisation benefits accrue from the presence of several actors and sectors in the same geographical area. Localisation benefits refer to the utility of firms owing to the presence of other firms in the same industrial sector.

Finally, there is a long tradition of seeing the accessibility of regions to matter for economic development (Hirschman 1958; Myrdal 1957). Regions close to markets are better off than those located further away from centres. Accessibility in terms of high quality connections (infrastructure) to centres alleviates the disadvantage of a peripheral location. Accessibility depends on the location of geographical areas with respect to markets and the state of the infrastructure. In other words, accessibility is a factor related to agglomeration, since large agglomerations tend to have high accessibility due to the size of their own markets.

In fact, all these four dimensions of competitiveness are closely related to one another. To begin with, human capital is regarded as a crucial factor for economic growth in a modern knowledge-based society. In particular, human capital is at the heart of innovative behaviour, which is the source of technological progress. Groundbreaking innovations, in turn, usually take place at a higher intensity in large agglomerations than at the periphery (Kangasharju and Nijkamp 2001; Freeman 1990). Finally, agglomerations tend to have high accessibility due to the size of their own markets and high quality connections to other agglomerations.

Without radical changes, the development of these aspects is slow. For example, the level of human capital does not improve quickly without extensive migration. Similarly, innovations take time to realise and infrastructure cannot be built overnight. Agglomeration, in turn, is a result of long-term competitiveness.

In fact, overall competitiveness is determined by previous competitiveness that has resulted, for instance, in in-migration and growth in employment and production volume, i.e., an increased level of agglomeration. In other words, improvement of competitiveness and growth of geographical areas take place simultaneously, feeding each other, and leaving the direction of causation bi-directional.

There are also other sources of development. These include social capital (Kajanoja and Simpura 2001; Putnam 1993; Putnam 1995), regional policy measures (Tervo 1991) and possible regional differences in the efficiency of the public sector. We have been forced to leave out these dimensions of competitiveness for reasons of data availability.

7.3 Construction of the Index

Our conceptual model suggests that the competitiveness of subregions in Finland is determined by human capital, innovativeness, agglomeration and accessibility. This subsection describes 16 variables that have been selected to measure these four dimensions of competitiveness. Apart from three exceptions, each variable was measured in 1999.

7.3.1 Variables

Human capital is usually approximated by educational variables (Barro and Sala-i-Martin 1995). The regional distribution of people with some secondary education is relatively even in Finland. The greatest variation can be found in the number of highly educated, having at least 13 years of education. Therefore, our first variable for human capital is the number of highly educated residents in a subregion. Moreover, not only the stock, but also the stream to human capital is regarded as important. Therefore, secondly and thirdly, a stream to human capital is approximated by the number of students and that of technical students. Finally, we extend here the typical way in which human capital is measured. We consider the characteristics of labour force as an integrated part of human capital. Consequently, we added two further variables that capture these characteristics. Our fourth variable is the size of the working-age population (15–64) and the fifth is the participation rate, both of which measure the labour supply potential in a subregion.

Since resources devoted to the acceleration of technological progress are seen as a highly important factor of competitiveness, we include the number of patents and the amount of R&D to capture the innovativeness of subregions. As patenting tends to vary strongly between years, we take the average of the number of patents between 1995–99. R&D expenditures are those measured in 1999. Thirdly, we have recently developed a measure for the proportion of establishments in a subregion that have been innovative during the years between 1985 and 1998 (Alanen et al. 2000). This variable measures the number of actual innovations, measured by subject- and object-based methods. Our final variable of innovativeness is the proportion of value added produced in high technology sectors. Although this is not a direct measure of innovativeness, it tells the proportion of value added that is produced in sectors where innovativeness is even more important than elsewhere in the economy. For reasons of data availability we have measured this variable in 1996.

As suggested by new economic geography, agglomeration and localisation economies are highly important factors of competitiveness. We have used population density as a measure of the general state of agglomeration. When this variable is transformed into an indicator, it reveals size differences between subregions (see the next subsection). Secondly, we have measured the proportion of workers in sectors where external economies, and therefore the regional tendency for concentration, are large. These sectors include manufacturing, wholesale and retail trade and private services, and exclude agriculture, the public sector and construction. A third variable considers the presence of so-called supporting industries as a vital ingredient for success. We measure this presence as the proportion of workers in business services. Finally, in addition to agglomeration, localisation benefits are also important. We approximate the extent to which subregions can have localisation benefits by the size of the largest sector in subregions.

Ease of access to other areas is traditionally seen as an important factor for economic development. We have three variables for accessibility. Firstly, we have measured the road accessibility of subregions with respect to markets as the road distance of each subregion to every other, weighted by the size of subregions. Another variable measures the distance from the airports, weighted by the size of airports. Finally, we have measured the number of existing international connections of firms, as these connections are seen as one of the most important ways in which innovations and new ideas diffuse. This is measured by the proportion of establishments in a subregion engaged in foreign trade.[2]

---

[2] Rail accessibility is not taken into account for three reasons. First, most of the trade between subregions is carried out on roads. Second, rail accessibility is not seen as an important factor for competitiveness in a modern economy; road and air accessibility dominate. Third, data were unavailable for rail traffic at the subregional level.

7.3.2 Formation of Indicators, Standardisation and the Weighting Scheme

We have two types of variables. One type is comprised of variables of absolute numbers, such as the number of students or patents, and the other contains proportional variables, such as the rate of participation. As the subregions differ greatly in size, we first divide the variables of type I by the population. In practice, these indicators are formed by dividing the proportion of subregion i from the indicator X by the proportion of subregion i from the total population P, multiplied by 100:

$$\text{indicator } X_i = 100 \ (x_i/X)/(p_i/P) \tag{3.1}$$

where capital letters are the total values for Finland. In the case of proportional variables we simply divide the value for each subregion by that for the whole country, multiplied by 100. For each variable the value 100 refers to whole of Finland, and the index shows the value for each subregion relative to the whole country. The purpose of each indicator is to reveal the strength of subregions relative to others.

The same mean for each indicator is not sufficient for comparability, however. Without standardisation, the indicators with a larger standard deviation would have obtained larger implicit weight than those with smaller standard deviations. As such, differences in the ranges of indicators would indicate large implicit differences in weights (Fig. 7.1). Without standardisation, the number of technical students (indicator 4) and the amount of R&D (indicator 6) would have the highest weights in the index. This is not appealing, however; we would like each indicator to have an equal weight.

In order to legitimate comparability, we standardised the dispersion of indicators by relating each indicator to its own standard deviation and multiplying all indicators by the same scalar to spread the common range wider. In practice, this was conducted in the following fashion. First, the mean of each indicator was returned to zero by subtracting 100 from the mean value. Then, each value was divided by the standard deviation of the indicator in question. As a consequence, the range of each indicator, as well as that of the total index, collapses. In order, to make the index visually more appealing, the range was artificially spread wider by multiplying each value by an arbitrarily chosen scalar, the same for all. Finally, the mean was returned to 100.

This standardisation changes neither the information content of indicators, the correlation between the indicators nor that between indicators and various outcome variables introduced below. After standardisation, each indicator has approximately similar weight in indices, and the ranges of the index and various subindices are visually easy to read.

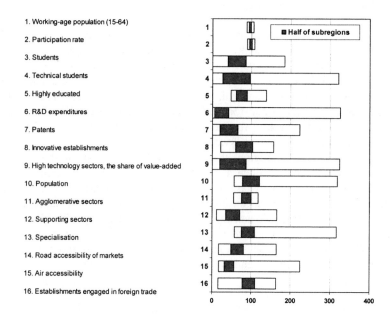

1. Working-age population (15-64)
2. Participation rate
3. Students
4. Technical students
5. Highly educated
6. R&D expenditures
7. Patents
8. Innovative establishments
9. High technology sectors, the share of value-added
10. Population
11. Agglomerative sectors
12. Supporting sectors
13. Specialisation
14. Road accessibility of markets
15. Air accessibility
16. Establishments engaged in foreign trade

Fig. 7.1. Distributions of Non-Standardised Indicators

In summary, all 16 variables are transformed into 15 indicators (the number of students and that of technical students form one indicator).[3] There are four indicators for human capital, innovativeness and agglomeration, and three for accessibility. The total index for competitiveness is formed by these four sub-indices. Within each sub-index each indicator has equal weight and within the total index each sub-index is considered equal. In other words, all indices were computed as the non-weighted average of indicators or sub-indices. For example, in the total index the implicit weight of each sub-index is 0.25.

7.4 Description of the Index

As mentioned above, the mean of the index is 100, which refers to the whole of Finland. The values for the 85 subregions range from 59.4 to 133.9; i.e., the range is 74.5 index points. Due to the way in which the index is constructed, the level of index scores is meaningless. However, the rank order and the distances of subregions from each other give valuable information. This section describes the rank order of subregions and the main features of the index and sub-indices.

---

[3] The average of these two variables is one of the indicators in our human capital index. In other words, we think of technical students as having an effect on human capital that is equal to that of the number of all students.

7.4.1 Rank Order of Subregions

The capital subregion, Helsinki, is the most competitive subregion in Finland (Fig. 7.2). The index score for Helsinki is 133.9, whereas that for the least competitive subregion, Kärkikunnat, it is 59.4. The triumph of Helsinki was expected due to its capital status and the fact that more than a quarter of the Finnish population lives there and one-third of value added is produced there. Therefore, it is natural that Helsinki has the highest value for agglomeration and accessibility. For innovativeness, which is the weakest feature of Helsinki, the subregion is in fifth place behind Salo, Oulu, Tampere and Jyväskylä.

From the total of 85 subregions there are only 10 that are above the average in the competitiveness index. Since a university is located in 7 of them (Helsinki, Turku, Tampere, Jyväskylä, Vaasa, Oulu and Lappeenranta), the success of these subregions is apparently based on human capital. The other three subregions are strong in innovativeness (Salo and Etelä-Pirkanmaa) and accessibility (Porvoo).

The remaining subregions have a lower than average index value for competitiveness. Broadly speaking, subregions in Southern Finland are more competitive than those located in Northern and Eastern Finland (Fig. 7.2).

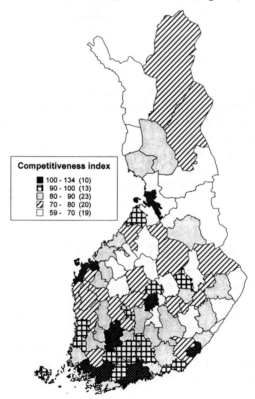

Fig. 7.2. The Competitiveness Index

7.4.2 Characteristics of the Competitiveness Index

One major feature of this index is that the sub-indices are highly correlated, im-
plying that to a large extent they measure similar things (Table 7.1). The highest
correlation coefficient is that between human capital and agglomeration (0.86),
whereas the lowest correlation is found between innovativeness and accessibility
(0.64).

Table 7.1. Correlation Matrix of Sub-indices

	Human capital	Innovativeness	Agglomeration	Accessibility
Human capital	1.00			
Innovativeness	0.76	1.00		
Agglomeration	0.86	0.80	1.00	
Accessibility	0.68	0.64	0.71	1.00

This indicates that if a subregion has one high sub-index, other indices also
tend to be high. This feature of sub-indices is illustrated in Fig. 7.3, which gives
the contribution of each sub-index to the total index value. Only 4 subregions have
a higher-than-average value for each sub-index, whereas the majority of subregions, 59 of them, have sub-index values that are all lower than the average. There
are 22 subregions where some sub-indices are higher and some lower than the average.

We consider this finding to provide evidence that regional development is subject to cumulative causation, since subregions that have a high value in one sub-
index also tend to have high values in other sub-indices. This supports the view
that the improvement of one aspect of competitiveness tends also to improve other
aspects.

Another related feature of the index is that the size of weights does not matter
much. When the total index is compared with alternative indices, where the weight
of each sub-index in turn is increased to one half (the other sub-indices sharing the
other half), the average change in the value of index across the subregions was
2.05 index points. This can be regarded as a rather low figure, as the range of the
non-weighted index is as high as 74.5 points (from 59.4 to 133.9). Changes in the
weight structure also only slightly changed the correlation between the alternative
indices and the non-weighted index, the correlation coefficient being 0.99 on average (the average correlation over four differently weighted indices and the non-
weighted one). The same applies to the rank correlation. Alternatively weighted
indices changed the rank order of subregions on average by 3.3 steps, which also
seems to be a low figure, as the total number of subregions is 85. The rank correlation coefficient between the non-weighted and alternative indices is 0.98 on average.

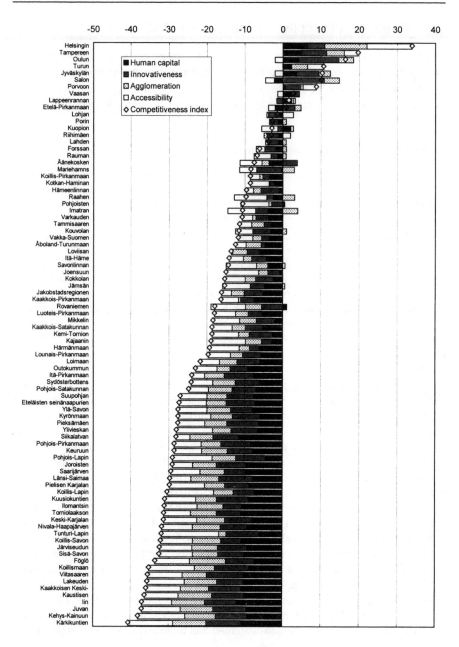

Fig. 7.3. Contribution of Sub-indices and Deviation of Competitiveness Index from 100.

The minor effects of various weights support the result obtained above: the sub-indices are highly correlated. Otherwise, a higher weight on one sub-index would have altered the rank order and index values of subregions more clearly.

There are some clear changes, however. At the highest, the index value for Salo increases by 11.1 index points when the innovation sub-index is weighted at the expense of others. This shows that the competitiveness of Salo is highly dependent on innovativeness, and Salo somewhat lags behind in other dimensions of competitiveness, the total index being above average, however. More generally, the value of the index changes by more than 5 points for only three subregions when human capital is weighted at the expense of others, whereas that of six subregions changes when innovativeness is over-weighted. In terms of agglomeration and accessibility, the corresponding number of subregions is six and thirteen, respectively.

These changes leave the changes in the rank order of subregions rather small. At the highest, weighting the agglomeration sub-index raises the rank position of Tunturi-Lappi by 22 steps. Otherwise, the five largest changes in the rankings are between 5 and 14 steps. If the rankings are illustrated by a five-category scale, as in Fig. 7.2, even the largest changes would mainly yield only one-class alterations, since the class-size is 17 in a five-class categorisation of subregions.

An implication is that the more the index of a subregion changes due to the alterations in weights, the higher the potential bias in the index value for a particular subregion. Therefore, our index gives a potentially more biased result for subregions with more uneven sub-indices.

Finally, the competitiveness index appears to be very stable over time. When the index for 1999 is compared to its 1995 counterpart,[4] neither correlations nor rank correlations between the index or sub-indices change to any noticeable extent. The mean change in the index value over subregions is 1.3 points between 1995 and 1999, whereas that in rank order is 2.4 steps (the index range being 74.5 points among 85 subregions). Minor changes between 1995 and 1999 imply that the index illuminates the long-term competitiveness of subregions.

There are a few exceptions, however. While the changes in index values remain rather low, ranging from –4.9 to +7.3, there are a few noticeable changes in the rank positions, due to close distances between the index values of subregions. At one extreme Siikalatva rises 20 positions between (7.3 index points) 1995 and 1999, and at the other Sisä-Savo drops by 13 positions though its index points drop 2.4 points only. One major reason for the rise of Siikalatva is in the accessibility. The proportion of firms engaged in foreign trade has dramatically increased between 1995 and 1999. This is partially due to the small total stock of firms within the subregions; a small absolute change in the number of exporting and importing firms can yield a high relative figure. Sisä-Savo declines because of a minor drop in innovativeness, agglomeration and accessibility.

---

[4] Note that for data availability reasons both indices, for 1995 and 1999, include identical indicators for patents and innovations.

7.5 The Index and Regional Development

So far we have been describing the construction of the index and some features of it. Now we will check how well the index and sub-indices correlate with most common variables of regional economic well being and development.

7.5.1 The Index and Long-term Development

Per capita gross domestic product (GDP) is the most common and perhaps the easiest measure for economic well being. This measure is not the optimal when the interest is focused on people living in the area concerned. For this reason we also use per capita personal income subject to taxation as a measure of economic well being. For comparisons we construct our outcome variables in a similar fashion to our indicators. As mentioned above, we expect the correlation to be rather high, due to cumulative causation and related processes. Per capita GDP and personal income describe the outcome of long-term competitiveness of subregions, since the level of the variables tend to be high for subregions that have been competitive for a long period of time.

Due to the long-term perspective we are able to scrutinise the cross-section correlation of the index and two outcome variables. It turns out that in 1999 the correlation between the index and per capita GDP is 0.79 and that between the index and personal income is as high as 0.92 (Table 7.2). Correlations between sub-indices and outcome variables are high as well. At the lowest, the correlation between accessibility and per capita GDP is 0.55, whereas at the highest, the correlation between agglomeration and personal income is 0.88.[5]

---

[5] The correlation between the index and the level of unemployment appears to be negative (–0.80). Among the sub-indices, accessibility correlates the most with unemployment (–0.54); unemployment is the highest in subregions where accessibility is the poorest. Other sub-indices correlate clearly less with unemployment (about –0.30).

Table 7.2. Coefficients of Correlation Between the Indicators and Outcome Variables

	Per capita GDP	Per capita personal income
The competitiveness index	0.79	0.92
Human capital	0.71	0.87
- Working-age population (15–64)	0.60	0.74
- Participation rate	0.60	0.79
- Students	0.49	0.51
- Technical students	0.49	0.51
- Highly educated	0.65	0.85
Innovativeness	0.77	0.76
- R&D expenditures	0.73	0.63
- Patents	0.57	0.64
- High technology sectors (share of value-added)	0.61	0.59
- Innovative establishments	0.59	0.60
Agglomeration	0.80	0.88
- Population	0.62	0.81
- Agglomerative sectors	0.74	0.82
- Supporting sectors	0.56	0.70
- Specialisation	0.50	0.29
Accessibility	0.55	0.77
- Road accessibility of markets	0.48	0.72
- Air accessibility	0.51	0.77
- Establishments engaged in foreign trade	0.34	0.39

The correlation between the total index and outcome variables is higher than that between each sub-index and outcome variable; the index measures something more than the sub-indices alone. As far as per capita GDP and separate indicators are concerned, the correlation with R&D expenditures is the highest. In contrast, the lowest correlation is found with the number of business links to abroad. For per capita personal income the correlation with highly educated population is the highest, whereas that with specialisation is the lowest. In general separate indicators correlate more with personal incomes than GDP.

The same finding is shown by the plot of outcome variables (y-axis) against the index (x-axis) (Figs. 7.4 and 7.5). The subregions are closer to the regression line in the case of personal income than GDP. In a simple regression, the index explains 84% of the variation in personal income. In a GDP regression, the index explains 62 % of the variation.

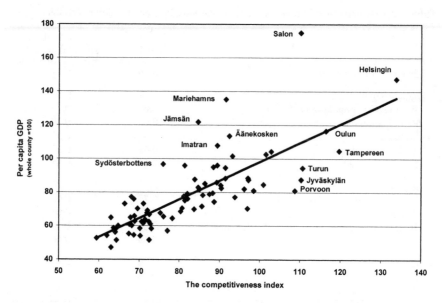

Fig. 7.4. The Index and Per Capita GDP (1999)

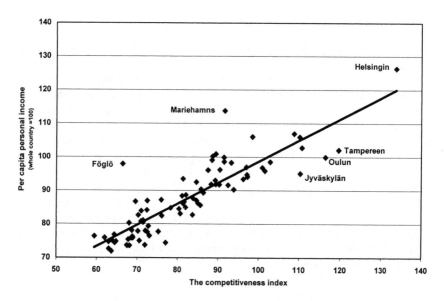

Fig. 7.5. The Index and Per Capita Personal Income (1999)

A poorer fit of GDP regression is partially explained by a higher annual volatility of GDP than that of personal income. For 8 subregions the standard deviation of per capita GDP between 1990–99 varied clearly more than for the others (Fig.

7.6). GDP of these subregions depends crucially on one firm. Note that although specialisation is accounted for in the index, dependence on one firm is not. Salo depends on one firm in the telecommunication industry, Jämsä, Imatra, Äänekoski and Sydörterbottens kustregion depend on a single firm in the paper industry, Raahe has a firm in the metal industry, Porvoo has one in oil manufacturing, and finally Kemi-Tornio has one in the paper and the metal industry. When a dummy variable for these subregions is added to a regression of per capita GDP, the rate of explanation rises from 62 to 73%.

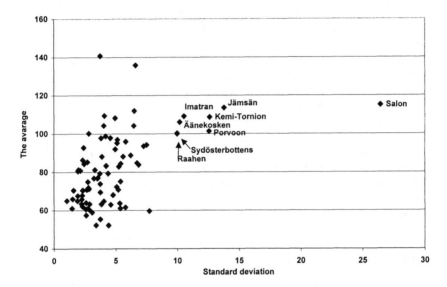

Fig. 7.6. The Mean and Standard Deviation of Per Capita GDP (1990–99)

Note, however, that these simple regressions do not reveal the causal relationship between the index and economic development. As mentioned above, we cannot determine which comes first: improved competitiveness or economic growth. Instead, they are interrelated processes and evolve simultaneously. In addition, this simultaneous development is more obvious in some sub-indices than others. For example, the fact that some subregions have formed into centres of agglomeration can be a result of their constantly higher-than-average economic growth in the past. This circularity cannot be taken into account in the above regressions. The mere purpose was to describe the extent to which the index and the two outcome variables happen to be related to each other.

7.5.2 The Competitiveness Index and the Short-term Growth

Although our index is essentially a long-term indicator of competitiveness, we have also checked how well it explains economic growth during the past few years. In this context, we are interested in several outcome variables, such as growth in per capita GDP and personal income and the number of employees, and the level of unemployment and migration.

A general finding is that the index is clearly less associated with the short-term variables than the long-term ones (Table 7.3). The correlation between the index of 1995 and a change in GDP, personal income and employment between 1995–99 is 0.33, 0.76 and 0.72, respectively. This is as expected, since long-term competitiveness cannot explain short-term shocks or unexpected phenomena. For example, Kangasharju and Vihriälä (2000), using shift share analysis, found that one half of growth across subregions can be explained by regional variations in sectoral composition, and the other half of growth is subject to random disturbance, competitiveness and related factors.

Among several short-term variables the index of 1995 correlates most strongly with the rate of migration relative to the population between 1995–99, the correlation coefficient being as high as 0.80. Again, the index is less closely associated with a change in per capita GDP than one in per capita income or employment. The same finding also applies to sub-indices. This is also an expected finding, since competitiveness should show up first in employment and then in value added, and personal income has less idiosyncratic variation between the years than the value added for small labour market areas. Change in employment is most closely associated with human capital sub-index, whereas changes in GDP and personal income have the largest correlation with innovation. The correlation between accessibility and GDP change is surprisingly low, 0.19 (Table 7.3).

Table 7.3. Coefficients of Correlation between the Indicators in 1995 and Chances in Outcome Variables between 1995–99

| | Between 1995–99, change in | | | |
	GDP	Personal Income	Employment	Migration (1995–99)
Index 1995	0.329	0.756	0.720	0.802
Human capital 95	0.258	0.672	0.712	0.748
Innovativeness 95	0.437	0.725	0.610	0.700
Agglomeration 95	0.286	0.683	0.639	0.664
Accessibility 95	0.200	0.638	0.631	0.768

7.6 Conclusion

In this paper we constructed an index for regional competitiveness. Our index consists of available and measurable statistical indicators for 1995 and 1999. We found that the index is relatively robust in the sense that small changes in the weighting of indicators do not greatly alter the rankings of subregions. When we examined the performance of various subregions, the constructed index was highly correlated with the most natural long-term measures of success and welfare. The correlation with shorter-term outcome variables, such as growth in employment, was also significantly positive, but clearly lower than that with long-term variables. This suggests that our index is essentially a long-term indicator of competitiveness. This is supported by another finding, according to which the index values and rankings of subregions changed only a little between 1995 and 1999.

Our findings suggest that economic success tends to attract and accumulate other positive factors that further accelerate growth and development. In this respect, our findings support early views of regional development, which describe economic development by means of cumulative causation and vicious cycles.

References

Aghion P, Howitt P (1998) Endogenous growth theory. MIT Press, Cambridge MA

Alanen A, Huovari J, Kangasharju A (2000) Constructing a new indicator for regional impact of innovativeness. In: European Commission (2000) Innovation and enterprise creation: Statistics and indicators. Innovation Papers 18: 229–233

Barro RJ, Sala-i-Martin X (1995) Economic growth. McGraw-Hill, New York

Begg I (1999) Cities and competitiveness. Urban Studies 36: 795–810

Cambridge Econometrics (1998) Regional competitiveness indicators. Final report submitted to DG XVI of the European Commission, Cambridge

Department of Trade and Industry (1997) Regional competitiveness indicators: A consultation document. London

European Commission (1999) Sixth periodic report on the social and economic situation and development of the regions of the European Union. Luxemburg

Freeman C (1990) Economics of innovation. Edward Elgar, Brookfield

Fujita M, Krugman P, Venables AJ (1999) Spatial economy. MIT Press, Cambridge MA

Hirschman AO (1958) The strategy for economic development. Yale University Press, New Haven

International Institute for Management Development (2000). World competitiveness yearbook. Lausanne

Kajanoja J, Simpura J (2001) Social capital – global and local perspectives. VATT Publications 29, Helsinki

Kangasharju A, Nijkamp P (2001) Innovation dynamics in space: Local actors and local factors. Socio-Economic Planning Sciences 35: 31–56

Kangasharju A, Vihriälä V (2000) Laman vaikutus aluekehitykseen. Pellervo Economic Research Institute, Working Papers 39, Helsinki

Kresl PK (1995) The determinants of urban competitiveness: a survey. In: Kresl PK, Gappert G (eds) North American cities and the global economy. Sage, London, pp 45–68

Krugman P (1997) Pop internationalism. MIT Press, Cambridge MA

Krugman P (1995) Development, geography and economic theory. MIT Press, Cambridge MA

Krugman P (1996) Making sense of the competitiveness debate. Oxford Review of Economic Policy 12: 17–25

Krugman P (1991) Geography and trade. MIT Press, Cambridge

Marshall A (1920) Principles of economics. Macmillan, London

Massachusetts Technology Collaborative (2000) Index of the Massachusetts innovation economy 2000. Westborough, Massachusetts

Mikkonen K (1995) Kansainvälistyvän Suomen alueelliset menestystekijät. University of Vaasa, Tutkimuksia 190, maantiede 33, Vaasa

Myrdal G (1957) Economic theory and underdeveloped regions. University Paperbacks, London

Ottaviano G, Puga D (1998) Agglomeration in the global economy: A survey of the 'New Economic Geography'. The World Economy 21: 707–731

Porter M (1996) Competitive advantage, agglomeration economies and regional policy. International Regional Science Review 19: 85–90

Porter M (1998) Competitive advantage of nations. Macmillan, London

Porter M, Stern S (1999) The new challenge to America's prosperity: Findings from the innovation index. Council on Competitiveness, Washington DC

Putnam RD (1993) Making democracy work: Civic traditions in modern Italy. Princeton University Press, Princeton

Putnam RD (1995) Bowling alone: America's declining social capital. Journal of Democracy 6: 65–78

Siebert H (2000) The paradigm of locational competition. Kiel Discussion Papers 367, Kiel

Solow R (1956) Investment and technical change. In: Arrow K, Karlin S, Suppes P (eds) Mathematical methods in the social sciences Stanford University Press, Palo Alto Stanford

Stern S, Porter M, Furman, JL (2000) The determinants of national innovative capacity. NBER Working Paper 7876, Cambridge MA

Swan T (1956) Economic growth and capital accumulation. Economic Record 32: 334–361

Tervo H (1991) Studies on the economic case for and effects of regional policy. Jyväskylä Studies in Computer Science, Economics and Statistics 17, Jyväskylä

World Economic Forum (2000) Global competitiveness report 2000. Geneva

8 Geographic Spillovers of University Research: on Patent Activities of the High Technology Sectors in Austria[1]

Manfred M. Fischer and Attila Varga

Department of Economic Geography & Geoinformatics, Vienna University of Economics and Business Administration, Vienna, Austria

8.1 Introduction

New economic growth theories may be simply described as an attempt to revive the notion of increasing returns within a theoretical framework that retains the cardinal virtues of the neo-classical systems. Accumulation of knowledge and its spillover into productive capacity is a central theme in these theories (see Romer 1986, 1990; Grossman and Helpman 1991). An interesting aspect has been the renewed interest in the geographic scope of the spillovers between knowledge creation and its economic application, or in other words, the extent of Marshallian spatial externalities, as identified in the new economic geography (see Krugman 1991, 1999).

The notion of knowledge spillovers is used to capture the phenomenon that some of the economic benefits of R&D activities accrue to economic agents other than the party that undertakes the research (Cohen and Levinthal 1989). Recently, there has been much interest in spillovers from universities to firms (see, e.g., Jaffe 1989). While the fact that knowledge spills over is rather uncontroversial, substantial disagreement exists whether such spillovers are geographically bounded or not (see Karlsson and Manduchi 2001 for a review). Indeed the mechanism by which university research spills over into the generation of inventions and innovations by private firms is not well understood. If the mechanism is primarily journal publications, then proximity and location are probably unimpor-

---

[1] The authors gratefully acknowledge the grant provided by the Jubiläumsfonds of the Austrian National Bank, and the support received from the Department of Economic Geography & Geoinformatics at the Vienna University of Economics and Business Administration and the Austrian Research Centers Seibersdorf. They also wish to express their thanks to Walter Rohn (Austrian Academy of Sciences), Christian Rammer, Doris Schartinger, Norbert Böck (Austrian Research Centers Seibersdorf), Werner Hackl (Austrian Chamber of Commerce) and Karl Messman (Austrian Central Statistical Office, Vienna) for assisting in certain phases of data collection.

tant in capturing the benefits of spillovers. If, however, the mechanism is informal academic discussions with researchers at universities, then geographic boundaries to knowledge spillovers, particularly tacit knowledge, may play a crucial role.

It is the objective of this contribution to shed some further light on this issue, or in other words, on geographically mediated spillovers of university research that characterise local innovation systems. Our interest is focused on spillovers to corporate knowledge production in the high technology sectors in Austria where knowledge spillovers from university research are likely to play the most important role. Corporate knowledge is difficult to define and even more difficult to measure. We follow Jaffe (1989) and others in using patents as a qualitative and rather direct indicator of invention to proxy the output of the knowledge production process.

We refine the standard knowledge production function by modelling research spillovers as a spatially discounted external stock of knowledge. This enables us to capture intra- and inter-regional spillovers.

The chapter is organised into five remaining sections. In the section that follows, the analytical framework applied to model geographically mediated research spillovers is introduced. Next the data set is outlined, and model specification and estimation issues are briefly highlighted. Subsequently, the results are presented. A brief summary and evaluation of the findings concludes the chapter.

8.2 The Knowledge Production Function Framework

Following the standard literature in the field, we assume that corporate knowledge production in the high technology sectors essentially depends on two major sources of knowledge: industrial R&D performed in the high technology sectors and university research (that is, the knowledge pool of basic research available to the high tech sectors). Academic research will not necessarily result in useful knowledge for every industry. But scientific knowledge from certain academic institutes is expected to be more important for high technology industries. To capture the relevant pool of knowledge, scientific fields were assigned to the high technology industries as an aggregate (see App. 8.A), using the survey of industrial R&D managers by Levin et al. (1987).

Knowledge is measured in terms of patents, and university research and industry R&D in terms of expenditures. We use patents as a quantitative and rather direct indicator of invention. But we are aware that the use of patent counts to identify the effect of spatially mediated spillovers is not without pitfalls. The usage might be particularly sensitive to what Scherer (1983) has termed the propensity to patent. There is evidence that the propensity to patent does not appear to be invariant across industries. For example, technology in the pharmaceuticals sector allows easy copying of newly developed drugs, and thus patent protection is essential. In other sectors, such as, for example, aerospace, the propensity to patent is typically smaller.

The conceptual framework for analysing geographic spillovers from university research on regional knowledge production is derived from the knowledge production function introduced by Griliches (1979) that relates the output measure of the knowledge production process (that is, patents in our study) to the above two input measures. We depart from the classical approach by modelling knowledge spillovers in the form of a spatially discounted external stock of knowledge and employing spatial econometric tools for model specification and estimation. The model is based on a modified Cobb-Douglas production function and reads in log-linear form as follows:

$$\log K_i = \alpha_0 + \alpha_1 \log \Omega_i + \alpha_2 \log \Phi_i + \alpha_3 Z_i + \varepsilon_i \qquad (8.1)$$

with

$$\log \Omega_i = \log(R_i + A_i^R) = \log(R_i + \sum_{j \neq i} R_j \, d_{ji}^{-2}) \qquad (8.2)$$

and

$$\log \Phi_i = \log(U_i + A_i^U) = \log(U_i + \sum_{j \neq i} U_j \, d_{ji}^{-2}) \qquad (8.3)$$

where $i = 1, ..., N$ indexes the spatial unit of observations (N=72, political districts in this study), K is measured in terms of patents as proxy for new corporate knowledge generated by high tech firms, R is industry R&D and U university research (measured in terms of expenditures). A_i^U is an accessibility measure to university knowledge with a distance decay parameter equal to 2 (see Sivitanidou and Sivitanides 1995) for each industry R&D district ($j \neq i$) in the national innovation system of Austria. d_{ji} is the distance between j and i as perceived by high tech industry located in i to get in touch with knowledge producers at university in j. A_i^R is defined in an analogous manner to capture potential interregional knowledge spillovers between R&D laboratories located in j and i.[2] Z is a variable that measures the concentration of high technology production (measured in terms of high tech employment in the national total) and attempts to capture agglomeration economies. ε is a vector of stochastic error terms.

It is important to note that university research spillovers are modelled as an external stock of knowledge, represented by variable Φ (see Eq. (8.1)). Variable Φ consists of two components (see Eq. (8.3)). The first captures knowledge spillovers that do not reach beyond the geographic boundaries of the political district,

---

[2] Note that the introduction of A_i^R and A_i^U, respectively, serves also the purpose of over-soming the technical problem caused by the fact that universities are located in only 7 out of the 99 political districts. The solution is achieved at the loss of a clear distinction between intra- and inter-regional spillovers.

and the second those that transcend the geographic scale of the political district. The accessibility measure assumes that these follow a clear distance decay pattern. A positive and significant coefficient for α_2 indicates the presence of localised geographic spillovers from university research on regional knowledge production. The higher the value of this coefficient, the more intense the effect of university-to-firm knowledge flows on regional knowledge production. By contrast, the level of significance of α_1 would suggest that all knowledge production is generated internally to the high tech sector, with or without co-operation between R&D laboratories (variable Ω in Eq. (8.1)). This does not preclude the presence of additional externalities, that is, the presence of agglomeration economies as measured by means of the variable Z.

8.3 The Data

We adopt the political district as the spatial unit of observation in our study. A count of corporate patent applications is used as the dependent variable in our model. The data come from the Austrian Patent Office. Postal code information made it possible to trace patent activity back to the district of knowledge production. In the case of multiple assignees, we followed the standard procedure of proportionate assignment. At the sectoral scale, the patent data were assigned to the two-digit International Standard Industrial Classification (ISIC)-system. The patent data refer to the application year 1993 following Edwards and Gordon (1984) to assume a time lag between the time when a particular R&D project starts (1991) and the moment it leads to an invention. We consider patents in six 'high technology' sectors, broadly defined as Computers & Office Machines (ISIC 30); Electronics & Electrical Engineering (ISIC 31–32); Scientific Instruments (ISIC 33); Machinery & Transportation Vehicles (ISIC 29, 34–35); Oil Refining, Rubber & Plastics (ISIC 23, 25), and Chemistry & Pharmaceuticals (ISIC 24). These six categories contain most of the three- and four-digit ISIC sectors that are typically categorised as high technology sectors. But with the two-digit ISIC sectors it is virtually impossible to designate industries as pure high technology. To the extent that the sectoral mix in these sectors shows systematic variation over space in its 'pure' high tech content, our results on the relationship between patents and research could be affected. But we are confident that we will be able to detect such systematic variations by means of specification tests for spatial effects (see Anselin 1988a).

We used the MERIT concordance table between patent classes as defined by the International Patent Classification (IPC) and ISIC industrial sectors (see App. 8.B) to match the patent data with the two-digit ISIC codes that form our high technology sector (see Verspagen, et al. 1994). It assigns the technical knowledge in the patent classes to the industrial sector that corresponds best to the origin of this knowledge. For example, knowledge about a machine for food processing will be assigned to machinery (ISIC 29) and not to the food sector.

The independent variables come from different data sources. The Austrian Central Statistical Office was the source for variable Z that accounts for agglomeration economies and is measured by the share of high technology employment 1991 in the national total. The R&D expenditure figures stem from an R&D survey for manufacturing firms conducted by the Austrian Chamber of Commerce in 1991. The data received were broken down by the Industrial Classification System of the Chamber. Unfortunately, this scheme can be matched with the International Standard Classification System only at the fairly broad two-digit level and, thus, impeded the definition of the high technology sector on the more appropriate three-digit or four-digit level.

The independent variable U is measured in terms of university research expenditures in 1991. A breakdown of these figures by scientific field is needed to link these fields to the high technology sectors. Unfortunately, data with such a breakdown are not available in Austria. But the Federal Ministry for science and research has been able to provide national totals of university research expenditures for broad scientific areas (natural sciences, technical sciences, social sciences, humanities, medicine, agricultural sciences) in 1991 as well as data on the number of professional researchers (university professors, university assistants and contract research assistants) disaggregated by the scientific areas mentioned above and by political districts so that research expenditures of scientific fields/academic disciplines could be estimated and associated with corresponding two-digit ISIC high technology sectors. Postal code information was used to trace university research activities back to the district of knowledge production.

We use a Cobb-Douglas specification for our knowledge production function. The implied log-linear form (see Eqs. (8.1)–(8.3)) creates a practical sample selection problem in so far that only observations for which all the variables are nonzero can be utilised. Thus, our final data set included only those political districts for which there were patents and R&D expenditures available. This results in 72 observational units that cover 100 percent of the university research expenditures (1991), 93.3 percent of the industry R&D activities (1991) and 99.96 percent of the patent applications (1993) in the high tech sectors. The data used are listed in App. 8.C.

8.4 Model Specification and Estimation Issues

The use of a cross-sectional sample may lead to spatial dependence (also termed spatial autocorrelation) and, thus, cause serious problems in specifying and estimating our knowledge production regression model (8.1)–(8.3). We assess this by means of a Lagrange Multiplier (LM) test using six different spatial weight matrices that reflect different a priori notions of the spatial structure of dependence:

- the simple contiguity weights matrix (CONT),
- the inverse distance weights matrix (IDIS1),
- the square inverse distance weights matrix (IDIS2), and

- distance-based matrices for 50 km (D50), 75 km (D75) and 100 km (D100) between the administrative centres of the political districts.

This test is used to assess the extent to which remaining unspecified spatial knowledge spillovers may be present in the knowledge production function model. Spatial dependence can be incorporated in two distinct ways into the model: *first*, as an additional regressor in the form of a spatially lagged dependent variable *WK*, or *second* in the error structure. The former is referred to as a *Spatial Lag Model* and the latter as *a Spatial Error Model*. The *Spatial Lag Model for Knowledge Production* can be expressed in matrix notation as

$$K = \rho\, W K + X\, \alpha + \xi \tag{8.4}$$

where K is a (72,1)-vector of observations on the patent variable, WK is the corresponding lag for the (72,72)-weights matrix W, X is a (72,M)-matrix of observations on the explanatory variables Ω, Φ and Z including a constant term (extended model: $M = 4$), with matching regression coefficients in the vector α. ξ is a 72 by 1 vector of normally distributed error terms, with mean 0 and constant homoskedastic variance σ^2. ρ is the spatial autoregressive parameter. WK is correlated with the disturbances, even when the latter are i.i.d. Consequently, the spatial lag term has to be treated as an endogenous variable and proper estimation procedures have to account for this endogeneity. Ordinary least squares (OLS) will be biased and inconsistent due to the simultaneity bias (Anselin 1988a).

The second way to incorporate spatial autocorrelation into the regression model (8.1)–(8.3) is to specify a spatial process for the disturbance terms. The resulting error covariance will be non-spherical; ordinary least squares, while unbiased, will be inefficient. Different spatial processes lead to different error covariances with varying implications about the range and extent of spatial interaction in the model (see Anselin and Bera 1998). The most common specification is a spatial autoregressive process in the error terms that results in the following *Spatial Error Model for Knowledge Production*:

$$K = X\, \alpha + \xi \tag{8.5}$$

with

$$\xi = \lambda\, W\, \xi + \eta \tag{8.6}$$

that is a linear regression with error vector ξ, where λ is the spatial autoregressive coefficient for the error lag $W\xi.X$ is a (72, 4)-matrix of observations on the explanatory variables, α a (4,1)-vector of regression coefficients. The errors ξ are assumed to follow a spatial autoregressive process with autoregressive coefficients, and a white noise error η.

The similarity between the Spatial Error Model (8.5)–(8.6) and the Spatial Lag Model (8.4) for regional knowledge production complicates specification testing in practice, since tests designed for a spatial lag specification will also have power against a spatial error specification, and vice versa. But as evidenced in a large number of Monte Carlo simulation experiments in Anselin and Rey (1991), the joint use of the Lagrange Multiplier tests for spatial lag and spatial error dependence suggested by Anselin (1988a, b) provides the best guidance for model specification. When both tests have high values indicating significant spatial dependence in the data, the one with the highest value (that is the lowest probability) will indicate the correct specification.

8.5 Empirical Results

Table 8.1 presents the results of the cross-sectional regression of the geographic knowledge production function for the 72 Austrian political districts. All variables are in logarithms. The first column of the table reports the results obtained by estimating the Basic Model (8.1)–(8.3), while the second column summarises the results for the *Spatial Error Model*. For the Basic Model (8.1)–(8.3) a diagnostic test for heteroskedasticity was carried out, using the White (1980) test. In addition specification tests for spatial dependence and spatial error were performed, utilising the Lagrange Multiplier tests. These tests for spatial autocorrelation were computed for six different spatial weights matrices (CONT, IDIS1, IDIS2, D50, D75, and D100) as mentioned in the previous section. Only the results for the most significant diagnostics are reported in Table 8.1. All estimations and specification tests were carried out with the SpaceStat software developed by Anselin (1995).

The starting point of modelling was the Basic Model for Regional Knowledge Production as expressed in the Eqs. (8.1)–(8.3). It confirms the strong significance of university research spillovers, industry R&D and agglomeration effects on the level of patent activity in the high technology sectors in a political district. As mentioned in Sect. 8.2, we interpret the influence of Φ on patent activities at the district level as evidence of the existence of geographically mediated university research spillovers. The regression yields highly significant and positive effects for both university research and industry R&D (at $p<0.01$), confirming similar results obtained in US studies (see, for example, Jaffe 1989; Anselin, Varga and Acs 1997). There is a clear dominance of the coefficient of industry R&D over university research, indicating an elasticity that is about two times higher. But agglomeration effects appear to be most important.

No evidence of heteroskedasticity was found, but the Lagrange Multiplier test for Spatial Error Dependence shows a strong indication of misspecification. Thus, the correct interpretation should be based on the spatial error model that removes any misspecification in the form of spatial autocorrelation. The significant parameter of the error term (λ), the significant value of the Likelihood Ratio test on spatial error dependence as well as the missing indication for spatial lag dependence and heteroskedasticity (Breusch-Pagan test) are taken as evidence for the correctness of the model. There is little change between the interpretation of the two models, which is to be expected. The main effect of the spatial error autocorrelation is on the precision of the estimators, but in this case it is not sufficient to alter any indication of significance.

Table 8.1. Regression Results for Log (Patent Applications) at the Level of Austrian Political Districts ($N = 72$, 1993)

Model	Basic Model (OLS)	Spatial Error Model (ML)
Constant	3.741***	3.315***
	(0.783)	(0.764)
Log Ω	0.211***	0.213***
	(0.065)	(0.064)
Log Φ (University Research Spillover)	0.100***	0.130***
	(0.037)	(0.037)
Log Z	0.512***	0.438***
	(0.125)	(0.121)
Spatial Autoregressive Coefficient		0.366*
		(0.190)
Adjusted R^2	0.672	0.699
Multicollinearity Condition Number	21.341	21.341
White Test for Heteroscedasticity	8.839	
Breusch-Pagan Test for Heteroscedasticity		2.277
Likelihood Ratio Test for Spatial Error Dependence		2.863 (D100)
LM Test for Spatial Error Dependence	3.444 (D100)	
LM Test for Spatial Lag Dependence	0.889 (D75)	0.382 (IDIS2)

Notes: Estimated standard errors in parentheses; critical values for the White statistic respectively 5 and 9 degrees of freedom are 11.07 and 16.92 ($p = 0.05$); critical value for the Breusch-Pagan statistic with 3 degrees of freedom is 7.82 ($p = 0.05$); critical values for Lagrange Multiplier Lag and Lagrange Multiplier Error statistics are 3.84 ($p = 0.05$) and 2.71 ($p = 0.10$); critical value for Likelihood Ratio-Error statistic with one degree of freedom is 3.84 ($p = 0.05$); spatial weights matrices are row-standardised: D100 is a distance-based contiguity for 100 kilometers; D75 a distance-based contiguity for 75 kilometers; D50 a distance-based contiguity for 50 kilometers; IDIS2 inverse distance squared; only the highest values for a spatial diagnostics are reported; * denotes significance at the 10 percent level, ** significance at the 5 percent level and *** denotes significance at the one percent level

In sum the maximum likelihood (ML)-estimators in column 2 of Table 8.1 can be reliably interpreted to indicate the influence of university research on patent activity in a political district, not only of university research in the district itself, but also in the surrounding districts. The geographic boundedness of university research spillovers is linked to a distance decay effect.

8.6 Conclusions and Outlook

Our empirical results unequivocally indicate the presence of geographically mediated knowledge spillovers from universities that transcend the geographic scale of the political district in accordance with our conceptual framework. The results also demonstrate that such spillovers follow a clear distance decay pattern. But these externalities appear to be relatively small in comparison to the agglomeration effects identified. It is also important to emphasise that the statistical relationship is only suggestive. More detailed estimation of university data will be required to determine if the university research spillover effects materialise in reality.

The findings are important in that they highlight the relevance of modelling knowledge spillovers in form of a spatially discounted external stock of knowledge. They also demonstrate the importance of carefully specifying spatial effects by employing spatial econometric tools.

References

Anselin L (1988a) Spatial econometrics: Methods and models. Kluwer, Dordrecht

Anselin L (1988b) Lagrange multiplier test diagnostics for spatial dependence and spatial heterogeneity. Geographical Analysis 20: 1–17

Anselin L (1995) SpaceStat Version 1.80 User's Guide. Regional Research Institute, West Virginia University, Morgantown

Anselin L, Bera A (1998) Spatial dependence in linear regression models with an introduction to spatial econometrics. In: Ullah A, Giles D (eds) Handbook of applied economic statistics. Marcel Dekker, New York, pp 237–289

Anselin L, Rey S (1991) Properties of tests for spatial dependence in linear regression models. Geographical Analysis 23: 112–131

Anselin L, Varga A, Acs Z (1997) Local geographic spillovers between university research and high technology innovations. Journal of Urban Economics 42: 422–448

Breusch T, Pagan A (1979) A simple test for heteroskedasticity and random coefficient variation. Econometrica 47: 1287–1294

Cohen WM, Levinthal DA (1989) Innovation and learning: The two faces of R&D. Economic Journal 99: 569–596

Echeverri-Carroll EL, Brennan W (1999) Are Innovation Networks Bounded by Proximity? In: Fischer MM, Suarez-Villa L, Steiner M (eds) Innovation, networks and localities. Springer, Berlin, pp 29–49

Edquist C, Rees G (2000) Learning regions and cities: Learning in regional innovation systems – A conceptual framework. Paper Presented at the International Workshop on Knowledge, Complexity and Innovation Systems, Vienna

Edwards K, Gordon T (1984) Final report. Characterization of innovations introduced on the U.S. market in 1982. Prepared for the U.S. Small Business Administration, The Futures Group

Fischer MM (2001) Innovation, knowledge creation and systems of innovation. Annals of Regional Science 35: 199–216

Fischer MM, Fröhlich J, Gassler H. (1994) An exploration into the determinants of patent activities: Some empirical evidence for Austria. Regional Studies 28: 1–12

Griliches Z (1979) Issues in assessing the contribution of research and development to productivity growth. Bell Journal of Economics 10: 92–116

Grossman G, Helpman E (1991) Innovation and growth in the global economy. MIT Press, Cambridge MA

Jaffe AB (1989) Real effects of academic research. American Economic Review 79: 957–970

Karlsson C, Manduchi A (2001) Knowledge spillovers in a spatial context – A critical review and assessment. In: Fischer MM, Fröhlich J (eds) Knowledge, complexity and innovation systems. Springer, Berlin, pp 101–123

Krugman P (1991) Increasing returns and economic geography. Journal of Political Economy 99: 483–499

Krugman P (1999) The role of geography in development. International Regional Science Review 22: 142–161

Levin RC, Klevorick AK, Nelson RR, Winter SG (1987) Appropriating the returns from industrial research and development. Brookings Papers on Economic Activity 3: 783–820

Romer P (1986) Increasing returns and long-run growth. Journal of Political Economy 94: 1002–1037

Romer P (1990) Endogeneous technological change. Journal of Political Economy 98: 72–102

Saviotti PP (1988) Information, entropy and variety in technoeconomic development. Research Policy 26: 843–856

Scherer FM (1983) The propensity to patent. International Journal of Industrial Organisation 1: 107–128

Sivitanidou R, Sivitanides P (1995) The intrametropolitan distribution of R&D acitivities: Theory and empirical evidence. Journal of Regional Science 25: 391–415

Varga A (1998) University research and regional innovation: A spatial econometric analysis of academic technology transfers. Kluwer, Dordrecht

Verspagen B, Moergastel T, Slabbers M (1994) MERIT Concordance Table: IPC-ISIC (rev.2). MERIT Research Memorandum 2/94-004, Maastricht Economic Research Institute on Innovation and Technology, University of Limburg

White H (1980) A heteroskedastic-consistent covariance matrix estimation and a direct test for hetereoskedasticity. Econometrica 48: 817–830

Appendix 8.A Linking Scientific Fields/Academic Disciplines to the 2-Digit High Technology Sectors

ISIC Category	Industry Sector	Associated Scientific Fields/Academic Disciplines
30	Computers & Office Machinery	Fields connected with Information Technologies: Micro-Electronics, Automation and Robotics, Computer Sciences, etc.
31–32	Electronics & Electrical Engineering	Electrical Engineering, Micro-Electronics, Technical Mathematics, Automation and Robotics, Computer Sciences, etc.
33	Scientific Instruments	Engineering Fields such as Mechanical Engineering, Electrical Engineering, Micro-Electronics, Automation and Robotics, Technical Mathematics, Computer Sciences, Physics-Related Fields, Medicine-Related Fields, Biology-Related Fields, Materials Sciences, etc.
29,34–35	Machinery & Transportation Vehicles	Engineering Fields including Mechanical Engineering and Electrical Engineering, Heat Science, Thermodynamics, Material Sciences, Computer Sciences, Technical Mathematics, Astronomy, Transport Science
23,25	Oil Refining, Rubber & Plastics	Chemistry-Related Fields including Materials Sciences, Chemical Engineering and Care Chemistry except for certain sectors such as Quantum Chemistry, Biochemistry and Geochemistry
24	Chemistry & Pharmaceuticals	Chemistry-, Pharmaceuticals- and Medicine-Related Fields including Microbiology, Pharmaceutical Chemistry, Biochemistry, etc.

Source: On the basis of the survey of industrial R&D managers by Levin et al. (1987); only the most important academic disciplines (scientific fields) are listed

Appendix 8.B Assignment of Patent Classes to the High Technology Sectors at the 2-Digit ISIC-Level

ISIC Category	Industry Sector	IPC Patent Classes
30	Computers & Office Machinery	B41J, B41L (50%), G06C, G06E, G06F, G06G, G06J, G06K, G06M, G11B, G11C
31–32	Electronics & Electrical Engineering	A45D (40%), A47J (80%), A47L (40%), A61H (30%), B03C, B23Q (10%), B60Q, B64F (20%), F02P, F21H, F21K, F21L; F21M, F21P, F21Q, F21S, F21V, F27B (10%), G08B, G08G, H01B, H01F, H01G, H01H, H01J, H01K, H01M, H01R, H01S, H01T, H02B, H02G, H02H, H02J, H02K, H02M, H02N, H02P, H03M, H05B, H05C, H05F, H05H, G08C, G09B (50%), H01C, H01L, H01P, H01Q, H03B, H03C, H03D, H03F, H03G, H03H, H03J, H03K, H03L, H04A, H04B, H04G, H04H, H04J, H04K, H04L, H04M, H04N, H04Q, H04R, H04S, H05K
33	Scientific Instruments	A61B, A61C, A61D, A61F, A61G (90%), A61H (40%), A61L (60%), A61M, A61N, A62B (50%), B01L, B64F (10%), C12K (25%), C12Q, F16P (60%), F22B (20%), F22D (20%), F22G (20%), F22X (20%), F23N, F23Q (10%), F24F (20%), F41G, G01B, G01D, G01F (60%), G01H, G01J, G01K, G01L, G01M, G01N, G01P, G01R, G01S, G01T, G01V, G01W, G02B, G02C, G02F, G03B, G03C, G03D, G03G, G03H, G04B, G04C, G04F, G04G, G05B, G05C, G05D, G05F, G05G, G06D, G07B, G07C, G07D, G07F, G07G, G09G, G12B, G21F, G21G, G21H, G21K, H05G
29,34–35	Machinery & Transportation Vehicles	A01B, A01C, A01D, A01F, A01G (10%), A01J (80%), A01K (30%), A21B, A21C, A21D (30%), A22B (50%), A22C (70%), A23C(10%), A23G (10%), A23N, A23P, A24C, A24D (50%), A43D, A61H (30%), A62B (30%), B01B, B01D, B01F, B01J, B02B (50%), B02C, B03B, B03D, B04B, B04C, B05B (50%), B05C (95%), B05D, B05X (50%), B06B, B07B, B07C, B08B, B09B (25%), B22C (10%), B23Q (70%), B25J, B27J, B28B (60%), B28C (60%), B28D (70%), B29B (80%), B29C (80%), B29D (50%), B29F (80%), B29G (50%), B29H (50%), B29J (40%), B30B, B31B, B31C (90%), B31D (80%), B31F (80%), B41B, B41D, B41F, B41G, B42C (50%), B60C (20%), B65 B,

		B65C, B65G (40%), B65H, B66B, B66C, B66D, B66F, B66G, B67B (50%),B67C, B67D, C02F (30%), C10F, C12H, C12L, C12M, C13C, C13G, C13H, C14B (50%), C14C (50%),D01B (50%), D01C (50%), D01D (50%), D01F (50%), D01G (50%), D01H (50%), D02D, D02G (50%), D02H (50%), D02J (50%), D03D (50%),D03J, D04B (50%), D04C (50%), D04D (50%), D04G (50%), D04H (50%), D06C, D06F (70%), D06G, D06H (70%), D21F, D21G, E01B (50%), E01C (50%), E01H (80%), E02D (30%), E03B (30%), E04D (25%), E21B (45%), E21C, E21D (50%), F01B, F01C, F01D, F01K, F01L, F01M, F01N, F01P, F02B, F02C, F02D, F02F, F02G, F02K, F03B, F03C, F03D, F03G, F03H, F04B, F04C, F04D, F04F, F15B, F15C, F15D, F16C, F16J (80%), F16K, F16N, F16T, F23B, F23C, F23D, F23G, F23H, H23J, F23K, F23L, F23M, F23Q (60%), F23R, F24F (80%), F24J (30%), F25B, F25C, F25D, F25J, F26B, F27B (90%), F27D, F28B, F28C, F28D, F28G, F41A, F41B, F41C, F41D, F41F, F41H (50%), F42B, F42C, F42D (50%), G01F (40%), G01G, G21J
23,25	Oil Refining, Rubber & Plastics	A47G (50%), A47K (40%), A61J (40%), A62B (20%), B29H (50%), B60C (80%), C10B, C10C, C10G, C10L, C10M, D06N (50%), F42D (50%)
24	Chemistry & Pharmaceuticals	A01M (20%), A01N, A61J (30%), A61K (95%), A61L (40%), A62D, B09B (75%), B27K (70%), B29B (20%), B29C (20%), B29D (50%), B29F (20%), B29G (50%), B29K, B29L, B41M (15%), B44D (50%), C01B, C01C, C01D, C01F, C01G, C02F (50%), C05B, C05C, C05D, C05F, C05G, C06B, C06C, C06D, C06F, C07B (95%), C07C (95%), C07D (95%), C07F (95%), C07G (95%), C07H (90%), C07J, C07K, C08B, C08C, C08F, C08G, C08H, C08J, C08K, C08L, C09B, C09C, C09D, C09F, C09G, C09H, C09J, C09K, C10H, C10J, C10K, C10N, C11B (50%), C11C (50%), C11D, C12D (90%), C12K (75%), C12N (80%), C12P (50%), C12R (10%), C12S, C14C (50%), E04D (25%), F41H (50%)

Note: The assignment is based on the MERIT concordance table (Verspagen, Moergastel and Slabbers 1994) between the International Patent Classification (IPC) and the International Standard Industrial Classification of all economic activities (ISIC-rev.2) of the United Nations. The percentages in brackets in the last column of the table give the share of the patents in the IPC-class assigned to the accessory ISIC-category if not all patents in the IPC-class are assigned to the corresponding ISIC-category. A percentage of 80%, for example, therefore means that all patents in the IPC-class are assigned to the corresponding ISIC-category

Appendix 8.C Patent Applications (1993), Industry R&D (1991) and University Research (1991) for 72 Austrian Political Districts

Political District	Patent Applications (Variable K)	Industry R&D (Variable R)	University Research and Out-of-District Access to University Research (Variable Φ)
Eisenstadt-Umgebung	3.00	35.45	1.24
Neusiedl am See	3.00	7.29	1.38
Oberpullendorf	1.00	3.80	0.52
Klagenfurt (Stadt)	19.50	3.29	36.14
Villach(Stadt)	8.00	16.16	0.13
Hermagor	1.00	0.34	0.09
Sankt Veit an der Glan	1.00	3.16	0.26
Spittal an der Drau	4.00	0.41	0.10
Villach Land	6.50	35.01	0.14
Wolfsberg	2.00	6.24	0.35
Feldkirchen	2.00	0.35	0.20
Krems (Stadt)	2.50	17.74	0.71
Sankt Pölten (Stadt)	7.50	21.34	1.01
Waidhofen (Stadt)	3.00	6.60	0.31
Wiener Neustadt (Stadt)	5.00	14.24	1.65
Amstetten	16.00	87.49	0.37
Baden	27.50	360.98	4.80
Gänserndorf	3.00	14.33	3.19
Korneuburg	12.50	46.70	9.82
Mödling	22.40	213.57	12.97
Neunkirchen	10.00	61.54	1.01
Sankt Pölten (Land)	3.50	4.61	1.45
Scheibbs	1.00	4.98	0.42
Tulln	2.80	34.12	3.29
Waidhofen an der Thaya	1.00	1.20	0.28
Wiener Neustadt (Land)	6.60	11.75	1.55
Vienna-Umgebung	14.60	323.08	25.35
Linz (Stadt)	62.30	1144.26	218.16
Steyr (Stadt)	28.60	1123.43	0.36
Wels (Stadt)	12.50	30.87	0.44
Braunau am Inn	8.50	14.73	0.13
Gmunden	19.10	103.77	0.20
Grieskirchen	10.00	49.42	0.24
Kirchdorf an der Krems	12.30	7.21	0.25
Linz-Land	10.70	111.67	2.74
Perg	13.00	26.41	0.44
Ried im Innkreis	5.30	11.96	0.17
Rohrbach	3.00	3.11	0.22
Schärding	5.00	10.34	0.14
Steyr-Land	8.00	10.43	0.28

Vöcklabruck	43.80	318.82	0.20
Wels-Land	5.00	77.04	0.28
Salzburg (Stadt)	34.30	36.70	117.1
Hallein	8.10	107.28	0.53
Salzburg-Umgebung	23.80	20.92	0.70
Zell am See	5.00	4.57	0.12
Graz (Stadt)	84.30	399.49	1195.15
Bruck an der Mur	4.30	9.17	1.09
Deutschlandsberg	5.50	93.80	0.97
Feldbach	1.00	2.08	0.81
Fürstenfeld	2.00	12.38	0.61
Graz-Umgebung	8.50	347.15	8.75
Hartberg	1.00	5.53	0.65
Judenburg	12.00	42.26	0.38
Knittelfeld	3.00	20.34	0.48
Leibnitz	4.00	2.23	1.09
Leoben	3.00	5.93	98.51
Liezen	4.00	25.22	0.22
Mürzzuschlag	1.00	9.84	0.55
Voitsberg	10.00	7.88	1.57
Weiz	4.00	123.45	1.68
Innsbruck-Stadt	9.00	5.54	852.03
Innsbruck-Land	29.40	39.07	8.38
Kitzbühel	7.00	15.91	0.18
Kufstein	9.00	329.98	0.25
Lienz	3.00	8.73	0.08
Schwaz	15.00	80.21	2.58
Bludenz	1.00	17.86	0.06
Bregenz	12.00	66.74	0.04
Dornbirn	11.00	146.49	0.04
Feldkirch	14.00	90.23	0.05
Vienna	383.70	6999.29	3345.06

Notes: Industry R&D and University Research were measured in terms of expenditures; all figures are in millions of 1991 ATS; Patent and industry R&D data refer to high technology industries; University research data include those academic institutes that are expected to be important for the high technology industries; Universities are located in seven political districts: Vienna, hosting six universities, Graz (Stadt), Innsbruck (Stadt), Salzburg (Stadt), Linz (Stadt), Klagenfurt (Stadt) and Leoben; all the other political districts have only out-of-district access to university research. Sources: Patent data were compiled from the Austrian Patent Office database; Industry R&D data were compiled from the 1991 Industry R&D Survey of the Austrian Chamber of Commerce; University research data were estimated on the basis of information provided by the Austrian Federal Ministry for Science and Research.

9 High Technology Employment and Knowledge Spillovers

Zoltan J. Acs[1], Felix R. FitzRoy[2] and Ian Smith[2]

[1]University of Baltimore, Baltimore, MD, USA; [2]University of St. Andrews, St. Andrews, Scotland, UK

9.1 Introduction

Informal, as well as econometric evidence, suggests there is a close association between high technology employment and major research universities in the United States (Acs 2002). Typically cited are the links between Stanford University and Silicon Valley or MIT and Route 128. Such a nexus has scarcely emerged in Europe except in the form of a few fledgling research parks such as Cambridge, England (Lumme et al. 1993; Cooke and Simmie 2002), and the capitol region of Norway (Wiig-Aslesen, this volume). Formal tests conducted by Jaffe (1989) provide econometric evidence for the real effects of academic research in terms of its spillover to corporate patenting activity. In addition, papers by Jaffe, Trajtenberg, and Henderson (1993), and Almeida and Kogut (1997) demonstrate the significant degree of localisation of these knowledge externalities with respect to patent citations.

However, spillovers from university research to commercial innovation are not the only effects of relevance to theory and policy. The ultimate economic interest lies chiefly in the product markets and jobs that are generated by R&D. This is a question of considerable policy importance (Business Week 1994) which has only been discussed systematically to date by Beeson and Montgomery (1993) who, in contrast to our results, find no statistically significant effect of university research and development expenditures on high technology employment shares.

In a previous paper, Acs et al. (1999) found considerable evidence that disaggregated data by industry sector appears to deal with the nonrandom selection problem that appeared in aggregated data. Second, it is clear that detection of R&D spillovers to employment requires the matching of industry clusters to relevant university departments. Aggregate data are simply too course to provide an appropriate testbed. Finally, a further result is that real wages and employment are positively related ceteris paribus. This result is quite surprising; however, it is consistent with two important features of high technology industries, increasing returns and, within industries, specific skills and imperfect mobility of labour. The aim of this chapter is to further test for robustness the existence of this effect using a two stage least squares model.

The discussion is organised into five sections. The first outlines discursively the theoretical background. The second section provides a preliminary analysis of the data. We use unique annual data for six high technology sectors in 37 American Standard Metropolitan Statistical Areas (SMSAs) for the period from 1988 to 1991 to investigate the relationship between university R&D expenditure and employment. Jaffe (1989) used American states as his geographical unit of analysis. This has drawbacks in those cases where state borders cut through economic areas or where states contain several large cities. Our use of SMSA data should clearly subject the theoretical argument for spillovers based on spatial proximity to a more precise test. The model is specified and estimation issues are discussed in section three and, in the fourth section, the econometric results are reported and discussed. Given the inclusion of real wages in the employment function, we apply simultaneous estimation techniques to study university R&D spillovers on high technology employment over time and across cities, while controlling for common macroeconomic effects. A final section concludes the paper. Consistent with studies showing R&D spillover effects on innovation at the state level, we find robust evidence that university R&D is a statistically significant determinant of city high technology employment and some evidence for employment effects of innovation.

9.2 Theoretical Background

There are two related hypotheses explaining the development of high technology clusters in the vicinity of major university R&D activity.

9.2.1 Research Spillovers

The first explanation argues that university research is a source of significant innovation-generating knowledge that diffuses initially through personal contacts to adjacent firms, especially those based in a science park (Lever, this volume). Since both basic and applied university research may benefit private enterprise in various ways, it induces firms to locate nearby. Lund (1986), in a survey of industrial R&D managers, confirms the proximity of university R&D as a factor in the location decision due to the initial spillover from neighboring university research to commercial innovation. Of course, as research results are used and disseminated, the learning advantage created by close geographic proximity between local high technology activity and the university would fade but these learning lags may be long. Information flows locally and therefore, through a variety of channels discussed below, more easily and efficiently than over greater distances (Fromhold and Schartinger, this volume). There is a growing body of evidence that supports this hypothesis, especially in the United States.[1] Spillovers from university R&D to patent activity in the same state have been identified econometrically by Jaffe (1989). Acs et al. (1992, 1994), Audretsch and Feldman (1996) and Anselin et al. (1997, 2000) reinforce this result with, instead of patents, a more direct measure of economically useful knowledge production, namely the number of innovations recorded in 1982 by the US Small Business Administration from the leading technology, engineering and trade journals. Likewise, Nelson (1986), using surveys of research managers finds university research to be a key source of innovation in some industries, especially those related to the biological sciences where he finds some degree of corporate funding of university projects. University research spillovers may be a factor which explains how small, and often new, firms are able to generate innovations while undertaking generally negligible amounts of R&D themselves.[2] There is econometric evidence for this result based on data from both the United States (Acs et al. 1994) and Italy (Audretsch and Vivarelli 1996).

Despite the presumed advantages of geographical proximity for receiving spillovers, the mechanisms by which knowledge is transferred are not well understood. Information flow is usually attributed to the use of faculty as technical consultants and post-graduate students as research assistants, the use of university facilities, informal communication between individuals at trade shows, industry conferences, seminars, talks and social activities, or joint participation in commercial ventures by university and corporate scientists through contracted research projects. The latter has grown in importance since the late 1970s as the universities established formal Offices of Technology Transfer (or Licensing) to foster interaction with industry and the commercialisation of research results. This partly reflects pressure applied by US government agencies to universities, for economic growth reasons, to hasten technology transfer from their laboratories to the private sector (Parker and Zilberman 1993). Federal Acts passed in the early 1980s also promote knowledge spillovers. The Stevenson-Wydler Technology Innovation Act of 1980, for example, encourages co-operative research and technology transfer and the 1981 Economic Recovery Tax Act gives tax discounts to firms that provide research equipment to universities. Some universities have created industry consortia to help fund research. Firms pay membership fees to join these consortia and in return benefit from access to the research output and have some voice in the research agenda. Such channels would be expected to flourish given that universities as public institutions do not face the same incentives as private corporations to keep research results secret. In both the San Francisco Bay and Boston areas, for example, the introduction and growth of the biotechnology industry is a direct result of university R&D spillovers. Presumably, the chief benefits of geographical

---

[1] Shachar and Felsenstein (1992) report evidence from studies conducted in Europe and Japan which show very few benefits arising from the close physical proximity of high technology firms to a local university.

[2] It should be noted that R&D is not a good measure of small firm inputs into knowledge production since such inputs often arise informally without the support of an R&D laboratory.

proximity to the spillovers' source consist of a reduction in both the transaction costs of knowledge transfer and in the costs of commercial research and product development. As a caveat, it ought to be noted that we do not argue that proximity is a necessary condition for spillovers to occur, only that it offers advantages in capturing them (see Fischer and Varga, this volume).

9.2.2 The Labour Market

The second university-based explanation of clustering highlights the provision of a pool of trained and highly qualified science and engineering graduates. The high level of human capital embodied in their general and specific skills is another mechanism by which knowledge is transmitted (Beeson and Montgomery 1993). To the extent that they do not migrate, such graduates may provide a supply of labour to local firms or else a supply of entrepreneurs for new start-ups in the high technology sector (Link and Rees 1990). Some evidence for this latter link is provided by Bania et al. (1987, 1993) who, using cross-section data, find a significant effect of university research expenditure on new firm start-ups. Over a longer time period Simon (1998) and Simon and Nardinelli (2002) provide evidence of the importance of human capital and the employment growth of metropolitan areas. University scientists themselves, of course, may provide the entrepreneurial input, working part-time as directors of their own start-up companies, or even leaving academia to take positions in high technology firms. Parker and Zilberman (1993, p. 97) report, for example, that MIT has incubated about 40 biotechnology firms since the late 1980s. Shane (2002) and Lumme et al. (1993) in their study of academic entrepreneurship in Cambridge (England) identified 62 high technology companies whose business idea was based on the exploitation of knowledge developed or acquired in either a university or a research institute. However, even if university research is either negligible or irrelevant to industry, university training of new industrial scientists alone may be sufficient to generate local labour market spillovers. Nelson (1986, p. 187), for example, notes that industrial interest in academic departments of physics is confined mainly to their output of potential industrial scientists rather than to their research results.

A university and its associated science park may also play an important signalling role in locational choice (Shachar and Felsenstein 1992) in the sense that they signal the presence of local technological capacity. Thus, firms may be attracted even if the university spillovers are not in fact that great (see Wiig-Aslesen, this volume).

9.3 Preliminary Data Analysis

As is well known, no disaggregated employment data at the MSA level exists for the United States. The employment and wage data used in this study come from the U.S. Department of Labor, Bureau of Labor Statistics (BLS). The data are reported to BLS by the State Employment Security Agencies (SESAs) of the 50 states as part of the Covered Employment and Wages Program (i.e., the ES-202 report). Employers in private industry provide SESAs with quarterly tax reports for an average of 90 million wage and salary workers in approximately 5.9 million reporting units. These reports covered approximately 98 percent of total wage and salary civilian employment and provide a virtual census of employees and their wages for nearly all sectors of the economy. This study utilises specialised data runs for 36 MSAs and 32 three-digit SIC industries. There are disclosure limitations of the data. Because individual records cannot be revealed, for cities and industries where there are only a few employers, the data are not available. This limits both the number of cities and the number of industries that can be studied with BLS data. We could have studied most of the 300 MSAs, however, we would *not* have been able to study specific high technology industries because of disclosure problems. Therefore, in order to study R&D spillovers, the study is limited to cities that have a large number of high technology industries. The advantage of this approach is that we are able to study those cities that are dominated by high technology industries and test for spillovers.

Our data for university research expenditures follow the common approach in the literature and are compiled from the National Science Foundation Survey for Scientific and Engineering Expenditures at Universities and Colleges for the various years. The innovation variable comes from the U.S. Small Business Administration Innovation DataBase. The data set is compilation of innovations that were introduced to the U.S. market in the year 1982 based on an extensive review of new product announcements in trade and technical publications. The data are disaggregated at both the industry and MSA level. For a discussion of their limitations see Edwards and Gordan (1984), Feldman (1994), Varga (1998) and Acs et al. (2002).

The first step[3] is to identify the high technology sectors. We proceeded by selecting those with a relatively high ratio of R&D to industry sales. Thirty two three-digit Standard Industrial Classification (SIC) industries were identified in this way, and then grouped into the six sectors detailed in Table 9.1: Biotechnology and Biomedical, Information Technology and Services, High Technology Machinery and Instruments, Defence and Aerospace, Energy and Chemicals, and High Technology Research. This latter sector refers to development and testing services carried out by the private sector. It is necessary research for the successful commercialisation of university research. While it is widely recognised that SIC codes have their limits in identifying high technology industries, they are still widely used because there are no easy substitutes.

Next, we selected the 22 most important SMSAs for these industries, most of which also have major university R&D activity. For comparison and sample variation we also include 15 additional SMSAs with only minor university research.

The relationship between university R&D and high technology employment can be analysed in a preliminary fashion using scatter diagrams. Both variables

---

[3] See Acs (1996) for a detailed description.

display great variation across metropolitan areas though there is a clear positive association between them. The simple correlation coefficient is 0.60. University research expenditure and high technology employment are both high in the major cities of Los Angeles, Boston, New York and Baltimore.

We next plotted high technology employment against the number of scientists and engineers per 100 workers by SMSA. The motivation is that the stock of university science graduates with good general and specific skills influences the location of a high technology cluster. Empirically the association with high technology employment is not that strong. The simple correlation coefficient is 0.26. Austin, San Jose, Seattle and Raleigh have a high share of engineers and scientists relative to the level of high technology employment. In other words, the labour quality is relatively high in these SMSAs. In contrast, the large number of employees in Los Angeles appears to be concentrated in low-skilled occupations.

9.4 Empirical Specification

9.4.1 The Model

In spite of data limitations, we estimate a parsimonious structural labour market model. The main missing variable is a proxy for product demand faced by high technology firms, such as sales, which is not available for individual SMSAs. Our initial specification for the employment equation is written down in natural logarithms as:

$$EMP_{m\,t} = a_0 + a_1 W_{mit} + a_2 RD_{mi} + a_3 POP_{mt} + a_4 HK_m + a_5 INNOV_m + aX + u_{1mit} \quad (9.1)$$

where m indexes SMSA, i indexes industry, and t indexes time: $m=1,...,37$; $i=1,...,6$; and $t=1988,...,1991$. EMP_{mit} refers to high technology employment and W_{mit} is the corresponding annual real wage per employee, defined as nominal wages deflated by the appropriate industry producer price index. Since the panel includes only four years of annual data, cross-sectional variability dominates[4]. For this reason, attempts to estimate equations specified in terms of employment *growth* rates proved fruitless.

For reasons of data availability, RD_{mi}, university R&D, is specified for only a single year, 1985. Given the time span of our data set, it seems reasonable that the use of R&D inputs dated in 1985 provides an appropriate lag for the knowledge externality to be transmitted into commercial products and employment. Edwards and Gordon (1984), for example, find that innovations made in 1982 resulted from

---

[4] Inclusion of a lagged dependent variable in Eq. (9.1) yielded a coefficient of almost unity and impaired the explanatory power of most other variables, suggesting a relative lack of movement in employment over time.

inventions made on average 4.2 years earlier. The R&D data include industry-funded university research, a component which rarely exceeds 10% of the total and is usually considerably less. Notice that RD_{mi} varies by both SMSA and industry. Total university R&D spending in each city is desegregated by broad science department and allocated to each of the six industries. This is appropriate, given substantial differences in the commercial applicability of university research across academic departments. Thus employment data by industry sector are linked to the relevant component of university research expenditure. The assignment of university department to industrial sector is listed in Table 9.2. This is close to Jaffe (1989) but it is doubtless not the only plausible allocation.

POP_{mt} refers to city population and controls for local market size. Of course, the market extends beyond SMSA boundaries but we do not have a more appropriate measure of demand. The number of scientists and engineers as a proportion of the labor force of each SMSA represents the potential human capital or quality of the labor force, available for employers, HK_m. Data are only available for a single year, 1989. $INNOV_m$ is a simple count of the number of innovations by MSA in 1982, the year for which this variable has been collected. It attempts to control for the effect of pre-existing commercial innovation that leads to product development and marketing with substantial time lags, on subsequent employment levels. Finally X represents a vector of industry, state and annual time dummies. These control for effects specific to each which may not have been captured by the continuous variables.

Since employment and real wages are jointly determined in the labour market, Eq. (9.1) should be estimated by a simultaneous method. The corresponding real wage level equation is given by:

$$W_{mit} = b_0 + b_1 W_{mi,t-1} + b_2 EMP_{mit} + b_3 HK_m + b_4 CW_{mit} + bX + u_{2mit} \qquad (9.2)$$

This includes the average SMSA hourly wage CW_{mit} and a lagged dependent variable in addition to human capital. Rank and order conditions indicate that both the wage and employment equations are over-identified. Two stage least squares (2SLS) is therefore adopted as the method of estimation. Table 9.3 presents the main summary statistics by variable for the 37 MSAs in aggregate.

Table 9.1. Industry Groupings

Biotechnology and Biomedical
- Medicinals and botanicals (283)
- Medical instruments and supplies (384)
- Ophthalmic goods (385)

Defence and Aerospace
- Ordnance and accessories (348)
- Aircraft and parts (372)
- Guided missiles and space (376)
- Search and navigation equipment 381)

Information Technology and Service
- Computer and office equipment (357)
- Electronic distribution equipment (361)
- Audio and video equipment (365)
- Communications equipment (366)
- Electronic components and accessories (367)
- Communication services (489)
- Computer and data processing services (737)

Energy and Chemicals
- Crude petroleum and natural gas(131)
- Industrial inorganic chemicals (281)
- Plastic materials and synthetics (282)
- Industrial organic chemicals (286)
- Miscellaneous chemical products (289)
- Petroleum refining (291)

High Technology Machinery and Instruments
- Engines and turbines (351)
- Construction and related machinery (353)
- General industrial machinery (356)
- Electrical industrial apparatus (362)
- Household appliances (363)
- Electric lighting and wiring (364)
- Miscellaneous electrical equipment and suppliers (369)
- Measuring and controlling devices (382)
- Photographic equipment and supplies (386)

High Technology Research
- Research, development and testing services (873)

Source: Office of Management and Budget, Standard Industrial Classification Manual, 1987, Washington DC, 1988.

Table 9.2. Correspondence of University Departments and Industries

Industry	University Department
Biotechnology and Biomedical	Life Sciences
Information Technology and Services	Maths and Computer Sciences
High-Technology Machinery and Instruments	Environmental Sciences and Engineering
Defence and Aerospace	Engineering and Physical Sciences
Energy and Chemicals	Physical Sciences
High Technology Research	All Hard Sciences

9.4.2 Sample Selection Bias

The disclosure limits of the BLS data outlined earlier may potentially introduce a selection bias in the results. This arises since the data are suppressed in those MSAs where high technology employment is low. A nonrandomly selected sample is, therefore, effectively imposed by the BLS. This bias can be resolved econometrically by constructing a joint model which represents both the employment equation and the selection process determining when the dependent variable is observed. In effect we have a selection rule which states that employment is only reported if it exceeds an unobserved disclosure threshold, EMP^*_{MIT}. Thus the model may be described statistically as follows:

$$EMP_{MIT} = \beta_\_ X_{MIT} + u_{MIT} \qquad (9.3)$$

$$EMP^*_{MIT} = \gamma_\_ Z_{MIT} + \varepsilon_{MIT} \qquad (9.4)$$

$$EMP_{MIT} \text{ observed only if } EMP_{MIT} \geq EMP^*_{MIT}$$

where $(u_{MIT}, \varepsilon_{MIT})$ are i.i.d. drawings from a bivariate normal distribution with zero mean, variances σ^2_u and σ^2_ε, and covariance $\sigma_{u\varepsilon}$. If this covariance is nonzero, the OLS estimates of β will be biased. X_{MIT} and Z_{MIT} are vectors of independent variables. The dependent variable EMP^*_{MIT} is unobserved but has a dichotomous observable realisation I_{MI} which is related to EMP^*_{MIT} as follows:

$$I_{MIT} = 1 \text{ if and only if } EMP_{MIT} \geq EMP^*_{MIT}$$

$$I_{MIT} = 0 \text{ if and only if } EMP_{MIT} < EMP^*_{MIT}$$

Eq. (9.3) applies to the selected sample of 36 cities and summarises the specification in Eq. (9.1). Additional data were obtained on the right hand side variables for a further 77 MSAs which are nonselected in the sense that no high technology employment data were available for these cases. The additional observations permit correction of the sample selection bias introduced by the censoring of the dependent variable using the two-stage estimation procedure proposed by Heckman (1979). In the first stage the parameters of the probability that an MSA will be in the selected sample of 36 cities are estimated from a probit analysis of Eq. (9.3) using the full sample of $36 + 77 = 113$ cities. From these estimates the values of the inverse of Mills' ratio, denoted $\hat{\lambda}_{MIT}$, are computed for each observation in the selected sample. The second stage is to estimate the employment Eq. (9.2) by OLS with $\hat{\lambda}_{MIT}$ as an additional explanatory variable. It has been shown by Heckman and others that this correction term is a proxy variable for the probability of selection, measuring the sample selection effect arising from undisclosed observations on employment. This procedure gives consistent estimates of the parameters of Eq. (9.3).

Note that Z_{MIT} is a subset of X_{MIT}. Since the non-disclosure problems, which apply to employment likewise, afflict the wage data, the wage variable is excluded from the Z_{MIT} vector in the selection equation. The probability of hi-tech employment disclosure is likely to be strongly related to city size, which is proxied here by the population variable. In addition, the innovation and university R&D variables are included. Human capital was badly determined in all probit equations and so dropped from the unmatched specification.

Table 9.3. Summary Statistics by Variable

Variable	Maximum	Minimum	Mean	Standard Deviation	Coefficient of Variation
EMP_{mit}	219500	67	15537	24713	1.59
W_{mit}	60114	7822	30920	7564	0.24
POP_{mt}	8978000	636000	2341200	1931900	0.83
RD_{mi}	479314	0	46655	73905	1.58
HK_m	6.39	0.76	2.72	1.14	0.42
$INNOV_m$	384	4	54.76	76.58	1.4
CW_{mit}	14.22	7.07	11.35	1.29	0.11

9.5 Empirical Results

Three sets of results are reported. First, aggregate high technology employment equations by MSA are estimated over a four-year time period. Corresponding to the aggregate construction of the employment variable, total university R&D expenditures are specified on the right hand side. Second, employment and university R&D are disaggregated and matched up by industry sector in a two stage least regression. Third, sectoral employment equations are estimated for each of our six industry clusters.

9.5.1 Aggregated Unmatched Equations

Column (1) of Table 9.4 reports the aggregate OLS estimates of Eq. (9.1) in which the six high technology industries clusters are pooled to form a single sector. The equation includes both state and time fixed effects to control for unmeasured state and time specific factors. The coefficients on the fixed effects are not tabulated but their joint significance cannot be rejected by an F-test. The equation was estimated in natural logarithms over the four-year period 1988 to 1991 using 144 observations (4 years x 36 cities). The coefficients should therefore be interpreted as elasticities. Three lags are specified for the university R&D variable of which the first clearly has the strongest impact. Restricting the second and third lags to zero and re-estimating the equation gives the results reported in column (2). The coefficients have the expected signs and are statistically significant at the 5% level using a one tail test. In particular the R&D elasticity of employment is 0.11 with a t-ratio of 3.51. To check for the robustness of the results, the equation was respecified by substituting the stock of research and development for the flow measure. This generated virtually identical parameter estimates. To correct for any possible simultaneity between employment and real wages, the equation was also estimated using lagged wages. Again, however, the results were very similar and are not presented.

These simple OLS estimates provide a baseline from which to assess the impact of sample selection on the employment equation. Column (3) of Table 9.4 reports the coefficient estimates of the disclosure probability equation estimated by maximum likelihood probit on the full sample of 113 MSAs over the four-year period. The population, innovation and R&D variables are statistically significant at conventional levels, and the equation correctly predicts disclosure status in 88% of cases. Column (4) lists the estimated coefficients of the employment equation corrected for sample selection and again controlling for state and time fixed effects. The key difference from the results of the uncorrected equation in column (2) is the statistical insignificance of the R&D variable. Moreover, its coefficient has fallen considerably from 0.11 to 0.04 suggesting a substantial initial upward bias. Under the null hypothesis of no selection bias, the coefficient of the estimated inverse Mills' ratio, $\hat{\lambda}_{MIT}$, has a t-distribution. Using a simple t-test, we cannot reject the null. However, omitting the university R&D variable from the employment equation overturns the initial statistical insignificance of the sample selection effect and increases its absolute value as reported in column (5). This outcome implies that there is a sample selection problem for these data. The absolute t-statistics in parentheses are based on White's heteroskedastic consistent estimates of the standard errors since, in the presence of selection bias, the usual OLS estimates of the standard errors of the estimates of β are also biased.

The significance of the coefficient on R&D in the probit equation demonstrates that the magnitude of total university R&D in an MSA has a strong and direct effect on the probability of employment disclosure but only affects aggregate high technology employment indirectly through the disclosure term, $\hat{\lambda}_{MIT}$. Therefore, R&D may appear to be a statistically significant important determinant of employment when an OLS regression is fit on the selected sample as in column (2); this is the consequence of nonrandom sample selection. The negative sign on the selection term, $\hat{\lambda}_{MIT}$, indicates that, controlling for all observed effects, an MSA for which high technology employment is disclosed will have lower employment than an MSA with similar characteristics for which it remains undisclosed. With respect to the remaining coefficients, a comparison of column (5) with column (2) indicates that they are overstated if sample selection is ignored.

9.5.2 Disaggregated Equations

Table 9.5 reports the 2SLS estimates of Eqs. (9.1) and (9.2). OLS estimates are listed for comparative purposes, though it will be noted that the coefficients do not differ much from their 2SLS counterparts. Student t-ratios are in parentheses. The coefficients on the fixed effects are not tabulated, but for the employment equation, their joint significance cannot be rejected by an F-test. Taking the fixed effect groups separately, none fail a variable deletion test.[5]

Each 2SLS equation was estimated in natural logarithms over the three-year period 1989 to 1991 using 666 observations (3 years x 6 sectors x 37 cities). The coefficients should therefore be interpreted as elasticities. Statistically the wage and employment equations are satisfactory and, with one notable exception, have the expected signs, though not all are significant at conventional levels.

The central result is a positive and statistically significant coefficient on the R&D variable in the employment equation. Although the magnitude of the employment elasticity is small (0.08), this is evidence of a direct spillover of university research on the high technology employment. In unreported regressions, we found the same result when the dependent variable is specified in terms of high technology employment share, in striking contrast to the statistically insignificant coefficient reported by Beeson and Montgomery (1993).[6]

A further result is that real wages and employment are positively related ceteris paribus. This is counter to our theoretical priors based on the perfectly competitive model. Dropping the wage variable did not markedly affect the signs and significance of the remaining regressors so this outcome does not vitiate our spillover story. Neither re-estimating as single equations using OLS nor as random effects models produced major differences in the results. So the estimates are robust with respect to estimation technique.

At first blush, this result is quite surprising. However it is quite consistent with two important features of high technology industries. First, output markets with continual product innovation and imperfect information are far from the traditional model of perfect competition. It follows that some proxy for product demand should be included in the employment equation but such a variable was not available. Thus we are estimating a reduced form rather than a true structural demand model. Second, specialised skills are often required in high technology sectors. Locational advantages that attract high technology firms may also generate shortages of skilled workers that lead to higher wages. Other wages typically follow to maintain differentials. The positive correlation between high technology employ-

---

[5] All equations were also estimated with coarser regional instead of state fixed effects, yielding very similar results, though the R&D employment elasticity was smaller in this model. White standard errors to control for heteroscedasticity differed little from the reported results.

[6] Note that Montgomery and Beeson omit real wages and prior innovations from their employment equation. They do, however, include several variables to control for the effects of other area attributes on local labor market conditions, which we capture using state dummies.

ment and wages thus probably reflects the crucial shortages and imperfect mobility of skilled labour that has been the subject of much policy discussion and concern. Equally plausible, and without relying on market imperfections, it may simply be the demand for products produced by the most skilled and highly paid workers that has grown most rapidly.

The university-based labour market spillover story has weaker support. The proportion of engineers and scientists in a city, the human capital variable, is statistically insignificant in both the employment and wage equations. These results are inconsistent with research on employment growth in general (Simon 1998; Simon and Nardinelli 2002). However, most other studies have not looked at this level of human capital. Our population and technical innovation variables, however, are both well determined.

Table 9.4. Aggregate High Technology Employment Estimates

Dependent variable	(1) EMP_{MT} OLS	(2) EMP_{MT} OLS	(3) I_{MT} Probit	(4) EMP_{MT} OLS	(5) EMP_{MT} OLS
constant	13.19	13.2	−14.32	13.32	13.28
	(3.1)	(3.17)	(−8.73)	(3.97)	(3.85)
W_{MT}	−0.77	−0.77	−0.68	−0.61	
	(−1.84)	(−1.89)	(−1.87)	(−1.83)	
$RD_{M,T-1}$	0.12	0.11	0.56	0.04	
	(0.59)	(3.51)	(6.21)	(0.49)	
$RD_{M,T-2}$	−0.02				
	(−0.08)				
$RD_{M,T-3}$	0.01				
	(0.07)				
POP_{MT}	0.21	0.21	1.04	0.2	0.19
	(2.66)	(2.70)	(5.85)	(1.61)	(1.70)
HK_M	0.48	0.48		0.48	0.48
	(4.3)	(4.35)		(5.21)	(5.28)
$INNOV_M$	0.65	0.65	0.19	0.62	0.61
	(9.83)	(9.97)	(2.00)	(10.21)	(10.36)
$\hat{\lambda}_{MT}$				0.2	−0.32
				(-0.82)	(−4.78)
adjusted R^2	0.88	0.88		0.88	0.88
estimated st. err.	0.278	0.276		0.276	0.275
n	144	144	452	144	144

Notes: (i) absolute *t*-statistics are in parentheses; (ii) all variables are in natural logarithms; (iii) n is the number of observations; (iv) unreported dummy variables for time and state are also included in each of these regressions except the probit in (3).

Table 9.5. Disaggregated 2SLS High Technology Employment and Wage Function Estimates with Industry, States and Time Fixed Effects

Dependent Variable	(1) EMP_{mit} OLS	(2) EMP_{mit} 2SLS	(3) W_{mit} OLS	(4) W_{mit} 2SLS
constant	−20.4	−23.19	1.26	1.29
	(−10.34)	(−9.29)	(5.85)	(5.45)
W_{mit}	2.52	2.78		
	(14.21)	(12.28)		
RD_{mi}	0.08	0.08		
	(7.89)	(6.73)		
POP_{mt}	0.37	0.39		
	(3.8)	(3.46)		
HK_m	0.004	−0.03	0.01	0.01
	-0.03	(−0.21)	(1.00)	(1.00)
$INNOV_m$	0.25	0.22		
	(3.11)	(2.39)		
EMP_{mit}			0.01	0.01
			(3.89)	(1.82)
$W_{mi,t-1}$			0.86	0.85
			(47.03)	(32.54)
CW_{mit}			0.07	0.07
			(1.11)	(1.15)
adjusted R^2	0.62	0.62	0.93	0.93
estimated standard error	0.851	0.849	0.069	0.069
n	888	666	666	666

Notes: (i) t-statistics are in parentheses; (ii) all variables are in natural logarithms; (iii) n is the number of observations; (iv) unreported dummy variables for industry, time and state are also included in each of these regressions.

9.5.3 Industry Matched Equations

We have also estimated employment functions separately for each of the six high technology industries. The mean SMSA employment, wage and R&D in each sector is listed in Table 9.6 and the equation estimates are provided in Table 9.7. The R&D coefficients are positive and statistically significant (or near significant) in all but the Energy and Chemicals industry. A plausible explanation is that Energy and Chemicals represents a rather traditional industry dependent on both raw materials and products that are much more costly to transport than the inputs of other sectors. Access to port facilities, and other transport infrastructure, is thus likely to be much more important in the location decision, weakening considerably the role of the R&D variable.

Although the results for prior innovation are mixed in terms of statistical sign and significance, it is the university R&D effect and human capital that are our key variables of interest, which is most consistent. The coefficients are largest in the Defence and Aerospace and High Technology Research sectors. These results are consistent with prior research and indicate that both knowledge spillovers and wages are important determinants of high technology employment.

Table 9.6. Mean SMSA Employment, R&D and Wages by Industry

Industry	Employment	R&D($1000)	Wages($)
Biology and Biomedical	5934	68937	25412
Defense and Aerospace	22101	33948	33374
Energy and Chemicals	8215	15459	38237
High Technology Research	7886	127444	26616
Information and Technology Ser.	33082	7109	34396
High Tech Machinery & Instruments	16004	27032	27483

9.6 Conclusions

Previous empirical work on R&D spillovers has focussed on their relationship with innovation and patent counts at the level of individual U.S. states. With new data for 37 American Standard Metropolitan Statistical Areas including the main university R&D centers we have found a statistically significant and robust spill-over to employment in five high technology sectors, after controlling for state fixed effects. This confirms the popular view of high technology clusters and provides the first quantitative evidence that academic research has a positive local high technology employment spillover at the city level. A further result is that innovation was also strongly related to high technology industry employment after a long time lag, again a plausible but hitherto untested proposition.

These results are clearly of relevance for regional policy. They provide support for the importance of high technology clusters in the U.S. and possible lessons for Europe and Japan where such clusters are much less well-developed and where there is less evidence of the localisation of knowledge spillover, at least in the semiconductor industry (Almeida and Kogut 1997). In spite of dramatic declines in the costs of information transmission, local spillovers underline the importance of personal contacts and face-to-face communication in transferring scientific progress into jobs and products. Clearly more research is required on the nature of the transmission process as well as on the skill composition of high technology employment and the relationship of training and skills to wages and employment in local labour markets. Another significant unexplored issue is the role of rent sharing in an industry where human capital is particularly important. Our short panel precluded any dynamic analysis but longer time series could throw light on the determinants of high technology employment growth that have generated the distribution and composition of existing clusters.

Table 9.7. Industry 2SLS High Technology Employment Function. Estimates with State and Time Fixed Effects

	EC	DA	ITS	HTR	BB	HTM
constant	−13.84	−90.48	1.89	−9.68	−3.84	−39.47
	(−1.27)	(−6.83)	(0.55)	(−4.62)	(−1.09)	(−5.81)
W_{mit}	1.75	9.75	0.3	0.89	0.85	4.13
	(1.60)	(7.49)	(0.88)	(4.49)	(2.52)	(6.75)
RD_{mi}	0.005	0.25	0.01	0.14	0.08	0.09
	(0.23)	(8.47)	(1.55)	(15.49)	(4.28)	(6.02)
HK_m	−0.43	−1.57	0.54	0.68	−0.33	−0.54
	(−1.66)	(−3.94)	(5.02)	(7.78)	(−1.97)	(−2.94)
POP_{mt}	0.71	−0.12	0.17	0.85	0.24	0.71
	(3.12)	(−0.49)	(2.19)	(13.0)	(1.89)	(4.53)
$INNOV_m$	−0.08	−0.42	0.78	−0.04	0.32	0.15
	(−0.51)	(−1.75)	(11.97)	(−0.72)	(3.18)	(1.37)
adjusted R^2	0.86	0.79	0.94	0.97	0.85	0.86
estimated st. error	0.53	0.769	0.231	0.196	0.383	0.356
n	111	111	111	111	111	111

Notes: (i) t-statistics are in parentheses; (ii) all variables are in natural logarithms; (iii) n is the number of observations; (iv) unreported dummy variables for time and state are also included in each of these regressions. Key: EC: Energy and Chemicals, DA: Defense and Aerospace, ITS: Information and Technology Services, HTR: High Technology Research, BB: Biology and Biomedical, HTM: High Technology Machinery and Instruments

The second and initially somewhat surprising result is the strong positive correlation between wages and employment in high technology industries. This association is apparent in all equations and appears to be quite robust. Our view is that the positive partial correlation in the employment equation could arise from two sources that are not mutually exclusive: omitted variables and skill aggregation. However, these results are consistent with endogenous growth theory and increasing returns.

The most important omitted variable is the absence of a demand or sales variable in the employment function. This equation therefore essentially captures a labour supply relationship. For example, if the demand for products produced by the most highly skilled, and paid, labour grows fastest due to innovation, government procurement or whatever, employment and real wages would be positively related in a regression which would not control for demand effects. Likewise, if there are shortages or bottlenecks of key skilled personnel, their wages would rise with demand for their products or services to include a scarcity rent.

A complementary explanation relates to the heterogeneity of skill categories in the high technology sector. It is obviously rather crude to estimate employment demand implicitly assuming a single, homogenous category of labour. There exists both skilled and relatively unskilled employment in the high technology sector and the demand for these categories may move in different directions.

Naturally, university knowledge spillovers are not the only reason for high technology clusters. Other forces for localisation are quite strong. They would include the development of specialised intermediate goods industries, economies of scale and scope, and network externalities. With respect to the latter, innovations by different producers may be complementary, yielding related new products or processes when combined. On these questions too, further research is called for.

References

Acs ZJ (2002) Innovation and the growth of cities. Edward Elgar, Cheltenham

Acs ZJ (1996) American high technology clusters. In: De la Mothe J, Paquet G (eds) Evolutionary economics and the new institutional political economy. Pinter, London, pp 183–219

Acs ZJ, Anselin L, Varga A (2002) Patents and innovation counts as measures of regional Production of New Knowledge. Research Policy, forthcoming

Acs ZJ, Audretsch DB, Feldman F (1994) R&D Spillovers and recipient firm size. Review of Economics and Statistics 76: 336–340

Acs ZJ, Audretsch DB, Feldman F (1992) Real effect of academic research: Comment. American Economic Review 82: 363–367

Acs ZJ, FitzRoy FR, Smith I (1999) High technology employment, wages and university R&D spillovers: Evidence from US cities. Economics of Innovation and New Technology 8: 57–78

Almeida P, Kogut B (1997) The localization of knowledge and the mobility of engineers. Management Science 45: 905–917

Anselin L, Varga A, Acs ZJ (1997) Local geographic spillovers between university research and high technology innovations. Journal of Urban Economics 42: 422–448

Anselin L, Varga A, Acs ZJ (2000) Geographic spillovers and university research: A spatial econometric perspective. Growth and Change 31: 501–515

Audretsch DB, Feldman MP (1996) Knowledge spillovers and the geography of innovation and production. American Economic Review 86: 630–640

Audretsch DB, Vivarelli M (1996) Small firms and R&D spillovers: Evidence for Italy. Small Business Economics 8: 249–258

Bania N, Eberts R, Fogarty M (1987) The role of technical capital in regional growth. Paper presented at the Western Economic Association Meetings.

Bania N, Eberts R, Fogarty M (1993) Universities and the start-up of new companies: Can we generalize from Route 128 and Silicon Valley? Review of Economics and Statistics 75: 761–766

Beeson P, Montgomery E (1993) The effects of colleges and universities on local labor markets. Review of Economics and Statistics 75: 753–761

Business Week (1994) Why are we so afraid of growth? May 16th: 62–72

Cooke P, Simmie J (2002) The Competitiveness of cities: Knowledge, innovativness and entrepreneurship. Centre for Advanced Studies, Cardiff University

Edwards KL, Gordon TJ (1984) Characterization of innovations introduced in the US market in 1982. The Futures Group

Feldman M (1994) The geography of innovation. Kluwer Academic Publishers, Boston

Fromhold-Eisebith M, Schartinger D (this volume) The knowledge base, innovation and urban economic growth. In: Acs ZJ, De Groot HLF, Nijkamp P (eds) The emergence of the knowledge economy: A regional perspective, Springer Verlag, Berlin

Heckman JJ (1979) Sample selection bias as specification error. Econometrica 47: 153–162

Jaffe AB (1989) Real effects of academic research. American Economic Review 79: 957–970

Jaffe AB, Trajtenberg M, Henderson R (1993) Geographic localization of knowledge spillovers as evidenced by patent citations. Quarterly Journal of Economics 100: 577–598

Krugman P (1991) Increasing returns and economic geography. Journal of Political Economy 99: 483–99

Lever B (this volume) The knowledge base, innovation and urban economic growth. In: Acs ZJ, De Groot HLF, Nijkamp P (eds) The emergence of the knowledge economy: A regional perspective, Springer Verlag, Berlin

Link AN, Rees J (1990) Firm size, university based research, and the returns to R&D. Small Business Economics 2: 25–31

Lund L (1986) Locating corporate R&D facilities. Conference Board Report No. 892, Conference Board, New York

Lumme A, Kauranen L, Autio E, Kaila MM (1993) New technology based companies in cambridge in an international perspective. Working Paper No. 35, Small Business Research Centre, University of Cambridge

Nelson RR (1986) Institutions supporting technical advance in industry. American Economic Review 76: 186–89

Parker DD, Zilberman D (1993) University technology transfers: Impacts on local and U.S. economies. Contemporary Policy Issues 11: 87–99

Shachar A, Felsenstein D (1992) Urban economic development and high technology industry. Urban Studies 29: 839–55

Shane S (2002) Selling university technology: Patterns from MIT. Management Science, forthcoming

Simon CJ (1998) Human capital and metropolitan employment growth. Journal of Urban Economics 43: 223–243

Simon SJ, Nardinelli (2002) Human capital and the rise of American cities, 1900-1990. Regional Science and Urban Economics 32: 59–96

Varga A (1988) University research and regional innovation: A spatial econometric analysis of academic knowledge transfer. Kluwer Academic Publishers, Boston

10 Universities as Agents in Regional Innovation Systems. Evaluating Patterns of Knowledge-Intensive Collaboration in Austria

Martina Fromhold-Eisebith and Doris Schartinger

ARC Seibersdorf Research GmbH, Division Systems Research Technology-Economy-Environment, Austria

10.1 Introduction

The use of universities as providers and promoters of know-how in the interests of regional economic innovativeness is a longstanding objective of technology policies throughout Europe. Calls for local knowledge and technology transfer (TT), meaning the deliberate and purposeful transfer of know-how from academia to practical applications, have recently been revived by the notion of regional innovation systems. In a normative sense, this emphasises the need for continuing inter-organisational interaction to induce industrial innovation, attributing major importance to institutions of higher education and R&D for effective local system dynamics (Edquist 1997; Cooke et al. 1998; De la Mothe and Paquet 1998). A range of policy measures aims to promote this interaction, such as the establishment of transfer offices at universities, specific public support programs, or science and technology centres to 'incubate' new enterprises run by academics.

However, ways in which to measure and evaluate the outcome and efficiency of TT linkages and their (regional) economic relevance are still a matter for debate (Tornatzky 2001; Bozeman 2000; Rappert et al. 1999; Charles et al. 1998; OECD 1998). Despite a vast number of case studies on university regions in European countries (for recent examples, see Braun and Voigt 2000; Charles 2000; Cooke et al. 2000; Jones-Evans and Klofsten 1997), important conceptual and methodological issues – only rarely discussed in these works – still need further exploration. Above all, this relates to the question of how to analyse the significance of TT to existing firms. TT assumedly represents an important contribution by universities to regional innovation systems, and may take a variety of forms ranging from casual informal conversation to permanent structures, such as the establishment of joint research laboratories. Integral assessments of TT should take into account not only the various forms of TT, but also regional peculiarities and actor characteristics. In particular, information on regional TT should be interpreted against the background of how the *provision* of applicable know-how by local universities relates to regional economic *receptiveness* to such transfers.

In contrast to this integral view, in recent years most of the studies on TT (see Varga 2000a, for an overview) have focused on partial aspects of TT, such as the detailed analysis of science-industry links in narrowly defined fields of research and technology (so-called "high-tech" industries, see Meyer-Krahmer and Schmoch 1998; Acs et al 1994; Bania et al. 1993; Rees 1991), on the aggregate effect of university research on knowledge production in firms (Varga 2000b; Anselin et al. 1997; Jaffe 1989), or on certain types of knowledge interaction such as citations of university research in firm patents (Almeida and Kogut 1995; Jaffe et al. 1993), personnel mobility (Hicks 2000; Almeida and Kogut 1995; Bania et al. 1992), joint publications (Hicks et al. 1996), and spin-off formations of new firms by university staff (Parker and Zilberman 1993; Kelly et al. 1992; Shachar and Felsenstein 1992). TT has also been examined with a strong focus on the use of new technology from universities (i.e., patents, prototypes) by firms (see Bozeman 2000, for an overview).

One major omission of surveys of the regional relevance of university-industry collaboration is that they collectively neglect crucial framework factors and indicators that significantly influence the valuation of regionalised data in the transfer projects as such. Focusing on those aspects, this chapter introduces a concept that tries to derive a more adequate evaluation of the extent to which universities contribute to regional innovation systems by knowledge-intensive collaboration with firms. The main questions addressed are:

- Which indicators should be considered in order to assess the degree to which a region already benefits from TT between universities and local industry?
- Consequently, are there ways to identify less than optimal integration of universities into regional innovation systems and underuse of transfer potential?

The chapter is organised as follows: After a brief discussion of the limitations of standard approaches assessing the regional impact of universities as know-how providers for industry, a conceptual framework is presented that suggests a set of indicators and information which should be eclectically combined when 'evaluating' (in a more qualitative than quantitative sense) the regional relevance of TT from academia within a regional innovation system. The concept is subsequently applied to an empirical case study that attempts to evaluate the significance of TT from two Austrian Universities of Technology (Vienna and Graz) to their respective regions, centring on data collected by Austrian universities on their R&D collaboration with firms. In this respect, the study represents a complementary approach to the chapter by Fischer and Varga on regional knowledge spillovers from Austrian universities; this may specifically enrich the debate on suitable methodologies. Finally, conclusions are drawn with respect to the conceptual and political issues which seem relevant for the general question of regional innovation analysis.

10.2 Limitations of Standard Approaches and Indicators on the Regional TT Impact of Universities

Three main approaches can be taken to evaluate the regional economic impact of TT from universities, involving macro, meso or micro levels of analysis, focusing either on large sets of compared regions, particular regions and universities, or on individual firms and collaboration projects in a particular region. Each is associated with different objectives and sets of indicators. They all have their merits, but also their limitations, and a complete account can only be composed eclectically, if at all. Actually, there seems to be no way to comprehensively and unequivocally identify the contributions of university-industry interaction to innovativeness, as Bozeman (2000, p. 627) concedes in his recent review of TT and economic effects: "The impacts are usually numerous and they are almost always difficult to separate from other parts of organisational life".

The macro perspective includes, firstly, studies that follow the knowledge production function approach, and secondly, studies that try to measure and evaluate knowledge flows and interactions between a number of universities and regions. Knowledge production function studies econometrically measure the correlation between R&D input and other data on universities and innovation-related output indicators – mostly patents – over a wide number of regions (e.g., the chapter by Fischer and Varga in this book; Anselin et al. 2000). They provide some evidence that spatial proximity matters in the sense that the co-location of academia and industry in the same region is associated with sector-specific innovative outcomes. However, there is no proof that the resulting innovations and registered patents have in fact emerged from real contact and collaboration between university and firms. This makes any differentiation between the impact of universities on regional innovativeness or industrial dynamics and those of other, possibly more influential factors, problematical. For this reason, and because of the fact that the widely used indicator of patent activities varies considerably between sectors and organisations regardless of their R&D intensity and innovativeness (e.g., Owen-Smith and Powell 2001), the results produced by many knowledge production function studies remain rather superficial. Furthermore, as these studies are aimed at assessing the aggregate university effect on innovation activities, the analysis does not allow for the evaluation of concrete TT processes.

There are, however, studies at the macro level that choose a different approach in that they attempt to track real contacts and interactions between universities and industry over a number of regions by means of either "paper trails" (Krugman 1991) or surveys. Jaffe et al. (1993), for instance, analyse the spatial distribution of patent citations in relation to that of the cited patents. Audretsch and Stephan (1996) investigate the regional affiliation patterns of university scientists with biotech firms. Both studies therefore account for actual flows of knowledge and reveal differentiated evidence for geographically limited benefits provided by universities to industry.

Other macro studies based on survey data on university-industry collaboration attempt to establish which determinants significantly favour the interaction, comparing a larger number of projects, academic institutions and industries (for recent work on Austria see Schartinger et al. 2001a and 2001b). These studies confirm the assumption that certain structural features of both university departments and the economy have an impact on the formation of knowledge-intensive linkages, which bears some policy relevance. However, questions of regional impact and region-specific patterns of collaboration have not been explored using the Austrian data available – they are discussed below. Although other investigations have also endeavoured to compare the percentages of regional academia-industry interaction for various universities (Allesch et al. 1988), such evaluations have not gone beyond establishing that the regional orientation of TT varies widely between academic fields and university locations.

Most of the research into the regional TT impact of universities draws on the meso level of analysis, and is sometimes comparative (Tornatzky 2001; Braun and Voigt 2000; Charles 2000; Cooke et al. 2000; Charles et al. 1998; Fromhold-Eisebith 1992a). This approach offers the best method of taking institutional and regional specifics into account in the process of assessment. Relevant studies attempt to quantify or qualitatively assess the actual relationships between certain universities and industrial partners in the region and beyond, and are based on information about recorded interactions. Their main conclusions are often derived from comparing the volume of regional flows with that of other spatial units or the total. Data on different modes of university-industry interaction may also be included, revealing a functionally and spatially differentiated picture. (For instance, the regional volume usually tends to be much higher in collaborative graduation theses or consulting projects for industrial partners than in contracted R&D.) Although this may reveal the relative significance of regional users of local academic expertise, most studies lack any further analysis of whether or not the numbers calculated indicate a satisfactory volume of TT. The assessment concept introduced below shows how ambiguous – or even almost meaningless – data on relative volumes of regional TT actually is, and that additional framework indicators are needed to clarify the situation.

Another limitation of regional studies is that they still do not capture the innovative effects actually emerging from the university-industry interactions identified. For instance, many patents generated in the course of R&D collaborations do not necessarily indicate the creation of a newly marketed product or a substantially improved production process. The financial value of a TT project linking academia and industry does not strictly correlate to the business benefit for the user firm. (The results of low-cost material tests may prevent a company from suffering exorbitant production losses, whereas often the outcome of major R&D projects does not translate into greater market success or increased profit.)

The extent to which university-industry interactions really lead to innovative results and industrial progress can only be determined by means of (aggregated) micro analysis based on surveys of individual firms and specific TT projects (for approaches along these lines, see Gonard 1999; Rappert et al. 1999; Gee 1993; Bleaney 1992). This involves establishing which benefits have actually accrued to the firm receiving know-how in each case of collaboration. But here research runs up against insurmountable limits on the acquisition of information. Many companies directly collaborating with universities are unable to clearly ascribe certain innovative consequences to such interaction, much less to quantify them or to ascertain all the relevant future implications. Written surveys are usually too vague concerning questions of effect to reveal truly comprehensive results. Thus, no regional investigation will ever manage to obtain a rate and quality of response high enough to allow the construction of a complete regional balance sheet of industrial benefits from university collaboration. Nevertheless, an attempt should be made to push forward the frontiers of knowledge in this area.

10.3 A Concept for Evaluating the Regional Relevance of TT from Universities

The authors' approach to evaluating regional university-industry collaborations draws mainly on the meso level of analysis, focusing on particular regions and taking local specifics into account. The methodology presented here (based on Fromhold-Eisebith 1992b) argues that three main categories of indicators must be eclectically combined in order to allow an assessment of the extent to which a region and its innovation system have already made use of the TT potential of a resident university, bearing in mind the limited scope for realisation. The same main categories are used in studies applying the methodology of interaction models for a different – but related – purpose, i.e., identifying determinants for the extent of TT within a spatial area (see for example Schartinger, Rammer et al. 2001). These categories relate to the following sets of indicators (see Fig. 10.1 for an overview):

- The first attempts to 'measure' regional TT as such, determining regional numbers and, above all, relative volumes for several means of recorded university-industry interaction and collaboration. (While numbers of projects with regional partners certainly represent an important quantitative indicator, calculated relative volumes are usually better suited to pinpoint the regional relevance of links.) (See Audretsch and Stephan 1996.)
- The second assesses the framework of knowledge supply, characterising the *provision* of regionally suitable know-how by the respective university.
- The third addresses the regional capacity to resonate academic knowledge, permitting a rough estimate of the *receptiveness* of the economic region to impulses from academia.

The main question that this approach attempts to answer is whether the relative volume of regional TT from a university to firms indicates that the role of the institution within the regional innovation system is adequate or inadequate. This in turn depends largely on an evaluation of the extent to which the university is actually able to contribute, given its potential of knowledge transfer in relation to the *receptiveness* of the economic region to such a transfer. An example may serve to illustrate this. Even when an investigation reveals that a university plays a small role in regional transfer, from a regional perspective this may still be positively interpreted if the structure of the regional economy makes it unreceptive to the large amount of know-how and assistance provided by the academic institution.

Universities offer many options for TT to industry with respect to the first set of indicators. These range from various types of R&D partnerships (such as those listed in OECD 1998) over formal or informal consulting, the provision of sophisticated testing and measuring facilities and of well-sorted scientific libraries to an array of people-bound or people-oriented kinds of transfer in the area of higher and further education, not to forget the important aspect of spin-off entrepreneurship (Schartinger, Rammer et al. 2001; Bozeman 2000; Charles et al. 1998; Parker and Zilberman 1993; Fromhold-Eisebith 1992a).

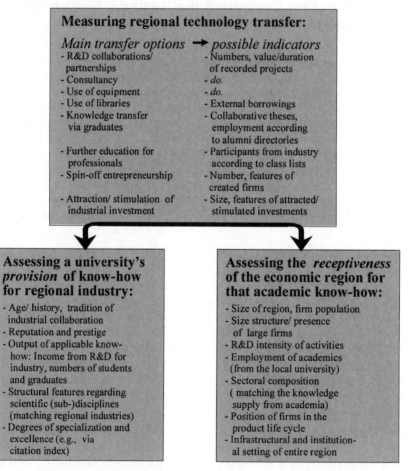

Measuring regional technology transfer:

Main transfer options ➤ *possible indicators*
- R&D collaborations/   - Numbers, value/duration
  partnerships   of recorded projects
- Consultancy   - *do.*
- Use of equipment   - *do.*
- Use of libraries   - External borrowings
- Knowledge transfer   - Collaborative theses,
  via graduates   employment according
     to alumni directories
- Further education for   - Participants from industry
  professionals   according to class lists
- Spin-off entrepreneurship   - Number, features of
     created firms
- Attraction/ stimulation of   - Size, features of attracted/
  industrial investment   stimulated investments

Assessing a university's *provision* of know-how for regional industry:
- Age/ history, tradition of industrial collaboration
- Reputation and prestige
- Output of applicable know-how: Income from R&D for industry, numbers of students and graduates
- Structural features regarding scientific (sub-)disciplines (matching regional industries)
- Degrees of specialization and excellence (e.g., via citation index)

Assessing the *receptiveness* of the economic region for that academic know-how:
- Size of region, firm population
- Size structure/ presence of large firms
- R&D intensity of activities
- Employment of academics (from the local university)
- Sectoral composition (matching the knowledge supply from academia)
- Position of firms in the product life cycle
- Infrastructural and institutional setting of entire region

Fig. 10.1. Sets of Indicators for Assessing the Regional Relevance of University-Industry Collaborations / TT. Source: Compilation by the authors

Any comprehensive evaluation of regional TT emanating from a university should therefore include various indicators, depending on the availability and accessibility of reliable data (see Fig. 10.1). TT resulting from R&D collaboration, for instance, can be captured by recording the number of projects, the location of industrial partners, and project value or duration. The regional transfer of highly qualified graduates might be assessed by analysing alumni directories, or by using knowledge from libraries by looking at records of external borrowing. Only when such a 'patchwork' of data is compiled can an investigation approximate the requirements of objectively assessing the role of a university within a regional innovation system. However, there will always be some dimensions of TT which may be partly reconstructed qualitatively, but which can barely be observed, much less measured. Of course, this does not mean that they are not essential for the functioning of an innovation system.

The second set of indicators relating to assessing the provision of know-how by universities should ideally cover aspects of its history, reputation and tradition of industrial collaboration, data on the volume of output relating to R&D activities as well as education, and information on the structural composition of scientific fields and research specialisations (Fig. 10.1). The latter are particularly important because they indicate the extent to which the university is oriented towards research issues of relevance to (regional) industries. On the one hand, the scientific disciplines are associated with different scopes and scales of possible practical application, with advantages for the engineering sciences, and above all for mechanical engineering (Schartinger et al. 2001a; Allesch et al. 1988). The question of matching fields of expertise of university departments and a larger number of local firms must also be taken into account with respect to regional impacts. On the other hand, the nature and degree of research specialisation determines the necessary coverage of the resulting TT, in accordance with the sectoral specialisations of regional industry (Fromhold-Eisebith 1992a and 1992b). Yet, impartially determining the degrees of academic specialisation or excellence is a difficult and delicate task that may only be suitably tackled by analysing science citation indices. It is important to include this aspect since the more specialised a university department becomes, the more seldom it is represented within the university setting of that country. Consequently, the spatial range of its TT flows to industrial recipients is necessarily wider, and its share in the regional transfer process is probably smaller. (This connectivity is illustrated by the examples of university departments and aircraft construction or parallel computing.)

This brings us to the third set of indicators that addresses the important issue of the structural receptiveness of a region's economy to TT stimuli from its university. It acknowledges and emphasises the fact that the ability of industries to respond to the transfer of academic know-how, i.e., the ability and propensity of firms to enter into external R&D collaboration, depends not only on spatial proximity, but also on certain structural and sectoral qualities (e.g., Fritsch and Lukas 2001; Rappert et al. 1999). In the first place, the size of the (defined) region is a determining factor, particularly with respect to the resident population of firms. In the following we concentrate only on the characteristics of companies constituting a regional economy, since these are most relevant to the question of R&D collaboration between a university and existing firms. The prerequisites for the institutional and infrastructural features of a region *per se* are not considered, despite their high importance for some other kinds of TT (the existence of technology parks favours the foundation of academic spin-off firms, for instance).

As research into technology diffusion and the behaviour of firms with respect to R&D collaboration has shown, particularly active and absorptive companies are characterised by certain structural features (Fritsch and Lukas 2001; Ewers and Fritsch 1987). On the one hand, the size of a firm plays a major role, since it is mainly larger firms with greater financial potential that engage in external knowledge acquisition. On the other hand, a firm's absorptive capacity (Cohen and Levinthal 1989, 1990), i.e., its propensity for and interest in collaborating with academia, correlates positively to its own involvement in corporate R&D and employment of highly qualified university graduates. In these cases, common interests and a 'common language' with academia substantially ease interaction, overcoming some of the barriers that are usually encountered between the 'work cultures' of universities and companies. Thus regions that boast large numbers of big firms as well as large numbers of firms performing R&D feature a much higher receptiveness to TT from academia than those that do not.

As mentioned above, the sectoral composition of regional industry sets the parameters for collaboration in several respects, depending on the structures for the provision of academic know-how. By nature, the intensity of R&D varies widely between economic sectors, as does their need for inputs of external know-how (Rappert et al. 1999; Faulkner and Senker 1994). Receptiveness to TT from academia is much higher in a university region characterised by a high accumulation of firms in technology-driven and knowledge-intensive industries (such as electrical or automotive engineering, chemical and pharmaceutical industries, engineering consulting) than in a locality based mainly on low-tech industries. A high relative volume of regional TT can be expected as a logical consequence particularly where the sectoral specialisations of companies located in a region correspond closely to the scientific specifics of a nearby university, and a low relative volume should evoke considerable political concern. However, a firm's current position in the product life cycle also plays a role in its actual demand for external inputs of know-how, regardless of sectoral characteristics.

Although the methodology presented here may improve the evaluation of regional university-industry collaboration, the caveat remains that the conclusions derived can only be vague and qualitative. Even when accurate statistical information is available for the structures of know-how-provision by universities as well as for the sectoral and structural features of regional economies, it will never be possible to quantitatively compare and assess actual local relative volumes of recorded TT against 'maximum potential relative volumes' with respect to the optimal exploitation of transfer possibilities based on structural constellations. Too many imponderable factors obfuscate the picture, such as psychological and personality factors enforcing (personal networks) or retarding contacts (entrepreneurial phlegm), irrespective of questions of technical correspondence. However, the following empirical section sets out to indicate the possibilities inherent in this methodological concept.

10.4 Evaluating Regional Patterns of Knowledge-Intensive University-Industry Collaboration in Austria

The approach is subjected to preliminary empirical testing in an evaluation of the regional patterns of TT from two Austrian technical universities (a first test was actually conducted much earlier for the German University of Technology in Aachen; Fromhold-Eisebith 1992a). Due to necessary limitations, the case study presented here can only consider one type of TT, and is restricted to a comparative evaluation for Graz and Vienna Universities of Technology (TU)) (see Schartinger, Rammer et al. 2001 for an analysis of various forms of TT from twelve major Austrian universities against the background of the structural characteristics of Austrian industry and the Austrian university scene). In this chapter, we draw on a reasonably comprehensive database of all official (i.e., officially recorded) research projects carried out by these two universities (AURIS database). Results on regional transfer volumes are interpreted against a background of information about the provision of applicable know-how by the universities, on the one hand, and the structural features of the regional economy on the other. This data is jointly analysed and interpreted according to the general assumptions discussed above, searching for evidence to confirm their validity.

To begin with, a brief general introduction of the objects of the investigation is given which outlines the major features of the Vienna and Graz regions and their respective TUs. Differences in the size and position of the study areas within the administrative hierarchy are also pointed out inasmuch as they are relevant to the interpretation of TT data. As a state (Bundesland) within the Austrian federal system, the capital city of Vienna easily ranks first with respect to size and concentration of political, intellectual, and economic power. According to the statistics for 2000 (all the following data is taken from the websites of the respective economic chambers: http://wko.at/wien), Vienna has a population of about 1.6 million people and altogether roughly 35,700 enterprises with nearly 490,000 employees. The city of Graz, although ranking second nationally, is much smaller, with 238,000 inhabitants and something over 6,400 enterprises employing almost 94,000 people. It only has the status of a political district, although it is the capital of the federal state of Styria. The latter has a total population of 1.2 million people, 24,800 enterprises, and 307,200 employees. The two study regions may therefore only be truly comparable at state level. In the case of Vienna, the surrounding federal state of Lower Austria is characterised by strong functional interdependencies with the national capital. As Vienna's hinterland, the area enriches the city's functional region by almost 1.4 million people, 36,000 businesses, and 412,000 employees.

One quality that unites the cities of Vienna and Graz is their role as outstanding centres of higher education, with a high concentration of potential particularly in the former (Fröhlich and Gassler 1999; Rohn 2000). Within the academic scene of each location, Graz TU is of much higher relative importance than Vienna TU because the latter is only one of a handful of larger local universities. In absolute terms, however, Graz TU is a lot smaller than Vienna TU. Whereas the former currently has about 11,000 students and 550 staff in research and teaching, the latter has over 19,000 students and roughly 1,000 scientific staff. However, to resume our central line of argumentation, the relative volumes of official regional TT to industrial partners are strikingly similar compared to these interregional and inter-organisational differences.

10.4.1 Regional Volumes of Knowledge-Intensive University-Industry Collaboration

Table 10.1 presents data on the relative spatial distribution of national and international partnerships in research projects undertaken with firms by Graz TU and Vienna TU. The numbers are calculated from the AURIS database, which provides information on all officially recorded research projects carried out by universities with counterparts in industry or science. By January 1999 a total of 3,656 joint research projects had been listed for the two TUs under investigation. These involved a total of 12,865 individual partnerships with firms or other research organisations (since many projects include several partners, the analysis focuses on partnerships rather than projects). In the main, the details regarding type and location of project partners provided by the database can be picked up for this analysis. (Unfortunately, this information cannot be statistically weighted by project value or duration.)

One of the main weaknesses of the AURIS database is that university departments are not obliged to report all of their research projects to the organisational unit collecting the data. Thus the inclination to report is likely to vary among departments. Academic units that carry out many research collaborations probably tend to report only projects exceeding a critical mass of budget and duration, whereas departments with fewer activities in this field may actually report every project conducted, regardless of size. Since local collaborations are usually smaller in volume than non-local ones (Fromhold-Eisebith 1992a), this may have implications for the assessment of regional TT as well. This is probably generally slightly underrepresented in the AURIS database. Additionally, university departments are often requested not to disclose any information on joint research projects by their industrial project partners. Information on project content as well as the identity of the collaborating company is therefore often kept secret. Despite these drawbacks, the database appears to provide a useful source for identifying and (comparatively) analysing the spatial patterns of co-operation between Austrian universities and their partners. At all events, this is the best and most comprehensive information available. Although the absolute numbers of partnerships may be inaccurate, structural characteristics of collaboration, such as the organisational composition and spatial patterns, should roughly correspond to reality, bearing in mind the limitations mentioned above.

Of the 12,865 partnerships of Graz and Vienna TUs, 1,460 (= 11 percent) relate to joint research projects with firms. This indicates the comparatively low propensity of these universities – particularly Vienna – to collaborate with industry in purely scientific relationships. Table 10.1 indicates the spatial distribution of the project partnerships with firms, showing the relative volumes for several spatial units. Although it would also be desirable to compare the absolute numbers of TT ventures for both universities, inconsistencies in the data set provided (widely differing temporal delimitation of data collection) prevent this. (Anyway, crude project numbers are a rather inadequate means of evaluation, since the size and economic impact of projects may vary considerably.) At first sight, the structural situation of both Graz and Vienna TUs seems quite similar. The former reports an impressive 22 percent of its project partnerships with firms in the relatively small city of Graz alone, and almost 33 percent with those in Styria as a whole. Vienna TU has roughly 30 percent of its industrial partnerships within the city limits, with partners in Lower Austria adding a negligible amount to this figure. Both universities – Vienna TU more so than Graz TU – engage to an even greater extent in projects with industrial partners in other countries. Although these figures may substantially overemphasise the actual situation due to the selective reporting routines of these universities (which surely favour their most prestigious external projects), one may infer that of the two universities, Graz TU, collaborates to a considerably higher extent with Austrian partners than Vienna TU.

Table 10.1 Spatial Distribution of Project Partnerships with Firms (in per cent)

Location of industrial partner	Graz TU	Vienna TU
Own political district	22.19	29.62
Surrounding region[a]	10.31	1.14
Rest of Austria	23.75	12.27
Abroad	35.94	54.25
Not possible to localise	7.81	2.72
Total [b]	100.00	100.00

Notes: [a]For Graz TU: state of Styria without the political district of Graz: for Vienna TU: state of Lower Austria. [b]A total of 1,460 partnerships were analysed. Due to the differing temporal delimitation of data collection, absolute numbers of partnerships should not be compared for both TUs and therefore are not reported here. Source: AURIS. Authors' own calculations.

Although these figures seem to already represent the final result of this evaluation, a more thorough assessment should take them only as a point of departure. The essential question is whether the relative volumes calculated for Graz TU and Vienna TU in fact indicate a similarly (un)satisfactory situation with respect to R&D collaboration with regional industry. As will be shown below, the numbers presented do not suffice to answer that question. The fact that Graz TU achieves this relative volume of regional TT despite the smaller size of its industrial population clearly indicates that such figures hardly have any intrinsic analytic value, and need to be further embedded in the framework indicators. They must also be assessed against information on the provision of academic know-how for regional industry.

10.4.2 Provision of Know-how for Regional Application by the Universities Investigated

There are several factors that should be taken into consideration in evaluating the possibilities of a university to provide know-how for regional industrial innovativeness in accordance with our methodological approach (Fig. 10.1). However, only the most crucial one is examined here. It relates to knowledge supply structures with respect to the disciplines and fields of research represented at Graz TU and Vienna TU. The relevant information is shown in Fig. 10.2, which compares the supply structures of both organisations using the indicator of authorised posts, i.e., fixed scientific and teaching staff. University employment by fields of research may be said to reflect to a high degree a political desire to support certain research activities, and is fairly stable over time for each institution. Thus, the figures for 1997 are likely to be representative of a longer period.

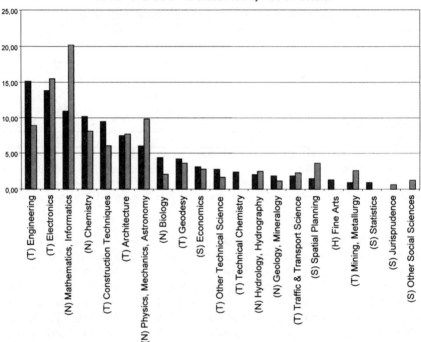

Fig. 10.2 The Knowledge Supply Structure: Authorised Posts per Field of Research. Source: Working Reports by Heads of Department 1997. Authors' own calculations. Graz TU: *n*= 549. Vienna TU: *n*=977.

This figure shows that both universities display roughly the same patterns of activity, despite their different sizes. As technical universities they are both relatively well endowed with disciplines of high practical relevance, and therefore offer quite good potential for (regional) TT.

However, a more detailed look at the figure reveals that Vienna TU appears to specialise particularly in the natural sciences, especially mathematics and informatics as well as physics/mechanics/astronomy. In contrast, Graz TU shows a slightly stronger focus on the academic fields of engineering and construction technology. This may lead us to infer that Graz TU has more to offer for immediate industrial application, while Vienna TU places greater emphasis on basic research with rather long-term perspectives for TT to (regional) economic agents. Although the discrepancies are rather small, they may help to explain why Graz TU is able to achieve a slightly higher relative volume of industrial collaboration with regional and national partners than Vienna TU. Against this background, it may be speculated that Graz TU should actually be able to collaborate even more with local partners because of the comparatively favourable know-how provision structures. However, we still need to take a closer look at the sectoral characteristics of regional industry in order to more adequately assess the possibilities for regional collaboration.

In addition to the information given in the chart, it would be desirable to include data on university researchers financed by third parties, i.e., external orders. This indicator should more adequately reflect the amount of academic R&D services provided to firms, and would therefore be better suited for comparing the differing supply structures of both universities. However, our data sources do not provide reliable information on this aspect. Even more importantly, the degree of scientific specialisation and excellence in major fields of scientific specialisation at Graz TU and Vienna TU cannot be assessed either, despite the major consequences which this may have for the expected geographical coverage of the supplies of academic know-how (see the theoretical considerations above).

10.4.3 Regional Receptiveness to the Transfer of Know-how from Technical Universities

As stated above, the Vienna agglomeration offers a substantially larger number of industries than either the city of Graz or the state of Styria. This may be an initial indication that the receptiveness of Vienna to TT from the local TU must be rated higher than in the case of Graz. Nevertheless, the relative volume of regional industrial collaboration is a mere 30 per cent for Vienna TU (Table 10.1). At this stage of the analysis, this is open to two possible interpretations. Firstly, this may indicate that the situation and role of the organisation within the regional innovation system are rather unsatisfactory (confirming the findings of Rohn 2000). Secondly, despite large numbers of local projects, Vienna TU may make an important contribution to the regional system in absolute terms, but is generally much more oriented towards extra-regional and international collaboration. Thus, further information is needed with respect to more meaningful indicators in order to verify our assumptions. Since the distribution of firm size does not differ substantially between the regional industries of Vienna and Styria (in both areas, a similarly large number of firms fall within the group of rather small enterprises with 20 to 49 employees), this indicator is not examined in any detail.

Fig. 10.3 illustrates the sectoral distribution of industrial R&D personnel (manufacturing only) in Vienna, on the one hand, and the state of Styria, on the other. The relative volumes of sectoral R&D employees in each (greater) region are given with respect to the industrial structures of the regional economy, and the industrial structures of the national economy. This data permits better evaluation of the absorptive capacity of local manufacturing firms of input from the local TU. (However, knowledge-intensive services are left out due to data limitations.) In order to ensure a more accurate assessment, the sectors depicted are sorted and categorised according to degree of technology intensity, making a distinction between high technology sectors, partly high technology sectors, medium high technology sectors, medium-low technology sectors, and low technology sectors.[1] This relates to the assumption formulated above that industrial sectors with a particularly high technology intensity are more inclined to maintain linkages with the local TU than others. Especially in the case of multi-technological products, several disciplines may have to complement each other in order to achieve innovation. These various kinds of knowledge can rarely be provided by a single firm, making interaction with external partners more likely.

In terms of crude numbers, Vienna has far more industrial R&D personnel than the greater Graz region (nearly 6,700, against fewer than 1,600). As Fig. 10.3 shows, both regions feature concentrations of technology-driven industries. In Vienna 73 percent of manufacturing R&D personnel are in the TV, Radio and Telecommunications sector (nace 32), which accounts for about 90 percent of total Austrian R&D personnel in this industry. Moreover, the city accounts for almost 60 percent of nation-wide R&D activities in Other Motor Vehicle industries and over 40 percent in the Medical, Precision and Optical Instruments sector. Vienna stands out as well with respect to the Chemical Industry and some medium-high technology sectors, such as the Electrical/Electronics Industry. By contrast, Styria is relatively strong in Office Machinery Production, where the region boasts about 90 percent of all R&D personnel in the whole of Austria. Furthermore, Graz and Styria, respectively, exhibit a high degree of specialisation in the Motor Vehicle Industry and Engineering, while TV, Radio and Telecommunication as well as the medium-low technology Basic Metal and Metal Products industries are also significant. Altogether we conclude that, with respect to the differing R&D profiles of the study regions, the Vienna region reveals a higher technological intensity than the Graz region.

---

[1] This follows the technology classification of the OECD (1999). We also introduce the category 'partly high technology' because our database does not separate either the Pharmaceutical Industry from the Chemical Industry (nace 24), or Aircraft Production from Other Motor Vehicle Industries (nace 35).

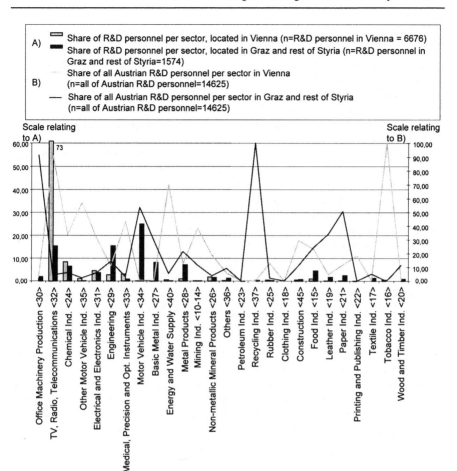

Fig. 10.3 R&D in the Manufacturing Sectors in Vienna and Graz / Styria. Source: Statistics Austria, Strukturleistungserhebung 1995. Authors' own calculations.

This result underscores the assumption that the relative volumes of regional R&D collaboration with industry have to be evaluated against the background of a region's sectoral composition. Although industry in Vienna has a higher techno-logical intensity, the TU's relative volume of regional R&D collaborations is quite low, confirming our conclusion the Vienna TU is comparatively weakly oriented towards its own region (regardless of the considerable value which this TT may have for local recipients). This is in line with more generalised conclusions by other authors (Fröhlich and Gassler 1999; Rohn 2000; Diez 2001), and is espe-cially true by comparison with Graz TU and its surrounding region.

A final example provides additional evidence that the regional collaboration of Graz TU and Vienna TU is manifestly influenced by the specific structures of their regional economies. Figs. 10.4a and 10.4b give a more detailed picture of the sectoral distribution of the project partnerships of both universities with firms in their (greater) regions, again calculated from AURIS data. In order to track consistencies with the composition of regional industry, we display the relative volumes of collaboration partners per sector alongside the respective relative volumes of sectoral R&D personnel (taken from Fig. 10.3).

The results are twofold. Firstly, the collaboration profiles of the two universities differ considerably, although they appear to be characterised by similar patterns of specialisation in terms of personnel allocation (Fig. 10.2). This illustrates the necessity of looking beyond crude relative volumes of regional TT collaboration in order to assess the function of a university within its regional innovation system. Secondly, these collaboration profiles to some extent reflect the sectoral composition of the respective regional industries in relation to the data on R&D activities.

This is mainly evident for Graz TU (Fig. 10.4b). The university has a particularly high relative volume of regional TT co-operation in the fields of Motor Vehicle Industry, Mechanical Engineering and Basic Metal Industries. This corresponds quite well to the distribution of industrial R&D personnel in the surrounding region. For Vienna TU, on the other hand, the relative volumes of project partnerships per sector seem to correlate significantly less with those of regional R&D employees (Fig. 10.4a).

This can be explained partly by the fact that this organisation focuses more on collaborations with partners in service industries (e.g., Producer-Related Services, Recreational Activities), which rather reflect the economic structure of the national capital, but are not captured in the database on R&D personnel.

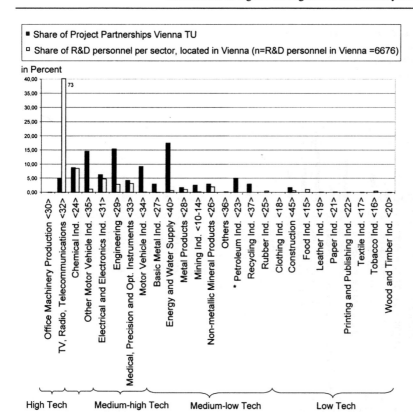

Fig. 10.4a Sectoral Distribution of Regional Project Partnerships of Vienna TU with Firms Compared to that of Industrial R&D Personnel in Vienna. Source: AURIS. Authors' own calculations.

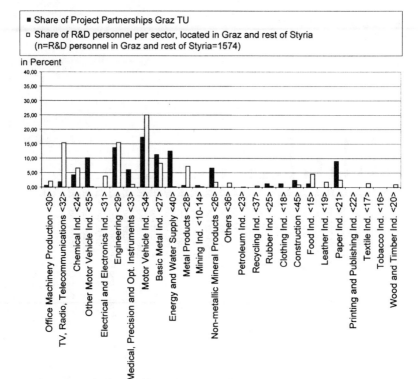

Fig. 10.4b Sectoral Distribution of Regional Project Partnerships of Graz TU with Firms Compared to that of Industrial R&D Personnel in Styria. Source: AURIS. Authors' own calculations.

Considering the relatively strong position of the Chemical Industry, the Electrical and Electronics Industry, and the Medical, Precision and Optical Instruments sector, the collaboration activities of Vienna TU appear to be coherent with the R&D potential of the Vienna region as well. In some sectors both universities show a disproportionately high propensity to collaborate locally (e.g., Energy and Water Supply, Other Motor Vehicle Industry; Vienna TU only: Engineering; Graz TU only: Paper Industry, Non-metallic Mineral Products). In other sectors, however, TT relationships fall far below expectations. For instance, both TUs display strikingly little orientation towards regional firms in the TV, Radio and Telecommunications sector. Does this indicate a crucial gap in local university-industry collaboration, or are there other explanations? At all events, such conclusions from integral data analysis definitely provide a focused point of departure for more detailed empirical investigations and policy considerations.

10.5 Conclusions

Although the empirical evidence provided above with respect to knowledge-intensive collaboration of two Austrian technical universities with regional firms may only be fragmentary, it does suffice to underscore how important it is to consider several sets of indicators when analysing the role of a university in its regional innovation system. In addition to information on relative volumes of regional knowledge transfer to industry, information on structures for the *provision* of academic know-how for regional applications and on factors relating to regional economic *receptiveness* to such transfers must also be included in order to obtain a better basis for evaluation. The examples of Graz TU and Vienna TU clearly illustrate that similar relative volumes of regional university-industry collaboration are not necessarily equivalent to similar ratings for these organisations as collaboration partners for local industry. A more realistic evaluation can only be obtained when the specific features of the respective universities and regional economies are also taken into account. Against this background it would appear that the regional collaboration activities of Vienna TU are apparently below those of Graz TU in relative terms (however, this does not explicitly indicate the inferior quality of university R&D as such).

Within this framework, the objective of this chapter is to prove the necessity of a multi-dimensional approach to assessment, and to suggest a methodological solution rather than to fully demonstrate the empirical application of such a method. In order to do this properly, it would be necessary to capture and display more indicators – those named in our conceptual approach – than could be done within the limited space of this chapter. We nevertheless hope to have made a constructive contribution to the general debate on how to approach the objectives of regional innovation analysis, offering some options, but also indicating the limitations of measurability. Our methodological elaboration may also help in the design of regional transfer policies and facilitate the checking of their results. This may put the discrepancies between political expectations and the realistic possibilities of regional university-industry collaboration into perspective.

References

Acs ZJ, Fitzroy F, Smith I (1994) High technology employment and university R&D spillovers: Evidence from US cities. Paper presented at the 41st North American Meeting of the Regional Science Association International, Niagara Falls

Allesch J, Preiß-Allesch D, Spengler U (1988) Hochschule und Wirtschaft: Bestandsaufnahme und Modelle der Zusammenarbeit. Verlag TÜV Rheinland, Cologne

Almeida P, Kogut B (1995) The geographic localisation of ideas and the mobility of patent holders. Paper presented at the Conference on Small and Medium-Sized Enterprises and the Global Economy, Organized by CIBER, University of Maryland

Anselin L, Varga A, Acs ZJ (1997) Local geographic spillovers between university research and high technology innovations. Journal of Urban Economics 42: 422–448

Anselin L, Varga A, Acs ZJ (2000) Geographic and sectoral characteristics of academic knowledge externalities. Papers in Regional Science 79: 435–443

Audretsch DB, Stephan PE (1996) Company-scientist locational links: The case of biotechnology. American Economic Review 86: 641–652

Bania N, Calkins L, Dalenberg R (1992) The effects of regional science and technology policy on the geographic distribution of industrial R&D laboratories. Journal of Regional Science 32: 209–228

Bania N, Eberts R, Fogarty M (1993) Universities and the startup of new companies: Can we generalise from Route 128 and Silicon Valley? Review of Economics and Statistics 75: 761–766

Bleaney MF (1992) What does a university add to its local economy? Applied Economics 24: 305–311

Bozeman B (2000) Technology transfer and public policy: A review of research and theory. Research Policy 29: 627–655

Braun G, Voigt E (eds) (2000) Regionale Innovationspotentiale von Universitäten. Rostocker Beiträge zur Regional- und Strukturforschung 151. Rostocker Beiträge zur Regional- und Strukturforschung 15: 41–65

Charles DR (2000) Universities and regions: An international perspective. Paper presented at the Annual Conference of the Society for Research into Higher Education 'HE Futures: Policy Prospects & Institutional Change', University of Leicester

Charles DR, Rappert B, Webster A, Widrum P (1998) The commercialisation of university research in the local economy: Institutional practices and benefits analysis. SATSU Working Paper Series, Anglia University, Cambridge

Cohen WM, Levinthal DA (1989) Innovation and learning: The two faces of R&D. Economic Journal 99: 569–596

Cohen WM, Levinthal DA (1990) Absorptive capacity: A new perspective on learning and innovation. Administrative Science Quarterly 35: 128–152

Cooke P, Manning C, Huggins R (2000) Problems of systemic learning transfer and innovation – Industrial liaison and academic entrepreneurship in Wales. Zeitschrift für Wirtschaftsgeographie 44: 246–260

Cooke P, Uranga MG, Etxebarria G (1998) Regional systems of innovation: An evolutionary perspective. Environment and Planning A 30: 1563–1584

De la Mothe J, Paquet G (eds) (1998) Local and regional systems of innovation. Kluwer Academic Publishers, Dordrecht

Diez JR (2001) Innovative links between industry and research institutes – How important are they for firm start ups in the metropolitan regions of Barcelona, Vienna and Stockholm? In: Koschatzky K, Kulicke M, Zenker A (eds) Innovation networks. Concepts and challenges in the European perspective, Physica-Verlag, Heidelberg, pp 93–108

Edquist C (ed) (1997) Systems of innovation: Technologies, institutions and organisations. Pinter, London

Ewers H-J, Fritsch M (1987) Unterschiede zwischen frühen und späten Übernehmern computergestützter Techniken im verarbeitenden Gewerbe der Bundesrepublik Deutschland. Wirtschaftswissenschaftliche Dokumentation der TU Berlin, Discussion Paper 119, Berlin

Faulkner W, Senker J (1994) Making sense of diversity: Public-private sector research linkages in three technologies. Research Policy 23: 673–695

Fritsch M, Lukas R (2001) Who cooperates on R&D? Research Policy 30: 297–312

Fröhlich J, Gassler H (1999) Das Innovationssystem Wiens und Ansatzpunkte für technologiepolitische Strategien. In: Schmee J, Weigl A (eds) Wiener Wirtschaft 1945–1998: Geschichte – Entwicklungslinien – Perspektiven. Peter Lang, Frankfurt and

8: Geschichte – Entwicklungslinien – Perspektiven. Peter Lang, Frankfurt and Vienna (Seibersdorf Research Report OEFZS-S-0004)

Fromhold-Eisebith M (1992a) Wissenschaft und Forschung als regionalwirtschaftliches Potential? Das Beispiel von Rheinisch-Westfälischer Technischer Hochschule und Region Aachen. Informationen und Materialien zur Geographie der Euregio Maas-Rhein, Beiheft Nr. 4. Maas-Rhein Institut für Angewandte Geographie, Aachen

Fromhold-Eisebith M (1992b) Meßbarkeit und Messung des regionalen Wissens- und Technologietransfers aus Hochschulen. In: Niedersächsisches Institut für Wirtschaftsforschung (ed) Erfolgskontrollen in der Technologiepolitik. NIW-Workshop 1992, Hannover, pp 117–136

Gee RE (1993) Technology transfer effectiveness in university-industry cooperative research. International Journal of Technology Management 8: 652–675

Gonard T (1999) Public research-industry relationships: Efficiency conditions in current innovation. International Journal of Technology Management 17: 334–350

Harmon B (1997) Mapping the university technology transfer process. Journal of Business Venturing 12: 423–434

Hicks D (2000) Using innovation indicators for assessing the efficiency of industry-science relationships. Paper presented at the Joint German-OECD Conference 'Benchmarking Industry-Science Relations', Berlin

Hicks D, Isard P, Martin B (1996) A morphology of Japanese and European corporate research networks. Research Policy 25: 359–378

Jaffe AB (1989) The real effects of academic research. American Economic Review 79: 957–970

Jaffe AB, Trajtenberg M, Henderson R (1993) Geographic localisation of knowledge spillovers as evidenced by patent citations. Quarterly Journal of Economics 108: 577–598

Jones-Evans D, Klofsten M (1997) Universities and local economic development: The case of Linköping. European Planning Studies 5: 77–93

Kelly K, Weber J, Friend J, Atchinson S, DeGeorge G, Holstein W (1992) Hot spots: America's new growth regions are blossoming despite the slump. Business Week 29: 80–88

Krugman P (1991) Increasing returns and economic geography. Journal of Political Economy 99: 483–499

Meyer-Krahmer F, Schmoch U (1998) Science-based technologies: University-industry interactions in four fields. Research Policy 27: 835–851

OECD (1998) Trends in university-industry research partnerships. STI Review 23: 39–65

OECD (1999) OECD science, technology and industry scoreboard. Benchmarking knowledge based economies. OECD, Paris

Owen-Smith J, Powell WW (2001) To patent or not: Faculty decisions and institutional success at technology transfer. Journal of Technology Transfer 26: 99–114

Parker DD, Zilberman D (1993) University technology transfers: Impacts on local and US economies. Contemporary Policy Issues 11: 87–99

Phillips FY, Eto M (1998) University research and technology transfer: Featuring special section. Technological Forecasting and Social Change 58: 205–265

Rahm D (1997) Patterns of university-industry interaction. In: Lee YS (ed) Technology transfer and public policy. Quorum Books, Westport, pp 125–138

Rappert B, Webster A, Charles DR (1999) Making sense of diversity and reluctance: Academic-industrial relations and intellectual property. Research Policy 28: 873–890

Rees G (1991) New information technologies and vocational education and training in the new information technologies in the European community. Background Report, Commission of the European Communities, Cardiff

Rohn W (2000) Forschungseinrichtungen in der Agglomeration Wien. Stellung im Innovationsprozess und Einbindung in innovative Netzwerke. Verlag der Österreichischen Akademie der Wissenschaften, Vienna

Sargeant A, Sadler-Smith E. Dawson A (1998) University collaboration and regional economic development – Exploring the potential. Local Economy 13: 257–266

Schartinger D, Rammer C, Fischer MM, Fröhlich J (2001a) Knowledge interactions between university and industry in Austria: Sectoral patterns and determinants. Research Policy, forthcoming

Schartinger D, Schibany A, Gassler H (2001b) Interactive relations between universities and firms: Empirical evidence for Austria. Journal of Technology Transfer 26: 255–268

Schmoch U (1999) Interaction of universities and industrial enterprises in Germany and the United States: A comparison. Industry and Innovation 6: 51–68

Shachar A, Felsenstein D (1992) Urban economic development and high technology industry. Urban Studies 29: 839–855

Tornatzky LG (2001) Benchmarking university-industry technology transfer: A six year retrospective. Journal of Technology Transfer 26: 269–277

Varga A (2000a) Local academic knowledge transfers and the concentration of economic activity. Journal of Regional Science 40: 289–309

Varga A (2000b) Regional economic effects of university research: A survey. Working Paper, Department for Economic Geography and Geoinformatics, University of Economics and Business Administration, Vienna

Vedovello C (1998) Firms' R&D activity and intensity and the university-enterprise partnerships. Technological Forecasting and Social Change 58: 215–226

11 ICT and Knowledge Challenges for Entrepreneurs in Regional Economic Development

Roger Stough, Rajendra Kulkarni and Jean Paelinck

The Mason Enterprise Center, School of Public Policy, George Mason University, Fairfax, Virginia, USA

11.1 Introduction

This paper examines the knowledge needs of entrepreneurs in a regional context with particular emphasis on the information and communication technology (ICT) industry sector. The paper begins by clarifying and defining the basic concepts. This is followed by the introduction of the entrepreneurial fountain as a model of the entrepreneurial milieu and as a framework for examining factors that influence the expansion and contraction of knowledge and entrepreneurial activity. The role knowledge plays in entrepreneurial discovery and action is thus examined and the implications are examined. The paper ends with a set of conclusions and recommendations for future research.

Knowledge has many meanings ranging from raw information or data to understanding and comprehension. In this paper the knowledge concept is on the understanding end of this spectrum. It means know-how, comprehension, understanding, judgement, insight, wisdom and learning. These attributes are central to the role entrepreneurs play in discovering new products and processes, and creating and implementing plans to produce them. The knowledge needs of entrepreneurs drive the development of new and valued organisations and institutions, and influence behaviour patterns of entrepreneurs including their business location decisions. Both of these topics are of concern here.

Like knowledge, entrepreneurs have been defined in many ways. A rather generic definition after Stevenson et al. (1992) has been adapted for this paper. Stevenson and his colleagues see entrepreneurs as creating unique packages of resources to exploit opportunities. The weakness of this definition is that it fails to sufficiently emphasise the importance of discovery (Fiet 1996) in the entrepreneurial process. The entrepreneurial process then is that which discovers opportunities and creates resource packages leading to the exploitation of the opportunities. Morris et al. (2001) characterise this process in six steps: opportunity identification (discovery); concept development; determining resource requirements; resource acquisition; concept implementation and management; and, harvesting the venture or the fruits of the venture (Fig. 11.1).

As a concept, entrepreneurship holds an interesting and provocative position in the economics literature. In mainstream neo-classical economics it has received at best minimal attention because there is little or no incentive for the entrepreneur to assume the risk of creating new products or processes when only average profits are possible (see Fiet 1996; Jacobson 1992). This is the outcome when equilibrium (Marshall 1961) conditions (information and allocational efficiency) are assumed. Thus, with marginal rates of return for all buyers and sellers equal (Fiet 1996) there is no incentive for the entrepreneur to assume the risk of creating new products or processes. The Austrian economics view assumes that the economy is at all times in a state of disequilibrium (Schumpeter 1971). This enables entrpreneurs to exploit market imbalances and thereby earn above average or pure profits. Acquiring knowledge and information about opportunities associated with the related imbalances are therefore opportunities for above average profits. The Austrians provide the motivational argument for entrepreneurial discovery and behaviour.

From a policy perspective entrepreneurship may be viewed as a supply-side phenomenon. On the supply side, transportation infrastructure serves to reduce transaction costs in a regional economy. Like transportation infrastructure, entrepreneurship and the (soft) infrastructure that supports it may be viewed as contributing to regional economic performance (job creation, revenue and tax generation) by reducing the transaction costs of creating new products and services. Concern here is with the role of knowledge and information in the entrepreneurial process and related entrepreneurial infrastructure policy.

The concept of region employed is the functional region. With this view regions are defined in terms of their functions, e.g., cultural, economic, political, etc. In this case concern is with functional economic regions. Such regions are often defined in terms of their fields of economic or cultural influence, e.g., service hinterlands and labour fields represented by commuting patterns. Metropolitan regions or development corridors are examples of functional economic regions.

The final concept requiring some elaboration if not clarification is the information and communication technology (ICT) sector. This sector is composed of a wide range of product and service technologies including computer hardware, software and services and a host of telecommunications functions that include wire or wireline, wireless, satellite products and services. In a fundamental sense it includes the fusion of these ICT components into a local, regional, national and global infrastructure that has increasingly contributed to destabilisation of most organisations and institutions in society.

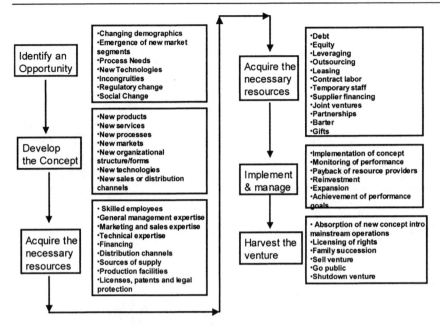

Fig. 11.1. Framework of Entrepreneurial Process. Source: Adapted from Morris, Kuratko and Schindehutte, Entreprenuership and Innovation, Feb. 2001, p. 40

ICT has enabled major reductions in transactions costs across most processes in society including such diverse ones as trade, politics, religion, education, sales, construction, recreation, and so on. Consequently, it has grown rapidly (Figs. 11.2–11.4). ICT functions as a new generic technology that has impacted society both broadly and deeply. As such, it may be viewed as a mega-innovation wave that has moved not only the economy of the industrial period from near equilibrium conditions but other societal systems as well. ICT has, in essence, destabilised the near equilibrium conditions of an earlier time and contributed to conditions of greater disequilibrium. The importance of ICT is thus that it has created prime conditions for entrepreneurial discovery and action.

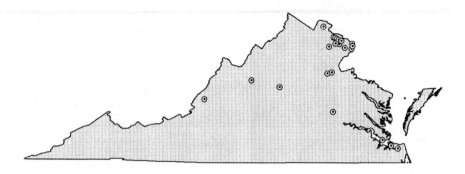

Fig. 11.2. Technology Firms by Location in 1970

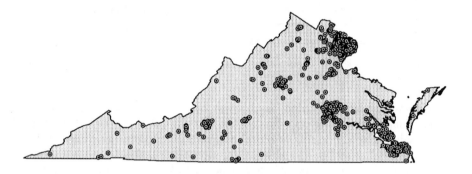

Fig. 11.3. Technology Firms by Location in 1998

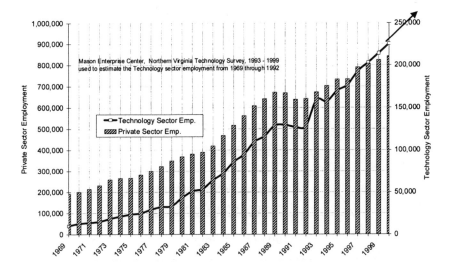

Fig. 11.4. Technology and Private Sector in Northern Virginia: 1969–2000

11.2 The Entrepreneurial Fountain

At any given time in a region entrepreneurial potential may be symbolised by a fountain that spawns a few high potential ventures at the apex and houses a multitude of loosely formed ideas, thoughts and concepts for new ventures at the base (Fig. 11.5). The base of the fountain may be thought of as composed of entrepreneurial turbulence in that it is here that entrepreneurial discovery is occurring with, in many cases, nothing more than a filmy view of a business or technical concept. As such ideas gain structure and definition they may be viewed as moving up in the pyramid and therefore moving from idea/discovery on through the various stages of the process (see Figs. 11.1 and 11.5). The entrepreneurial fountain is a stylised model where components of the entrepreneurial process are ordered sequentially from idea generation to execution. However, the process in reality is quite messy with a good bit of overlap and counter-ordering of components.

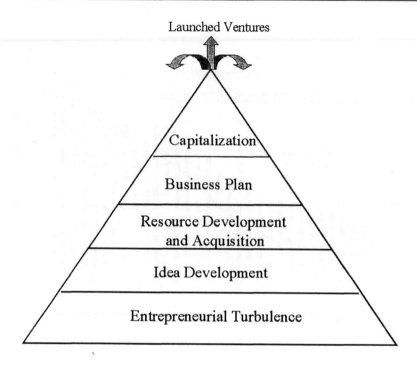

Fig. 11.5. Entrepreneurial Fountain: Static Model

It is well understood that the level of entrepreneurial activity varies by location and by time (Acs et al. 1999). This can be symbolised for a specific region by an expansion or contraction of the fountain (Fig. 11.6). In a general way the size of the fountain for any given region will depend on various factors including population, industrial structure, and wealth.

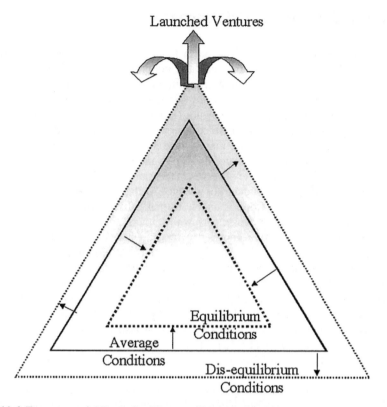

Fig. 11.6. Entrepreneurial Fountain: Change or Dynamic Model

But given the view of entrepreneurship adopted in this paper the fountain should be larger the stronger the disequilibrium conditions and smaller the more conditions tend toward equilibrium. It may be argued that ICT has destabilised the economic structure of earlier decades. This has increased risk and uncertainty, a risk and uncertainty that is reflected in a rise in entrepreneurial activity. That much of the entrepreneurial activity of the 1990s was financed by non-traditional investment is indicative of higher risk and disequilibrium conditions. But these were background conditions that impacted all regions. So why have some regions' ICT sectors expanded greatly during recent decades while others have lagged or regressed? Recent research of firm formation rates suggests that human capital and market size (agglomeration) are central attributes impacting the level of entrepreneurial activity (Armington and Acs 2000). R&D infrastructure also appears to be important in some if not many cases. Certainly, entrepreneurial infrastructure must also be important. But entrepreneurial infrastructure has not been examined systematically although there is a vast literature on what is needed to create new firms.

11.3 The Entrepreneurial Process

The entrepreneurial process is depicted in Figs. 11.1–11.5. At the foundation of the process lies the discovery of ideas and opportunities for new ventures. Fiet (1996) identifies four different roles for entrepreneurs in the discovery process: risk bearer (Cantillion 1931); innovator (Schumpeter 1936, 1939, 1942, 1947, 1961 and 1971); risk bearer and innovator (Baudeau 1910); and Arbitrageur (Kirzner 1973, 1979a, and 1979b). The risk bearer uses knowledge (from past experience or acquired) to reduce risk; the innovator to creatively combine factors of production; the risk bearer/innovator as above; and the arbitrageur to identify opportunities for risk arbitrage. He observes that what each has in common is the acquisition of specific risk reducing knowledge. At the same time, some would-be entrepreneurs are diverted from or unable to make discoveries because of uncertain returns from potential investments while others are not. In Fiet's view the ability to make cost effective knowledge investments is what enables entrepreneurs to envision discoveries necessary for venture development. He takes issue with the view that entrepreneurs have a special ability, are smarter, more diligent or more alert and focuses his analysis on the assumption that entrepreneurs, in a fundamental sense, reduce risk by knowledge they have or acquire and how they process and evaluate this knowledge. But knowledge acquisition can become a sunk cost and purchasing the wrong information also exacts a time cost. Thus, from this perspective, Fiet (1996, p. 420) defines an entrepreneur as "someone who optimizes the tradeoff between investing too much or too little in specific, risk-reducing signals (knowledge)."

Fiet then sees the use and acquisition of knowledge as central to the definition of entrepreneurs and to the foundation of the entrepreneurial process. We must ask then under what conditions are entrepreneurs able to best identify opportunities and at the same time optimise the processing of risk reducing signals in the discovery process? One hypothesis is offered by the Austrian economists who would view periods (contexts) with high levels of economic disequilibrium and thus periods of high risk as generating more opportunities for entrepreneurs (Fig. 11.6). Additionally, the literature suggests that contexts (regions or times) where information and knowledge (especially tacit) are widespread, communication infrastructure (associations and other venues for exchanging knowledge) is well developed for evaluating it, and the population is highly educated also provide optimal conditions for the entrepreneur. Regions with high quality human capital and high levels of agglomeration of economic activity would therefore be more likely to exhibit high levels of entrepreneurial activity. In periods of greater risk and therefore disequilibrium these conditions would be amplified.

Regions with these general attributes would be expected to have additional attributes and deeper entrepreneurial infrastructure. First, such regions are likely to have or be in the process of creating advanced levels of entrepreneurial infrastructure. Figs. 11.7–11.9 depict, in increasing complexity, the components of such infrastructure.

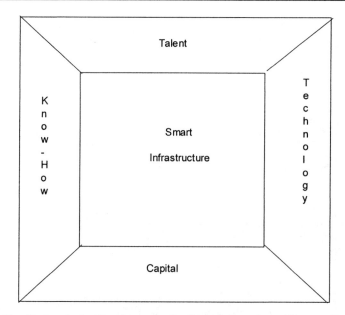

Fig. 11.7. Key Factors in the Development of a Smart Infrastructure (Source: Smilor and Wakelin 1990)

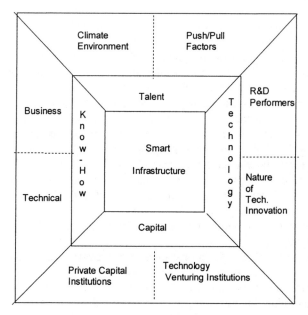

Fig. 11.8. Environmental Conditions (Source: Smilor and Wakelin 1990)

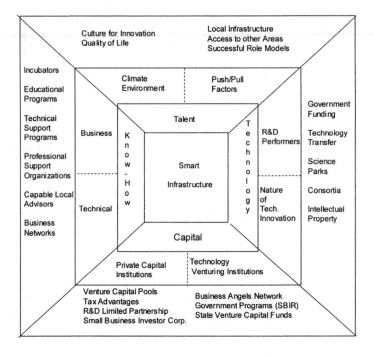

Fig. 11.9. Policy Implications (Source: Smilor and Wakelin 1990)

Additionally, as agglomeration and human capital become greater, so would the variety and number of supporting organisations and institutions. For example, in the U.S. National Capital Region, there were 3 formal incubators in 1997; today there are more than 50, symbolising the explosion in ICT new enterprise start-ups that occurred there in the mid and late 1990s. In a study of angel and venture capital organisations in the state of Virginia it was found that the number, range and diversity of capital organisations increased considerably as the analysis moved from the far rural hinterlands to the urbanised Northern Virginia part of the state. The point of these examples is to suggest that entrepreneurial discovery and venture development levels in a region depend a great deal on the level of infrastructure available to the entrepreneur. As this infrastructure grows the ability to acquire risk-reducing information increases thereby reducing a knowledge challenge of the entrepreneur.

Second, in such regions functional dependence among the different ICT subsectors would be expected to be expressed with a fair amount of spatial or geographical clustering. A case study of three ICT intensive regions in the U.S. is undertaken to examine this hypothesis. A view implied if not asserted in the industrial clustering literature (Rosenfeld 1997; Bergman, Feser and Sweeney 1996; Held 1996; Saxenian 1994; Porter 1990) is that the proximal location of would-be entrepreneurs in such clusters increases knowledge sharing and exchange and thereby reduces risk. This in turn improves the probability of successful venture development. If this is the case one would expect to find a strong positive relationship between ICT sub-sector functional dependence levels and levels of their spatial clustering. A case study of three ICT intensive regions in the U.S. is undertaken to examine this hypothesis.

11.4 Geographic and Functional Clustering and Entrepreneurial Risk: Case Study

Establishment-specific data for 33 ICT sub-sectors (see Table 11.1) in three U.S. metropolitan areas (Austin, Texas; Boston Massachusetts; and Washington D.C.) are examined to test a hypothesis that the more functionally dependent ICT subsectors are, the more tightly clustered they will be in geographic space. The importance of this hypothesis stems from the above conceptual analysis that argued that knowledge acquisition reduces risk and promotes greater entrepreneurial activity. These regions have been selected because they all have large ICT sectors of different sizes and thus serve as good examples for illustration purposes.

The data for this study include establishments by ICT sector (SIC number) and the respective geographical co-ordinates and centres of mass of each subsector (source: own computations); Figs. 11.10–11.13 reproduce that information graphically.

Recognising that innovation and entrepreneurial activity often occur through combining different technologies or processes, knowledge acquisition in ICT would then likely occur more fully and rapidly in the more interdependent ICT sectors. Such functional clustering should be manifested in corresponding spatial clustering. In short, the greater the functional dependence between two ICT sectors the greater (closer) they will tend to cluster spatially or geographically. The purpose of this case study is to test this proposition (for an earlier version of this analysis see Stough et al. 2001).

Table 11.1 lists the ICT sectors selected for this analysis (Stough et al. 2000; data derived from Business Analyst 1.1, 1999, http://www.esri.com). The 33 4-digit SIC sectors were selected based on earlier work (Stough et al. 1998).

The MSAs that have been analysed are:

- the Austin – San Marcos (TX) MSA;
- the Boston (MA and NH) MSA;
- the Washington – MD – VA – WV MSA.

They are designated by A, B and W, respectively. Table 11.1 provides the data for the number of plants observed in each MSA; they total 2,141 (A), 8,313 (B) and 8,503 (W) respectively.

The subsequent parts of the case study present a more analytical description of the observed patterns.

Table 11.1. Number of Establishments by SIC by MSA

SIC Category	SIC	Austin MSA	Boston MSA	Wash. MSA
Electronic Computers	3571	34	103	83
Computer Storage Devices	3572	6	34	15
Computer Terminals	3575	7	31	18
Computer Peripherals	3577	33	195	62
Calculating and Accounting Machines	3578	0	9	7
Office Machines	3579	2	14	11
Telephone and Telegraph apparatus	3661	11	78	62
TV and Cable comm. equipment	3663	14	99	91
Electron Tubes	3671	1	13	3
Printed Circuit Boards	3672	32	167	29
Semiconductor and related devices	3674	49	130	17
Electronic Capacitors	3675	0	4	1
Electronic Resistors	3676	1	4	0
Electronic coils and transformers	3677	1	19	62
Electronic connectors	3678	3	19	1
Electronics components, nec	3679	46	219	60
Magnetic and Optical Recording Media	3695	14	40	36
Radio Telephone Communications	4812	52	203	217
Telephone Communications, exc. Radio	4813	206	531	640
Telegraph and other Communications	4822	12	38	49
Radio Broadcast Station	4832	44	168	159
Television Broadcast Station	4833	11	53	91
Cable and other pay TV services	4841	35	170	118
Communication services, nec	4899	33	77	138
Computer Programming Service	7371	560	2157	2049
Prepackaged Software	7372	216	816	547
Computer Integrated Systems design	7373	174	806	1236
Data Processing and Preparation	7374	140	405	561
Information Retrieval Services	7375	37	120	155
Computer Facilities Management	7376	4	19	38
Computer rental and leasing	7377	8	56	45
Computer maintenance and repair	7378	83	342	379
Computer related services, nec	7379	272	1174	1523
Total		2141	8313	8503

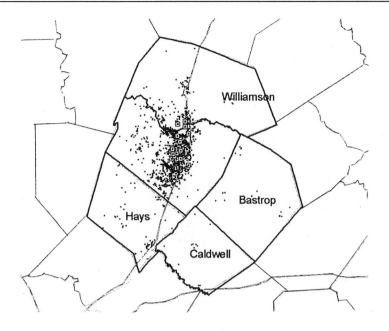

Fig. 11.10. ICT in Austin-San Marcos (TX) MSA

Fig. 11.11. ICT in Boston (MA-NH) NECMA

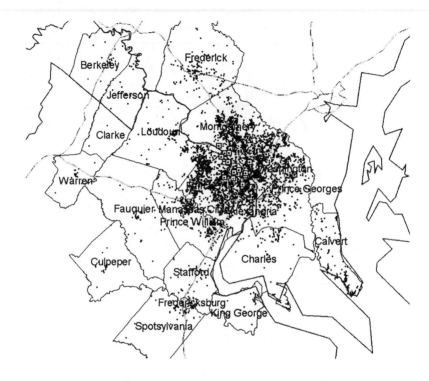

Fig. 11.12. ICT in Washington D.C. (VA, MD, WV and Wash. D.C.) CMSA

11.4.1 Inter-MSA Comparisons

The first coefficient to be computed is what can be termed a Tinbergen-coefficient; it is derived from Tinbergen-Bos spatial economic equilibrium analysis in terms of "centres" and "systems" (Paelinck 1997), centres being defined as spatial clusters of activities, systems as spatial combinations of centres.

The Tinbergen coefficient is defined as the relative number of sectors present in an observed centre:

$$t_k = n_k/n \tag{11.1}$$

where, n is the total number of sectors analysed (in casu 33) and n_k the number of sectors effectively observed in a given centre k $(k=1,2,3)$.

For A, B, and W, respectively, the t_k's were .9394, 1 and .9697, with only 2 sectors being absent in A and 1 in W (see Table 11.1).

The establishments' density by population and by area were also computed for each technology sector. The results are as follows: the number of plants per 100 thousand population are 187 (A); 140 (B) and 179 (W); the number of plants per square mile are 0.50 (A); 1.23 (B) and 1.29 (W); showing the effects of different centre sizes and population densities.

The average number of plants per sector is 65 (A), 252 (B) and 258 (W), with coefficients of variation (standard deviations divided by the respective means) of 1.7481, 1.7337 and 1.8408.

In these global terms, and taking into account the standardising deflators (population and surface) the results point at a certain, though not complete, degree of homogeneity in the general (still not spatial) patterns observed.

This relative homogeneity is confirmed by the matrix of correlation coefficients and its eigenvalues; still in the ABW-order the correlation matrix is {1, .9883, .9485; 1, 9648; 1} with eigenvalues of 2.9345, .0558 and .0097; it is known that if $n-1$ eigenvalues out of n are near zero, the overall correlations are extremely high (positively or negatively, but in the present case positively as the simple correlation coefficients show).

A measure of the overall correspondence might be the largest eigenvalue divided by the sum of the eigenvalues, in casu 2.9345/3=.9786. Figs. 11.13–11.15 reproduce those observations graphically.

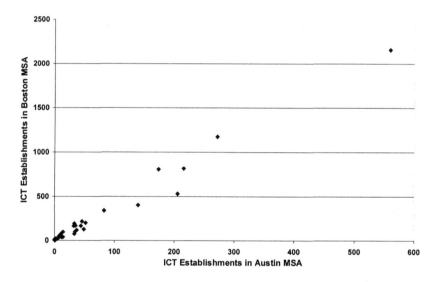

Fig. 11.13. Boston vs. Austin MSA: ICT Sector Establishments

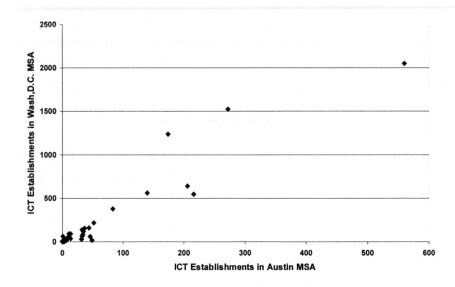

Fig. 11.14. Wash. D.C. vs Boston MSA: ICT Sector Establishments

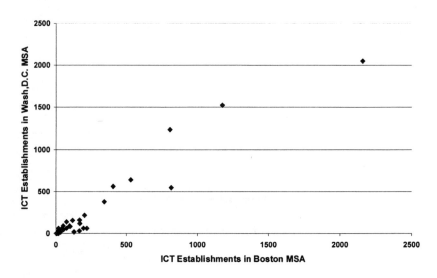

Fig. 11.15. Wash. D.C. vs Austin MSA: ICT Sector Establishments

11.4.2 Intra-MSA Analyses

Spatial analysis requires the introduction of topological elements; these are now introduced in terms of relative positions (co-ordinates) and distances; the distances have been defined as Manhattan distances (sum of the absolute differences of the respective x and y co-ordinates), a rather realistic metric for the study of urbanised areas.

11.4.3 Characteristic Coefficients

A first indicator of the intra-MSA spatial structure is the average distance (total distance depending on the number of establishments) separating the establishments analysed, divided by the square root of the metropolitan area in square miles (this is to ensure dimensional homogeneity of the numerator and denominator); the resulting A, B an W indicators are respectively .0437, .0692 and .0727, showing different orders of magnitude of mutual internal relative accessibility. Average distances are .0446, .0952 and .0977, confirming the previous observation.

Returning to Figs. 11.10–11.12, one can visualise the (unweighted) centres of gravity of the hi-tech activities present; noticeable are the differences in shape of the spread of those centres, a fact which is submitted to further mathematical analysis.

To better understand these spatial linkings, the following approaches are proposed:

- compute the Hausdorff distances (Hausdorff 1962, pp. 166) between all the plants belonging to different activities; this allows a comparison of the relative closeness of the sectors involved, and to examine the hypothesis that more centrally clustered sectors have higher input (supply chain) dependencies (measured, e.g., by the sum of the corresponding input coefficients) through correlation analysis;
- conduct a nearest neighbour analysis in terms of the average nearest neighbour distances between plants belonging to different sectors, and apply again the above analysis of the relationship to the input coefficients.

As an intermediate investigation, the distances between the sectoral centres of gravity referred to above were used, together with aggregated summed input coefficients (taken from the Survey of Current Business 2000); Table 11.2 shows the aggregation.

The simple correlation coefficients between distances and the summed input coefficients were –.5008 (A), –.7335 (B) and –.3890 (W), showing all of them to be negative relations between distances and summed input coefficients, as expected.

The strongest relation was observed in the Boston area. Once more, this is only an intermediate investigation; additional analyses are required at more disaggregated levels.

Table 11.2. Aggregation of Sectors

Input-output code	Sector	SIC
51	Computer and office equipment	357
56	Audio, video and communication equipment	365–366
57	Electrical components and accessories	367
66	Communications, except radio and TV	481, 482, 484, 489
73A	Computer and data processing services	737

11.5 Conclusions and Implications

This paper has examined the knowledge challenges of the entrepreneur in the ICT industries with a focus on the regional scale. The knowledge challenges were introduced with a metaphor called the entrepreneurial fountain showing that information and knowledge challenges exist from the idea or discovery stage through to successful venture development. At the discovery stage the knowledge challenge is to identify and select an idea or concept that can be fruitfully developed. Once the idea is targeted or selected, a plan for the associated venture must be developed. The business plan development process offers a very different type of challenge for the entrepreneur than at the idea discovery stage. During this stage the entrepreneur must clearly define the product(s) or service(s) create a business model, create defensible market and financial forecasts, build a management plan, acquire some top management personnel and develop a capitalisation plan. At the implementation stage investors must be approached and financial backing secured, management must be recruited and hired if not done during the planning stage, market development must occur, and financial, personnel and information management systems must be initiated. In sum, the entrepreneurial process creates continuously changing and diverse knowledge challenges as the entrepreneur moves from the discovery to the venture deployment stage.

As noted in the paper the demand for knowledge and its use in the entrepreneurial process is likely greater during periods that are characterised by disequilibrium conditions. In general, investment in regional infrastructure to address entrepreneurial knowledge needs is probably greater under disequilibrium conditions. Regions that provide greater infrastructure to support the various knowledge needs associated with the process should outperform other regions that make lesser investments in such infrastructure.

The concept of smart infrastructure is used to describe the types of actions, organisations and policies that are needed to support entrepreneurs in general and their knowledge needs in particular. These are not restated here but it is useful and important to note that the type of infrastructure needed to support entrepreneurs' knowledge needs varies from the discovery stage to the implementation stage. At the discovery stage entrepreneurs need informed people to help them assess and evaluate their venture concept. Associations, workshops and venture counsellors (e.g., like those found in Small Business Development Centres) are more important. Once the concept has been defined and targeted business development counsellors and educational workshops and programs (e.g., NextLevel and FastTrack) are important in helping the entrepreneur create the business plan. Effective business plan development requires considerable knowledge about business processes (finance, market research and market development, technology evaluation and technical development, personnel, hiring, and information management). Most entrepreneurs need assistance to develop the knowledge necessary to build an effective business plan to exploit their concept. Finally, experienced management must be secured to ensure effective execution of the business model and plan once the venture is capitalised. In short, regions that provide broad and deep entrepreneurial infrastructure will better support entrepreneurial development and therefore are likely to perform better in terms of job and wealth creation.

Knowledge acquisition, transfer and learning for entrepreneurs should be higher where functional and spatial clustering are high. An analysis of the spatial and functional clustering of ICT industries in three metropolitan regions confirmed that sectors that are more functionally dependent tend to be more closely clustered geographically. This is consistent with the conclusion from other research that firm formation rates increase as agglomeration and internal accessibility levels increase (Acs et al. 1999).

This is a preliminary analysis of the knowledge challenges of entrepreneurs and how this influences and contributes to regional economic development. All aspects of the analysis beg for deeper and more thorough treatment. Follow-up research needs to further elaborate on the entrepreneurial fountain and undertake an examination of regional variation in the associated components of entrepreneurial infrastructure. The spatial analysis needs to be disaggregated to provide additional insight into the relationship between functional and spatial clustering.

References

Acs ZJ, Carlsson B, Karlsson C (1999) Entrepreneurship, small & medium-sized enterprises and the macroeconomy. Cambridge University Press, Cambridge UK

Armington C and Acs ZJ (2000) The determinants of regional variation in new firm formation. University of Baltimore, School of Business, Mimeo, Baltimore

Baudeau N (1910, originally 1767) Réduction et incertitude de risque. In: Dubois A (ed) Premier introduction a la philosopic economique. Paris

Bergman E, Feser E, Sweeny S (1996) Targeting North Carolina manufacturing: Understanding the State's economy through industrial cluster analysis. UNC Institute for Economic Development, Chapel Hill NC

Cantillon R, Higgs H (1931, originally 1755) Istais sur la nature da commeertc in general. Macmillan, London

Fiet JO (1996) The informational basis of entrepreneurial discovery. Small Business Economics 8: 419–430

Hausdorff F (1962) Set theory. Chelsea Publishing Company, New York

Held JR (1996) Clusters as an economic development tool: Beyond the pitfalls. Economic Development Quarterly 10: 249–261

Kirzner IM (1973) Competition and entrepreneurship. University of Chicago Press, Chicago

Kirzner IM (1979a) Perception opportunity and profit: Studies in the theory of entrepreneurship. University of Chicago Press, Chicago

Kirzner IM (1979b) Comment: Efficiency error and the scope of entrepreneurship. In: Rizzo MJ (ed) Time uncertainty and disequilibrium. Lexington Books, Lexington, MA

Marshall A (1961) Principles of economics. Macmillan, London

Morris MH, Kuratko D, Schindehutte M (2001) Towards integration: understanding entrepreneurship through frameworks. International Journal of Entrepreneurship and Innovation 2: 35–49

Paelinck JHP (1997) Two studies in Tinbergen-Bos systems. Oikonomika 34: 1–22

Porter M (1990) The competitive advantage of nations. Basic Books, New York

Rosenfeld SA (1997) Bringing business clusters into the mainstream of economic development. European Planning Studies 5: 3–23

Saxenian AL (1994) Regional advantage: Culture and competition in the Silicon Valley and Route 128. Harvard University Press, Boston

Schumpeter JA (1936) The theory of economic development: An inquiry into profits, capital, credit, interest and the business cycle. Harvard University Press, Cambridge MA

Schumpeter JA (1939) Business cycles. McGraw-Hill, New York

Schumpeter JA (1942) Capitalism, socialism and democracy. Harper & Roe, New York

Schumpeter JA (1947) The creative response in economic history. Journal of Economic History 7: 149–159

Schumpeter JA (1961) The theory of economic development. Oxford University Press, New York

Schumpeter JA (1971) The fundamental phenomenon of economic development. In: Kilby P (ed) Entrepreneurship and economic development. Free Press, New York, pp 43–70

Smilor RW and Wakelin M (1990) Smart infrastructure and economic development: The role of technology and global networks. In: Kozmetsky G, Smilor RW (eds) The technolopolis phenomonen. IC^2 Institute, The University of Texas at Austin, pp 53–76

Stevenson H, Roberts M, Grousbeck I (1992) New business ventures and the entrepreneur. Irwin Publishing, Chicago

Stough RR, Kulkarni RG, Riggle J (2000) Technology in Virginia's regions, Appendix A. The Virginia Center for Innovative Technology, Herndon, VA

Stough RR, Kulkarni R, Riggle J, Haynes K (2001) Technology and Industrial Cluster Analysis: Some New Methods. In: Higano P, Nijkamp P, Poot J, van Wijk JJ (eds) The region in the new economy. Ashgate, London

Survey of current business (2000) Bureau of Economic Analysis, U.S. Dept of Commerce. Washington DC. (http://www.bea.doc.gov/bea/pubs.htm)

12 Newcomers and Innovation in the U.S. Telephone Industry – Then and Now[1]

Pat Norton

Movieu.net, Marblehead, Massachusetts, USA

12.1 Introduction

To what extent has digital convergence pushed the U.S. to a new phase of the Information Age, one favouring scale and scope over entrepreneurial newcomers? As we consider this question, what stands out is the similarity between the communications revolution of the late 19th century and today's digital revolution. In both eras, challenges by entrepreneurs from peripheral U.S. regions led to an accelerated deployment of new technologies.

This paper surveys the role of innovation and entrepreneurship in the evolution of the U.S. telephone industry. Under the Kingsbury Commitment of 1914 AT&T survived as a private, regulated monopoly (Sect. 12.2.) For 50 years the symbiosis of monopoly, network interconnection, and basic research seemed organically preordained. But after 1960 a series of entrepreneurial challenges attacked the monopoly. The result was the 1982 court decision requiring AT&T to turn its local telephone business over to seven regional "Baby Bells" (Sect. 12.3). Today, the four surviving Baby Bells seem to have emerged as the winners under the terms of the Telecommunications Act of 1996, despite its goal of opening the playing field to newcomers. By implication, the era of convergence and consolidation may offer less range for the kind of entrepreneurial experimentation by newcomers and outsiders that helped spawn the New Economy (Sect. 12.4).

Three related strands in the article are (1) advances in technology, (2) the inherent tension between standard setting and innovation, and (3) the shifting aims of federal regulation. Accordingly, we might preface the account with a framework for thinking about the telephone as an episode in the history of landmark inventions.

The framework appeared in a September 1999 article, "Landmark Inventions of the Millennium", by Herb Brody, the editor of *Technology Review*. His list included 10 discoveries, ranging from the compass to the transistor. While any such

---

[1] I have benefited greatly from the insights and encouragement of Junfu Zhang and William Latham III. Any errors are my own.

list could be debated on specific entries, it would be hard to dispute Brody's emphasis on information and communications technologies (which I italicise):

1. the compass
2. the mechanical clock
3. the glass lens
4. *the printing press*
5. the steam engine
6. *the telegraph*
7. *electric power*
8. *wireless communication*
9. antibiotics
10. *the transistor*

Half of the ten breakthroughs thus refer to information and communication. Three – the telegraph, electricity, and wireless – cluster in roughly the latter part of the 19th century. But what of such other landmarks as the telephone, television, or the Internet? In Brody's view, each followed more or less routinely from one of the 10 seminal breakthroughs: the telephone from the telegraph, television from radio, and the Internet from the transistor.

In that light, the telephone can be viewed as one of a series of breakthroughs that began with the telegraph before 1850 and continue to this day. The Scottish-born inventor of the telephone, Alexander Graham Bell, initially referred to his project as a "harmonic telegraph" because it was intended to permit multiple telegraphic messages on one line. In a separate but linked trajectory, the transistor was invented at Bell Labs in 1948 as a device to facilitate switching of telephone calls. What it led to, however, was the gradual replacement of analog by digital messages and media – and the stage of digital convergence.

Bell travelled from his base in Boston to demonstrate his fledgling telephone at Philadelphia's Centennial Exposition in June 1876. The effect was to make clear, as Tom Standage puts it in his history of the telegraph, *The Victorian Internet*, "that telegraphy was merely one of many applications of electricity" (Standage 1998, p. 199). In other words, communicating by means of variations in electric current or electromagnetic waves proceeded from the telegraph to the telephone and the phonograph and then to wireless modes, culminating in radio after 1920.

In each era, the Victorian Revolution and today's digital revolution, similar issues arose as to the rules of the competitive game, the role of government regulation, and the balance to be struck between standard-setting and technological progress. For that reason, it is instructive to recall the formation of the original Bell System – and the federal government's attempts to advance the public interest while also responding to highly organised and well-financed private interests.

12.2 The Rise of the Bell System: 1876–1934

The creation of the Bell System as a regulated monopoly can be understood as a play in three acts. (1) From 1876 to 1894, the System developed as a monopoly behind patent protection. (2) From 1894 to 1914, competition prevailed. (3) Under the Kingsbury Commitment at the end of 1913, the federal government chartered the Bell System as a private, regulated monopoly – but one that remained largely unregulated. This transition period ends with the Communications Act of 1934. It renamed the Federal Radio Commission (FRC) as the FCC and brought "the beginning of real regulation at the federal level" (Mueller 1997, p. 157).

12.2.1 The Temporary (Patent-Based) Monopoly: 1876–1894

From 1876 to 1894, the American Bell Telephone Company held a monopoly based on the inventor's elegant patents. After an early struggle with Western Union (the telegraph monopoly) and its ally Thomas Edison, the authority of Bell's patents led to an agreement between the two companies that gave Bell interests clear sailing. In all, the Bell System undertook 600 successful patent defences without a single courtroom defeat (John 2000, p. 93).

There would be five key components of the new system, and the first four emerged right away (Fig. 12.1). These were the telephone itself, the line connecting the telephone to the rest of the world (forming "the local loop"), a central exchange (with switchboards), and the trunk line between local exchanges. While the very first calls used dedicated point-to-point lines, by 1878 the first commercial switchboards were up and running in New Haven and Chicago (Burlingame 1940, p. 113). Rather than sell the telephones outright, the Company manufactured and leased them, charging a flat monthly fee to household subscribers.

The expense of manufacturing (but not selling) the units, together with the costs of creating exchanges and grids, led to a series of strategic decisions. First, Bell and his backer (and father-in-law) Gardner Hubbard raised capital from Boston financiers, including in particular William H. Forbes. Then the Company instituted a policy of licensing – and imposing standards on – independent operating companies, which would incur start-up costs in their own localities. Finally, in 1881 the Company obtained a controlling interest in Western Electric, the foremost U.S. manufacturer of electrical equipment, and gave it exclusive rights to supply the Company with telephones.

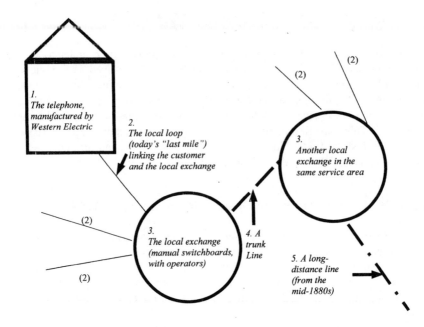

Fig. 12.1. The Five Elements in the Initial Bell Network

Where was component (5), the long-distance or inter-city line, in all this? Initially, the transmission lines permitted only a 20-mile calling range before the signal attenuated. By 1884, however, a long-distance line linked Boston and New York. As head of the by now renamed American Bell Telephone Company, the visionary Theodore Newton Vail championed the goal of complete system integration, whereby every telephone subscriber could connect with every other.

The following year (1885) Vail's vision found its way into the certificate of incorporation of the American Telephone and Telegraph Company (AT&T), initially a wholly owned subsidiary for long distance. He pledged that AT&T would "connect one or more points in each and every city...and also by cable and other appropriate means with the rest of the known world" (Burlingame 1940, pp. 118–119). Eventually, in 1899, a reorganisation made AT&T "the parent firm, with full control over the federation of manufacturing facilities, operating companies, and research and development laboratories that together came to be known as the Bell System" (John 2000, p. 87).

12.2.2 Dual Service Drives Rapid Development: 1894–1914

Once the competitive floodgates opened in 1894, independents proliferated, especially in the South and Midwest. Most sold the phones – not leased them – and charged lower monthly service rates, sometimes through economising devices like the party line (one line for multiple users). Newcomer and independent phone operating companies challenged and until perhaps 1907 held their own against the Bell System, forcing the System to extend its service far wider than it had before – and to charge lower rates.

The spur to the industry's rapid development over the two decades was the lack of inter-connection between Bell and its competitors. The key point: where Bell co-operated with independent local providers by offering interoperability, there was no incentive for Bell to expand its network. (Such affiliated independents were numerous and widespread and must be distinguished from *competing* independent service providers.) Only the prod from competing, non-connected local providers forced Bell to expand its coverage.

After 1897 both the Bell System and the competing independent companies resolved to develop non-interconnecting systems. The resulting "access competition" became the norm, with "competing telephone exchanges operating in more than half of all American cities with populations larger than 5,000" during the years 1900–1910 (Mueller 1997, p. 81).

As Richard R. John has written, "The independents greatly expanded the market for telephony and forced Bell to extend its network at an unprecedented rate". He points out that the number of telephones per capita went from four per 1,000 in 1891 to 82 by 1910. Between 1894 and 1914 "Bell installed ten times as many telephones as it had in the period between 1876 and 1893" (John 2000, p. 94).

What, then, went wrong? Why did the competing independents experience increasing difficulty, finally signing off – as most did – on the Kingsbury Commitment of 1914? In light of recent research, we can dispose of three plausible but superficial explanations quickly. These are the (1) natural monopoly, (2) superior-technology, and (3) long-distance interpretations of the triumph of the Bell System.

The first among the specious explanations is the natural-monopoly argument. *Local telephone service was not the standard textbook version of a natural monopoly.* A natural monopoly is defined in theory as an industry in which long-run average costs fall over the entire feasible range of output. However, owing in part to switching problems, beyond a certain moderate subscriber base, average costs began to rise[2] (John 2000, p. 94; Mueller 1997, p. 15).

Second, and by extension, for its own reasons, the Bell System resisted automated switchboards, the heart of the central exchange. Long after the automated switchboard had been devised (as the story goes, by an irritated undertaker in St. Louis who felt slighted by a Bell operator), the System stuck to the labour-intensive system of regimented female operators. For one thing, the System had huge sunk costs in the manually operated switchboards. For another, the original

---

[2] This awkward reality poses a paradox when viewed from traditional antitrust perspectives (in essence: "two networks cost more to install than one"). An alternative perspective on dual-service provision during the build-out of early telephone service begins with the demand side and with network externalities (see Mueller 1997, Chap. 3). What the latter analysis comes down to is lower rates for consumers and lower profits for local-service providers.

Bell marketing model posited the telephone as a tool for the upper middle-class household, in which personal servants were the norm. Operators fit into that norm.

In any case the effect was the one predicted by Kenneth Arrow in a classic article 40 years ago. According to the Arrow Effect, *the industry leader has a vested interest in slowing the pace of technological change*. In this case, and throughout the 20th century, the Bell System's willingness to support basic research coexisted with a reluctance to abandon outmoded practices (Arrow 1962).

Third, and despite our impressions today, the long-distance monopoly of AT&T did not play much of a part. Long-distance service with interoperability between big-city markets held little or no importance to the great majority of customers. If a household subscriber wanted to call long distance, the long-distance phone at the drug store or post office or some other public facility could be used, the traditional practice in much of Europe. Even among business subscribers, most continued to prefer the much less expensive telegraph for long-distance communication (Mueller 1997, p. 73).

What, then, did happen to lead not only the Bell System but even the competing independents to agree to the Kingsbury Commitment? In outline, four overlapping tendencies coalesced to yield the monopoly solution:

1. Vail's conception of complete interoperability, as summarised in his slogan, *"One system, one policy, universal service"*, offered a coherent and compelling vision, as a rallying cry and organising principle – the "network mystique" (John 2000, p. 87). The slogan gathered added force as "toll callers", i.e., those trying to call within a given metropolis but across separate exchanges, added their voices to the call for interconnection.
2. A watershed in the competitive phase occurred in 1907, when none other than J. P. Morgan (at the time, a one-man Federal Reserve System, a lender of last resort in the financial panic of that year), aligned himself with the Bell System. This decade was the era of what used to be called "Finance Capitalism", and J. P. Morgan was the finance capitalist par excellence. The combination of his resources and Vail's strategy proved decisive.
3. Armed with Vail's network mystique and Morgan's money, AT&T's troops fanned out far and wide to lobby in state legislatures for "higher technical standards". The standards exceeded what was needed, but they served the desired result of raising costs for the competing independents, hastening their demise. It is in this sense that "the state governments helped it fend off potential challengers between 1894 and World War I" (John 2000, p. 95).
4. In the end, many competing independents also supported the Kingsbury Commitment. Whatever their own inefficiencies or under-capitalisation, the overriding fear that led them to give in to AT&T's victory was the perceived alternative: nationalisation. Along with AT&T, they too feared the prospect of a government-operated telephone service, of the kind that would indeed be adopted in every other comparable economy.

On December 19, 1913, AT&T Vice-President Nathan Kingsbury sent a letter to the Justice Department that sounded like a concession to the Department's antitrust concerns. AT&T agreed to relinquish its holdings in Western Union (the telegraph monopoly), to stop acquiring any more competitors, and to selectively open up long-distance lines to competing local exchanges. The apparent "commitment" to dual-service and competition, however, was hedged by technicalities and within a few years would be ignored.

The Kingsbury Commitment was but one of several momentous policy events of 1914. That year also saw the Clayton Antitrust Act, the founding of the Federal Trade Commission, and the founding of the Federal Reserve System. In the context of a last Progressive burst of pre-World War I reforms, one writer comments, "The antitrust-inspired Kingsbury Commitment was a shrewd tactical move by AT&T, in that it deflected antitrust pressures but did not undermine the company's superior position in access competition..." (Mueller 1997, p. 134). He concludes that by 1921, the monopoly was a fait accompli.

12.2.3 From Radio to the FCC: 1914–1934

Wireless technologies came into practical use at the turn of the century, reaching fruition after a spectacular series of discoveries on the part of European scientists such as Hertz, Henry, and Maxwell – and the 20-year-old Italian entrepreneur, Marconi (Levinthal 1998). "In 1899, an experimental Marconi apparatus on an English lightship sent out what we now call SOS signals for aid to helpless ships", a function the world would come to know when the Titanic went down on the night of April 14, 1912 (Burlingame 1940, pp. 439–440). The first trans-Atlantic wireless transmission linked Cape Cod in Massachusetts and the U.K. just after 1900.

Wireless looms large in the early history of U.S. telephone regulation, on two counts. First, as commercial radio broadcasting exploded on the scene in the 1920s, the need soon arose for a regulator to allocate frequencies on the electromagnetic spectrum. In response, Congress created the Federal Radio Commission in 1927. A few years later, in 1934, it would be renamed as the Federal Communications Commission, with a mission to regulate long-distance phone service as well (see Fig. 12.2).

The second connection is that in their technology, today's mobile telephones are, in effect, radios. "All 2-way wireless handsets are in reality radios with transmitters and receivers. Radios transmit energy into the air" (Dodd 2000, pp. 318–319). That is what wireless telephones do. By extension, today's controversies over finding new spectrum space for broadband wireless services in the U.S. reflect legacies of decisions made as early as the 1920s.

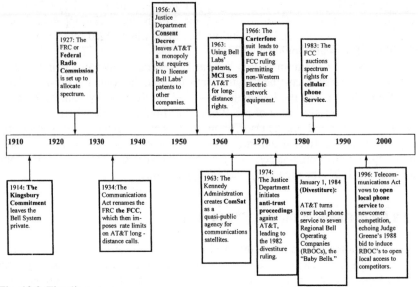

Fig. 12.2. Timeline

Early Radio: Tower of Babel

In 1920 Westinghouse Electric began radio broadcasts of music from an antenna in East Pittsburgh, Pennsylvania. In November 1920 the East Pittsburgh station, KDKA, broadcast the news of Warren G. Harding's election as President, an event taken to denote "the first public broadcast". At that point, Westinghouse announced that it would produce and sell radios to the public. Part of the revenue from selling receivers went to setting up three more stations in Springfield, Massachusetts, New York City, and Chicago.

General Electric, another early radio manufacturer, followed suit in its headquarters city, Schenectady, New York. Incidentally, this was the home of the first formal U.S. R&D lab. Whereas GE's R&D lab was formed in 1900, AT&T's legendary Bell Labs would not occur until 1925 (for details, see Buderi 2000).

As with the Internet, the question remained how the broadcasts might make money, not just sell radios (or computers). While it was only slowly recognised, the answer sprang from the first KDKA broadcasts.

As in a marketing experiment, the question was, "Who is the audience, and what can we sell them?" As to that first audience, wireless hobbyists had been active since the turn of the century. The early KDKA audience thus consisted of ham-radio operators (mainly adolescent boys). In response to their enthusiasm for the initial music broadcasts, the company sent buyers out to local record stores for more material to broadcast. One store lent the station records but asked to have its name mentioned on the air. For better or worse, this was the germ of the idea.

As luck would have it, AT&T owned the station that first generalised this concept in 1922. Its fledgling New York City station, WBNY, hired an ad agency and solicited businesses for general-purpose advertising, to be featured during broadcasts of popular music (Burlingame 1940, p. 451). Why is this "synergistic" event lost in the mists of industrial history? Eventually, for fear of antitrust prosecution, AT&T got out of the radio-station business.

1927: The Federal Radio Commission Allocates Spectrum

The number of radios in use jumped from an estimated 60,000 in 1922 to 6.5 million five years later, in 1927. As a witness to the spectacle observed later, "the years from '22 to '27 were frantic ones...competition ran riot...Everywhere, as stations multiplied...soap and Shakespeare failed to come through because gum and Gershwin were in the way" (Burlingame 1940, pp. 451–452).

The only regulatory precedent was a 1911 federal law requiring any wireless transmitting station to obtain a public license. Something more had to happen to resolve property rights over the airwaves. In response to a public outcry about the crowding of transmissions on the same frequency, Congress in 1927 created the Federal Radio Commission, the forerunner of the FCC.

The broadcast technology then in use was limited to AM (amplitude modulation). Following international convention, the spectrum the FRC allocated for AM transmission ran from 500 to 1500 kilohertz, or thousands of cycles per second. This low frequency (.5 to 1.5 megahertz or MHz) reflected the primitive electronic sophistication of receiver technology at the time. Some other portion of the spectrum could have been used, had receivers been more sensitive – as when FM (frequency modulation) debuted 15 years later in the FCC-allocated range of 88 MHz to 108 MHz.

Thus the origin of radio and television spectrum allocation in the U.S. To this day American AM radio stations range from 500 to 1500 (and FM from 88 to 108) on the dial.[3] As for television, as noted at the outset it is technologically an offshoot of radio (both being expressions of wireless). Its assigned bandwidth in the U.S. after about 1940 would include 54–88 MHz, 174–220 MHz, and above.

In its primary mission of eliminating overlapping broadcasts, the FRC was a complete success. What else constituted the initial broadcasting regulator's assignment? "The commission demanded continuity during normal listening hours, specified equipment and stated minimum power requirements in watts" (Burlingame 1940, p. 452). As to censorship, Burlingame observed succinctly in

---

[3] The FRC assigned each licensed radio station's frequency within a given market area (typically a town or city). Depending on the power a station used for transmission, the signal might carry beyond a city to surrounding countryside – but not by much. The AM spectrum band of 1,000 kilohertz (from 500 to 1,500) permitted 96 distinct broadcast frequencies or channels of about 10 kilohertz each. Somewhat arbitrarily, given the vast size of the U.S., Congress limited the number of stations the FRC could license to fewer than 700.

1940 that the advertisers saw to that: "It is one thing to offend a citizen. It is another to offend a potential customer" (Ibid.).

The Communications Act of 1934

As President Franklin Roosevelt's New Deal began, the House Committee on Interstate and Foreign Commerce conducted a year-long study of monopoly in broadcasting. It focused on RCA, Western Union, and AT&T – which remained as yet unregulated at the federal level, despite its status as *"more powerful and skilled than any state government with which it has to deal"* (House Committee on Interstate and Foreign Commerce 1934, quoted in Mueller 1997, p. 156 emphasis added). Preoccupied with railroad regulation, the Committee recommended creating a new federal agency to regulate broadcasting and interstate telephone service.

As already noted, the name-change that created the FCC signalled "the beginning of real regulation at the federal level" in the telephone industry (Mueller 1997, p. 157). The FCC controlled spectrum allocation and had oversight of both broadcasting (i.e., radio) and interstate telephone communications. Its purview was confined to long-distance calls, which at the time amounted to little more than two percent of all calls.

Real regulation began with the 1934 Act, an event embedded in the context of the Depression and New Deal reform. Between 1934 and 1944, the FCC required AT&T to reduce long-distance telephone rates. By the end of World War II, something like a full-blown coalescence of interests and views marked the FCC, state regulators, and AT&T.

In the view of a contemporary observer, all this – the coalescence of interests as between the monopoly and the regulators, and the elimination of competition within the telephone industry – had the flavour of historical necessity:

> Thus the organization of the Bell System was merely a part of the whole collectivist phase. The 'greatest good to the greatest number' was the result. If individuals lost opportunity for private profit, if free competition dropped out of existence, if personal 'ruggedness' lapsed, so it did in most departments of industrial and commercial activity during this whole tightening of society (Burlingame 1940, p. 118).

Granting this conclusion for the sake of argument, an obvious question follows. *What would it take to alter this sense of AT&T's inevitability?*

12.3 Newcomers and Innovation, 1963–1996

For the 50 years after the creation of the FCC in 1934, AT&T practiced a cost-plus pricing relationship that encouraged lavish capital expenditures, but – despite all Bell Labs' patents – not much innovation in telephone service. In *the old regime*, long-distance calls were transmitted as (1) analog messages in the form of electrical signals over (2) copper wire. As with Alexander Graham Bell's original calls, each conversation occupied (3) the entire circuit for the duration of the call.

In the course of the 1960s, this "circuit-switched" system would be joined by an alternative technology developed by the Pentagon, "packet-switching", a digital technology to be used in the Defense Department's ARPAnet and later Ethernet and the Internet. By 1970, wireless packet-switched transmission would succeed.

But even before then, another radical alternative to conventional long distance had appeared – microwave transmission. It would provide the first great break with the Bell System's reliance on copper wire to connect telephone users.

12.3.1 Microwaves and MCI (Chicago-St. Louis, 1963)

As an outgrowth of radar and its development during World War II, microwave communications came into use in the late 1940s (Fig. 12.3). By 1948 the Western Union Telegraph Company deployed line-of-sight antenna towers about 30 miles apart from Washington, D.C., to Boston, Pittsburgh, and points in between. The Western Union network soon spread nation-wide. The implication was that voice messages could also be relayed wirelessly. Microwave "telegraphy" was and is a powerful medium for transmission of voice, data, and video signals – not just dots and dashes.[4] When would someone venture onto the stage to try to use the then not-quite-new technology for voice telephone messages?

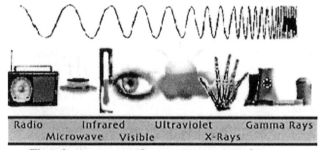

Fig. 12.3. Microwaves in the Electromagnetic Spectrum

The answer came in 1963 when John Goeken petitioned the FCC for the right to provide long distance service within the Midwest. His company was Microwave Communications, Inc. As suggested by the Western Union telegraphic network,

---

[4] Microwaves lie on the 4 gigaherz (4,000 MHz) band of the electromagnetic spectrum, just before infrared and then visible light. Hence microwaves are shorter ("micro") and higher-frequency than cell phones, which operate at about 950 or, for Personal Communication Services (PCS) phones, 1,900 MHz. This range also lies above the unregulated transmission bands for wireless local area networks (LANs) at around 2,500 MHz. In the 4,000 MHz microwave band 800 telegraph or 40 voice channels are available.

Goeken's plan was to use the microwave portion of the spectrum to relay signals wirelessly from one tower to another along a route from Chicago to St. Louis.

AT&T fought the petition, recognising that an alternative medium of long-distance telephony would destroy its monopoly position. In the end AT&T lost. Renamed in 1968, and with a new president (William McGowan), MCI brought suit against AT&T on the grounds that it was an illegal trust designed to prevent competition. *In 1971 the FCC authorised MCI to provide long-distance service*, the first competition AT&T had experienced since 1914. (Ultimately, in 1997, MCI would be bought for $37 billion by WorldCom, a financial conglomerate.)

The meaning of this now familiar event is that the "new" technology for long-distance voice communication had been around for 15 or 20 years. But it awaited an entrepreneurial champion, and in practice that meant someone from outside either Western Union or AT&T. Table 12.1 lists this episode along with the six additional examples to be discussed now.

Table 12.1. Newcomer Innovations in U.S. Telecommunications after 1960

Event	Location	Outcome
1. (1963) Microwave Communications, Inc. (MCI) sues AT&T	Chicago-St. Louis	First non-AT&T long-distance service since 1914
2. (1963) Syncom satellites	California	The "Clarke Belt": geostationary COMSAT satellites
3. (1966) Carterfone challenges Bell System equipment requirement	Texas	Part 68 FCC rule allowing non-Bell System components
4. (1970) Alohanet	Hawaii	Wireless packet-switched messages, wireless local area networks (WLANS)
5. (1978) Hayes Modems	Georgia	Smart PC modems
6. (1980s) McCaw Cellular	Washington State	Creation of first U.S. national cellular network, later purchased by AT&T
7. (1990s) Qualcomm's CDMA	California	Code division multiple access, now the "3G" standard for wireless data and voice communication

12.3.2 Harold Rosen and GEO Satellites (California, 1963)

As early as 1945 Arthur C. Clarke (author of the novel *2001*) had suggested in *Wireless World* magazine that a satellite at the right distance from the earth could appear to hover over a single spot on the earth's surface, in a "geosynchronous" earth orbit (GEO) at the equator. In reality, the seemingly stable orb circles the earth once every 24 hours. But since the earth rotates once in the same interval the satellite appears to hold a fixed position relative to the ground.

The advantage of such "geostationarity" was the simplicity of staying in contact with a ground base. A single dish on the ground could hone in on the overhead satellite, avoiding the hand-off issues that arise in tracking a vehicle hurtling from one time zone to another. Clarke therefore emphasised the dramatic telecommunications advantages of a GEO communications satellite. What would it take to make Clarke's vision a reality?

The answer that emerged in the mid-1960s was that geostationarity hinged in part on the size of the satellite to be launched. It required an orbit just under 24,000 miles up (22,300 to be exact), about the same elevation as the earth's circumference. To reach that lofty orbit, extremely powerful rockets would be required (see Fig. 12.4).

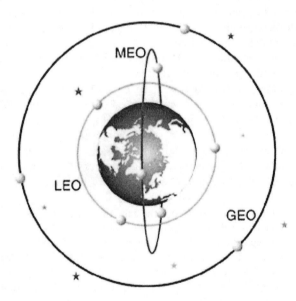

Fig. 12.4. Low, Middle and Geosynchronous Earth Orbits

In any case, as a regulated monopoly, AT&T was prepared to spend whatever it took, confident that any costs could be passed on to its telephone customers. Accordingly, it envisaged not a GEO system but what today would be termed a MEO (middle earth orbit) network of from 50 to 130 satellites 7,000 miles up, to be launched a dozen at a time by huge rockets. The satellites would be tracked by some 25 ground stations around the world. This was Bell Labs' proposal for Telstar, as outlined in a 1961 article by J.R. Pierce.

As a 1995 NASA (U.S. National Aeronautics and Space Administration) history recalls, the expense to be borne by AT&T was not a concern to the monopoly:

> The cost of such a system would be high, Pierce estimated it at $500 million in his 1961 article, but that was not a detriment from AT&T's standpoint. As a monopoly at the time, AT&T's rates were regulated. These rates included an amount that allowed AT&T to recover its costs as well as make a profit. The costs of the satellite system would be passed on to consumers just as the high costs of undersea cables were. *Higher cost investments by the monopoly allow higher [absolute] profits, so the complex Telstar system was attractive to AT&T* (Glover 1995, online, emphasis added).

NASA launched the first Telstars, and AT&T reimbursed the $6 million launch costs.[5] But then, in a policy shift on August 31, 1963, President Kennedy signed the Communication Satellite Act giving a monopoly on international satellite transmissions not to AT&T but to COMSAT, a newly created quasi-public corporation.

Telstar, while a public-relations triumph, had been an unnecessarily complicated and expensive proposition. The problem was the lack of geosynchronicity – which required a greater altitude. As a chartered monopoly, AT&T was virtually a nation unto itself, with the resources to match. But for other private companies to put up communications satellites, lift-off costs posed a formidable obstacle. How to keep a communication satellite small and light enough to make launch costs economic – while still attaining orbits at 22,300 miles up?

As developed by Harold Rosen, an engineer working at Hughes Aircraft in California, the solution to the puzzle turned out to be "spin-stabilisation". This is the principle by which a spinning football or bullet travels farther.[6] After two years of experimentation with a small, light, spinning satellite (and one failed launching, in which Syncom 1 failed to transmit), Rosen's project came nearer to fruition in July of 1963. At about 80 pounds (less than half the weight of Telstar I), Syncom 2 reached an orbit at a height of 22,300 miles – though still not quite

---

[5] The payoff for both organisations came July 10, 1962, with the first live trans-Atlantic TV transmission by Telstar I of U.S.-originated pictures in France. The result was a public-relations coup for AT&T, NASA, and the U.S. Owing to radiation from U.S. and Soviet nuclear tests, Telstar I sustained damage that ended its role within six months of launch. Before long, AT&T would launch Telstar II, also in MEO, in May of 1963. But by that time, the Kennedy Administration had already taken away the company's monopoly on commercial satellites.

[6] The setting for Harold Rosen's breakthrough had more than a touch of Hollywood. An engineer from Louisiana with a Ph.D. from the California Institute of Technology, he worked for Hughes Aircraft in California. This was the creation of eccentric movie mogul and aviator Howard Hughes – famous among other things for his Spruce Goose, a giant wooden aircraft that could barely get off the ground. Ironically, Hughes Aircraft was commissioned by NASA's Goddard Space Flight Center to come up with satellites light enough to make GEO launches feasible.

stationary relative to the equator. Finally, on August 19, Syncom 3 was launched in a geostationary orbit in time to broadcast the Tokyo Olympics around the world in 1964.

This and subsequent successes led COMSAT to conclude that geostationarity could work. Accordingly, COMSAT launched the geo-stationary Intelsat system and Hughes Aircraft became the world's largest manufacturer of commercial communications satellites. "Without government creation of Comsat, AT&T would be building its own medium-altitude satellites" (Glover, online). Instead, the "Clarke Belt" around the equator, 22,300 miles up, now contains some 150 GEO communications satellites.

Today geostationary communications satellites are old hat, and the new drama resides in such low-earth-orbit (LEO) schemes as Teledesic and GlobalStar.[7] Hughes' satellite division has been acquired in the meantime by General Motors. Harold Rosen remains unknown to the general public. But it was his creative insight, as put into practice in an environment that encouraged bold gambles, that made Clarke's 1945 vision a reality.

12.3.3 The Carterfone (Texas, 1966)

Even before MCI sued AT&T as a trust in 1968, a small, specialised electronics company struck the first telling legal blow. The issue was not provision of telephone service, but manufacture and use of compatible equipment. Up to that point, and in line with the Kingsbury Commitment, AT&T subsidiary Western Electric was the sole provider of every telephone and every component used anywhere in the Bell System. The predictable result was that however spectacular the discoveries in Bell Labs, changes in the telephones or peripherals proceeded at a glacial pace.

All this would change with the Carterfone case. "In 1966 a small Texas company called Carterfone invented a simple device that allowed two-way radios to connect to a telephone line" (Derfler and Freed 2000, p. 30). In other words, workers and managers in an oil field or other worksite could use walkie-talkie devices that could also hook up to the local and national AT&T networks. The fact that the connection took place through an "acoustic coupler" meant that it stayed within the limits of the law.

At that time, then, federal law prohibited the use of any non-AT&T equipment at any point in the Bell system. The Carterfone device, however, posed a quirky test of the law. The acoustic coupler linked the two-way radios to the Bell System network via sound, rather than actual physical contact. In other words, the Carterfone was a cradle (or "coupler") that held a telephone handset connected to the

---

[7] The drawback, as the sometimes awkward gaps in live TV interviews from Afghanistan to the U.S. revealed in late 2001: at 22,300 miles up, the speed of light creates a half-second transmission time up and back, a lag lengthened when multiple satellite relays occur.

network. The cradle could receive and relay messages from a two-way radio and from the handset.

AT&T's battery of lawyers swung into action to prevent the connection. They labelled it a corruption of the network. Two years later the FCC reached a decision that can now be seen as the first step toward deregulating the industry. Third-party equipment like the Carterfone could be used to connect to the Bell system, provided steps were taken to safeguard network integrity.

The next step was a ruling by the FCC in 1975 that any equipment meeting certain standards or specifications could hook up to the Network's lines. The guidelines published in 1977 are known as "Part 68" and refer to "Connection of Terminal Equipment to the Telephone Network" (hence the reference on the bottom of nearly all modems and telephones used in the U.S., asserting compliance with Part 68).

As Derfler and Freed explain, "The FCC's Part 68 rule opened a floodgate of new equipment" (p. 31). Now consumers could buy their own telephones instead of renting one from AT&T. Innovation was unleashed as well in peripherals: modems, answering machines, and cordless units.

The effect resembled that of the PC revolution in the 1980s relative to IBM's traditional vertical ("end-to-end") organisation of the mainframe market. After about 1985, the computer industry would experience a horizontal reorganisation. The various hardware and software components of computing would become specialised "horizontal" tiers within which companies would compete by innovating. In Andrew Grove's ski-equipment metaphor, competition among suppliers in each specialised horizontal tier sparked innovations up and down the layers – in skis, boots, and bindings. Meantime *uniform standards* assured compatibility across tiers when it came time for the consumer to pick and choose the best skis, boots, and bindings, typically from different suppliers (Grove 1993, p. 57).

From 1977 on, a similar acceleration marked telephone and network equipment. To that extent, "The telephone industry itself was turned upside down..." (Derfler and Freed, p. 31).

12.3.4 Alohanet (Hawaii, 1970)

Through the 1960s, both local and long-distance telephone calls continued to use analog (that is, sound-wave) signals. By contrast, computers handled information digitally, by converting everything into 0's and 1's, as in the telegraph's Morse Code a century earlier. The linking device for sending data over the telephone from dumb terminals to mainframes was a rudimentary AT&T modem.[8]

The packet-switched paradigm originated at a military think-tank, the RAND Corporation, in Santa Monica, California in 1962 (Dodd 2000, p. 244). In its original, hard-wired version, it enabled direct communication from one computer to another, without reliance on intervening modems. The concept was put into

---

[8] As countless manuals remind us, the word "modem" refers to the device that *mo*dulates and *dem*odulates messages from digital computers to analog telephones and back.

practice in the late 1960s when the Defense Advanced Research Projects Agency (DARPA or ARPA) commissioned the small consulting firm of Bolt, Baranek, and Newman (BBN) in Cambridge, Massachusetts, to create a decentralised national communications network that could survive a first-strike missile attack on Washington, D.C.

BBN worked with Professor Leonard Kleinrock at UCLA (the University of California at Los Angeles). Together they succeeded in setting up a system for handling messages coded as 0's and 1's via a refrigerator-sized "router" at UCLA toward the end of 1969. The first functioning packet-switched network linked the Stanford Research Institute, UCLA, the University of Utah, and the University of California at Santa Barbara.

The very next year, 1970, saw the first successful wireless version of packet-switching in a project to link the Hawaiian Islands. It is said that this sudden adaptive improvement in the new technology occurred when Norman Abramson, a professor of engineering at Stanford University in California, relocated to Hawaii in the late 1960s so he could spend more time on a surfboard (Segaller 1998, Chap. 4). ARPA then funded his idea for a system of mobile radios (as found then in taxi-cabs or police cars) to be used in fixed sites to connect seven computers on four of the Islands.

A decisive step in the project was to find a way for a single wireless frequency to carry packets of 0's and 1's simultaneously in both directions. (The two-way radios then in use in police cars or taxis could handle only one direction at a time: hence the "Roger" or "over-and-out" punctuation to relinquish the channel.) The problem: what if the individual packets collided or otherwise interfered with each other?

Abramson's solution? Randomness in transmission, combined with resending any packets that did not arrive successfully. "So if the source radio didn't get an acknowledgement, it assumed the packet had gotten garbled; it retransmitted the packet later at a random interval" (Hafner and Lyon 1996, p. 220). The analogy sometimes offered is of two people talking in a telephone conversation: if they both speak at the same time, they tend to stop, until one speaks again, uninterrupted.

The progression that finds today's "wi-fi" (or "802.11b") wireless-local-area-networks thus began with Abramson's Alohanet all the way back in 1970.

12.3.5 The Hayes Modem (Georgia, 1978)

Then there was the modem itself. As with all things telephonic, AT&T had set the standard unilaterally for its modems. Their main use was to link dumb terminals in time-sharing systems to mainframes elsewhere. The 300 bits-per-second (not kilobytes, but individual bits!) Bell 103 modem and its successor the 212a (1200 bps) left a great deal to be desired, not only in speed but also in quality. The 212a, for example, was "very susceptible to noise and signal degradation on the telephone circuit". However, with the break-up in 1984, "AT&T was no longer in a position to dictate standards to the rest of the industry" (Derfler and Freed 2000, p. 59).

In any case, by this time a major breakthrough had occurred in Georgia, where the first "smart" modem had been introduced. The Great Idea Finder website has a capsule summary on PC modems that highlights the contribution:

Dennis C. Hayes invented the PC modem in 1977, establishing the critical technology that allowed today's online and Internet industries to emerge and grow. He sold the first Hayes modem products to computer hobbyists in April of 1977 and founded...Hayes Corp. in January of 1978. Hayes' quality and innovation resulted in performance enhancements and cost reductions that led the industry in the conversion from leased line modems [that is, leased from AT&T] to intelligent dial modems – the PC modem.

All this happened in Georgia, where Hayes had received a degree from the Georgia Institute of Technology. Eventually, in 1998, and partly from competition from "Hayes Compatible" modems produced by other companies, the company went out of business. But thanks to Hayes, from the outset the PC revolution included smart modems for communication. As a result, the infrastructure required for the Internet to become a household utility 15 years later would be available to everybody: a PC, a telephone line, and a Hayes-compatible modem.

12.3.6 From Cellular to a National Network (Washington State, 1987)

The evolution of mobile phone technology points up the disconnect between Bell Labs' inventive prowess and AT&T's capacity to capitalise on the invention. Two researchers at Bell Labs came up with the cellular vision in the early 1960s. In the end, AT&T wound up buying a nation-wide cellular network from Seattle's McCaw Cellular for $11.5 billion. If researchers at Bell Labs in New Jersey could invent cellular, why did AT&T end up having to buy a national cellular network from the McCaw family in Seattle?

As the MIT Archives recall, in 1962 when Richard Frenkiel and Joel Engel teamed up at Bell Labs, "only a few hundred people in a typical city had car phones". They were expensive (perhaps $2,500) and the service was hard to connect to because so few channels were available. In this pre-cellular regime, the paucity of radio channels meant that only 20 or 30 calls at a time could take place in a locality. Frenkiel, Engel, and a team of almost 200 other engineers came up with a new approach, one that created 1,000 channels for each existing one.

As to the team concept, Frenkiel has focused the issue with a modest disclaimer, occasioned by the many awards and honours he and Engel have won: "It is hard for any one person to seem like he is responsible for anything. As I said, hundreds of people were working on it in my company alone." This appealing observation gets at the duality of corporate R&D, as practised at IBM, Xerox, or AT&T. On the one hand, teams of research scientists and engineers provide a tremendous depth and range of technical talent. On the other, bureaucratic buffers and corporate controls tend to prevent their research breakthroughs from becoming successful new products.

The breakthrough the Frenkiel-Engel team had is known today by the term "frequency re-use". Their insight was to divide a city into spatially limited geometric cells, each containing most of the channels that before had blanketed the entire city. That *shrinking of each cell's area made the number of conversations on a given frequency a function of the number of cells in the city.* As long as the signal was sufficiently low-powered, it could be used in different cells (meaning, specifically, non-adjacent ones) without risk of interference.

In Fig. 12.5, for example, each cell uses one-seventh of the available frequencies. The nesting pattern assures that none of the frequencies used in one cell overlaps with the frequencies in any of the six adjacent cells. In this scheme, *each frequency is thus used only in non-adjacent cells, minimising interference.* The Frenkiel and Engel team then tackled such technical problems as (1) how a central control station could locate a car within the city and (2) how to achieve the "hand-off" of a signal when vehicles crossed cell boundaries.

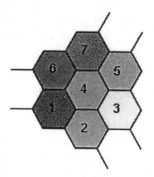

Fig. 12.5. Each Hexagonal Cell Uses 1/7 of Available Frequencies

The proposals Engel and Frenkiel made to the FCC in the 1970s cleared the path for the rollout of the U.S. cell-phone networks of the 1980s. By then, however, AT&T was handing over local telephone service to the seven regional Bell operating companies (RBOCs), the Baby Bells.

The 1984 divestiture decree left AT&T as a long-distance provider. But despite the new medium of wireless cellular, the company expected only a million U.S. cell-phone customers by 2000. Accordingly, it left wireless development to others. In fact, the number of U. S. cell-phone users in 2000 exceeded 109 million.

The FCC granted cellular permits in local markets to two competing carriers. In practice this meant the regional Baby Bell incumbent and an outsider.

Enter Craig McCaw. "The man who really made the cellular business come alive was a young horse trader and negotiator extraordinaire, Craig McCaw" (Young 1998). As noted, Seattle's McCaw created the rudiments of America's first nation-wide commercial wireless network – which he and his brothers (John, Bruce, and Keith) then sold outright to AT&T for $11.5 billion in 1993. As the spin-off AT&T Wireless, it now rivals Sprint and McCaw's own Nextel as the most complete U.S. wireless network.

When the FCC auctioned cell phone licenses in 1983, McCaw and partner Wayne Perry bid for and won a number of licenses, including one for Seattle.[9] From that point, McCaw unloaded the cable business and used the proceeds to buy up local cellular licenses around the country. He acted "in the belief that customers would be attracted to any service that allowed them to roam freely...The value of such freedom seemed obvious to a man who preferred flying, kayaking, sailing, and camping in remote regions of western Canada to working in his office" (Feder 2000).

Aided by junk-bond financing arranged by Michael Milken's Drexel Burnham Lambert, McCaw bought licenses in California, Pennsylvania, Minnesota, and Colorado after 1987. The climax came in 1989 when he paid $3.4 billion for Lin Broadcasting's licenses in Los Angeles, New York, Philadelphia, Houston, and Dallas (Young 1998).

The result was a cellular network covering three-fourths of the U.S. population, serving five million subscribers, and generating over $1 billion a year in revenue. But another legacy was a heavy debt load in a temporarily lulled industry. So in the early 1990s Craig and his brothers sold the whole network to AT&T.

12.3.7 Qualcomm, San Diego, and the 2G Wars (California, 1989)

The next step entailed the development of a *global* wireless communication network. It began, indirectly, in Green Bay, Wisconsin. In October of 1988 Irwin Jacobs, CEO of San Diego's Qualcomm, signed a contract with a Wisconsin trucking firm for Qualcomm's OmniTracs service. The company would then use the revenue from the system of truck-tracking to develop its dark-horse digital wireless technology (McLain 1998, online).

In the poetic language of telecommunications, their advance is known today as CDMA, for "code-division-multiple-access". In CDMA, "multiple access" is attained on a given frequency by means of "code-division". The technique operates at low power, so that batteries and phones can be smaller. It also permits the most efficient known usage of a given frequency. To that extent, a given band of the electromagnetic spectrum can host more high-quality transmissions.

The upshot is that CDMA has emerged as one of the two dominant standards worldwide (along with its cousin, Europe's GSM – Global Standard for Mobile Communications) for incipient third-generation (3G) wireless broadband voice

---

[9] McCaw's business adventures began too early. As a 19-year-old Stanford student he came home to Seattle on vacation to find his father J. Elroy dead from a stroke. At that point Craig (who is severely dyslexic and uncomfortable behind a desk) took primary responsibility for running the family business, a local cable television company where he had held summer jobs (Feder 2000). Under his direction, the company would then go on in the 1970s to acquire paging businesses as well. At the same time, aggressive expansion plans by other cable operators around the country seemed to limit the prospects for the family's Seattle cable business, which peaked at 450,000 in the early 1980s (Young 1998).

and data. But first it had to establish its credibility as a technology capable of re-placing first-generation (analog) cell phones.

As background, Louis Jacobs and Andrew Viterbi spurred San Diego's emer-gence as a global centre for wireless through an incubator named Linkabit. They were two MIT-educated engineers who became professors in Southern California, then eventually abandoned academia to make a go of the business. Jacobs left MIT for the University of California at San Diego in 1966. Before long, he and Viterbi, then a professor at UCLA, founded Linkabit. It would prove a company compara-ble to Silicon Valley's Fairchild Semiconductor as a source of numerous future spin-offs. In 1986, Jacobs and Viterbi left Linkabit to found Qualcomm. Then the OmniTracs truck-tracking service positioned the company to explore the corridors of what would become CDMA.

That brings us to the 2G wars, the rivalry among competing digital wireless voice technologies. Well into the 1990s CDMA was scorned in favour of the pre-vailing digital wireless standard, TDMA. (Now the first initial stands not for code but for "time": multiple access on a given frequency was attained by "time divi-sion"). Pushed by the U.S government and by Europe's telecommunications con-sortium, several big U.S. telecommunications players adopted TDMA in the early 1990s as the standard for digital cell phone service

The principle of TDMA can be readily grasped. As a *digital* technique it could compress the bits or packets in a message and process them. It improved on *ana-log* cellular by processing messages so they needed only a fraction of a second for every second used by an analog message on the same frequency. The process ini-tially tripled the capacity of each analog channel. Various tweaks and refinements raised the multiple to 10 times as many digital transmissions per channel as analog transmissions.

In contrast, the CDMA technique Jacobs and Viterbi developed is by no means easy to understand. Now the technique is to code each message at its origin, send it out over a broad bandwidth, and rely on the digital signal processor in the phone at the other end to capture the right message out of the air and de-code it. What makes that a formidable task is that the airwaves will simultaneously hold many other messages at the same time – on the same band of frequencies. As George Gilder puts it, the technique can be likened to a cocktail party where every conver-sation is in a different language, so that the interlocutor screens out all conversa-tions but the one she understands (Gilder 2000, Chap. 8).

As noted above, the payoff from CDMA is a lower power requirement and a more efficient use of spectrum. The lower power requirement means that batteries need recharging less often and can be smaller, permitting smaller and lighter handsets. The greater spectrum efficiency comes about because CDMA can pack three to six times more channels into a given band of spectrum than TDMA. Once the technical problems were sorted out by the late 1990s, then, the tide began to turn in favour of CDMA.

In 2000 the International Telecommunications Union made variants of CDMA the basis for all five suggested standards for 3G, slated to offer broadband Internet services on mobile telephones. By 2002 TDMA was being phased out completely in the U.S. by either CDMA or a new CDMA-based version of Europe's GSM.

The lack of a uniform U.S. standard has turned out to be a cloud with a silver lining. The cloud is more obvious. It is the frustration Americans have felt over the lack of a comprehensive nationwide wireless network. The silver lining is CDMA, an unlikely breakthrough in wireless technology that permits better mobile phones. The episode paralleled HDTV in the early 1990s. Then Japan's companies under MITI had committed to a single (analog) technology, only to be leapfrogged by better digital approaches subsequently developed by U.S. companies.

Not that we wish to paint too rosy a picture of the effectiveness of the U.S. approach to telecommunications policy. In the U.S., as in Europe, government policies appear to have made things worse in recent years.

12.3.8 The 1996 Act: End of an Era?

For the moment, the U.S. telecommunications industry is drowning in capacity. One reason for the glut: the Telecommunications Act of 1996 encouraged start-up companies to enter the industry, but it failed to guarantee a level playing field.

To be sure, the ostensible aim of the Act was to open local service provision to newcomers. In the words of then FCC Chair William E. Kennard, "The Telecom Act is the foundational document for a world where monopoly has been replaced with competition...." (Quoted in Dodd 2000, p. 107).

As Dodd observes of the Act, "This situation has built-in conflicts: The Bell telephone companies are expected to help their competitors gain a stronghold in their territories" (Ibid.). In theory, optimal access fees might have provided the right incentives for cooperation. In practice, the four remaining Baby Bells –Verizon, SBC, Bell South and Qwest – resisted (technically, Qwest is the Baby Bell, U.S. West, after it was taken over by a much smaller company).

In an echo of access competition between 1900 and 1914, the four incumbent companies tend to control the local loop or "last mile" – the access to households given by local telephone service (see Fig. 12.1). It was hoped in 1996 that fiber optic, wireless, and cable TV offered alternative routes of access. But the incumbents have tended to block newcomers from using their local-loop lines to provide such new broadband services as the Digital Subscriber Line (DSL). In any case, several of the major *wireless* providers that might be expected to compete with the Baby Bells are owned or controlled by them.

As a result, complaints about consumer telephone service are increasing in much of the U.S. Qwest and SBC in particular have gone on aggressive takeover campaigns that have led to diminished local-service competition, deteriorating quality, and higher rates (see Young et al. 2002, p. 1).

Ironically, another symbol of the continued strategic value of the local loop is AT&T. The slimmed-down *mater familias* has placed its bets on cable TV as a means of regaining the local-loop it lost in the 1984 divestiture. Its profits now derive mainly from its cable-based TV and broadband Internet services.

In combination, and after all the 20th-century's advances in technology, these tendencies recall the landscape of 1900–1914: a regime that favors incumbents and drives newcomers out of business.

NextWave and Europe's 3G Auctions

Consider, in this regard, the FCC's problems with bankrupt NextWave's spectrum rights. NextWave was a wireless start-up that bid successfully for 3G spectrum rights in a 1996 FCC auction. But in a preview of Europe's 3G auctions a few years later, NextWave paid too much. Before long it went bankrupt. Opinion remains divided as to whether NextWave was a serious company or merely a speculator in the 1996 bidding. But it was not alone:

> After some of the winners of the FCC's broadband personal communications spectrum auction in May 1996 went bankrupt as a result of the debt they incurred, U.S. courts actually gave protection to the failed companies on the grounds that they had been defrauded into overbidding by the FCC's rosy scenario (Cukier and Hibbard 2000, p. 290).

Accordingly, a federal court ordered the FCC to buy back NextWave's spectrum rights for $6 billion (at the time of this writing, the outcome awaits a decision by the U.S. Supreme Court, because in late 2001 the U.S. Congress refused to fund the $6 billion settlement). Had it gone through the proposed settlement would have turned newcomer spectrum over to incumbent bidders. To that extent NextWave provides further evidence of the failure of the 1996 Act.

From a European perspective, the Next Wave saga might seem merely comic. In the wake of the 1996 FCC auctions, British economists tailored an elaborate, game-theory-influenced auction scheme to induce maximum bids from companies wishing to buy 3G spectrum rights in the U.K. The auction mechanism worked so well that it was emulated on the Continent, garnering $130 billion for Europe's governments. In effect, a tax of $130 billion was imposed at the beginning of the race to roll out 3G networks, before the added cost of building the networks.

While some governments have since relented, the British and German governments are standing firm on the $79 billion they are owed from the auctions. Some observers see the result as a decisive setback for the European Union's goal of matching the U.S. in cutting-edge technologies by 2010. According to Declan Ganley, president of GrowthPlus Ireland and an advocate for returning some of the auction money

> Where is the capital to feed Europe's growth industries? A lot of it disappeared down the 3G sinkhole... [in] one of the biggest nationalizations of private capital since the Russian Revolution (Kapner 2001).

12.4 Convergence and Creative Destruction

The eclectic and surprisingly successful U.S. approach to technological development has pivoted on start-ups and newcomer firms. In practice, such newcomers tended to hail from the South and West, where institutions, attitudes, and industrial structures stimulated entrepreneurial experimentation (Norton 1986). For the moment, however, this decentralised, market-based approach to technology development seems to have foundered, at least within the telecommunications sector.

I conclude now by noting the play of competing forces: (1) the apparent restoration of oligopoly power and (2) the possibility of continued newcomer challenges. The issues can be framed in terms of convergence and creative destruction.

12.4.1 Convergence

A useful angle on the parallels between 1900 and the present comes from Schumpeter's famous construct, Long Waves of Creative Destruction. In one rendition, the technology regimes accompanying such 50- or 55-year waves were electricity a century ago and the digital revolution now (see Table 12.2).

Table 12.2. Long Waves of Creative Destruction

1	Industrial Revolution (1787–1842)	cotton textiles, iron, steam power
2	The Bourgeois Kondratieff (1842–97)	railroadisation
3	The Neo-Mercantilist Kondratieff (1897–1939)	electricity, automobiles
4	The Cold-War Kondratieff (1939–89)	defence, TV, mainframes
5	The Information Age (1989–)	PCs, telecommunications, entertainment

Source: reproduced from Norton (2001, p. 41). Based on Kuznets (1940, p. 257) for items 1–3

The defining characteristics of the current regime, the Information Age, can be stylised under five tendencies (as listed in Norton 2001, p. 40). Together, the tendencies create a context for convergence of formerly separated activities and industries:

- *Digitisation*, through which all information can be reduced to 0's and 1's, or on-off states on a transistor.
- *Moore's Law*, which states that the amount of information that can be stored on a microchip doubles every 18 months.
- A *Law of Increasing Bandwidth* (also known as Gilder's Law), a tendency (though less regular than Moore's Law) for telecommunications carrying capacity to double or triple each year via wireless and fibre-optic technologies.
- *Metcalfe's Law*, that the costs of adding a user to a network increase linearly, while benefits expand with the square of the number of users.
- *Packet-switching* as the digital transmission technique referred to earlier, the basis for the TCP/IP conventions behind the Internet.

What is new about the Information Age, in this framework, is "the ability to do things in a digital way" (Byrnes 1998).

How, specifically, does digitisation promote convergence? According to David B. Yoffie (1997), convergence can be defined as "the unification of functions – the coming together of previously distinct products that employed digital technologies...[enabling] the same infrastructure to accommodate manipulation and transmission...of voice, video, and data" (Quoted in Chandler and Cortada 2000, p. 287). The examples thus begin with the telephone and the computer, but soon range to television and beyond. Convergence, whether in 1900 or 2000, erases the boundaries between existing industries, cancelling out initial barriers to entry.

Still, incumbent firms may benefit from convergence by virtue of their end-to-end delivery systems. In addition, as William Baumol observes of Creative Destruction in telecommunications, the *"beneficiaries from the new technology are at least in part those whose older products are displaced"* (Baumol 2000, p. 22, emphasis added). The implication is that most innovations in the telecommunications sector in recent years may have benefited incumbents as much as newcomers.

Chandler and Cortada (2000) also discern a shift of the pendulum back toward large corporations in communications and media. In a survey of the role of information in U.S. economic development, they point out that during the 20th century, windows of entrepreneurial opportunity within electronics and computing opened only three times: (1) radio in the 1920s, (2) data-processing following IBM's System 360 and Digital's PDP minicomputers, and (3) the PC revolution.

Then the windows to entrepreneurial opportunity close:

> Since the mid-1980s, opportunities for entrepreneurial start-ups in hardware arose primarily in the production of specialized niche products or for...[suppliers] to the large established core companies. So if history is any guide, a small number of complex enterprises, particularly those experienced in building systems, will continue to lead in commercializing the hardware for today's Information Age (Chandler and Cortada 2000, p. 289).

By this reading it is not just regulatory failure that seems to have cleared the way for a restoration of oligopolistic firms in the U.S. telephone industry and in media. Both capital requirements and the organisational advantages that accrue to some large, mid-life companies may make the first decade of the 21st century resemble the industrial landscape a century earlier. The Baby Bells, Microsoft, and AOL-Time Warner are obvious candidates to thrive in this phase of the Information Age – an era of consolidation.

12.4.2 The Necessity of Newcomer Firms

Then again, any such idea of a corporate restoration may be shortsighted, or at best misleading. Insofar as the present moment is technologically dormant, incumbent firms would seem to have the advantage relative to newcomers. As

Schumpeter famously observed, however, "technological possibilities are an un-charted sea" (1942, p. 118).

Our chronology of the U.S. telephone industry seems to point to a clear conclusion. When new technological possibilities present themselves – in whatever as yet unsuspected ways – only newcomer firms can fully explore their potential. It was true of local U.S. telephone service in 1900. It was true in the series of challenges against the Bell System after 1963. In a different but more familiar example, it was true also of the microprocessor after 1971, as the PC revolution amply demonstrated.

The open question, by this reading, is when the next round of radical or disruptive innovations will begin, not whether new firms will drive their development.

References

Arrow KJ (1962) The economic implications of learning by doing. Review of Economic Studies 29: 155–73

Baumol W (2000) Innovation and creative destruction. In: McKnight LW, Vaaler PM, Katz RL (eds) Creative destruction: business survival strategies in the global Internet economy. MIT Press, Cambridge MA, pp 21–38

Brain M (2001) How stuff works. Hungry Minds, Inc., New York

Brain M, Tyson J (2001) How cell phones work. Available online at www.howstuffworks.com

Brody H (1999) Landmark inventions of the millennium. Encarta Yearbook

Buderi R (2000) Engines of tomorrow. Simon & Schuster, New York

Burlingame R (1940) Engines of democracy: inventions and society in mature America. Charles Scribner's Sons, New York

Chandler AD Jr (1990) Scale and scope. Harvard University Press, Cambridge

Chandler AD Jr, Cortada JW (2000) The information age: continuities and differences. In: Chandler AD, Cortada JW (eds) A nation transformed by information. Oxford University Press, Oxford, pp 281–299

Christensen, CM (1997) The innovator's dilemma: when new technologies cause great firms to fail. Harvard Business School Press, Boston

Cukier KN, Hibbard J (2000) Spectrum shortage. Red Herring, October: 284–290

Derfler FJ Jr, Freed L (2000) How networks work (millennium edition). Que, Indianapolis

Dodd, AZ (2000) The essential guide to telecommunications. Prentice-Hall, Upper Saddle River, New Jersey

Encarta Encyclopedia (2001) MCI WorldCom, Inc. Available online at www.encarta.com

Feder BJ (2000) Can Craig McCaw keep his satellites from crashing? The New York Times on the web, June 4

Forbes.com (1999) Sun, fun, and Ph.D.s, too. Available online at www.forbes.com/forbes/1999/0531/6311220a_print.html

Gilder G (2000) Telecosm: how infinite bandwidth will revolutionize our World. The Free Press, New York

Glover DR (2000) NASA experimental communications satellites. Available online at roland.lerc.nasa.gov/~dglover/sat/satcom2.html#Echo

Grove A (1993) How Intel makes spending pay off. Fortune, February 22: 57–61

Hafner K, Lyon M (1996) Where wizards stay up late: the origins of the Internet. Simon and Schuster, New York

John RR (2000) Recasting the information infrastructure for the industrial age. In: Chandler AD, Cortada JW (eds) A nation transformed by information. Oxford University Press, Oxford, pp 55–105

Kapner S (2001) Europe's wireless vision is dashed. New York Times, December 17

Kuznets S (1940) Schumpeter's business cycles. American Economic Review June: 257

Levinthal D (1998) The slow pace of rapid technological change: gradualism and punctuation in technological change. Industrial and Corporate Change 7: 217–247

McClain TJ (1998) San Diego's romance with telecommunications. San Diego Metropolitan Magazine, available online

MIT Inventor of the Week Archives (2001) Cellular technology (Frenkiel RH, Engel JS). available online

MIT Inventor of the Week (2000) Harold A. Rosen: geosynchronous satellite. The Lemelson-MIT Program's Invention Dimension, available online

Mueller ML Jr (1997) Universal service: competition, interconnection, and monopoly in the making of the American telephone system. MIT Press and AEI Press, Cambridge, MA and Washington DC

Norton RD (1986) Industrial policy and American renewal. Journal of Economic Literature 24: 1–40

Norton RD (2001) Creating the new economy: the entrepreneur and the U.S. resurgence. Edward Elgar, Cheltenham, UK

Schumpeter J (1942, 1962) Capitalism, socialism, and democracy. Harper & Row, New York

Segaller S (1998) Nerds 2.0.1: a brief history of the Internet. TV Books, New York

Seitz P (2001) Inventor Harold Rosen: his perserverance helped the world connect faster. Investor's Business Daily online edition, May 23

Standage T (1998) The Victorian Internet. Berkeley Books, New York

Young JS (1998) Craig McCaw –The Wireless Wizard of Oz. Forbes.com, available online

Young S, Dreazen YJ, Blumenstein R (2002) As SBC wars with regulators, local phone competition stalls. The Wall Street Journal, February 11, p 1

13 The Spatial Industrial Dynamics of the ICT Sector in Sweden

Charlie Karlsson and Johan Klaesson

Jönköping International Business School, Jönköping, Sweden

13.1 Introduction

At the Lisbon European Council meeting of 23–24 March 2000, the European Union put itself forward to a new strategic goal: "to become the most competitive and dynamic knowledge based economy of the world capable of sustainable economic growth with more and better jobs and greater social coherence". As part of this goal a comprehensive eEurope action plan was set up and approved at the Feira European Council meeting. The aim of the action plan is to advance Europe further on the road to the new, digital economy.

The Lisbon meeting expressed strong concerns about Europe's competitiveness in the new knowledge-based economy. It noted in particular that Europe was lagging compared to the United States in information and communication technologies (ICT). This lagging concerns investments on both the producer and consumer side in ICT hardware and software as well as the development of ICT services more generally. This continuous lagging over the 1990s in such knowledge investments coincided with Europe's lagging growth and productivity performance compared to the US. However, the comparison between the US and Europe, instructive as it may seem at first glance, hides a very differentiated picture within the EU. While Europe as a whole seems to have been slow in its transition towards the new, digital economy, some of the smaller European economies (such as Ireland, Finland, and Sweden, and to a lesser extent the Netherlands) actually witnessed a rapid uptake in computer, Internet and mobile phone use and ICT investments more generally over the second half of the 1990s, accompanied by a remarkable growth and employment performance over those same years.

Some of these smaller countries like, e.g., Sweden, also had an important ICT niche-producing sector with a substantial manufacturing involvement in ICT production. It seems highly probable that this substantial involvement in ICT production can be a primary explanation for why these smaller countries witnessed a more rapid diffusion of ICT goods and services throughout their economies. Hence, it seems as if they appeared better equipped to exploit some of the new digital growth opportunities than the larger countries within the EU, as if they adapted faster existing "old" economic activities to the new e-business environment and more generally as if they learnt more from the new opportunities to exploit those advantages across the European Union. Furthermore, the policy makers in these countries appear to have been more aware of the increasingly limited degrees of freedom of their national policy actions, for example, liberalising more rapidly their national telecommunications monopolies.

A rapid diffusion of ICT goods and services throughout an economy on both the producer and the consumer side is critically dependent upon that those industries that supply the relevant hardware and software also diffuse rapidly over the system of functional regions in an economy. This is not least true since a rapid adoption of new technologies is highly dependent upon face-to-face contacts between suppliers and customers.

It is well known and well documented that new, advanced products are to a large extent developed and first introduced at the market in the large metropolitan regions in the industrialised countries. In Sweden it is only the Stockholm region that really qualifies as belonging to this exclusive group of regions. However, the Stockholm region is the leading region not only in Sweden but also in the whole Nordic region. It is a major import node for new technologies and advanced, new products developed in other leading metropolitan regions in the world but also a major region in terms of R&D and product development, not least within the ICT sector.

To acknowledge the leading role of the Stockholm region in the ICT sector is not enough to explain the rapid diffusion of ICT in the whole Swedish economy. As part of such a fuller explanation it is necessary to understand how the ICT sector and the different industries within the ICT sector have penetrated the system of functional regions in Sweden.[1]

It is a well-established empirical fact that industries that have become strongly over-represented in the Stockholm region tend to have a strong tendency to grow in the rest of the country (Forslund 1996). However, it is less well established to what extent this is also true for the industries in the ICT sector and what the spatial diffusion patterns look like. Furthermore, there is a lack of explanations as regards the form of these diffusion patterns. To what extent do the spatial diffusion patterns follow a filtering-down model and to what extent do they follow a spatial product cycle model?

The exact form of the diffusion patterns is important, since it is mainly a filtering-down pattern that contributes to the broad spatial diffusion of ICT applications among customers. When analysing filtering-down patterns it is also interesting to study what role other characteristics of functional regions and their rank in the system of functional regions play for the decentralisation patterns that emerge. What role does the educational level of the labour force in different functional regions play? Does the presence of research universities in certain functional regions influence the decentralisation patterns?

Another set of interesting questions concerns the relationship between the different industries within the ICT sector. To what an extent can we talk about ICT

---

[1] Of course, the diffusion of ICT technology is to a high extent determined by changes on the demand side. However, supply side changes also play a significant role.

clusters? And what do these ICT clusters look like? Can we distinguish several different ICT clusters and do these clusters exhibit different decentralisation patterns?

The purpose of this paper is to analyse the spatial industrial dynamics of the Swedish ICT sector and the different industries within the sector. In doing so we will be able to determine if there is anything peculiar to this industry or if it behaves much like "ordinary" traditional sectors of the economy.

The rest of this paper is organised as follows. Section two presents a theoretical background to our empirical analysis. Important concepts in this section are urban regions, home market and increasing returns. These concepts will be discussed within the frameworks of two theories. These are spatial product life cycle theory and filtering-down theory. This discussion generates a few hypotheses that will be examined empirically. In section three the empirical analysis begins by determining the structure and development of the ICT sector during the nineties. Section four continues the empirical investigation, but now with an emphasis on spatial phenomena. The paper ends with a summary and conclusion of the main findings.

13.2 Spatial Industrial Dynamics of ICT Industries

13.2.1 The Leading Role of Leading Urban Regions

In the 1980s and early 1990s, some cyber prophets predicted that developments in ICT would kill distance and make urban regions superfluous (Cairncross, 1997). The basic idea was that ICT would enable a total spatial spread of economic activities and strongly reduce agglomeration economies. At the beginning of the 21st century, however, it has become clear that this picture is at least single-sided. There is increasing evidence that the digital revolution reinforces the position of leading urban regions (Hall 1998; Castells 1999). Leading urban regions are concentrations of knowledge – human resources, universities and R&D institutes – and knowledge constitutes the principal "input" in the digital economy. Leading urban regions are also leading centres of innovation but also host new economic growth sectors such as tourism and cultural industries. Leading urban regions are growing in importance as places where information is interpreted. The shift towards growing reliance on tele-mediated information, electronic transactions, and financial flows, as well as the continuing importance of fashion, art, the media, dance, consumption, leisure, research, collective consumption, travel, tourism, education, and governance place a premium on reflexivity, interpretation and innovation – the key assets of large urban regions (Storper 1996).

Many observers show that both the development and the application of ICT – infrastructure, hardware and software – occur first and foremost in or near urbanised economic core regions (Alles et al. 1994; Graham and Marvin 1996; Schmand et al. 1990; Shields et al. 1993). Many large urban regions in Europe including the Stockholm region host a relatively large and growing ICT sector (van Winden 2000). The developments within ICT have resulted in

- a dramatic decline in the price of information processing;
- a technologically driven digital convergence between communication and computer technology;
- a rapid growth in international electronic networking.

ICT allows for the codification of information and knowledge. As a consequence, ICT make codified knowledge more accessible to all sectors and all actors in the economy linked to information networks or with the knowledge how to access such networks (ter Weel 1999). Hence, it should be no surprise that the ICT revolution obviously is associated with the emergence of new location factors favouring some, mainly large urban regions more than others (van den Berg 1987; Mitchell 1999). International accessibility and quality of life seem to have become the key to attracting or retaining foot-loose companies and highly skilled labour. The diversity of the regional economy and the quality of the regional knowledge and innovation systems are other factors that seem to have become more important. Economic fortunes of urban regions tend to depend on the degree to which they manage to develop or extend their knowledge base, improve their accessibility, and offer a high quality of life. This implies that sustainable development is not only an ideal but also a precondition for future prosperity of urban regions.

Increased adoption of ICT is associated with newly emerging network structures between individuals, between companies but also between urban regions. Interaction in urban networks of all kinds has grown rapidly in the last decade, putting high pressure on inter- and intra-urban transportation systems. However, the ICT-revolution not only increases the (economic) importance of quality of life for urban regions, it also opens new ways for urban regions to improve the quality of life and accessibility (van den Berg and van Winden 2000; Mitchell 1999). Traffic information systems can contribute to reducing congestion and improving the quality of public transportation. New possibilities for home working may reduce commuting traffic, and so on. Taken together this means that ICT contributes in a self-reinforcing way to strengthening the competitive edge of large urban regions in developing and applying ICT.

13.2.2 The Decentralisation of ICT Industries

In the preceding section we established that the largest urban regions in the industrialised countries – and in the case of Sweden the Stockholm region – are the focal points of the digital economy. Not only do they host a strong ICT sector, there are also indications that they are leading in the application of ICT in other sectors. What, then, is the situation for smaller urban regions and for peripheral non-urban regions? Some tend over time to lose human resources to larger agglomerations and, hence, become less attractive for private sector companies, including companies in the ICT sector. Others find growth paths through specialisation in certain sectors of which the ICT sector could be one. Given this overall situation how does the digital economy develop in space, i.e., in the system of functional regions? An important purpose of the theory of spatial industrial dynamics is to try to explain why the economic milieu of a functional region can be advantageous for certain sets of economic activities and less advantageous for others, and why economic activities diffuse and/or relocate between functional regions. In the regional science literature two basic types of models have been employed to explain location patterns. Both of them can be extended to include dynamic change processes. The first type of models consists of central place system (CPS) models. CPS models focus on demand-based specialisation in the sense that regions that are large and dense can host a richer variety of output than smaller and less dense regions (Beckmann 1958, 1996; Tinbergen 1967). Within a CPS model it is the size of the set-up costs for each given product that determines the necessary size of a region's market area. When the market area is too small, the region will not host the activity in question. At a given point in time it is possible to identify certain high-rank products that are produced only in those urban regions where the accessible demand is large enough.

The second class of models consists of location advantage (LA) models. In LA models the specialisation pattern of regions is primarily supply based in the sense that the resource profile of each region determines its location advantages in a multi-regional system (Johansson 1997). Certain economic activities are based upon natural resources, which have to be extracted or harvested in the region where they are located. A standard LA model will predict where among available regions such resources will be harvested (Moroney and Walker 1966; Smith 1975). However, location advantages are not limited to the spatial location of natural resources but include all those localised, i.e., regionally trapped, factors which affect the location of economic activities in the form of birth, growth, decline and disappearance. They may also spring from increasing returns phenomena of various kinds: (i) agglomeration economies, (ii) localisation economies, and (iii) other specific resource advantages including internal economies of scale. Localisation economies may be described as "specialised external economies of scale" and can be associated with small as well as large functional regions. Agglomeration economies, which primarily are found in metropolitan regions, are based upon an abundance of positive supply externalities (Vernon 1960).

In this context one can observe that already Marshall (1920) identified three specific conditions, which explained why firms in a certain sector tend to be localised, i.e., why they could function more efficiently, and, hence, improve the regional economic milieu, when located near each other (cf. David and Rosenbloom 1990; Krugman 1991a and 1991b). Firstly, an industrial centre, and, in particular, a diversified urban region that is a centre for several industries allows a pooled (and robust) market for workers with specialised skills and varied competence profiles. Such a robust labour market benefits both workers and firms. Secondly, the same urban region can provide non-traded (public) inputs specific to each of its localised industries at lower costs, which affect the productivity and/or the cost level of firms in the region. Thirdly, new and subtle information about new production techniques, new products, and available suppliers and customers can spread more easily and accurately within a local environment and its intra-regional information networks than in distant networks. This generates market as well as technology spillovers (cf. Johansson and Wigren 1996; Malmberg et al. 1996; Malmberg and Maskell 1997). The same three conditions can also be applied to explain why the multiplicity and richness of a specific economic milieu (agglomeration diversity) simultaneously brings benefits to firms in many sectors (Norton 1992). Agglomeration economies are reinforced by the comparatively large and differentiated supply of producer services in metropolitan regions. The Marshall inspired arguments above mean that a specialised industrial centre can self-reinforce its location advantages for a specific industry (Arthur 1990; Krugman 1991c; Malmberg 1996). They also mean that a vital and multifaceted urban region can do even better. It can provide (i) a creative milieu (Andersson 1985), (ii) a diversified supply of various producer services, (iii) an intra-regional network for information flows about new production techniques, products, customers, and suppliers (Johansson et al. 1991), and (iv) a large and differentiated supply of labour categories. This enumeration of location attributes tends to emphasise intra-regional accessibility and the associated infrastructure. It also implies that the firms in a region mutually may constitute each other's production milieu characteristics. However, one should also add the importance of inter-regional interaction links and pertinent accessibility properties.

The filtering-down (FD) theory and spatial product life cycle (SPC) theory both offer dynamic explanations of the location behaviour of firms within a CPS- and a LA-framework, respectively. One major difference between the two theories is the following: the filtering-down theory stresses the hypothesis that industries filter down through the system of urban places in a hierarchical manner from locations of greater to locations of lesser industrial sophistication (Thompson 1969; Moriarty 1991). The spatial product life cycle theory, on the other hand, does not present any similar strict hypothesis concerning the spatial relocation pattern as products age (Karlsson 1988). In a dynamic CPS model, such as the filtering-down theory, technical change and/or demand change will influence commodities (or product groups) to shift position over time and thereby reshape the specialisation pattern of regions (Camagni et al. 1986). Standardisaion of products and routinisation of production may lower the set-up costs as well as the variable production costs. Market demand may also increase due to improvements in real income, changes in taste and outsourcing of activities from firms. As a consequence, activities may gradually "filter-down" or diffuse down the hierarchy of functional urban regions over time. In this way the "filtering-down" model refers to commodities, which spread from one level of an urban hierarchy to all functional regions at the subsequent lower level.

The spatial product life cycle theory that belongs to the family of dynamic LA models assumes that a high proportion of new products are initiated or imitated (at an early stage) in a leading functional, urban region with an opportunity-rich economic milieu. As production expands, products are standardised and production technique routinised and then relocation takes place. However, the number of followers is expected to be limited, since growing economies of scale prevent full decentralisation to many regions. According to this approach, changes in location are assumed to be supply-dependent also at the later stages of the product cycle

(Vernon 1960; Hirsch 1967; Andersson and Johansson 1984). Hence, this theory stresses the importance of external economies for the location behaviour during the life of a product. When relocation takes place, production may be concentrated in a small set of very specialsed regions. At this stage localisation economies which are very strong and which provide individual regions with a location advantage become essential (cf. Marshall 1920; Krugman 1991a).

Both SPC and FD theories assume that the development of a product or an industry follows a sequence with an introduction phase, a growth phase, and a maturing phase that takes the shape of an S-shaped growth curve.[2] The life cycle perspective makes it possible to see patterns in the continuously adjusting spatial structure as regards intra-urban as well as interregional development. As the life cycle concept is a dynamic concept, it is very useful for the analysis of a number of locational changes, because in reality firms are dealing with a dynamic market environment in the competitive struggle, i.e., competition is a dynamic process (Clark 1940). In particular, the life cycle concept seems to be a useful device to explain specific aspects of locational dynamics, especially in the case of interregional relocation processes for new sectors (Aydalot 1984).

In the following sections we emphasise the dynamics of product vintages as the force that drives the dynamic behaviour of SPC and FD models – a dynamic behaviour that supports the assumptions used in empirical lead-lag models (Forslund and Johansson 1995; Forslund 1996, 1997). The lead-lag model is formulated with the specific objective of generating hypotheses that can be tested empirically. It classifies economic activities in such a way that it is possible to refer to them as clusters of products with a synchronised location dynamics.[3] For a given system of functional urban regions, the model specifies for each type of economic activity (product), j, its average share, s_j, of all activities in the system of regions (measured in terms of employment or value added). The activity share of a particular region, r, is denoted by s_{jr}. The model identifies for a given multi-regional context a specific leading region (within the international system of leading regions), 0. The relative shares for this region, $\mu_{j0} = s_{j0} / s_j$, are used as predictive indicators. The basic hypotheses are associated with the locational leadership of region 0. The first says that economic activities with a high μ-value should be expected to grow in other regions in the given system of functional regions. The second says that activities with a low concentration in the leading region, i.e., activities with a low μ-value, should be expected to decline in other regions. The first assumption implies that new activities frequently are initiated and start to grow first in the leading region. The second assumption implies that leading regions lose employment in mature activities before other regions. Hence, they are leading also in the de-

---

[2] However, some activities may not show cyclical behaviour. This concerns in particular non-standardised activities including customised delivery of goods and services such that each delivery has new and individual attributes (Forslund 1997).

[3] The lead-lag model does not apply to activities, which have to be extracted or harvested in the region where they are located. However, their location requirements are characterised by standard location advantage models, which refer to comparative advantages of Ricardo type.

cline phase. As a consequence of the above assumptions, a set of sub-hypotheses can be formulated. For example, activities with both a high μ-value and fast growth are assumed to be non-routinised and refer to non-standardised products. They are also assumed to be R&D and knowledge intensive. Activities with a low μ-value are assumed to be routinised and price competing, with a very strong tendency to reduce the labour input coefficient. In the general case it is assumed that a high proportion of new products are initiated or imitated (at an early stage) in a leading region, which in the case of Sweden is the Stockholm metropolitan region. As the production expands, products are frequently standardised and production techniques routinised, which is referred to as product vintage dynamics. As new product vintages are introduced, the pertinent activities are relocated or diffused within the national system of functional urban regions. Analysing vintage process dynamics as the driving force in SPC and FD models, it is possible to show that a gradual change in location will take place. In that process the follower regions will host a growing share of activities for which the vintage renewal is dominated by standardisation and routinisation (Forslund and Johansson 1998). It should be emphasised that the diffusion process will be somewhat different in the two cases and these differences can be related to different underlying assumptions for the two models as regards the nature of the commodities and their distance sensitivity, with respect to intra- and inter-regional interaction.

An understanding of spatial industrial dynamics is fundamentally dependent upon knowledge of the time scale at which different regional factors change. In this paper the following time scale assumptions are made. First, the production factors of firms, such as installed capital and labour employed, adjust to market signals in a delayed way, i.e., they adjust slowly compared to the speed of change of the market signals themselves. The latter include prices, current input flows, sales volumes, and profits. Second, the economic milieu with its various location attributes adjusts on a slower time scale than the capital equipment of the firms. As a consequence, it can affect the production possibilities in a fundamental way and influence location dynamics as well. Third, the labour supply is assumed to adjust on a time scale slow enough to make the labour supply a component of the economic milieu. In summary: due to its slow pace of adjustment, the economic milieu of the various regions in the system of regions functions as the structure on which the fast game of interaction and competition is played. Because of this time scale difference, it may be assumed that the economic milieu of a region can attract and repel specific sets of transaction and production activities.

13.2.3 Home Market: Local Products and Global Products

Consider the system of functional urban regions. Some functional regions are specialised due to the existence of specific natural resources. Disregarding such location factors, this paper considers two types of endogenous specialisation: the first is a combination of home market size and internal economies of scale, the second is localisation economies (industry-specific external economies of scale). The term "external" signifies that firms and other organisations in a functional region together form an economic milieu, such that the efficiency conditions are improved for all firms. A functional region is in a fundamental way characterised by its density of economic activities, social opportunities, and interaction options. From the perspective of the individual firm, density is a positive factor to the extent that it creates accessibility to households, firms and other actors at the market place. The density may also relate to a specific industry. Such intra-industry density is an important phenomenon also in small municipalities belonging to medium-sized regions or to small, peripheral regions. Industry-wide density exists primarily in metropolitan or other large regions with a large home market for local products. Economic density can be interpreted as intra-regional accessibility, where "region" is defined as a functional region. However, in the discussion here it is not density *per se* but accessibility to resources and between economic agents that matters. Accessibility is obtained by an appropriate combination of density and infrastructure, and it is the dynamic interaction between these three factors that forms the core of urban regional development. If density increases and the infrastructure remains unchanged, congestion and other tension phenomena may follow. As a consequence, accessibility is reduced and the value of density declines. Infrastructure without matching density, on the other hand, represents only idle opportunities. Economic density can be interpreted as intra-regional accessibility within a functional region, i.e., accessibility to resources and between economic actors. CPS and FD models recognise density of purchasing power in a general sense. A dense region has an advantage in the production of goods and services with contact intensive sales. LA and SPC models, on the other hand, focus on the density of firms producing similar products (industrial clusters) and of input suppliers and labour categories, which are specialised with regard to the industrial cluster, i.e., on the external economies.

Suppose now a case with a product with a strongly non-linear spatial interaction cost curve. This situation creates a home market advantage for suppliers of such a contact-dependent product that it warrants talking about such a product as a local product. If the number of potential buyers within the home market region is large and if their purchasing power is high, then this constitutes a strong home market potential as discussed by Krugman (1980) and Davies et al. (1997). Economic activities with strong internal economies of scale will have a particular advantage of locating in a region with a large home market as defined here. Suppose also that for products with low distance sensitivity there exists another generalised interaction cost curve that is linear but with a slight positive slope. Such a curve may of course have a steep section further away, e.g., when the delivery of the product passes a language and/or a cultural barrier. However, within such borders the home market is extended, and there exist no significant home market effects for large urban regions. This latter type of products is here labelled global products and can be located in a much less restricted way than local products. In this case the location advantages will, in particular, depend upon the accessibility in the inter-regional transport networks. Consider now a firm that sells much of its output in distant export markets. Such a firm can be expected to have a customer interaction cost-curve of the second type described above. However, the same firm may have accessibility requirements as regards input suppliers. This latter type of accessibility concerns specialised labour inputs as regards skills and knowledge, specialised services including R&D, as well as current material inputs. Suppose now that these input suppliers have internal economies of scale. In that case these suppliers will have an incentive to locate in the same functional region as the exporting firm, if the demand in the region for their deliveries is large enough. If the exporting firm is not large enough, sufficient demand may be created if several firms of the same type locate in the same region. This would then represent a specialised demand density, which is big enough to match the internal scale economies of the input suppliers. This form of localisation economies represents one side of the LA model.

This emphasis on accessibility has an additional consequence. For a functional region with a narrow (sector-specific) specialisation, the critical accessibility concerns primarily those resources and actors that interact with the firms in the particular industry (industries). In this case it is a specific set of customers and a specific set of suppliers to which the accessibility networks need to be alert. For a region with a broad scope of specialisation, agglomeration accessibility applies. However, it is important to distinguish between two types of accessibility: intra-regional and inter-regional. Regarding intra-regional accessibility, consider a set of zones or nodes ($j = 1,...,m$) within an urban region r. The density of contact options of each zone, i.e., its contact value, is denoted by A_j. For a given infrastructure, $\hat{I}_r$, the intra-regional accessibility increases as the A_j-values are augmented, given that the infrastructure capacity is sufficient. As interaction increases and the capacity limits of the infrastructure are reached, congestion effects will emerge and, hence, the accessibility is reduced. For a given zone the accessibility to the other zones within the urban region can be described as follows:

$$a_{rj} = \sum_{k=1}^{m} \exp\{-\lambda_I d_{jk}\} A_k \qquad (13.1)$$

where d_{jk} represents some relevant distance measure and where λ_I signifies the distance sensitivity of economic actors. From Eq. (13.1) it is possible to calculate an average accessibility value $a_r = [a_{r1}+a_{r2}+...+a_{rm}]/m$. The latter value can also be interpreted as a measure of the overall density of the region. If the density is increased while the infrastructure remains unchanged, the product $\lambda_I d_{jk}$ will increase for each link (j,k), and this will reduce accessibility. Hence, in this way density and infrastructure capacity simultaneously determine accessibility.

The inter-regional accessibility, i.e., the accessibility between two regions s and r can be described by a formula which resembles Eq. (13.1). Using a_r as an indicator of region r's attractiveness, the accessibility between s and r is described by

$$a_{sr} = \exp\{-\lambda_{II} d_{sr}\} a_r \qquad (13.2)$$

Since Eq. (13.1) refers to very frequent intra-regional interaction and Eq. (13.2) to less frequent inter-regional interaction, consistency requires that $\lambda_I \gg \lambda_{II}$. Moreover, it may be recognised that $a_{ss} = a_s$. Also in this case, the measure is calculated contingent on the existence of sufficient infrastructure capacity. Congestion on the link (s,r) will increase the value of $\lambda_{II} d_{sr}$. Analysing different commodities it is possible to make a distinction between those commodities for which intra-regional accessibility dominates and those commodities for which inter-regional accessibility is more important.

13.2.4 Increasing Returns to Scale and Home Market

The home market concept was used above to make a distinction between local products and global products. In the current section the relationship between increasing returns to scale and home market is explored. Consider a CPS model in which there exists set up costs for all types of production. In this case the size of the set up costs for each given product will determine the necessary size of its market area. Regions whose market area is too small will not host the production in question. Products that need large market areas are therefore only produced in those functional urban regions whose accessible demand is large enough, i.e., that have a large market area. The (potential) market areas of urban regions belonging to class k are denoted by M_k. Intra-regional as well as the inter-regional accessibility to customers influence the size of M_k. A system of functional urban regions may be characterised by its ordering of sizes of market areas, such that $M_0 > \ldots > M_k > \ldots M_n$, where M_0 refers to the urban region with the highest rank and M_n to all urban regions of the lowest rank. Commodities (goods and services) with the highest rank are supplied only from the urban region of rank 0 and distributed over the system of urban regions. Commodities of rank k are supplied from several urban centres of rank k to all urban regions within the system of regions with a lower rank. Beckman (1996) presents a CPS model with equilibrium properties, such that the market size of an urban region attracts location of activities, which in turn attract population and determine the size of the urban region. Moreover, the market size for all ranks of the central place system is determined under complete interdependency (cf. Bos 1965; Tinbergen 1967). In the sequel, we follow an elaboration of the Beckmann model made by Johansson and Forslund (1997). Given the described urban system, a feasible location for a market-oriented firm (which supplies a given type of commodity) depends upon the cost function, which applies at a given point in time for the production of this commodity. A vintage index τ, which has the value 0 for a new activity (product) and which increases towards the value 1 as the product becomes more standardised and the activity is routinised, is introduced to determine the feasible location. Let $F(\tau)$ denote the fixed costs, including the non-variable part of the development costs, for a given vintage. Consider also the variable costs, which here may be approximated by a proportional cost component $c(\tau)Q$, where $c(\tau)$ is a fixed coefficient and Q denotes output (supply). This yields:

$$C(\tau) = F(\tau) + c(\tau)Q \tag{13.3}$$

Given this cost function, a firm supplying the pertinent commodity can locate in a region of category k, if it can break even there. For a given price p this is equivalent to the following condition:

$$\pi_k(p,\tau) = [p - c(\tau)]f(p)M_k - F(\tau) \geq 0 \tag{13.4}$$

where $f(p)$ is the individual demand function. From Eq. (13.4) it is possible to conclude that with a given price level that is the same across all urban regions, the activity can be established only in regions with a sufficiently large market area, as expressed by the variable Mk.[4] Or, in other words, the larger the set up cost $F(\tau)$ the larger the market area, i.e., the larger the home market needed to make production profitable *ceteris paribus*. The dynamics of this hierarchy may be studied by introducing a technical change process described by the technique vintage index τ. Consider technical change processes such that $F(\tau)$ decreases and that $c(\tau)$ do not increase as τ increases. This implies that an industry supplying a given commodity may initially have a feasible location in urban regions with k as the lowest rank. As the technique vintage index increases, a feasible location will gradually be found in urban regions of category $k+1$, $k+2$, etc. The reason is that it may become feasible to locate an activity at a new, lower level in the system of urban regions, when the set up costs change in such a way that $F(\tau+u)<F(\tau)$. Thus, the actual industry filters down the hierarchy of urban regions. A process where activities are relocated may also involve a price reduction, $p^*<p$, and a corresponding demand increase, $f(p^*)>f(p)$, where p^* is the equilibrium price when the vintage $\tau+u$ is introduced. This is equal to saying that as the effects of increasing returns diminish, the smaller the market area needed to make production profitable becomes. Hence, given the described technical change process, the location of all supply activities will filter down the hierarchy of functional urban regions. Generally speaking the filtering down process implies that when the location condition for a certain product changes so that urban regions of both size category k and $k+1$ become feasible, then all urban regions of rank $k+1$ are expected to be invaded by firms supplying the pertinent product.

For many production activities, in particular within manufacturing industry, a more realistic assumption regarding the technical change process is a change process where the set up cost $F(\tau)$ increases while the variable cost $c(\tau)$ decreases as τ increases. Assume initially that the product price remains constant as well as the market areas. Under these new assumptions the feasible location pattern may involve a filtering down process as well as a "filtering up" process. If the following condition holds when the vintage $\tau+u$ is introduced

$$[p-c(\tau+u)]f(p)M_k < F(\tau+u) \qquad (13.5)$$

production will "filter up" the hierarchy of the system of urban regions, i.e., the filtering down process might be reversed and new units might be set up at higher levels in the hierarchy of urban regions. If the opposite condition holds we obtain a filtering down process. Hence, under these assumptions stronger effects of increasing returns may lead either to a centralisation of production or a decentralisation. In a more realistic setting it must also be acknowledged that the changes in the cost structure may involve a price reduction that can trigger off a demand increase that is large enough to balance any "filtering up" tendencies. In the filtering down case a demand increase will of course speed up the filtering down process.

---

[4] All regions of rank k are assumed to have the same market size.

The technical change process may also lead the distribution costs (or the distance friction) to diminish due to, e.g., lower product weight, which would lead to an extension of the market areas. Then the following condition holds: $M_k(\tau+u)>M_k(\tau)$, which should counteract the "filtering up" process and stimulate the filtering down process depending upon the circumstances. The distribution costs (or the distance friction) may diminish due to other reasons than the technical change process. One obvious reason is improvements in the intra- and interregional infrastructure systems that lower the generalised transport costs, and, hence, increase the market area of each urban region. Assuming that only regions with a rank higher than k host a given type of production, that the market area of regions of the rank k increases from M_k to M'_k, and that all other variables stay constant, then regions of rank k will obtain the actual type of production established if

$$\pi(p,\tau)=[p-c(\tau)]f(p)M'_k - F(\tau)\geq 0 \qquad (13.6)$$

However, this condition is not a sufficient condition for production to be established in urban regions of rank k. It must be remembered that historically regions of rank $k-1$ or higher have supplied regions of rank k and lower with the actual products via interregional exports. Hence, newly established production in regions of rank k will always have to compete with imports from regions with a higher rank. This means that there is one more condition that must be fulfilled, namely that

$$[c(\tau)f(p)M'_k + F(\tau)]/Q < [c(\tau)f(p)M'_{k-1}]/Q \qquad (13.7)$$

where M'_{k-1} signifies the market areas of urban regions of rank $k-1$ after the improvements of the infrastructure systems. Thus, any discussions of establishing production in urban regions of rank k after an improvement of the infrastructure systems that extends the market areas of these regions must also consider that the same infrastructure improvement also extends the market areas of the old suppliers in urban regions of rank $k-1$. This discussion concerns the more short-run effects of an improvement of the infrastructure systems. In the long run ongoing improvements of the infrastructure systems may of course transform the whole system of urban regions, which not least the construction of the railway systems in different countries during the last century illustrates. Now return to condition (13.4) and assume that the vintage dynamics process makes a halt. Then free entry into the system can be assumed to generate an equilibrium solution such that profits are reduced towards zero. When n producers have entered a particular region, the profit function of each firm becomes

$$\{[(p-c(\tau))f(p)M_k]/n - F(\tau)\}\geq 0 \qquad (13.8)$$

13.2.5 Networks, External Economies of Scale, and Development Strategies

In Sect. 13.2.4 the relationship between increasing returns to scale and home market effects was explored within a CPS framework. In this section we consider a dynamic LA framework, i.e., an SPC framework, where the number of follower regions in the decentralisation process is expected to be limited. The limited number of follower regions is due to the fact that growing economies of scale will normally characterise the technique vintage development that makes products standardised and their production routinised. Hence, market demand can be satisfied by a limited number of production units. This means that instead of being dominated by market considerations, location choices will be dominated mainly by supply considerations. Thus, location decisions will be influenced by the external economies of scale offered by different regions that can give cost advantages as regards routine inputs (land, unskilled labour, and so on) and transport costs.

The SPC framework emphasises that at an early stage of the product cycle (i.e., when an activity has a low τ-value) the development benefits from intra-regional accessibility to both suppliers and customers tend to determine location. Hence, the starting phase of the cycle is sensitive to intra-regional accessibility and combines a demand side specialisation with a supply side specialisation and variation. As a consequence, an urban region with agglomeration economies provides the most advantageous milieu for the initiation of product cycles. At later stages, when the product is mature enough to be located in less advanced regions the supply side specialisation tend to dominate location and now the output is distributed to customers across a wide inter-regional system. Thus, at these later stages inter-regional accessibility is more important for location than intra-regional accessibility.

Let every product be associated with a τ-value, which is low for a young product or an early vintage and high for a late vintage. The former refers to non-standardised products, which require large shares of knowledge or development resources in the production process. A high τ-value refers to a late vintage with routinised (and usually automated) production and interaction activities, which are assumed to use small shares of knowledge resources. With routine input resources and development resources as the two input categories, the cost function in Eq. (13.3) can be extended as in Eq. (13.9). When focusing on a particular product group it is possible to consider the cost function in Eq. (13.9), which refers to a product vintage that is based on technique τ, and which is applied in a region r:

$$\phi_r(\tau) = \left[F_r(\tau)/x_r(\tau)\right] + L_r c_r(\tau) \tag{13.9}$$

where

$$c_r(\tau) = \rho_r a(\tau) + w_r b(\tau) \tag{13.10}$$

and where $\phi_r(\tau)$ denotes the average total cost, $F_r(\tau)/x_r(\tau)$ the average fixed cost associated with technique τ, L_r summarises the effects of the location advantages and the external economies of scale associated with production in region r

$(0<L_r\leq1)$, $L_r c_r(\tau)$ the average variable cost associated with using technology τ in region r, $a(\tau)$ the input coefficient (per unit delivered output) for routine input resources, and $b(\tau)$ the input coefficient for development resources, i.e., input resources for knowledge activities or knowledge production. It is assumed that the input coefficients are determined by the actual technique τ and are not dependent upon in which region the production takes place. The two price variables, p_r and w_r, on the other hand, are location specific. p_r denotes the price of routine inputs, and w_r the price of knowledge-intensive development resources. It is now assumed that the knowledge-intensity of products and production techniques declines as the technique-vintage and product-vintage indexes increase. To analyse the implications of this assumption a new variable – the knowledge ratio $-\beta(\tau)=b(\tau)/a(\tau)$ or simply $-\beta=b/a$ is constructed. In order to bring out the essential aspect of ageing product vintages it is assumed that the technical change process is driven by the change in τ. In line with the product cycle model in Johansson and Karlsson (1987) it is assumed that the routinisation of production increases as the product is getting more standardised. Consider now two stages of the product cycle development represented by two pairs of input coefficients (b^0, a^0) and $(\hat{b}, \hat{a})$. Let the technique (b^0, a^0) refer to a young product vintage and the second to a more mature one, so that

$$\beta^0 = b^0/a^0 > \hat{\beta} = \hat{b}/\hat{a} \qquad (13.11)$$

Consider now two regions, where the first region k is a metropolitan region and the second region h is a non-metropolitan region. The metropolitan region k is assumed to have lower prices (costs) of knowledge resources and higher prices of routine resources – in comparison with the non-metropolitan region h. In other words, it is assumed that $p_k>p_h$ and $w_k<w_h$. Consider then the production of a particular product, which initially is located in the metropolitan region k with $L_k c_k < L_h c_h$. Moreover, assume that the technique develops as specified in Eq. (13.11). According to the above assumptions, a shift in the variable cost advantage occurs when the knowledge-routine ratio reduces in such a way that $\beta^0 > (p_k - p_h)/(w_h - w_k) > \hat{\beta}$. However, a shift in the variable cost advantage between the two regions is not a sufficient condition for providing an incentive to relocate production. Therefore, let the assumptions above apply, and assume also that the product price is reduced to $\hat{p} < p^0$. Furthermore, assume that the set up cost increases to $\hat{F} < F^0$, when the knowledge-routine ratio shifts from β^0 to $\hat{\beta}$. A region h is a feasible location if

$$(\hat{p} - L_h \hat{c}_h)f(\hat{p})\widetilde{M}_h - \hat{F} \geq 0 \qquad (13.12)$$

where $\widetilde{M}_h$ denotes the size of the market area for a producer in region h.

$$\widetilde{M}_h = \sum_s \exp\{-\lambda d_{rs}\}v_s \qquad (13.13)$$

where v_s represents the size of the market in region $s \in U$. U denotes the relevant set of customer regions. d_{rs} denotes the distance between r and s in the network connecting regions in the entire area U. The above analysis can be extended to a system of regions. Assume that the internal economies of scale are substantial so that not all non-metropolitan regions have a home market that is large enough to make production profitable. Then it is natural to ask the following question: which regions will be chosen for setting up new production facilities when it becomes profitable to relocate production from the metropolitan regions? As can be seen from Eq. (13.12), this choice will be determined by the external economies offered by different non-metropolitan regions, the cost of the input factors in the different regions, and the size of the market area covered by each region.

13.2.6 Hypotheses

This paper is to a large degree exploratory and not basically targeted at the testing of hypotheses. However, based upon the theoretical discussion above we are able to formulate some preliminary hypotheses as regards the spatial dynamics of the ICT sector in Sweden.

H1: Given the general strength of the ICT sector in the Stockholm region we expect most industries in the ICT sector to exhibit a clear pattern of decentralisation in the Swedish system of functional regions.

H2: However, this does not mean that we expect every industry to show such a pattern, since some industries may be heavily dependent upon those for Sweden unique external economies offered by the Stockholm region. In particular, we expect industries with a high knowledge intensity to stick to the Stockholm region, since this region offers the best supply of well-educated labour of all regions in Sweden without any comparison.

H3: We expect manufacturing industries within the ICT sector to decentralise mainly according to a spatial product cycle pattern, since among other things large-scale establishments dominate these industries.

H4: We expect service industries within the ICT sector to decentralise mainly according to a filtering down pattern, since among other things small-scale establishments dominate these industries.

H5: Some service industries in the ICT sector to a high extent provide producer services to the manufacturing industries within the ICT sector. These service industries will follow the decentralisation patterns of the relevant manufacturing industries.

H6: We expect that within the ICT sector it is possible to identify clusters of industries that mainly follow the same decentralisation pattern.

13.3 The ICT Sector in Sweden

The first problem to address is how to define the ICT sector. The Swedish standard industrial classification system identifies about 750 independent industries (at the five-digit level). Following the classification suggested by the OECD (Definition for the Information and Communication Technology Sector), we identify 23 industries at the five-digit level as the ICT sector. Seven industries of these 23 are of a manufacturing type and the remaining 16 are more service oriented. The Table in App. 13.A gives information concerning code numbers and a brief description of the industries.

In Table 13.1 the number of persons employed in the 23 industries is presented. Total employment in Sweden in the ICT sector as a whole has developed from 135,595 in 1990 to 159,338 in 1998. This represents an increase of 18%. This increase is more impressive if one takes into account that during these same years total employment in all sectors fell from 4,485,400 in 1990 to 3,978,500 in 1998, that is a drop by 11%. Thus, this sector has been very successful in Sweden during the 1990s. However, not all sub sectors have increased in employment. Of the seven manufacturing sub sectors there are two that have decreased in employment. Those are industries *Manufacture of office machinery* and *Manufacture of computers and other information processing equipment.* In the latter industry the drop has been very substantial, over 80%. Of the services sub sectors seven industries have decreased their employment. In some cases the drop has been equally drastic. In particular, *Renting of office machinery and equipment including computers* experienced an employment drop of 78%.

Turning to the industries with increasing employment, the highest percentage increases in the manufacturing sub sector are recorded for *Reproduction of computer media* and *Manufacture of television and radio receivers, sound or video recording or reproducing apparatus and associated goods.* The first industry of these two has the highest increase, 324%, but in absolute numbers this only amounts to 107 employees. The second industry has an increase of 234% or in absolute numbers almost 3000 persons. In the services sub sector two industries stand out, these are *Retail sale of telecommunication equipment* with a percentage increase of 1290% and *Software supply* with an increase of 211%. Again the lower figure represents the highest absolute increase. The development of the first of these two service industries mirrors the expansion of the use of mobile phones. The second illustrates the widespread use of computers generating a demand for software.

Regarding number of plants, we observe that the number of plants has decreased in four of the manufacturing industries, i.e., for the majority of the manufacturing industries. Even if the number of plants has decreased in four service industries, the dominating picture is the rapid increase of the number of plants among the service industries. Thus, the number of manufacturing plants in general has decreased by 14% while the number of service sector plants has increased by 68%.

The average plant size is very much larger for the manufacturing sub sector than for the service sub sector. During the period average plant size has increased for five industries in the manufacturing sub sector. For the services sub sector average plant size has decreased for 10 industries. Overall, manufacturing plants have increased in size from an average of 52 to 64 employees and service sector plants have decreased in average size from 12 to 9 employees. Thus, it seems as if internal economies of scale are much more important for manufacturing than for service production.

Table 13.1. Employment, Number of Plants, and Average Plant size in 1990 and 1998

	E90	E98	ΔE%	Nopl90	Nopl98	ΔNopl%	Apls90	Apls98
22330	33	140	324	13	28	115	3	5
30010	1615	1578	-2	43	37	-14	38	43
30020	10800	2074	-81	345	206	-40	31	10
31300	4976	5142	3	57	86	51	87	60
32100	4580	8155	78	182	192	5	25	42
32200	25756	31174	21	187	167	-11	138	187
32300	1260	4206	234	122	99	-19	10	42
51142	379	271	-28	66	71	8	6	4
51652	1197	945	-21	156	151	-3	8	6
51653	6383	7334	15	778	795	2	8	9
52493	2131	2604	22	410	555	35	5	5
52494	112	1557	1290	33	267	709	3	6
64201	40917	27917	-32	1069	1671	56	38	17
64202*	–	862	–	–	66	–	–	13
64203	732	520	-29	37	36	-3	20	14
71330	1160	256	-78	145	51	-65	8	5
72100	985	1419	44	116	410	253	8	3
72201	19770	42606	116	3159	5958	89	6	7
72202	3383	10529	211	240	993	314	14	11
72300	5266	6238	18	344	397	15	15	16
72400	823	1112	35	20	65	225	41	17
72500	2205	2087	-5	436	340	-22	5	6
72600	1132	612	-46	123	131	7	9	5
Man	49020	52469	7	949	815	-14	52	64
Ser	86575	106869	23	7132	11957	68	12	9
Ict	135595	159338	18	8081	12772	58	17	12

Notes: E = employment, ΔE = change in employment in percent, Nopl = number of plants, ΔNopl = change in number of plants in percent, Apls = average plant size, *) Industry 64202 was not present in the 1990 data.

In Table 13.2 the Gross profit share, wage rate, value added per employee and quotient between value added and turnover are shown. These figures are given for each of the 23 industries, for the manufacturing sub sector and for the services sub sector, together with overall figures. For all four categories the overall service sector has higher values than the overall manufacturing sub sector. Thus, profitability, wages, productivity and value added divided by turnover. The last measure is intended to capture how much of the production process actually takes place within the industry. A high value of this indicator means that purchases from other industries are limited and vice versa. The three most profitable (high gross profit share) manufacturing industries are *Manufacture of electronic valves and tubes* and other electronic components, *Manufacture of television and radio transmitters and apparatus for line telephony and line telegraphy* and *Manufacture of television and radio receivers, sound or video recording or reproducing apparatus and associated goods*, having a gross profit share ranging from 0.15 to 0.17. The three most profitable service industries are *Radio and television broadcast operation, Cable television operation* and *Renting of office machinery and equipment including computers*, ranging from 0.28 to 0.34.

Table 13.2. Profitability, Wages, Value Added/Employee and Value Added/Turnover in 1996

SNI92	Gross profit share (average)	Wage rate (1000 SEK)	Value Added per employee (1000 SEK)	Value Added/ Turnover
22330	0.10	179	418	0.35
30010	0.12	312	510	0.37
30020	0.11	277	458	0.41
31300	0.09	254	401	0.32
32100	0.17	235	362	0.39
32200	0.15	258	275	0.19
32300	0.16	220	334	0.31
51142	0.10	249	487	0.16
51652	0.13	304	467	0.31
51653	0.10	318	472	0.15
52493	0.08	202	274	0.15
52494	0.07	217	269	0.15
64201	0.16	244	695	0.53
64202	0.33	375	670	0.66
64203	0.28	213	570	0.52
71330	0.34	234	814	0.46
72100	0.17	281	405	0.43
72201	0.16	329	477	0.48
72202	0.16	286	395	0.46
72300	0.15	310	385	0.42
72400	0.12	281	379	0.31
72500	0.08	263	404	0.41
72600	0.12	242	404	0.41
Man	0.13	248	394	0.34
Ser	0.16	272	473	0.38
Ict	0.15	264	449	0.36

The average wage rate is about ten percent higher in the service sector than in the manufacturing sector. However, the variation in wage rates among service sectors is larger than among the manufacturing sectors. The difference between the highest and lowest wage rate between manufacturing sectors is 133,000 SEK. The corresponding measure for the service sector is 173,000 SEK. The average productivity is about 20 percent higher in the service sector than in the manufacturing sector. The value added per turnover is much higher in service sectors than in manufacturing sectors especially if we disregard the wholesale and retail sale industries.

Table 13.3 depicts the share of the workforce with a high educational standard in the different industries. In this context a high educational standard means that the employee has three years or more of university (college) studies.

From Table 13.3 one can see that on average the workforce in service production has more education than in the manufacturing industries.

Table 13.3. Share of Workforce with High Education

SNI92	Share of highly educated workforce %	Education in relation to overall ICT
22330	17.1	82.6
30010	8.1	39.1
30020	19.5	94.2
31300	4.5	21.7
32100	10.7	51.7
32200	23.1	111.6
32300	9.0	43.5
51142	4.8	23.2
51652	22.2	107.2
51653	10.0	48.3
52493	6.1	29.5
52494	1.9	9.2
64201	10.9	52.7
64202	16.5	79.7
64203	9.8	47.3
71330	16.1	77.8
72100	20.3	98.1
72201	32.9	158.9
72202	33.9	163.8
72300	17.8	86.0
72400	20.7	100.0
72500	3.8	18.4
72600	20.3	98.1
Man	17.7	85.5
Ser	22.2	107.2
Ict	20.7	100.0

In the manufacturing group *Manufacture of television and radio transmitters
and apparatus for line telephony and line telegraphy* have the highest educational
level. For the service sectors there are two industries that stick out. These are
Software consultancy and *Software supply*. In these two industries one out of three
employees has more than three years of university training. Perhaps it is a bit surprising to note that there seems to be a quite poor correlation between educational
level and wage rate.

In Table 13.4 the shares of small and medium sized firms (SMEs) are recorded
for the different industries. The numbers are collected for firms with fewer than 20
employees and for firms with fewer than 200 employees. The table also distinguishes between shares of actual firms and shares of employment in these enterprises.

Table 13.4. Share of and Employment in Small and Medium Sized Firms in the Industries

	%SMEs (<20)90	%SMEs (<20)98	%E in SMEs (<20) 90	%E in SMEs (<20) 98	%SMEs (<200) 90	%SMEs (<200) 98	%E in SMEs (<200) 90	%E in SMEs (<200) 98
22330	100	96	100	77	100	100	100	100
30010	74	68	6	7	93	95	41	54
30020	86	89	10	34	96	100	28	80
31300	49	52	3	5	82	93	33	55
32100	87	78	13	8	97	95	38	30
32200	65	54	2	2	82	82	11	13
32300	85	76	29	8	100	93	100	31
51142	95	97	72	82	100	100	100	100
51652	90	94	41	61	100	100	100	100
51653	91	90	46	44	100	100	93	95
52493	95	96	65	72	100	100	100	100
52494	100	97	100	75	100	100	100	100
64201	62	81	11	21	97	99	66	82
64202	–	88	–	26	–	100	–	100
64203	68	86	26	28	100	100	100	100
71330	91	94	34	49	99	100	78	100
72100	95	97	22	68	99	100	42	100
72201	94	93	44	36	100	100	87	78
72202	88	88	25	30	99	99	68	78
72300	79	81	21	18	99	98	88	73
72400	65	85	8	23	100	98	100	81
72500	97	95	60	56	100	100	100	86
72600	90	93	44	55	100	100	100	100
Man	79	73	6	5	93	93	23	25
Ser	88	91	27	34	99	100	78	82
ICT	87	90	19	24	99	99	58	63

For the manufacturing sub sector the share of firms with fewer than 20 employees have declined from 79% to 73%. Total employment in these firms has also diminished. The share of manufacturing firms with fewer than 200 employees has remained constant at 93%, but with a slight increase in employment. The service sub sector, on the other hand has increased its share of firms with fewer than 20 employees; employment in this group has also increased. In the service sub sector there are virtually no establishments with more than 200 employees.

13.4 The Spatial Pattern and Dynamics of the Swedish ICT Sector

13.4.1 Similarities and Dissimilarities of Locational Patterns of Subsectors within the ICT Sector

In Table 13.5 the 23 industries comprising the ICT sector are divided into groups according to their locational similarity. That is, in each of the four groups, industries within the group tend to be more spatially associated than across groups. The classification is performed in the following way. For the year 1998 the specialisation quotient was calculated for each industry for each and every local labour market region (LA region) in Sweden. Thus, one obtained one variable for each industry, the values representing the localisation quotient for every LA region. Hence, the number of observations for each is 81, although for some regions and some industries the observed value is zero, since all industries are not present in each and every region. For the 23 variables (industries) all pair-wise correlation coefficients were calculated. Thus, one obtains (23*23–23)/2 = 253 correlation coefficients. These coefficients were ranked in a descending order. The highest rank was attributed to the two industries whose correlation between location coefficients was the highest. These two industries were considered to form the basis for the first group. Then all correlations were scrutinised in a descending manner. If any one of the two industries in each correlation coefficient was already grouped, then the other industry was also considered to belong to that group. If neither belonged to any group then they form a new group. This process was continued until all industries were assigned to groups. Thus, the end result is a grouping of industries according to the similarities of their location quotients over regions. Note that the process determines both the grouping and the number of groups.

Group I is dominated by service industries. Of the twelve industries in group I, only two are manufacturing industries. Group II consists entirely of service industries. Group III is divided equally between service and manufacturing. Group IV is a pure manufacturing group.

Group I consists of industries that are located rather evenly across regions. Half of the industries in this group consist of sales activities, renting and maintenance. These activities can be expected to be spread out with a high correlation to the business population and human population. *Software consultancy* and *Software supply* are industries that have a market wherever there are computers, that is, everywhere. *Manufacture of television and radio transmitters and apparatus for line telephony and line telegraphy* is a major industry in Sweden containing companies like Ericsson and its sheer size makes it likely to be spread out. Group II is a pure service group, but is of a more specialised nature and thus not as dispersed as group I. Group III is centred on computer hardware with manufacturing coupled with hardware consultancy and data base activities. Group IV is made up of more traditional manufacturing activities. To make the analysis of Table 13.5 more thorough it would be very useful to have data on input/output relations. It would then be possible to explore to what extent the groupings in the table are reflections of inter-industry linkages.

Table 13.5. Classification of the Industries According to Their Locational Similarities

Class	SNI92	Industry
	22330	Reproduction of computer media
	32200	Manufacture of television and radio transmitters and apparatus for line telephony and line telegraphy
	51142	Agents involved in the sale of office machinery and computer equipment
	51653	Wholesale of telecommunication equipment and electronic components
	52493	Retail sale of computers, office machinery and computer programmes
I	52494	Retail sale of telecommunication equipment
	64201	Network operation
	71330	Renting of office machinery and equipment including computers
	72201	Software consultancy
	72202	Software supply
	72300	Data processing
	72500	Maintenance and repair of office, accounting and computing machinery
	51652	Wholesale of computerised materials handling equipment
II	64203	Cable television operation
	72600	Other computer related activities
	30020	Manufacture of computers and other information processing equipment
	31300	Manufacture of insulated wire and cable
III	32100	Manufacture of electronic valves and tubes and other electronic components
	64202	Radio and television broadcast operation
	72100	Hardware consultancy
	72400	Data base activities
	30010	Manufacture of office machinery
IV	32300	Manufacture of television and radio receivers, sound or video recording or reproducing apparatus and associated goods

13.4.2 Localisation Patterns

This section is devoted to determining the spatial concentration of the different industries in the ICT sector and to determining if this concentration has been increasing or decreasing during the 1990s. This is accomplished by recording Gini coefficients and the number of regions where the industry is present in 1990 and 1998. Also, we record which three regions (out of 81) have the largest number of employees for each industry in 1998. The results of these calculations are presented in Table 13.6. A Gini coefficient of 0 signifies a state where the industry is as spread out as employment in general. A coefficient of 0.5 is an industry that is concentrated in one single region.

Table 13.6. The Gini Coefficient, the Number of Regions where an Industry is Present and the Three Most Important Regions (in Terms of Employment)

SNI92	Gini90	Gini98	Reg90	Reg98	Empreg98 (ranked)		
22330	0.39(2)	0.36(3)–	8	12+	Stockholm	Växjö	Göteborg
30010	0.40(1)	0.42(1)+	16	20+	Gnosjö	Katrineholm	Göteborg
30020	0.32(10)	0.29(11)–	58	52–	Stockholm	Göteborg	Linköping
31300	0.37(4)	0.40(2)+	26	35+	Hudiksvall	Karlskrona	Borås
32100	0.38(3)	0.33(6)–	35	49+	Stockholm	Karlskrona	Linköping
32200	0.33(8)	0.32(7)–	35	29–	Stockholm	Örebro	Linköping
32300	0.32(11)	0.35(4)+	34	29–	Stockholm	Linköping	Oskarshamn
51142	0.33(8)	0.29(10)–	17	20+	Stockholm	Malmö	Göteborg
51652	0.30(13)	0.24(15)–	26	28+	Stockholm	Göteborg	Uppsala
51653	0.25(16)	0.27(13)+	58	56–	Stockholm	Göteborg	Malmö
52493	0.16(20)	0.14(23)–	66	58–	Stockholm	Göteborg	Malmö
52494	0.35(7)	0.16(21)–	19	51+	Stockholm	Göteborg	Malmö
64201	0.12(22)	0.15(22)+	81	81	Stockholm	Göteborg	Malmö
64202	–	0.28(12)+	–	45+	Stockholm	Luleå	Sundsvall
64203	0.31(12)	0.30(9)–	25	15–	Stockholm	Göteborg	Karlskoga
71330	0.25(17)	0.33(5)+	41	20–	Stockholm	Borås	Malmö
72100	0.37(5)	0.22(17)–	30	46+	Stockholm	Göteborg	Malmö
72201	0.22(19)	0.21(19)–	72	79+	Stockholm	Göteborg	Malmö
72202	0.28(14)	0.21(18)–	40	55+	Stockholm	Göteborg	Malmö
72300	0.24(18)	0.23(16)–	43	51+	Stockholm	Göteborg	Malmö
72400	0.36(6)	0.31(8)–	8	17+	Stockholm	Göteborg	Ljusdal
72500	0.14(21)	0.16(20)+	59	48-	Stockholm	Göteborg	Linköping
72600	0.28(15)	0.25(14)–	33	33	Stockholm	Göteborg	Malmö
ICT	0.16	0.17+	81	81	Stockholm	Göteborg	Malmö
Man	0.26	0.26+	72	73+	Stockholm	Linköping	Örebro
Ser	0.14	0.17+	81	81	Stockholm	Göteborg	Malmö

Note: Gini90(98) = the Gini coefficient in 1990 (1998), Reg90(98) = the number of regions where the industry is present in 1990 (1998), Empreg98 = the three largest regions in terms of employment in 1998 (ranked from left to right)

First, it is evident from Table 13.6 that the manufacturing sub sector is more spatially concentrated than the services sub sector. Since we have two measures for spatial concentration we can check for which industries the two measures are in concordance with each other. A minus sign signifies a drop and a plus sign signifies an increase. The two measures are in concordance if their respective signs are different. Thus, we have fourteen out of twenty-three industries for which the two measures say the same thing. Of these ten are dispersing and four are concentrating. The three largest regions in Sweden are Stockholm, Göteborg and Malmö, in descending order. Ten of the industries have their three largest employment concentrations in these three regions. Of these ten nine follow the ranking of regional size. All of these ten industries are service sectors. This means that the manufacturing sectors do not follow this size order. However, all but two industries have their largest employment figures in the Stockholm region. The two industries that do not follow this pattern are Manufacture of office machinery and Manufacture of insulated wire and cable, both of which are more traditional manufacturing industries. According to the Gini coefficient for 1998 these two were the two most concentrated industries. Thus, we may conclude that they are dependent on some form of localisation economies.

13.4.3 Spatial Dynamics

In this section we are going to study the spatial change process of the investigated industries. Table 13.7 is constructed according to information that is available in Table 13.6.

Table 13.7. The 23 Subindustries in the ICT Sector Classified According to Gini Coefficient 1990 and Change of Gini Coefficient between 1990 and 1998

		Process 1990 to 1998		
		Concentrating	Dispersing	
State 1990	Concentrated	30010 31300 32300	22330 30020 32100 32200 51142	51652 52494 64203 72100 72400
	Dispersed	51653 64201 64202 71330 72500	52493 72201 72202 72300 72600	

We have recorded all the Gini coefficients for 1990 and 1998 and made a cross-classification according to the state in 1990 and the change until 1998. All industries with a Gini above average in 1990 where considered to be concentrated spatially; all the others were dispersed. If the Gini coefficient was larger in 1998 the industry was concentrating and, otherwise, dispersing. All manufacturing industries were considered concentrated in 1990. The ones that were dispersed are all service industries. Thus, we can observe a distinct pattern in Table 13.7. Industries that were concentrated in 1990 and even more concentrated in 1998 are all manufacturing industries. Industries that were dispersed in 1990 and more dispersed in 1998 are all service industries. Also, industries that were dispersed in 1990 but were concentrating until 1998 are all service industries. Thus, the only cell in Table 13.7 with a mix between manufacturing and service industries is the cell for industries that were concentrated in 1990 but were dispersing during the time period.

Table 13.8 presents the result of a regression analysis where we use regional size, in terms of population, to explain the competitive shift. In shift-share analysis the competitive shift is the difference between actual growth in employment and expected (average) growth. A positive competitive shift indicates that growth in a particular region has been larger than the national average.

Table 13.8. Regression Results: The Competitive Shift Component in the Different Industries and Regions Explained by the Regional Population In 1990

Industry	Intercept	Pop90	R^2	Industry	Intercept	Pop90	R^2
Ict	−285.85	0.0029*	0.46	52493	−10.47	0.00010*	0.33
	(−3.34)	(8.12)			(−2.63)	(6.24)	
Man	9.52	−7.6E-05	0.00	52494	−11.88	0.00026*	0.81
	(0.15)	(−0.29)			(−3.58)	(18.51)	
Ser	−293.31	0.0030*	0.62	64201	−69.64	0.00094*	0.62
	(−4.60)	(11.28)			(−3.51)	(11.34)	
22330	−2.49	3.1E-05*	0.55	64202	−10.10	0.00020*	0.80
	(−3.29)	(9.84)			(−3.86)	(17.82)	
30010	6.53	−6.2E-05	0.04	64203	−6.66	6.7E-05*	0.62
	(0.75)	(−1.68)			(−4.73)	(11.34)	
30020	−59.61	0.0013*	0.83	71330	−9.82	0.00016*	0.79
	(−3.96)	(19.81)			(−4.43)	(17.19)	
31300	41.50	−0.00039*	0.29	72100	−9.39	9.8E-05*	0.06
	(2.55)	(−5.73)			(−0.90)	(2.23)	
32100	−51.53	0.000603*	0.18	72201	−112.91	0.0020*	0.82
	(−1.48)	(4.13)			(−4.45)	(19.18)	
32200	−27.24	0.00032	0.03	72202	−65.95	0.0010*	0.72
	(−0.53)	(1.46)			(−3.77)	(14.30)	
32300	−11.34	0.00029*	0.33	72300	13.595	−0.00012*	0.14
	(−1.01)	(6.18)			(1.70)	(−3.53)	
51142	−1.22	1.36E-05*	0.23	72400	−1.85	2.3E-05	0.03
	(−1.82)	(4.82)			(−0.53)	(1.54)	
51652	6.38	−5.7E-05*	0.26	72500	−10.23	9.7E-05*	0.45
	(2.51)	(−5.33)			(−3.59)	(8.10)	
51653	−21.28	0.00021*	0.56	72600	−2.70	4.4E-05*	0.80
	(−4.28)	(9.98)			(−4.58)	(17.61)	

Note: Pop90 = Regional population in 1990, t-values are given in parenthesis, * indicates an estimate significant at the 5 % level

Of the 26 different regressions 22 are significant at the five percent level. For the significant regressions the R^2 ranges between 0.06 and 0.83. Of the 23 industries 17 have a positive relationship with regional size. This means that the larger the region, the larger the competitive shift. For three industries the same relationship is negative. That is, growth is larger the smaller the region. These three industries are *Manufacture of insulated wire and cable*, *Wholesale of computerised materials handling equipment* and *Data processing*. For ICT in general the relationship is positive. This is also true for the service industries. However, the regression for the manufacturing sub sector is not significant. Individually five out of seven manufacturing industries have a significant relationship. This means that the manufacturing sub sector shows a heterogeneous regional growth pattern between different individual industries.

In order to extent our analysis we would like to test the relationship between the regional locational dynamics of ICT industries and variables other than population. Other variables that we would like to test are regional ICT manufacturing employment, regional ICT services employment, accessibility to domestic airports, accessibility to international airports and the educational level of the regional population in 1990. Unfortunately it is evident from Table 13.9 that these variables are all highly correlated to regional population. Thus, they are also highly correlated among themselves. The correlation coefficients in Table 13.9 range from 0.872 to 0.986.

Table 13.9. Correlation Coefficients between Variables Characterising (LA) Regions

	Man90	Ser90	Dom	Int	Pop90	Edu90
Man90	1	–	–	–	–	–
Ser90	0.951	1	–	–	–	–
Dom	0.941	0.980	1	–	–	–
Int	0.949	0.986	0.978	1	–	–
Pop90	0.872	0.958	0.911	0.914	1	–
Edu90	0.900	0.976	0.941	0.949	0.972	1

Note: Man90 = number of employees in manufacturing sub sector 1990, Ser90 = number of employees in service sub sector 1990, Dom = Number of airport passengers 1998 (domestic), Int = Number of airport passengers 1998 (international), Pop90 = population in 1990, Edu90 = Number of inhabitants with higher education (more than three years of university training)

Since this is the case a multiple regression analysis is very likely to produce multicollinearity making it virtually impossible to interpret the effect of individual variables. In order to analyse their aggregate effect we construct an aggregate variable of the six individual variables using principal components analysis. We extract the first principal component, which is a linear combination of the original variables with the factor scores as coefficients. We call this constructed variable a regional characteristics variable (Regvar). In this way one is able to account for the effect of all variables; however, one cannot discriminate between the different variables once they are aggregated.

In Table 13.10 the result of the regressions with this regional characteristics variable as explanatory variable is presented. Table 13.10 is identical to Table 13.8 except for the use of a different explanatory variable. Also in this case the number of significant (at the 5% level) relationships is 22 out of 26. Moreover, it is regressions of the same industries that have insignificant results. The same industries as in Table 13.8 show a negative relationship. The only major difference between the results in Table 13.8 and Table 13.10 is in terms of the explanatory power. The R^2 ranges between 0.17 and 0.95. Overall, most R^2s seem to have increased by approximately 0.1. Five of the regressions have an explanatory power of over 90%, not leaving much room for improvement by alternative specifications.

Table 13.10. Competitive Shift Explained by Regional Characteristics Variable

Industry	Intercept	Regvar	R^2	Industry	Intercept	Regvar	R^2
Ict	23.58	685.22*	0.54	52493	0.58	22.90*	0.35
	(0.34)	(9.69)			(0.17)	(6.45)	
Man	1.45	−43.55	0.01	52494	15.45	59.44*	0.94
	(0.03)	(−0.76)			(8.85)	(33.86)	
Ser	26.26	743.72*	0.81	64201	30.31	231.25*	0.81
	(0.66)	(18.54)			(2.40)	(18.16)	
22330	0.82	7.75*	0.74	64202	10.64	45.26*	0.93
	(1.58)	(14.87)			(7.57)	(31.98)	
30010	5.3E-03	−12.90	0.03	64203	0.44	15.59*	0.73
	(0.00)	(−1.64)			(0.41)	(14.46)	
30020	73.02	282.10*	0.92	71330	7.13	37.70*	0.95
	(7.66)	(29.40)			(7.432)	(39.079)	
31300	3.4E-02	−98.50*	0.40	72100	0.97	35.57*	0.17
	(0.00)	(−7.30)			(0.11)	(4.03)	
32100	12.39	151.27*	0.24	72201	103.18	460.39*	0.91
	(0.41)	(5.03)			(6.34)	(28.09)	
32200	6.37	47.85	0.01	72202	45.30	221.95*	0.70
	(0.14)	(1.02)			(2.78)	(13.54)	
32300	19.60	68.93*	0.39	72300	1.01	−21.73*	0.10
	(2.05)	(7.16)			(0.14)	(−2.95)	
51142	0.22	2.74*	0.20	72400	0.53	3.44	0.02
	(0.36)	(4.45)			(0.17)	(1.09)	
51652	0.37	−16.05*	0.46	72500	3.8E-02	25.38*	0.67
	(0.19)	(−8.19)			(0.019)	(12.79)	
51653	0.81	49.92*	0.69	72600	1.92	9.54*	0.83
	(0.22)	(13.36)			(3.95)	(19.57)	

Note: Regvar = Regional characteristics variable, t-values are given in parenthesis, * indicates an estimate significant at the 5 % level

13.5 Summary and Conclusions

In this paper we have analysed the development of the ICT sector in Sweden during the nineties. In particular we have looked at the spatial pattern and dynamics of the sector. As a theoretical background we have introduced concepts like urban regions, home market and increasing returns. We have discussed two theories for the spatial structure of industries: the spatial product life cycle theory and the filtering-down theory. In section three and four the ICT industries are investigated empirically.

In the first non-spatial part of the analysis we found that ICT employment has increased from 1990 to 1998 despite the fact that overall employment in Sweden has decreased during this period. The service industries have increased their employment (+23%) more than the manufacturing industries (+7%). When it comes to the number of plants, the manufacturing sub sector has experienced a drop by 14%. The services sub sectors have increased in number of plants by 68%. Taken together this means that manufacturing plants have increased in size and that service plants have decreased in size. Thus, internal scale economies are more important for manufacturing.

The services sub sectors have a higher profitability, a higher wage rate, more value added per employee and a higher value of the quotient of value added to turnover. The higher profitability is probably one reason for the rapid expansion of the ICT service industries. The wage rate and value added per employee are probably explained in part by the fact that the educational level in services is higher than in manufacturing. The observation that value added divided by turnover is higher for the services than for manufacturing is a reflection of the fact that the major input in service production is human resources and human capital.

Employment in SMEs is increasing for the service sub sector. For the manufacturing sub sector employment is increasing in establishments that are smaller than 200 employees, but employment is diminishing in establishments smaller than 20 employees.

Next, we come to the empirical investigation into the spatial structure and dynamics during the period. We were able to divide the 23 industries into four groups according to their locational similarity. These four groups were not easy to interpret and more data and analysis have to be performed in this area.

The manufacturing sub sector is more spatially concentrated than the service sub sector. The service sub sector employment location is more correlated to regional population size than the manufacturing sub sector. This probably tells us that services follows more of a filtering-down pattern than the manufacturing sub sector. Moreover, industries that were relatively concentrated in 1990 and kept on concentrating during the period are all manufacturing sectors, and conversely industries that were relatively dispersed in 1990 and kept on dispersing further were all service industries.

In a regression analysis we found that regional size in terms of population was a good predictor of industrial change in terms of the competitive shift. Out of 26 regressions 22 were found with statistically significant results. However, for three of the regressions the relationship was negative. In order to find other regional factors with importance for spatial industrial change we constructed a *regional characteristics variable*. This second regression came out similar to the first one. The only real difference was a higher coefficient of determination.

One of the main conclusions one can draw from this exercise is that what is termed the ICT sector is not a very homogenous grouping of industries, not even within manufacturing and services, respectively. Another general conclusion is that there does not seem to be anything particular with respect to these industries compared to more traditional ones. They seem to follow patterns much the same as other industries.

References

Alles P, Esparza A, Lucas S (1994) Telecommunications and the large city – small city divide: evidence from Indiana cities. Professional Geographer 46: 307–316

Andersson ÅE, Johansson B (1984) Knowledge intensity and product cycles in metropolitan regions. WP–84–13, IIASA, Laxenburg

Andersson ÅE (1985) Creativity and regional development. Papers of the Regional Science Association 56: 5–20

Armstrong H, Taylor J (1993) Regional economics and policy (second edition). Harvester Wheatsheaf, New York

Arthur B (1990) Positive feedbacks in the economy. Scientific American 262: 92–99

Aydalot P (1984) Reversal of spatial trends in French industry since 1974. In: Lambooy JG (ed) New spatial dynamics and economic crisis. IRPA Yearbook 1984, Finnpublishers, Tampere, pp 41–62

Batten D, Karlsson C (1996) Infrastructure and the complexity of economic development. Springer-Verlag, Berlin

Beckmann M (1958) City hierarchies and the distribution of city sizes. Economic Development and Cultural Change 6: 243–48

Beckmann M (1996) The location of market oriented industries in a growing economy. Paper presented at the 5th World Congress of the RSAI in Tokyo

Bos HC (1965) Spatial dispersion of economic activity. Rotterdam University Press, Rotterdam

Cairncross F (1997) The death of distance. Harvard Business School Press, Boston MA

Camagni R, Diappi L, Leonardi G (1986) Urban growth and decline in a hierarchical system – A supply oriented dynamic approach. Regional Science and Urban Economics 16: 145–60

Castells M (1999) The rise of the network society. The information age: Economy, society and culture, Volume 1. Blackwell Publishers, Malden MA

Cheshire P, Gordon I (eds) (1995) Territorial competition in an integrating Europe. Avebury, Aldershot

Clark CA (1940) The conditions of economic progress. Macmillan, London

David P, Rosenbloom JL (1990) Marshallian factor market externalities and the dynamics of industrial location. Journal of Urban Economics 28: 349–370

Davies DR, Bradford SC, Weinstein DE (1997) Using international and Japanese regional data to determine when the factor abundance theory of trade works. American Economic Review 87: 421–446

Forslund U, Johansson B (1998) Specialisation dynamics in a system of functional regions. Paper presented at the Western Regional Science Association meeting in Monterey CA

Forslund U (1996) Industrial location – Interregional leads and lags in Sweden and Norway. Working Paper No 1, Swedish Institute for Regional Research, Östersund

Forslund UM (1997) Studies of multi-regional interdependencies and change. Licentiate Thesis, Division of Regional Planning, Royal Institute of Technology, Stockholm

Forslund U, Johansson B (1995) The Mälardalen: A leading region in Scandinavia. In: Cheshire P, Gordon I (eds) Territorial competition in an integrating Europe. Avebury, Aldershot, pp 3–27

Graham S, Marvin S (1996) Telecommunications and the city: Electronic spaces, urban places. Routledge, New York

Hall P (1998) Cities in civilization. Culture, innovation and urban order. Weinfield and Nicholson, London

Hirsch S (1967) Location of industry and international competitiveness. Oxford University Press, Oxford

Isard W Aziz IJ, Drennan MP, Salzman S, Thorbecke E (1998) Methods of interregional and regional analysis. Ashgate, Aldershot

Johansson B, Karlsson C (1987) Processes of industrial change: Scale, location and type of job. In: Nijkamp P, Fischer MM (eds) Urban and Regional Labour Markets. North-Holland, Amsterdam, pp 133–79

Johansson B, Wigren R (1996) Production milieu and competitive advantages. In Batten D, Karlsson C (eds) Infrastructure and the complexity of economic development. Springer-Verlag, Berlin, pp 187–211

Johansson B (1997) Regional differentials in the development of economy and population. In: Sörensen C (ed) Empirical evidence of regional growth: The centre-periphery discussion. The Expert Committee of the Danish Ministry of the Interior, Copenhagen, pp 107–162

Johansson B, Hultén S, Nilsson JE (1991) Infrastruktur, produktivitet och konkurrenskraft, i Infrastruktur och produktivitet. Expertutredning nr 9 till Produktivitetsdelegationen, Allmänna Förlaget, Stockholm

Karlsson C (1988) Innovation adoption and the product life cycle. Umeå Economic Studies No. 185, University of Umeå, Umeå

Krugman P (1980) Scale economies, product differentiation, and the pattern of trade. American Economic Review 70: 950–959

Krugman P (1991a) Geography and trade. MIT Press, Cambridge MA

Krugman P (1991b) Increasing returns and economic geography. Journal of Political Economy 99: 483–499

Krugman P (1991c) History and industry location: The case of the manufacturing belt. American Economic Review 81: 80–83

Lambooy JG (ed) (1984) New spatial dynamics and economic crises. IRPA Yearbook 1984, Finnpublishers, Tampere

Malmberg A, Maskell P (1997) Towards an explanation of regional specialization and industry agglomeration. European Planning Studies 5: 25–41

Malmberg A (1996) Industrial geography: Agglomeration and local milieu. Progress in Human Geography 20: 392–403

Malmberg A, Sölwell Ö, Zander I (1996) Spatial clustering, local accumulation of knowledge and firm competitiveness. Geografiska Annaler 78B: 85–97

Marshall A (1920) Principles of economics (eighth edition). Macmillan, London

Mitchell WJ (1999) Equitable access to the online world. In: Schön DA, Sanyal B, Mitchell WJ (eds) High technology and low-income communities: Prospects for the positive use of advanced information technology. MIT Press, Cambridge, MA, pp 151–162

Moriarty BM (1991) Urban systems, industrial restructuring, and the spatio-temporal diffusion of manufacturing employment. Environment and Planning A 23: 1571–1588

Moroney JR, Walker JM (1966) A regional test of the Heckscher-Ohlin theorem. Journal of Political Economy 74: 573–586

Nijkamp P, Fischer MM (eds) (1987) Urban and regional labour markets. North-Holland, Amsterdam

Norton RD (1992) Agglomeration and competitiveness: From Marshall to Chinitz. Urban Studies 29: 155–170

Schmand J, Williams FH, Wilson R (1990) The new urban infrastructure: Cities and tele-communications. Praeger Publishers, New York

Schön DA, Sanyal B, Michell WJ (eds) (1999) High technology and low-income communities: Prospects for the positive use of advanced information technology. MIT Press, Cambridge, MA

Shields P, Dervin B, Richter C, Soller R (1993) Who needs POTS-plus services? A comparison of residential user needs along the rural-urban continuum. Telecommunications Policy 17: 563–587

Smith B (1975) Regional specialisation and trade in the UK. Scottish Journal of Political Economy 22: 39–56

Sörensen C (ed) (1997) Empirical evidence of regional growth: The centre-periphery discussion. The Expert Committee of the Danish Ministry of the Interior, Copenhagen

Storper M (1996) The world of the city: local relations in a global economy. School of Public Policy and Social Research, University of California, Los Angeles

Ter Weel B (1999) Investing in knowledge: On the trade-off between R&D, ICT, skills and migration. MERIT, Maastricht University

Thompson WR (1969) The economic base of urban problems. In: Chamberlain NW (ed) Contemporary economic issues. Pichard Irving, Homewood IL, pp 1–47

Tinbergen J (1967) The hierarchy model of the size distribution of centres. Papers of the Regional Science Association 20: 65–68

Van den Berg L, van Winden W (2000) ICT as potential catalyst for sustainable urban development. European Institute for Comparative Urban Research, Erasmus University, Rotterdam

Van den Berg L (1987) Urban systems in a dynamic society. Gower, Aldershot

Van Winden W (2000) Three ICT clusters compared. Paper presented at the 40th Congress of the European Regional Science Association, Barcelona

Vernon R (1960) Metropolis 1985. Harvard University Press, Cambridge MA

Appendix 13.A Selected Industries Representing the Swedish ICT Sector

	Sni92	Industry
Manufacturing	22330	Reproduction of computer media
	30010	Manufacture of office machinery
	30020	Manufacture of computers and other information processing equipment
	31300	Manufacture of insulated wire and cable
	32100	Manufacture of electronic valves and tubes and other electronic components
	32200	Manufacture of television and radio transmitters and apparatus for line telephony and line telegraphy
	32300	Manufacture of television and radio receivers, sound or video recording or reproducing apparatus and associated goods
Service	51142	Agents involved in the sale of office machinery and computer equipment
	51652	Wholesale of computerised materials handling equipment
	51653	Wholesale of telecommunication equipment and electronic components
	52493	Retail sale of computers, office machinery and computer programmes
	52494	Retail sale of telecommunication equipment
	64201	Network operation
	64202	Radio and television broadcast operation
	64203	Cable television operation
	71330	Renting of office machinery and equipment including computers
	72100	Hardware consultancy
	72201	Software consultancy
	72202	Software supply
	72300	Data processing
	72400	Data base activities
	72500	Maintenance and repair of office, accounting and computing machinery
	72600	Other computer related activities
	Man	Aggregate of ICT manufacturing sectors (22330–32300)
	Ser	Aggregate of ICT services sectors (51142–72600)
	Ict	Aggregate of all ICT sectors

14 The Multimedia Industry: Networks and Regional Development in a Globalised Economy[1]

Gerhard Fuchs

Center for Technology Assessment, Stuttgart, Germany

14.1 Introduction

At the intersection of economic and social sciences, a specific type of research literature has developed, emphasising the embeddedness of economic activities in social contexts (see, e.g., Granovetter 1985; Grabher 1993a; Amin and Thrift 1995; Staber 1996b; Uzzi 1996). This literature is concerned with identifying the various institutional mechanisms by which economic activity is co-ordinated. It attempts to understand the circumstances under which the various mechanisms of co-ordination are chosen, and is interested in comprehending the logic inherent in the different co-ordinating mechanisms. The importance of networking of economic actors is one of the central topics in these discussions (cf. Hage and Alter 1997). Embeddedness in social structures may explain why network arrangements may persist in situations where, at first glance, other forms of governance (such as open markets) may appear more efficient. Mutual trust, social expectations and the forces of tradition may be powerful mechanisms for overriding opportunistic motives preventing the breakdown of co-operative relationships. So far, however, only little research has been done on the specific effects of certain types of networking of actors. Moreover, technological progress and changes in the global economic system cause us to analyse the question of the effects of certain network-like ties over and over again. In other words, and following Granovetter (1973), the question which ties are strongest remains to be constantly answered anew in relation to the specific research object.

If we analyse, for example, various sectors of industry, the answers will be different. In this chapter, I will discuss the issue of the importance of network ties for one specific sector of industry: multimedia. Multimedia is generally considered to be a future-oriented and still emerging industry. In this chapter I will look at the development of this sector from the perspective of economic regions. The research

[1] I would like to thank Monika Baumunk for the translation of parts of a German manuscript that were used for this chapter. Some of the basic arguments were developed in co-operation with Hans-Georg Wolf. His participation is greatly appreciated.

question is: what kind of inter-organisational ties between multimedia firms will most likely favour the development and growth of a multimedia cluster within a certain region?[2] I will focus on the difference between intraregional and extraregional ties. This question is to be seen against the background of a scientific as well as policy-oriented discussion on globalisation and regionalisation in the development of economic regions.

Simplifying this discussion, two patterns of argumentation can be distinguished. Each pattern identifies certain ties as crucial. The first argumentation pattern may be described as the 'regionalization thesis'. This thesis is often used in works on industrial districts and emphasises the importance of quantity and quality of intraregional networking not at least as a means to protect a region against the effects of globalisation.

At the same time as the regionalist argument, the second pattern of argumentation, the so-called 'globalisation thesis', was gaining in popularity. According to this pattern the embeddedness of economic flows in regional networks will decrease in importance and there will be a process of disembedding from regional contexts. According to the globalisation argumentation, an environment without any ties will develop as a consequence of globalisation on the one hand; on the other hand, and much more relevant in this respect, is the argument that certain, i.e., global, ties are crucial in the context of a globalised economy.

The regionalisation and the globalisation theses are frequently discussed as being contradictory or their relation is treated as a 'paradox' (see Boekholt and Van der Weele 1998; Huggins 1997). The point of view presented in this chapter is different: the medium- and long-term development of regional economic areas is dependent on a combination of regional and global ties. The combination of both kinds of ties is crucial. Without any doubt, there is a conflict between regional and global ties, but assuming a fundamental contradiction is misleading.

In the following section I will recapitulate the regionalisation and globalisation theses and characterise the strengths and weaknesses of regional and global ties. Then the different kinds of regional and global ties will be discussed as well as their meaning for the development of economic areas in general and for multimedia clusters in particular. The argument will be illustrated by analysing the example of multimedia production in the German state of Baden-Wuerttemberg. Finally, the argument will be summarised.

---

[2] An industrial cluster is a set of industries related through buyer-supplier and supplier-buyer relationships, or by common technologies, common buyers or distribution channels or common labour pools. A regional cluster is an industrial cluster in which member firms are in close geographic proximity to each other (Enright 1996).

14.2 Strengths and Weaknesses of Regional and Global Ties

14.2.1 Regional Ties

The importance of the regional context for economic development has always been emphasised. The basic argument can be traced back to Marshall's work on industrial districts at the turn of the century. Yet this regional context was given only little attention (see Scott 1995) until the rise of 'neo-regionalism' began about 15 years ago. The neo-regionalist research perspective consists of various approaches. In the beginning, there were studies on *industrial districts* of the so-called 'Third Italy' with a distinct pattern of flexible specialisation of primarily small companies. Later, regions with similar characteristics were found in other countries, e.g., Baden-Wuerttemberg (see Piore and Sabel 1984, Pyke and Sengenberger 1992). At the same time, the concept of an *'innovative milieu'* developed (Aydalot and Keeble 1988; Camagni 1991), describing a complex network of social relations within a limited area which promotes the learning aptitude and innovative ability of the respective region (see Camagni 1991). Similar arguments concerning the importance of the regional level in the development of economic systems, to generate innovations in particular, can be found in the literature on innovation systems, especially *regional innovation systems* (see Braczyk et al. 1998). Finally, works of Porter (1990), Krugman (1991), Enright (1996) and Fischer (1998) describe the conditions under which spatially concentrated *industrial clusters* with high productivity and competitiveness emerge.

These approaches are partly complementary, but also contradictory to a certain extent. This cannot be discussed in detail in this context.[3] Nevertheless, there are some basic arguments that can be extracted which are useful for the present discussion. A testable hypothesis could be the following: if there is a close network of companies and between companies and institutions in a certain region, the competitiveness and economic development of this region will be promoted. To emphasise the positive effects of networking, it can be said that, based on the standard literature on this subject, regional networks

- enable companies to use a common pool of resources (qualified labour, infrastructure, services of supporting institutions, etc.);
- help companies to exchange knowledge and to generate innovations; most important are 'technology spillovers' among the companies in a region and the possibility to pass on 'tacit knowledge' via networks (see Bramanti and Maggioni 1997);
- help them to be in close contact with clients or users and their special requirements;

---

[3] Storper (1997) provides a detailed survey of the competing approaches.

- facilitate labour division so that highly specialised firms can combine and pool competence.

The neo-regionalist research perspective discusses the strengths of regional networks or intraregional ties. But there has been a lot of criticism concerning this research work. Some authors found fault with the emphasis on a few outstanding and successful model regions and the neglect of 'normal regions' with less favourable conditions. It was also criticised that the regions were frequently described by using a neo-regionalist vocabulary and without giving any exact empirical verification, i.e., whether there were actually important characteristics to be found such as a structure of predominantly small firms and an intensive co-operation of companies (see Krumbein et al. 1994; Markusen 1996; Staber 1996a; Sternberg 1998; Voelzkow 1999).

Without any doubt, this criticism is partly justified and gives reason for a more differentiated handling of the neo-regionalist arguments. The strengths of intraregional networking are obviously only effective under certain regional and sectoral conditions. Regional networking seems to be advantageous

- in sectors with a high number of small and medium-sized enterprises (SMEs). A flexible co-operation with other firms may even replace – at least partially – the advantages of organisational size. Larger companies in contrast can hold necessary competence within their own organisation (see Almeida and Kogut 1997);
- in sectors with a high rate of technological change and a high degree of innovation. Works on innovation research prove (see Feldman 1994; Almeida and Kogut 1997; Gehrke and Legler 1998) that especially research- and knowledge-intensive industries show a tendency for spatial concentration;
- in sectors where predominantly little standardised but customer-specific products are manufactured and where the close contact between manufacturer and customer is particularly important (see Scott 1988).

As will be verified below, these conditions can – to a very high degree – be found in the multimedia industry. Thus the neo-regionalist approach may be principally applied to this industry and the strengths of regional ties are characteristic for this industry.

With innovation becoming more and more important for the success of regions and considering the assumption that innovation is highly dependent on information and knowledge, innovativeness also seems to imply the ability to access such highly intangible assets by way of networking. It is to be admitted that a precise definition of networks or networking is hard to find in the literature. The appeal of the concept seems to stem exactly from the fact that it encompasses important relationships that are difficult to summarise under a precise definition. Networking capacity at a very basic level can be seen as the disposition of actors to collaborate and communicate in order to achieve mutually beneficial ends. Actors in these networks can be employees as well as employers, companies, associations, public funding agencies, research institutes, etc. Yet, to what extent is the globalisation argument contradictory to the assumptions of the regionalist thesis?

14.2.2 Global Ties

The above-mentioned criticism argues that many regions or sectors profit only to a limited degree from regional ties as emphasised in the neo-regionalist research. An even deeper conflict exists between the 'globalisation thesis' and the neo-regionalist research perspective. The purest version of this thesis can be found in various popular publications (see Martin and Schumann 1996; Forrester 1997). In a more moderate form, the thesis is also developed in numerous publications of social scientists or economists (see Thurow 1996; Altvater and Mahnkopf 1996). Briefly summarised, the globalisation thesis argues that, because of the rapidly advancing globalisation, economic structures and flows are increasingly disembedded from regional contexts and regional embeddedness is becoming less important. According to the globalisation thesis, companies act on a global level and the most globalise companies become key actors whose strategies will increasingly determine the possibilities for development of certain regions. "Regions become the object of companies in the process of international restructuring" (see Iwer and Rehberg 1999). And for Amin (1993) the consequence is: "The meaning of place is becoming defined within the hyperspace of global corporate activity."

This perspective emphasises the importance of global ties. Quantity and quality of intraregional networking are no longer crucial but the integration of economic regions in worldwide networks. The position of regions in the organisational structures and networks of 'global players' determines the possibilities for economic development. Even the often analysed 'model regions' of industrial district research come under pressure due to globalisation (see Voelzkow 1999).

One possible strength of global ties is to counter the lack of flexibility in regional structures. As a matter of fact, the strengths of a distinct regional network may turn into weaknesses if they hinder the adjustment of regional economies to modified technological and economic conditions. This is also acknowledged by the neo-regionalist research perspective (see Grabher 1993a on the Ruhr region; Heidenreich and Krauss 1996 on Baden-Wuerttemberg). Regional economies frequently develop along stable trajectories. To leave these trajectories, impulses from outside are necessary. In this context, Camagni (1991) sees the special function of innovation networks as the chance for one innovative milieu to come into contact with others and to use these contacts to import new technological possibilities, organisational models and commercial ideas into the system as well as to protect it from 'death by entropy'.

For multimedia and other young growth industries in particular, this correlation is most significant. Comparing specific regions (see Braczyk et al. 1999), it becomes evident that the regions which developed exemplary strengths in mature industries do not necessarily have advantages concerning multimedia production structures. Existent and working networks in established industries do not guarantee a rapid growth in innovative future industries. Exogenous regional strategies become relevant, aiming at establishing competence in new sectors by attracting highly competent actors from outside of a certain region. In other words, global ties have special strengths for regions that want to tread new paths for which the previous economic and structural development did not offer favourable starting conditions. Global networking provides contacts for regions to sectoral 'centres of excellence' in research and development and connections to extraregional markets. Examples of such strategies will be presented later.

In a large part of the above-mentioned literature on the globalisation thesis, the strengths of global ties are emphasised less than the problems and risks from the viewpoint of economic regions, pointing out the restrictions of the regional ability to act proactively and the fragility of global ties. Regional policies are forced to provide attractive conditions for global players, probably leading to a process of competitive dumping among the regions (Iwer and Rehberg 1999). Moreover, globalised companies with weak ties to a specific location will probably remove business units from the region at short notice. The more important these business units are for the economic performance and employment of a regional economy, the more problems arise due to decisions to remove operations from the region.

14.3 The Combination of Regional and Global Ties as a Precondition for Successful Cluster Formation

The neo-regionalist research perspective emphasises the strengths of regional ties referring to regional success stories, whereas the globalisation thesis points to the importance of global ties referring to an increasing internationalisation of the economy. From the viewpoint of economic regions, however, regional and global ties must not be treated as alternatives. The thesis advanced in this chapter argues that the most successful regions in one economic sector are embedded in well-functioning regional as well as global networks. This is just one of four possible combinations for the intensity of regional and global networking (see Table 14.1). The undoubtedly simplified and stylised[4] distinction is derived from the perspective of certain regions. Talking about regions from now on, I will only refer to specific sectors within the region, however. Based on this assumption the following four-field table (see Table 14.1) is constructed. Table 14.2 summarises examples for the respective combination from literature.

14.3.1 Fragmented Isolated Regions

The situation of an economic area is particularly precarious if there is only little networking of regional companies and no significant integration in global networks. The situation of combined fragmentation (no intraregional networking) and isolation (no integration in global networks) is generally accompanied by serious

---

[4] For the sake of simplicity what is described in a four-field table is actually a combination of two continuous dimensions. Moreover, this depiction should not give the impression that regional and global ties as such are decisive for the potential for economic development of a region. Not taken into consideration are numerous factors that should also be noticed, i.e., exchange rates or basic political conditions.

weaknesses in the regional economic productivity, particularly with regard to the generation and adaptation of innovations. This combination may primarily be observed in connection with fundamental and radical changes, i.e., the situation of far-reaching social change in the transformation from a socialist to a capitalist economic system. Grabher's study (1995) on East German industry after reunification gives an example of a 'disembedded' transformation economy. Informal networks, extremely important in the (former) German Democratic Republic, broke down and economic relations with other Eastern European countries were strained by the monetary union. The integration of this region in West German and global networks gradually developed but its position within these networks remains weak.

Table 14.1. Combinations of Regional and Global Ties

		Regional Networks	
		weak	strong
Integration in global networks	weak	I Fragmented isolated regions	II Isolated industrial districts
	strong	III Cathedrals in the desert	IV Global regions

Table 14.2. Examples from Research

		Regional Networks	
		weak	strong
Integration in global networks	weak	I Different industries, former German Democratic Republic (Grabher 1995) and other transformation economies (Heidenreich 1999)	II Watch industry, Swiss Jura (Glasmeier 1995), coal and steel industry, the Ruhr area (Grabher 1993b)
	strong	III Information technology, Boston/Route 128 (Saxenian 1994); electronics industry, Scotland: (Molina and Kinder 1999)	IV Information technology and software, Silicon Valley (Saxenian 1994)

14.3.2 Isolated Industrial Districts

Regions that deserve the rank of an industrial district because of a distinct degree of intraregional co-operation but whose integration in global networks is weak are called 'isolated industrial districts'. Technological discontinuities are one cause that brings about the situation in which isolated industrial districts develop. The study of Glasmeier (1995) on the watch industry in the Swiss Jura may serve as an example. For a long time, this industry was a very efficient, productive and integrated complex of highly specialised companies, deliberately cutting itself off in the course of protectionist politics. In the 1970s, this complex did not adapt itself to the emerging quartz technology as quickly as necessary and therefore lost its leading technological position quickly. There are many more examples of 'declining industries', i.e., the coal and steel industry in the Ruhr area, where formerly strong intraregional ties turned weak later (see Grabher 1993b). The shipbuilding industry in many European regions could serve as an additional example.

Industrial districts may flourish over longer periods of time without any strong integration in global networks. Yet, without well-functioning global ties industrial districts increasingly risk being surprised or put under pressure by technological and organisational innovations developed by other regions. The risk is high because isolated industrial districts frequently have a high degree of specialisation leading to high productivity in a very limited field, which makes adaptation to modified conditions difficult. In addition, there are limits to the growth of the domestic market for industrial districts that are difficult to overcome without ties to global players.

14.3.3 Cathedrals in the Desert

The somewhat ironic label of 'cathedrals in the desert'[5] is given to those regions that are closely integrated in global networks by prominent global players but do not show the distinct intraregional integration and networking of companies typical of industrial districts. Integration in global networks is generally achieved by one or several large companies, represented in the region by head offices or other major company units.[6] These globalised companies are not competing with an integrated endogenous economic sector in the region.

As described by Saxenian (1994) one example is the information technology industry in the Route 128 area near Boston. This region accommodates globalised companies, e.g., DEC, but does not show any distinct regional networking structures. According to Saxenian, this is the reason why, some years ago, the region had much more trouble than Silicon Valley in adapting to changing conditions in the world market. The electronics industry of Scotland is another example. According to Molina and Kinder (1999) a remarkable electronics industry cluster developed in Scotland, based primarily on foreign direct investments. But the exter-

---

[5] Alternatively, regions in this field could be called, according to Hilbert et al. (1999) 'lonesome rider regions', or according to Markusen (1996), 'satellite platform districts'.

[6] In contrast to Markusen's (1996) notion of a 'satellite platform district', globally integrated companies in the proposed distinction must not necessarily be branches of companies with their headquarters in other regions. According to this distinction – but not to Markusen's – it is possible that a region accommodates a firm's head office but no distinct intraregional networks.

nally dominated companies are integrated into 'indigenous' companies to only a very limited extent;[7] intensive forms of co-operation, such as, in particular, the generation and exchange of innovative knowledge are still rare.

From the viewpoint of the regions the predominance of globally oriented companies produces desired as well as undesired consequences. Global contacts between companies provide the chance for a region to have, at least, access to external know-how, technological innovations developed elsewhere and foreign markets. How far this chance is really used is dependent on the position a region obtains in the location hierarchy of globalised companies. In case the region is just an 'extended assembly line', conditions are of course not as favourable as if the head offices with all strategic core functions such as research and development are established there. In both cases it is true that globally oriented companies remove capacities from a region earlier the less they are integrated in regional networks with other companies. The negative effects for a region with no distinct endogenous networks can be serious.

14.3.4 Global Regions

Regions with a close integration in global networks as well as distinct intraregional integration are called 'global regions', corresponding to the notion 'global city' (see Sassen 1994).[8] Successful global regions are those whose networks incorporate an adequate supply of quality knowledge resources, along with the ability and willingness of local firms to make use of external sources of knowledge with a clear focus on innovation (see Huggins 1997). Silicon Valley is an example of this kind of region: it accommodates companies obtaining a worldwide leading position in information technology and software industry and that are globally active. Very intensive and flexible forms of labour division as well as co-operation between companies and the employees in the region (see Saxenian 1991, 1994) may arise simultaneously.

Regions with both distinct regional *and* global ties are predestined to take the part of worldwide forerunner. Whereas regional ties facilitate competitive production clusters, global ties provide an input of external know-how and access to new markets and prevent a cluster from becoming inflexible.[9] A combination of regional and global ties therefore offers the most favourable conditions for a permanent capability of development for regional economic systems.

---

[7] Turok (1993, 1997) and McCann (1997) discussed the regional integration of the Scottish 'Silicon Glen'. According to McCann's argumentation of a comparatively high degree of regional embeddedness of the Scottish electronic industry, the assignment in our four-field table should be revised.

[8] Huggins (1997, p. 103) uses the description 'global region' for regions "which are able to integrate geographically restricted economies into the global web of industry and commerce".

[9] See the above-quoted argument by Camagni.

Some authors emphasise the importance of the combination of regional and global networks. Ernst concludes from his study on the information technology industry: "The dynamic coupling of domestic and international knowledge linkages is of critical importance for economic growth in a globalizing world" (Ernst 1999, p. 31). Similar comments are found in Storper and Harrison (1991, p. 411–420), Freeman (1995, p. 21), Markusen (1996), Freeman and Soete (1997, p. 315), Huggins (1997, p. 102) and Almeida and Kogut (1997, p. 29). The literature in general, however, is dominated by an analysis which focuses only on the study of networks on a specific spatial level. Literature that tries to analyse the interlinkages of networks on different levels is scarce.

Only a few regions are in the favourable situation of being called 'global'. Most troublesome from the viewpoint of other regions is the fact that it is extremely difficult to catch up with these forerunner regions. This is most obvious in the discussion of exogenous and endogenous development models. An investigation by Kim and von Tunzelmann (1998) on the Taiwanese information technology industry is very informative in this respect.[10] The dynamic growth of this industry was possible because Taiwan has functioning local and national network structures on the one hand and achieved an integration in the production networks of transnational information technology companies. According to Kim and von Tunzelmann the achievement to align these different network levels in Taiwan was decisive for success although this alignment was dependent on the coincidence of a number of favourable conditions, i.e., the possibility to use connections to the networks of native Taiwanese in the US information technology industry (see Saxenian 1997).

Another example of a successful regional catching-up strategy is the Irish software industry (see Fuchs and Wolf 1998b), a process only possible because of numerous favourable conditions (i.e., financial aid from EC and EU, an excellent educational level of the population and intensive governmental support for direct foreign investments). For a long time Ireland has been a 'branch plant economy' but during the past few years in addition to foreign companies (or partly because of them) a respectable endogenous potential has developed in the country's software industry. The strategy to develop a regional economic sector with the help of specific global ties was successful in Taiwan and Ireland. It is very difficult to reproduce these development paths in other regions. 'Global regions' must expect serious problems only in connection with fundamental change, i.e., technological paradigmatic change.

---

[10] According to Ernst (1999, p. 31) the Korean innovation system of information technology developed because of a "co-evolution of international and domestic knowledge linkages".

14.4 Regional and Global Ties in the Multimedia Core Industry

What does the proposed distinction mean for the multimedia sector? First of all, we may say that at present this sector is at a formative stage so that any analysis of organisational forms can only be preliminary. The assumption regarding the importance of both regional and global ties may be used in principle despite this restriction (see Table 14.3). But the positioning of regions in the four-field table in such a fluid sector is questionable and a shifting of assignments is very possible, but given the strength of path dependencies not very likely.

The multimedia sector has a very high number of young, small or even one-person companies in all regions. The fact that newly founded companies have more regional co-operation relations in comparison to older and larger companies (see Almeida and Kogut 1997; Fuchs and Wolf 1999) makes us expect fewer global ties in the multimedia sector than in other established economic sectors. Nevertheless, we observe significant differences between the regions which develop multimedia clusters. This aspect allows us to use our four-field distinction in a meaningful manner.

Table 14.3. Examples of the Multimedia Core Industry

Integration in global networks	Regional networks	
	weak	strong
weak	I	III
	North Eastern England (Cornford 1997), Saarland (Matthäi and Schmidt 1998)	Wales (Cooke and Hughes 1999)
strong	II	IV
	Guetersloh (Hilbert et al. 1999)	California (Scott 1998; Egan and Saxenian 1999)

The generation of multimedia products and services is an economic activity for which clear-cut industrial structures are being developed. During the past few years, a core of multimedia producers developed, focussing activities on generating products and services for multimedia (so-called multimedia agencies, CD-ROM producers and others). Companies from numerous related industries (particularly print media, audio-visual media, advertising, software, etc.) established around this core and, acting as multimedia producers, form the first periphery of the multimedia labour market. The second periphery consists of companies which use multimedia but which are not active as producers (see Fig. 14.1; Belzer and Michel 1998, p. 5; Fuchs and Wolf 1999, p. 8). Arguments in this paper concentrate on the multimedia core industry.

The emergence of an innovative economic sector such as multimedia is considered to be a fundamental and radical change resulting in a combination of fragmentation and isolation (Field I) in regions with unfavourable pre-conditions. With regard to Cornford's study (1997) this description is true of the region of North Eastern England. According to his analysis the possibility of integration in multimedia-related economic sectors is very unfavourable and there are comparatively few multimedia-producing small companies. These firms do not show any intensive form of co-operation and have only a few distinct contacts to extraregional or global market actors (they particularly lack a 'hub firm' making extraregional contacts). Cornford (1997, p. 9) concludes "that there is little chance of a substantial multimedia business emerging in the region". The multimedia sector of Saarland (Germany) shows similar traits. According to Matthäi and Schmidt (1998) this sector shows neither characteristics of an industrial district with a strong regional network nor does Saarland have large entertainment and media companies with strong global ties.

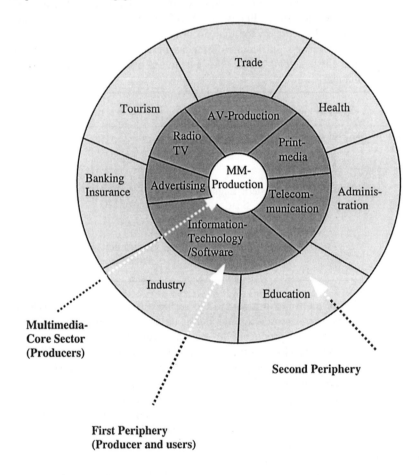

Fig. 14.1. Multimedia Producers and Peripheries

Regions where clusters of networking young and small multimedia companies developed, but where there are no global multimedia companies, belong to field II of our four-field table. This characterisation applies to the region of Cardiff and Wales for example. According to Cooke and Hughes (1999), a scene of predominantly smaller multimedia companies developed there, open to regional co-operation. Until now a strong integration in global networks is obviously not typical for the multimedia industry in Cardiff. Yet another kind of local embeddedness was very fruitful for growth, i.e., the demand for contents in the Welsh language. The industry originated largely, though not entirely, in the media sector in spin-off firms from the broadcasting industry. The development of the industry is supported by numerous public initiatives which seem to play an important role for the stabilisation of this mini-cluster. There is even a certain degree of multi-level governance from the grass roots and self-organisation, from city and regional authorities up to the European Union level offering support. There are more examples from other regions where a specific demand for regional culture and language helped to develop a multimedia industry (e.g., Finland). On the one hand these market niches provide favourable conditions for the growth of an industry; on the other hand, however, they also restrict the growth of these industries. Thus multimedia industries of field II will only be able to grow beyond a certain level if they succeed in achieving a more intensive integration in global networks.

As mentioned above, the majority of companies of the multimedia core sectors are small or medium-sized. Nevertheless some regions within the multimedia sector can be identified according to the pattern of 'cathedrals in the desert' (field III). In this case, global players are large companies of the first periphery of the multimedia sector, engaged in the multimedia core sector nowadays as well. The region around Guetersloh is an example (see Hilbert et al. 1999).[11] Bertelsmann, one of the worldwide leading media companies, has its head office there and company units based there are responsible for at least part of the company's multimedia activities. In its home region, Bertelsmann is the biggest employer. The Bertelsmann company units co-operate very intensively – for example in the form of customer-supplier relationships – but there are only few business relations to other regional firms. Knowledge transfer from Bertelsmann to other companies in the region or mobility of personnel moving from Bertelsmann to other regional companies rarely happens. This is the reason why the company's impact on the development of a regional multimedia cluster remains weak.

California (or more precisely, the Bay Area around San Francisco and Southern California around Los Angeles) is a typical example of a multimedia region in field IV. Scott (1998, p. 161) describes the Californian multimedia sector as "second to none in size, innovativeness and developmental potential" and claims that the region has assumed the "position of worldwide supremacy". Scott also emphasises the "double-sided local and global character of the industry": there are close and intensively used networks of multimedia firms as well as a strong global orientation and integration of the sector. The multimedia industry tends to settle in

---

[11] Guetersloh is a medium-sized city half way between Dortmund and Essen (ca. 75 km north-east of Dortmund).

dense transaction-intensive complexes made up of many small and medium-sized producers working together in tightly knit social labour divisions. At the same time, the commercial reach of the industry is effectively worldwide. Therefore Scott sees excellent development perspectives for the Californian multimedia industry even if he warns against complacency in view of other regions' efforts to catch up.

In Southern California the multimedia industry seems to have developed in close connection with the Hollywood entertainment complex and the creative design culture there. On the other hand the functional and local proximity to the high-tech milieu of Silicon Valley could serve for the expansion of the industry and access to valuable assets.

It must be emphasised – as shown in fields II and IV of our four-field table – that in many aspects the development of regional production structures in the multimedia core sector is similar to the characteristics of industrial clusters or industrial districts in general. This is remarkable because the central role of advanced and network-integrated information and communication technology in this sector might have suggested that spatial proximity is more or less insignificant. Available evidence, on the other hand, however, suggests that spatial proximity to customers and co-operation partners is important for multimedia firms as well (see Braczyk et al. 1999). Most multimedia projects require close and constant interaction between customer and producer. Thus, multimedia corporations are situated next to their biggest customers. For complex projects the predominantly small multimedia corporations depend on the input of partners, which – given the low degree of regulation and standardisation in this industry – should preferably also be nearby.

In the following section the argument related to the multimedia core sector will be exemplified by an analysis of the situation in Baden-Wuerttemberg.

14.5 Regional and Global Ties in the Multimedia Sector of Baden-Wuerttemberg

The question at the beginning was: what kind of interorganisational ties of multimedia companies in a certain region may provide for the development and growth of a regional multimedia cluster? With regard to worldwide regional efforts to support the development of clusters, this question gains a very practical relevance. Baden-Wuerttemberg, too, is making great efforts to become a multimedia location of extraregional importance. Baden-Wuerttemberg does not smoothly fit in one of the above-mentioned four categories. It is all the more interesting to consider this case in detail.

The thesis proposed at the beginning said that it is typical of the most successful regions of an economic sector to be integrated in well-functioning regional as well as global networks. One condition for a good start in multimedia is the existence of related industries. The situation in this case is not at all clear. There is no typical multimedia location in Baden-Wuerttemberg, although we have an outstanding number of publishing houses and electronics companies in Stuttgart. In this sense the presence of companies of the first periphery is remarkable. Yet, this is not of crucial importance for the location. Baden-Wuerttemberg is generally known as an industrially based economic region with the highest amount of industrial employment in comparison to Europe. Literature frequently emphasises the fact that there is a high degree of network integration of actors in the industrial core sectors (mechanical engineering and car manufacturing). There are numerous small and medium-sized companies strongly integrated in regional networks and there are a number of large companies integrated in global networks. In the relevant literature, Baden-Wuerttemberg has been described as an exemplary and – in this regard – frequently investigated region for a long time (see Voelzkow 1999). According to our distinction (see Table 14.1) Baden-Wuerttemberg in general would be a global region.

Experience shows that existing network structures are not necessarily of advantage for the development and growth of new sectors that are not closely linked to the core sectors. This does not mean that every successful region must be excellent in new fields of technology. But even successful model regions are faced with the danger of becoming inflexible. In the case of multimedia, we find multimedia producers almost everywhere in the meantime because they offer a service based on proximity to the customer, but concentrations of multimedia companies seem to develop only in a few conurbations with certain characteristics, which we can find in Baden-Wuerttemberg only to a very limited extent.

In the following you find a more detailed description of the situation of multimedia in Baden-Wuerttemberg. The results are based on two surveys carried out in multimedia companies in Baden-Wuerttemberg, on extensive field research as well as on the evaluation of secondary literature. The first result is: there are three clusters of multimedia producing companies in Baden-Wuerttemberg, i.e., Stuttgart, Mannheim/Heidelberg and Karlsruhe. The local concentration is in the core cities in the three regions.[12] There seems to be a city orientation among multimedia firms, a trend contrary to many other economic sectors where firms frequently choose locations outside city centres, thus causing a tendency to suburbanisation (see Eckert and Egeln 1997, p. 9).

The fact that there is a concentration of multimedia producers in three regions of Baden-Wuerttemberg makes a difference between this state and other German states where there is a higher concentration in one single region. Bavaria is an excellent example with a cluster in Munich (see Sträter 1999). The Baden-Wuerttemberg 'polycentrism' seems to have been an important politically and culturally supported context condition for the further development of multimedia production structures (see Fuchs and Wolf 1997a, p. 48).

---

[12] In 1997 a survey on multimedia companies was carried out (see Fuchs and Wolf 1998a), for which 128 addresses within the Stuttgart region were found (including the surrounding areas of Esslingen, Böblingen, Ludwigsburg, etc.). Of all these addresses, 38 were situated in the Stuttgart city centre (postal code 701XX). For a second wave of this survey in 1998 963 addresses were available from Baden-Württemberg as a whole, 95 of which were situated in the city centre of Stuttgart.

The surveys also show that companies engage in a dynamic and growing market. Actors in this market are primarily one-man businesses and small companies concerning turnover and staff but with enormous growth potential. A few larger firms among the surveyed companies are responsible for an average number of 9.43 of all regularly employed persons; the median is four. Larger companies are mainly playing an important role as customers for multimedia products.

Companies see their market in the region. Nationally or internationally oriented companies are more or less an exception from the rule. Therefore local customer solutions are developed for their specific needs. The necessary technological input is manageable. The market for business clients is developing dynamically and is more lucrative than the consumer market. The most important customers are the core industries predominant in Baden-Wuerttemberg. Multimedia employers are highly qualified and are looking for employees with high qualifications who are difficult to find on the market. Many firm foundations are team foundations in order to merge expertise from different fields. Entry barriers to the market are low and firm founders can survive by means of only a very small capital contribution in form of private savings or by the support of relatives.

In comparison to established industries of the Baden-Wuerttemberg economy, contacts to technology transfer institutions, advisory institutions etc., are below average (see Bechtle 1998).[13] Experience with these institutions is evaluated in an ambivalent way. An intensive exchange between educational institutions and companies is only possible in a few cases. The fact that the multimedia sector is a relatively young sector may certainly have caused this situation. This is also true of the relative importance of associations etc., in connection with the early development stage of the sector.

There is only little networking of companies. Networking of companies and related institutions (i.e., economic support, science etc.) is still in an early stage and not as highly developed as for dominant economic sectors. According to available information there are no signs of any specific regional specialisation. This kind of specialisation can be found in many other multimedia locations, however: for example in Duesseldorf with a close integration in the advertising and telecommunication industry, in Cologne in the orientation to film and television producers or in the concentration of computer-based training producers in Munich. Moreover, there seems to be no close connection to large and dominant companies or sectors in Baden-Wuerttemberg. The firms in Baden-Wuerttemberg are by far more regionally oriented than firms in other German media locations.

In comparison to multimedia locations in the US it is evident that standardized products are not of crucial importance at the moment; there is only little response from the consumer market. Globalisation or internationalisation of the business is still insignificant and financing strategies are very conservative. Venture capital, stock market flotation, etc. are hardly considered by these companies.

---

[13] Bechtle who investigated companies of the Baden-Wuerttemberg core industries such as mechanical engineering, etc. found out that 15% of the interviewed companies take advantage of the services of transfer institutions and 20%, services of regional universities and higher educational institutions.

To summarise characteristics, the Baden-Wuerttemberg region must – in view of multimedia – be described as a region with a weak regional network integration, with little specialisation and a weak integration in global networks (see Table 14.1). This describes the status quo only and need not determine further trajectories.

In assessing the situation in Baden-Wuerttemberg it is certainly interesting to see that the Stuttgart region accommodates numerous large companies in information technology (i.e., Alcatel-SEL, Bosch, Debis, Hewlett-Packard, IBM) that could become starting points for the development of regional networks with global significance. Based on the distinction introduced above (see Table 14.4), these companies belong to the first periphery.[14] Each of these companies is closely integrated in an international network. With the exception of IBM, these companies are not closely integrated in regional networks and in fact had only little influence on the development of the multimedia industry. This is contrary to the situation in Munich or Duesseldorf where large firms or venture capital investors could act as agents for global network integration.

There were numerous attempts to integrate so-called 'global players' in regional networks and use them as starting point for the development of the multimedia sector. The most prominent example for these efforts was the pilot project *Multimedia Services in Baden-Wuerttemberg*.[15]

The Stuttgart pilot project was an industrial policy project of the state government devoted to the network idea. The project idea was born in discussions with the Minister of Economics and managers of the 'local' electronics industry (Bosch, Alcatel-SEL, IBM and Hewlett-Packard). These top-level discussion meetings under the heading 'media economy' took place within the framework of a common initiative 'Economy and Politics'. During the stage of planning, the Ministry of Economics assumed that the Baden-Wuerttemberg industry would suffer from further losses in employment in the main business fields and that Baden-Wuerttemberg would participate in the growth of employment in the new sectors to a below average extent. The main actors agreed that there was need and justification for action: public actors were to aim at achieving more innovations, thus creating more employment in the future sector of 'multimedia'. It was the minister's intention not to define any objectives for the activities but, concerning the definition of objectives, to rely on a consensus of the social actors (companies, trade unions, etc.) to formulate them. The then minister Spöri saw the task of economic politics in the moderation of the process of finding a consensus and later in supporting a rapid realisation of the consensus, once achieved. To this extent the idea to carry out a pilot project corresponded with the consensus of the participants in the top-level discussion group. The role of government thus was to grant part of the money that was needed to carry out the project, a basis for coordination as well as security in a rapidly developing market (by organising a contract between the hardware companies and Deutsche Telekom).

---

[14] This is also true of the publishing sector.
[15] More details on the pilot project can be found in Fuchs and Wolf (1997b).

Hardware firms participating in the pilot project were interested in opening up new markets. Traditional telecommunication firms such as Bosch-Telecom and Alcatel-SEL were looking for new business fields in view of a decline in orders and prices in their core business. In combining the market of computer and telecommunication technology, HP and IBM saw various new market options. This group of companies intended to deliver to the network operator, the Deutsche Telekom AG (DTAG), hardware and software as well as to make technological offers available for service and content providers.

The DTAG had its own specific interest in the pilot project. The company owns a loss-making cable network which is not working at full capacity; the company is therefore looking for new areas of application. As a participant in the pilot project, the DTAG primarily wanted to test new offers for private customers via the network.

Summarising this constellation, we can say that the pilot project was supported by an alliance of large hardware companies that could be described as *global players,* the network operator DTAG, and the Ministry of Economics as initiator, moderator and partial financier. The actors' interests in the pilot project were divergent, but they agreed on a common arrangement for the pilot project with DTAG being responsible for the organisation.

After three years of preparatory discussions and prolonged negotiations as well as new technological developments, the DTAG and the Ministry of Economics declared the pilot project impracticable in October 1996. The official justification that the ordered technology was not available at the arranged date is only partially satisfactory. To postpone deadlines, especially in complex technological (software) projects, is the rule rather than the exception. Considering the fact that the order to carry out the project was only given in December 1995, the Stuttgart impatience needs even more explanation.

The strategic situation of the project became critical when assessments of the market volume for products of interactive television continuously and rapidly decreased and investment costs on the other hand soared in the period from 1994 to 1996. In the process some of the actors' calculations turned out to be wrong. The public was as much interested in the Internet as it was in 'normal' digital television. Moreover, the assessment solidified that the economic importance of business applications is to be rated higher than applications for private households. The construction of the project in Stuttgart (concentration on a cable-tv infrastructure) seemed to be problematic for the development of business applications and the complicated organisational structure of the project made a flexible response to spherical changes difficult.

Finally, it was not clarified to the very last moment which companies were to offer the different kinds of new services. Concerning service providers and contents developers, two major groups can be differentiated. On the one hand, there was a large number of regionally based organisations (i.e., consumer advice centers, trade unions, trade associations, etc.) showing great interest in participating in the pilot project, but from the very beginning these organisations were not involved in the planning owing to the project organisation (concentration on large hardware companies) and later refused to participate more or less voluntarily because of the high costs. The Ministry of Economics had excluded the possibility of supporting service providers and content developers within the framework of the pilot project. Actors with regional interest were faced with large nationally and internationally oriented service providers: private and public radio stations (Kirch, Bertelsmann, Suedwestfunk, etc.), mail-order firms (Kaufhof, Otto). Although the pilot project was intended to be supported by this group with contents as a focus, the project architecture corresponded only partially to their requirements. Service providers are interested in a relatively large and homogenous market and a marketing test under competitive conditions. Telekom, however, wanted to test a proprietary technology in Stuttgart and did not want to guarantee the portability of contents to other pilot systems.

It was decisive for the failure of the project that there was little integration and regional orientation of the network. The network proved to be too inflexible to cope with the changing environment. With the goal of supporting the multimedia industry, the focus of the project could have been changed and other partners admitted. This did not happen. With the failure of the project, the network, too, broke apart. The attempt to create a regional network intended to incorporate primarily the global players had failed. In the end the actors' interests were so divergent and determined by the companies' head offices and not by regional branches that regional industrial and political considerations were only of secondary importance. In this respect Ash Amin's quote from section 2.2 came true: regions play only an instrumental role for globally oriented companies. During the lifetime of the project there were only very spurious attempts to integrate regionally oriented companies into the network.

Attempts to make amends were made later. At the end of 1995 the media and film company of Baden-Wuerttemberg was founded, an institution acting as coordinating headquarters for numerous independent multimedia and technology projects. An important goal of this institution is to bring about the integration of actors in networks and to increase the attractiveness of Baden-Wuerttemberg as a location by means of sponsoring presence at fairs and public relations activities.

14.6 Conclusion

It has been demonstrated in this paper that successful economic regions can be characterised by certain constellations of global and regional network integration. The intensity of network integration is, however, different from sector to sector. What applies to the dominating companies of a respective region need not be valid for other industries at the periphery. The lack of ability to integrate in the dominating structures of a region makes it difficult for new sectors to achieve visibility and excellence. The case of multimedia in Baden-Wuerttemberg may serve as an example in this regard. The young multimedia sector succeeded only partially in integrating in existing structures and regional networks. But the case of Baden-Wuerttemberg also shows that there is a process of alignment and the chance to break up long established structures. Catching up with regions already advanced in multimedia is nevertheless a process difficult to handle, as there are many preconditions to the management of this kind of process. As the example of the failure of the Stuttgart pilot project for multimedia services showed, even ambitious and well-meant attempts to support network integration may fail. Politicians, too, must learn from experience about how far they can promote the interaction of regional and global ties in the multimedia production so that a region may profit from this.[16]

The fact that the innovation network analysed in this article failed to realise the innovation it had been established for does not imply that such networks are generally unsuited for supporting regional economic development. The lesson we can draw from this specific case is that regional innovation networks should meet the following criteria to make them likely to be more successful than the IVSS network:

- when establishing the network, great evaluative effort must be spent on choosing the specific innovation, the network is supposed to strive for;
- network members (firms, public and semi-public actors) must be carefully selected according to their strengths in the specific technological field the network addresses;
- if regionally based actors alone cannot provide the necessary competencies, links to pools of knowledge outside of the region are essential;
- a balance must be maintained between the need to limit the size of the network to keep it efficient and the need to keep the network open enough so that all the actors who may make important contributions to the innovation are included;
- the internal organisation of the network is crucial: the role of a mobilising actor is important, and a certain level of centralised co-ordination is necessary to guarantee the flow of information among the network members.

Even if a regional innovation network fulfilled all these requirements, it still might fail for other reasons: too high a technological and economic complexity of its task, unforeseeable changes in its economic, social and political environment, or a breakdown of the fragile co-operative relationships between potentially or actually competing firms. On the other hand, it is unlikely that the technological complexity in many fields of innovation is achieved without the co-operation in networks. Thus, if regions striving for economic regeneration attempt to foster innovations there may be few alternatives to supporting innovation networks. Only the future will tell whether it will be possible to establish strong regional and global network structures in the Baden-Wuerttemberg multimedia core sector so that the region will succeed in becoming an example of a 'global region' in this sector as well.

---

[16] It must be said that so far not much help is to be expected from the social sciences in this respect because the study of the relationships between regional and global ties in the process of regional development is still in a nascent state.

References

Almeida P, Kogut B (1997) The exploration of technological diversity and the geographic localization of innovation. Small Business Economics 9: 21–31

Altvater E, Mahnkopf B (1996) Grenzen der Globalisierung. Ökonomie, Ökologie und Politik in der Weltgesellschaft. Westfälisches Dampfboot, Münster

Amin A (1993) The globalization of the economy: An erosion of regional networks? In: Grabher G (ed) The embedded firm: On the socioeconomics of industrial networks. Routledge, London, pp 278–295

Amin A, Thrift N (eds) (1995) Globalization, institutions, and regional development in Europe. Oxford University Press, Oxford

Aydalot P, Keeble D (eds) (1988) High technology industry and innovative environments: The European experience. Routledge, London

Bechtle G (1998) Das Verhältnis von Organisation und Innovation: Wie reagiert die baden-württembergische Industrie auf die Krise der neunziger Jahre? Arbeitsbericht Nr. 124 der Akademie für Technikfolgenabschätzung in Baden-Württemberg, Stuttgart

Belzer V, Michel LP (1998) Der Multimedia-Standort Düsseldorf. Arbeitsbericht Nr. 98 der Akademie für Technikfolgenabschätzung in Baden-Württemberg, Stuttgart

Boekholt P, Van der Weele E (1998) Southeast Brabant: a regional innovation system in transition. In: Braczyk H-J, Cooke P, Heidenreich M (eds) Regional Innovation Systems. UCL Press, London, pp 48–71

Braczyk H-J, Cooke P, Heidenreich M (eds) (1998) Regional innovation systems. The role of governances in a globalized world. UCL Press, London

Braczyk H-J, Fuchs G, Wolf H-G (1999) Multimedia and regional economic restructuring. Routledge, London

Bramanti A, Maggioni MA (1997) The dynamics of milieux: The network analysis approach. In: Ratti R, Bramanti A, Gordon R (eds) The dynamics of innovative regions: The GREMI Approach. Ashgate, Aldershot, pp 321–341

Camagni R (1991) Introduction: From the local 'milieu' to innovation through cooperation networks. In: Camagni R (ed) Innovation Networks: Spatial Perspectives. Belhaven, London, pp 1–9

Camagni R (ed) (1991) Innovation networks: Spatial perspectives. Belhaven, London

Cooke P, Hughes G (1999) Creating a multimedia cluster in Cardiff Bay. In: Braczyk H-J, Fuchs G, Wolf H-G (eds) Multimedia and regional economic restructuring. Routledge, London, pp 252–268

Cornford J (1997) The myth of 'the' multimedia industry: Evidence from the North East of England (and beyond). Unpublished Draft Paper, Newcastle upon Tyne

Eckert T, Egeln J (1997) Multimedia-Anbieter in Westdeutschland: Existieren Cluster? Arbeitsbericht Nr. 76 der Akademie für Technikfolgenabschätzung in Baden-Württemberg, Stuttgart

Egan T, Saxenian A (1999) Becoming digital: Sources of localization in the Bay Area multimedia cluster. In: Braczyk H-J, Fuchs G, Wolf H-G (eds) Multimedia and regional economic restructuring. Routledge, London, pp 11–29

Enright MJ (1996) Regional clusters and economic development: A research agenda. In: Staber UH, Schaefer NV, Sharma B (eds) Business networks: Prospects for regional development. de Gruyter, Berlin, pp 190–213

Ernst D (1999) How globalization reshapes the geography of innovation systems: Reflections on global production networks in information industries. Unpublished Paper, Prepared for DRUID 1999 Summer Conference on Innovation Systems, Kopenhagen

Feldman MP (1994) The geography of innovation. Kluwer, Dordrecht

Fischer M (ed) (1998) Clusters and regional specialisation. On geography, technology and networks. Pion, London

Forrester V (1997) Der Terror der Ökonomie. Paul Zsolnay, Wien

Freeman C (1995) The 'national system of innovation' in historical perspective. Cambridge Journal of Economics 19: 5–24

Freeman C, Soete L (1997) The economics of industrial innovation. 3rd edition, Pinter, London

Fuchs G, Wolf H-G (1997a) 'Multimedia-land' Baden-Württemberg? In: Heidenreich M (ed) Innovationen in Baden-Württemberg. Nomos, Baden-Baden, pp 41–59

Fuchs G, Wolf H-G (1997b) Regional economies, interactive television and interorganizational networks: A case study of an innovation network in Baden-Württemberg. European Planning Studies 5: 619–636

Fuchs G, Wolf H-G (1998a) Multimedia-Unternehmen in Baden-Württemberg. Erfahrungen, Erfolgsbedingungen und Erwartungen. Arbeitsbericht Nr. 128 der Akademie für Technikfolgenabschätzung in Baden-Württemberg, Stuttgart

Fuchs G, Wolf H-G (1998b) The emergence of new industrial clusters –The role of regional governance in multimedia development: A comparison of California, Ireland and Baden-Württemberg. Current Politics and Economics of Europe 8: 225–255

Fuchs G, Wolf H-G (1999) Zweite Umfrage zu Multimedia-Unternehmen in Baden-Württemberg. Arbeitsbericht Nr. 141 der Akademie für Technikfolgenabschätzung in Baden-Württemberg, Stuttgart

Gehrke B, Legler H (1998) Regional concentration of innovative potential in Western Germany. Vierteljahreshefte zur Wirtschaftsforschung 67: 99–112

Glasmeier A (1995) Flexible districts, flexible regions? The institutional and cultural limits to districts in an era of globalization and technological paradigm shifts. In: Amin A, Thrift N (eds) Globalization, institutions, and regional development in Europe. Oxford University Press, Oxford, pp 118–146

Grabher G (1993a) Rediscovering the social in the economics of interfirm relations. In: Grabher G (ed) The embedded firm: On the socioeconomics of industrial networks. Routledge, London, pp 1–31

Grabher G (1993b) The weakness of strong ties: The lock-in of regional development in the Ruhr area. In: Grabher G (ed) The embedded firm: On the socioeconomics of industrial networks. Routledge, London, pp 255–277

Grabher G (1995) The disembedded regional economy: The transformation of East German industrial complexes into Western enclaves. In: Amin A, Thrift N (eds) Globalization, institutions, and regional development in Europe. Oxford University Press, Oxford, pp 177–195

Granovetter M (1973) The strength of weak ties. American Journal of Sociology 78: 1360–1380

Granovetter M (1985) Economic action and social structure: The problem of embeddedness. American Journal of Sociology 91: 481–510

Hage J, Alter C (1997) A typology of interorganizational relationships and networks. In: Hollingsworth RJ, Boyer R (eds) Contemporary capitalism: The embeddedness of institutions. Cambridge University Press, Cambridge, pp 94–126

Heidenreich M, Krauss G (1996) Das baden-württembergische Produktions- und Innovationsregime - Zwischen vergangenen Erfolgen und neuen Herausforderungen. Arbeitsbericht Nr. 54 der Akademie für Technikfolgenabschätzung in Baden-Württemberg, Stuttgart

Hilbert J, Nordhause-Janz J, Rehfeld D (1999) Between regional networking and lonesome riding: Different patterns of regional embeddedness in new media´s business in North Rhine Westphalia. In: Braczyk H-J, Fuchs G, Wolf H-G (eds) Multimedia and regional economic restructuring. Routledge, London, pp 131–154

Huggins R (1997) Competitiveness and the global region: The role of networking. In: Simmie J (ed) Innovation, networks and learning regions? Jessica Kingsley, London, pp 101–123

Iwer F, Rehberg F (1999) Mythos Region? – Clusterstrukturen und Diffusion regionaler Politikmuster unter der Bedingung internationaler Restrukturierung. In: Fuchs G, Krauss G, Wolf H-G (eds) Die Bindungen der Globalisierung. Interorganisationsbeziehungen im regionalen und globalen Wirtschaftsraum. Metropolis, Marburg, pp 329–361

Kim S-R, von Tunzelmann N (1998) Aligning internal and external networks: Taiwan's specialization in IT. SPRU Electronic Working Papers Series, Paper No 17, Falmer, Brighton

Krugman P (1991) Geography and trade. MIT Press, Cambridge

Krumbein W, Friese C, Hellmer F (1994) Industrial districts und 'Normalregionen' – Überlegungen zu den Ausgangspunkten einer zeitgemäßen Wirtschaftsförderpolitik. In: Krumbein W (ed) Ökonomische und politische Netzwerke in der Region. Beiträge aus der internationalen Debatte, Lit, Münster, pp 153–186

Markusen A (1996) Sticky places in slippery space – a typology of industrial districts. Economic Geography 72: 293–313

Martin H-P, Schumann H (1996) Die Globalisierungsfalle. Der Angriff auf Demokratie und Wohlstand. Rowohlt, Reinbek bei Hamburg

Matthäi I, Schmidt G (1998) Multimedia-Anbieter im Saarland. Arbeitsbericht Nr. 114 der Akademie für Technikfolgenabschätzung in Baden-Württemberg, Stuttgart

McCann P (1997) How deeply embedded is Silicon Glen? A cautionary note. Regional Studies 31: 695–703

Molina A, Kinder T (1999) From purposiveness to sustainability in the formation of multimedia clusters: Governance and constituency building in Scotland. In: Braczyk H-J, Fuchs G, Wolf H-G (eds) Multimedia and Regional Economic Restructuring. Routledge, London, pp 269–297

Piore MJ, Sabel CF (1984) The second industrial divide: Possibilities for prosperity. Basic Books, New York

Porter ME (1990) The competitive advantage of nations. Free Press, New York

Pyke F, Sengenberger W (eds) (1992) Industrial districts and local economic regeneration. International Institute for Labour Studies, Geneva

Sassen S (1994) Cities in a world economy. Pine Forge Press, Thousand Oaks

Saxenian A (1991) Local area networks: Industrial adaptation in Silicon Valley. In: Brotchie J, Batty M, Hall P (eds) Cities of the 21st century: New technologies and spatial systems. Longman Cheshire, Melbourne, pp 275–291

Saxenian A (1994) Regional advantage: Culture and competition in Silicon Valley and Route 128. Harvard University Press, Cambridge MA

Saxenian A (1997) Transnational entrepreneurs and regional industrialization: The Silicon Valley-Hsinchu connection. Paper presented on the Conference on Social Structure and Social Change: International Perspectives on Business Firms and Economic Life, Taipei

Scott AJ (1988) Metropolis: From the division of labor to urban form. University of California Press, Berkeley

Scott AJ (1995) The geographic foundations of industrial performance. Competition and Change 1: 51–66

Scott AJ (1998) From Silicon Valley to Hollywood: Growth and development of the multimedia industry in California. In: Braczyk H-J, Cooke P, Heidenreich M (eds) Regional innovation systems. UCL Press, London, pp 136–162

Staber UH (1996a) Networks and regional development: Perspectives and unresolved issues. In: Staber UH, Schaefer NV, Sharma B (eds) Business networks: Prospects for regional development. de Gruyter, Berlin, pp 1–23

Staber UH (1996b) The social embeddedness of industrial district networks. In: Staber UH, Schaefer NV, Sharma B (eds) Business networks: Prospects for regional development. de Gruyter, Berlin, pp 148–174

Sternberg R (1998) Innovative linkages and proximity – Empirical results from recent surveys of small and medium-sized enterprises in German regions. Working Paper No. 98-01, University of Cologne, Department of Economic and Social Geography, Köln

Storper M, Harrison B (1991) Flexibility, hierarchy and regional development: The changing structure of industrial production systems and their forms of governance in the 1990s. Research Policy 20: 407–422

Storper M (1997) The regional world: Territorial development in a global economy. The Guilford Press, New York

Sträter D (1999) Multimedia – Profiling and regional restructuring of Munich as an industrial location. In: Braczyk H-J, Fuchs G, Wolf H-G (eds) Multimedia and regional economic restructuring. Routledge, London, pp 155–182

Thurow LC (1996) Die Zukunft des Kapitalismus. Metropolitan-Verlag, Düsseldorf

Turok I (1993) Inward investment and local linkages: How deeply embedded Is Silicon Glen? Regional Studies 27: 401–417

Turok I (1997) Linkages in the Scottish electronics industry: Further evidence. Regional Studies 31: 705–711

Uzzi B (1996) The sources and consequences of embeddedness for the economic performance of organizations: The network effect. American Sociological Review 61: 674–698

Voelzkow H (1999) Die Governance regionaler Ökonomien im internationalen Vergleich: Deutschland und Italien. In: Fuchs G, Krauss G, Wolf H-G (eds) Die Bindungen der Globalisierung. Interorganisationsbeziehungen im regionalen und globalen Wirtschaftsraum, Metropolis, Marburg, pp 48–91

15 Small Key Tech-Knowledge Firms in Canada: Their Innovation Potential, Structure, and Spatial Adaptation

Brian Ceh

Department of Geography, Geology and Anthropology, Indiana State University, Terre Haute, USA

15.1 Introduction

There is greater awareness among scholars that innovative change is vital to the economic progress of firms and regions. While such change has previously been attributed to large companies (Freeman 1971, 1974), small firms have in fact developed half the new technology in several countries (Acs and Audretsch 1988). In this study, such firms are thought to be vital to the economic progress of economies, as envisioned by Schumpeter (1939), and those that are actively patenting new technology are considered to be key technology firms.

It is worthwhile to investigate SKT (small key technology) firms because they help maintain economic systems by filling and creating new market niches, threatening uncompetitive firms, encouraging competition, and even spurring new technological developments among their larger counterparts. In effect, these firms provide the economic turbulence and competition needed for industrial and economic regeneration (Acs and Audretsch 1990; Audretsch 1991). The possibility that small firms are contributing many new products is reinforced by the fact that their share of innovation exceeds their share of economic activity in terms of sales, employment, or value-added goods in the industrialised world (Shipman 1993).

Since small technology firms play an important role in shaping economies, expanding our understanding about these firms is worthwhile. Therefore, the purpose of this study is twofold. First, it will show what types of small firms have been patenting in Canada, the types of patents they developed, and where they conducted this activity from 1975 to 1990. Specifically, the location, industry, year of establishment, ownership, incidence of teams of inventors, and frequency of product or process inventing are examined for SKT firms in Canada to help meet the study's first objective. Additionally, these characteristics are analysed from a regional perspective. Studying several characteristics of SKT firms should provide new insight about their nature that otherwise would not be known if only one or two of their characteristics were studied.

The second goal of the study is to investigate whether three major findings in the literature on the geography of new technology describe the situation for SKT firms. The literature shows that spatial patterns of agglomeration, dispersion, and specialisation exist with respect to invention and innovation (Antonelli 1986; Feldman and Florida 1994; Ceh 1997a,b, 2001; Brouwer et al. 1999; Mitchelson 1999). However, it is uncertain if these same findings hold true for small firms and whether they are occurring concurrently, instead of as independent events. Small key technology firms could very well be forging their own distinct spatial patterns.

Recent works on the geography of invention and innovation (Feldman and Florida 1994; Mitchelson 1999; Ceh 2001) seem to reconfirm Pred's (1966) finding that metropolitan environments or urban agglomerations are important for inventive activity. In fact, the capacity of regions to invent has become evermore dependent on the agglomeration of specialised skills, knowledge, institutions, and resources that mould the technical infrastructure of regions (Feldman and Florida 1994). With respect to the dispersion of this activity, it is most likely to happen within large city regions, as documented by Antonelli (1986) in the province of Turin, Italy.

15.2 Measuring New Technology

While patents can be either protective or strategic in nature, it is unclear what portion of patents fall into these categories. If protective patents are eliminated from a data set, patents then become a "refined" measure of new technology. On the other hand, if protective patents are analysed, it can prove valuable since these patents can be used as a source of self-citation. In other words, important technologies are often "circled" with patents that typically cite the key invention in some way. These patents typically have similar descriptions or titles with one another or to the key invention. Arguably, the more pertinent an invention, the more likely a company will acquire additional, supporting patents (which may never be commercialised) to protect their new technology. Therefore, unfiltered patent data has a weighted element built into it and researchers can consider it for analysis.

Simply because innovation data measures new technology further along the product cycle does not inherently make it a better technological indicator. If businesses are reluctant to disclose some of their inventions in patent records, they could benefit less from presenting their new ideas or products in technology, engineering, and trade publications. Any form of new technology can be disclosed in trade publications. Ironically, the information on new technology in trade publications may be too extensive since all new products and processes, some of which have not been scrutinised by technical experts, are treated as equal forms of new technology. Another problem with using trade publications, and the like, to collect technology data is that trailing innovative firms are known to engage in strategic disclosure(s) to thwart rival patent applications (Lichtman et al. 2000). The danger here is that these disclosures, which typically make their way into trade publications, can be a source of perfidious information, particularly since many of the firms are not near the patent stage (Lichtman et al. 2000). One could very well be measuring lagging technology firms when analysing such data.

While patent citation is another beneficial way of measuring new technology, it does have some potential shortcomings. First, cited patents tend to cluster over space in favour of urban centres. Rural and periphery areas could potentially be under-represented. North and Smallbone (2000) recently found that small firms in rural locations, particularly in remoter areas, often derive inventive stimuli from their rural surroundings. Jaffe et al. (2000) also cite a large amount of noise in patent citation data. In fact, half of all citations in their study did not correspond to any perceived communication or perceptible technological relationship between the inventions.

Patent citation is a particularly useful way to show the localisation of knowledge (Jaffe 1993). If patents (including those that are not cited) were only a moderately strong spatial measure of new technology, there would be a moderate or weak correlation between the location of cited patents (which are technologically significant) and all patents for a given year. However, this is not shown to be true and Jaffe (1993) found a significant correlation between cited and all patents.

Small firm patent data is an ideal data source from which to study because small firms do not typically acquire protective patents. With costs increasing to patent, small firms will be less apt to patent trivial inventions or innovations. This is substantiated by the fact that no more than 12 percent of the small firm patents analysed for this study (for which industrial data were attained) were ignored because they lacked technological significance.

Patent information can be used by companies to measure the success of their R&D employees and spending. Because modest product or process changes can involve considerable R&D at the firm level, the number of patents generated, or lack thereof, will reveal an accurate picture of the situation. It is partly for these reasons that an exhaustive study on innovation and firm size had more consistent findings with those works using patent than R&D data (Audretsch and Acs 1991). While R&D information can help measure inputs to new technology and innovation data can help measure output, patent data is unique because it is both an input and output measure of new technology.

15.3 Methodology

If discovering the major characteristics of technology firms can help explain the geography of invention, inter-industry variations in patenting, or the relationship between invention and industry concentration or market structure, then studying the main characteristics of SKT firms should prove worthwhile. Because this study examines notable technological developments in small Canadian firms, these entities can be thought of as key technology firms. Considering that inventors typically patent several inventions in their lifetime (Firestone 1971), the data can also be thought of as displaying cumulative technological knowledge for key tech-knowledge firms.

In this study, any firm having less than 100 employees is deemed small. Those characteristics examined of small Canadian key technology firms are their location, industry, propensity to develop product or process inventions, need to use teams of inventors, ownership, and age (or year of establishment). Any firm having more than 50 percent of its equity held by a foreign company is deemed foreign-owned in this study.

Though small firms invent numerous products every year, some of the discoveries are minor in context. This paper analyses small firm inventions that had an acceptable level of significance. A case by case examination of the patent descriptions in the Record (Patent Office Record 1975/76, 1981/82, 1989/90) made it possible to screen patents. Interestingly, around 12 percent of the patents were ignored. It might seem complicated to screen patents, but it is in fact more labour intensive than anything. An investigation of the title and description of each patent application can reveal protective patents, for example. Approximately 150 small firm patents were found for each year, of which industrial data was attained for around 110 and of which nearly 88 percent were deemed significant. It should be noted that patents granted by the Patent Office to inventors employed in small firms are analysed as opposed to those assigned to small firms.

Canada's patent registries or records show what companies have been patenting in the country, the nature of their patents (i.e., products or processes), and how many inventors developed any single patented invention. Although patent records typically do not have much information on the characteristics of companies being granted patents, this study has overcome the problem with the support of industrial directories, which typically have information on the size, ownership, industry, location, and/or age of companies. Correlating the names of companies being granted patents with those in industrial directories can yield useful data. Since there is a small amount of information on the age of small Canadian key technology firms, it was necessary to collect such data from the Canadian Key Business directory for the years 1989 to 1991.

This study examines patent data in a temporal-spatial framework to help uncover which Canadian cities and regions had adequate conditions for small firms to invent and if the conditions changed from one period to the next. A temporal analysis is useful to understanding the different findings in the literature with respect to the characteristics of new technology firms, because different time periods should produce different technology conditions (Radosevic 1990). The periods chosen for analysis in the study are significant because they represent the Canadian economy during three industrial periods: Fordism (1970s), Restructuring (1980s), and Post-Fordism (1990s). While it is difficult to define each period with complete precision, Norcliffe (1994) details the restructuring period of the early to mid 1980s as substantial with respect to industry and labour in Canada. The restructuring period arguably precipitated the economic recession of the early 1980s and subsided during the unprecedented economic growth of the late 1980s.

Some comparisons are made between Canada's small and larger key technology firms to help reveal the relative inventive position of the small firms over time. It is contentious as to whether small or large firms are better at inventing. In all likelihood, both sizes of firms have inventive advantages. When times are economically buoyant, large firms likely have an inventive advantage over their smaller counterparts. However, during economically depressed periods, small firms can create strategic inventions and innovations, which can replace ageing, large firm technology. While there are considerable differences between large and small firms, it is a mistake, according to Baldwin (1995), to treat small firms as immune from the pressures to innovate.

The remainder of this study examines the typology of SKT firms in Canada by region and the geography of their patents from 1975 to 1990. In this study, the core region (of nearly 18 million people) is defined by an axis that is nearly 200 km wide between Quebec City and Windsor (Fig. 15.1) and the periphery is that area beyond the core. The major cities of the core are Toronto, Montreal, and Ottawa. Near Toronto is a cluster of smaller technology cities. They are Mississauga, North York, Kitchener, and Oakville.

Fig. 15.1. Canada's Core Region and Its Major Technology Centres

15.4 Characteristics of Small Canadian Key Tech-Knowledge Firms: A Regional Perspective

It has been argued that small firms cannot compete with large firms when it comes to inventing because their technical infrastructure and capital reserves are normally lower (Freeman 1974). However, technological advances have not been monopolised by large companies in Canada. Small firms have in fact patented 20 to 25 percent of the notable inventions from 1975 to 1990 (Fig. 15.2). While large

Canadian firms became less inventive by the end of the 1980s, small firms (those with less than 100 employees) developed a greater share of the nation's patented inventions (Fig. 15.2). The SKT firms were essentially averse to the turbulent industrial period of the 1980s.

New technology activity in the US is more geographically dispersed (Feldman and Florida 1994; Mitchelson 1999; Ceh 2001) with what has been found here (Figs. 15.3–15.4). The core or Quebec City-Windsor corridor had 76 percent of Canada's small firm patents from 1975 to 1990 (Fig. 15.3). Compared with 82% in Canada (Fig. 15.4), around 50 percent of all patents in the US originate in its manufacturing belt (Feldman and Florida 1994). Interestingly, much of the concentration in Canada favoured a single geographical area – the greater Toronto area. These findings are consistent with other works that show Canadian industrial creativity concentrating to an area within 100 km. of Toronto (Ceh 1996, 1997b; Manseau and Godin 2000). On a global scale, the area arguably has the same importance as other mid-sized technology regions, such as Silicon Glen.

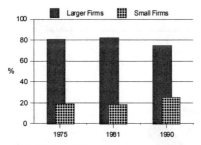

Fig. 15.2. Share of Firm Patents

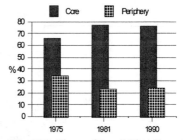

Fig. 15.3. Share of Small Firm Patents

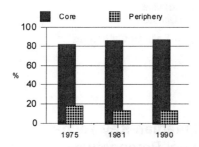

Fig. 15.4. Share of Firm Patents

The periphery's inventive situation would have worsened if it were not for the inventiveness of its small firms, which patented 47 percent of the region's firm inventions by 1990 (Fig. 15.5). This dependence on small firms for inventions was less apparent in the core where only 19 percent of the firm inventions were patented by small companies by 1990 (Fig. 15.6). Unlike what has happened in the

US, where entrepreneurial firms have rapidly emerged in peripheral areas (Wheeler 1990), Canada's periphery had only 23 percent of the country's small firm patents in 1990 (Fig. 15.3). This finding is surprising considering there is no evidence that the region had a disproportionately small share of the country's small firms. Further, the periphery had nearly 45 percent of the country's population during the 1980s (Statistics Canada 1981, 1986, 1991). The disparity here is inevitably due to smaller and more dispersed urban centres in the periphery and the fact that the periphery has yet to develop an incipient core.

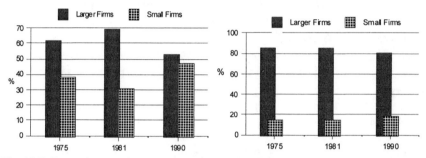

Fig. 15.5. Share of Patents in the Periphery   **Fig. 15.6.** Share of Patents in the Core

The inventive strength of the Montreal and Toronto areas lay with their readily apparent technological, services, financial, information, institutional, and headquarters environment. Conditions of this type are particularly important to small firms since they often rely on their regional surroundings for inventive stimuli (Radosevic 1990; Wever and Stam 1999).

However, these conditions, as will soon be discussed, did not exist throughout the Quebec City-Windsor corridor. As Lyons (1995) suggests, broad regional explanations cannot be used to describe the geography of small entrepreneurial firms. Overall, the spatial concentration of SKT firms found in this study parallels what Breschi (2000) found in Italy, a "spatial cumulativeness" of technological capability, and a situation where "regional embeddedness" (Camagni 1991) facilitates key knowledge regions, such as Toronto and Montreal.

To add to the periphery's dilemma, external information sources and professional and sectoral associations are more apparent in the core. Interestingly, small firms in Canada's periphery recently identified trade shows as the most important source of knowledge for the development of innovative goods and services (Schuetze 1998). Peripheral firms are at a disadvantage in this respect since many of Canada's trade associations and shows typically find themselves concentrated to the highly urbanised areas in the core.

Since the product life cycle is shortening, it has been hypothesised that the life of regional clusters of small high-tech firms might also be shortening, allowing for new regions of technology (Wever and Stam 1999). While this might be true in some industrialised countries, the Canadian situation, with its more concentrated spatial economic system, has had fewer possibilities for new regions of high technology at the broader regional level. In fact, in 1995, 80 and 55 percent of Canada's R&D took place within the core provinces of Ontario and Quebec and within Ontario by itself, respectively (Manseau and Godin, 2000). Further, the cities of Montreal and Toronto had 50 percent of the nation's total R&D (Manseau and Godin, 2000). With respect to small firm patents, they are equally concentrated to the Corridor (Table 15.1).

Table 15.1. Characteristics of Small Canadian Key Technology Firms by Core and Periphery, 1975–90

	Core						Periphery					
	1975		1981		1990		1975		1981		1990	
	A	B	A	B	A	B	A	B	A	B	A	B
Types of Inventions Developed												
Product	57	85.07	76	96.2	75	89.29	33	94.29	22	95.66	19	70.37
Process	10	14.93	3	3.8	9	10.71	2	5.71	1	4.34	8	29.63
Industry												
Mining	0	–	1	1.27	0	–	1	2.86	1	4.34	2	7.41
Food & Beverage	0	–	–	–	1	1.27	0	–	0	–	1	4.34
Wood	0	–	4	5.06	7	8.33	0	–	1	4.34	0	–
Paper	4	5.97	1	1.27	3	3.57	1	2.86	0	–	0	–
Construction	3	4.48	4	5.06	0	–	0	–	0	–	0	–
Chemical	11	16.42	6	7.6	13	15.48	4	11.43	2	8.7	3	11.11
Metal	17	25.37	12	15.19	10	11.9	9	25.71	7	30.43	6	22.22
Machinery	9	13.43	20	25.32	16	19.05	11	31.43	7	30.43	7	25.93
Electronics	7	10.45	7	8.86	17	20.24	1	2.86	2	8.7	1	3.7
Other Manufacturing	4	5.97	8	10.12	6	7.14	2	5.71	0	–	2	7.41
Services	12	17.91	15	18.98	12	14.29	6	17.14	2	8.7	5	18.52
Ownership												
Canadian	56	83.58	74	93.67	81	96.43	34	97.14	23	100	27	100
Foreign	11	16.42	5	6.33	3	3.57	1	2.86	0	–	0	–
American	6	8.96	4	5.06	2	2.38	1	2.86	0	–	0	–
European	5	7.46	1	1.27	1	1.19	0	–	0	–	0	–
Size of Research Teams												
One Inventor	58	86.57	53	67.09	60	71.43	26	74.28	15	65.22	18	66.67
Two Inventors	8	11.94	23	29.11	16	19.05	5	14.29	6	26.08	7	25.92
Three + Inventors	1	1.49	3	3.8	8	9.52	4	11.43	2	8.7	2	7.41
Total	67		79		84		35		23		27	

Note: A Total number of patented inventions; B Percent of patented inventions

The periphery came to depend on process technology to a greater extent by 1990, when 30 percent of its small firm patents were for process inventions (Table 15.1). This unusually high level of process inventing complements the region's orientation to the resource sector. A probable explanation for the decline of SKT firms in the periphery is that they operated in a smaller set of industries and showed more industrial-inventive specialisation compared to their counterparts in the corridor (Table 15.1). While 53 to 60 percent of the core's small firm inventions were patented in one of three sectors between 1975 and 1990 (i.e., chemical, machinery, services, electronics, or metal), the same happened for 74 to 77 percent of the periphery's small firm inventions (Table 15.1). Small periphery firms also under-invented in important sectors of the economy, such as electronics and chemical (Table 15.1). The core and periphery had, for example, 20 and 4 percent of their small firm inventions patented in the electronics industry in 1990, respectively (Table 15.1). These findings seem to collaborate with those showing that: 1) small firms frequently operate in industries that are technology oriented or have a high component of skilled labour (Rothwell and Zegveld 1985; Acs and Audretsch 1990) and, 2) industry-specific factors play a fundamental role in shaping the geography of innovation and that systematic relationships between spatial and sectoral patterns of innovation are real (Kleinknecht and Poot 1992; Breschi 2000). The type of spatial-economic system one is able to study needs to be noted, since those that are more concentrated, such as those of Canada, Australia, and Italy, are more likely to reveal core-periphery differences in the industry-specific and technology-specific factors of innovation.

Though a significant share of Canada's technology has been patented by foreign-owned companies during the past few decades (Ceh 1996), the situation is unapparent among SKT firms in both the core and periphery (Table 15.1). It is likely for this reason that the level of inventing among small Canadians firms did not decline during the 1980s. If small technology firms become increasingly foreign-owned, their ability to provide key technology during critical economic periods could be compromised, as happened with Canada's largest technology firms (Ceh 1997a).

The relative number of inventions being patented in some industrialised countries has been declining since the early 1900s (Ceh and Hecht 1990). Perhaps this inventive decline is not primarily due to a lack of inventive initiative, as initially suggested (Stafford 1952), but rather to the increasing standards or costs needed to invent at the technical, financial, and human levels. In this study, teams of inventors did patent a larger share of the inventions between 1975 and 1981 (Table 15.1). However, the level of human capital (or number of inventors) invested per invention did not increase between 1981 and 1990 in the core and it increased only modestly in the periphery (Table 15.1). SKT firms in Canada could very well be seeking external expertise and skills when developing new technology. Since small firms rarely have sufficient revenues to sustain long term in-house inventive and related types of activities, they often seek specialists, professional support, and explicit technical signals from elsewhere (MacPherson 1997). This would inevitably help them to increase their absorptive capacity for technical knowledge and inputs. The situation also reflects the fact that small Canadian firms still train a much smaller share of their employees for highly skilled tasks relative to their larger counterparts (Baldwin and Johnson 1995). Elsewhere, small firms in OECD countries are also having shortage problems with skilled personnel (OECD 1996).

It has been suggested that it is useful to classify small firms as "mice" or "gazelle" (Dennis et.al. 1994). The "mice" firms typically grow slowly and the "gazelle" firms grow quickly. It is the "gazelle" firms that are often thought of as newly established, small high-technology or entrepreneurial firms. Table 15.2 does not completely support the assertions of small high-technology firms being newly established. The 1960s and 1970s were when many of the SKT firms (in 1990) were established (Table 15.2). Some form of stability and/or maturity in the life of small firms, perhaps in the form of financial security or industry "know-how", is necessary for them to be key inventors. On average, the SKT firms were 23 years in age. (Canadian Key Business Directory 1989–91; PATDAT 1989, 1990). This finding provides some evidence that it is necessary to classify small firms as more than "mice" or "gazelle".

Table 15.2. Year Small and Larger Key Technology Firms were Established in Canada's Core and Periphery

	Small Firms		Larger Firms		Small Firms		Larger Firms	
	Core				Periphery			
	N	%	N	%	N	%	N	%
Pre 1950			54	48.22	1	8.33	8	32.00
1950–1959	6	13.04	9	7.14	2	16.66	5	20.00
1960–1969	16	34.78	14	12.50	2	16.66	5	20.00
1970–1979	14	30.44	22	19.64	2	16.66	2	8.00
1980–1990	10	21.74	14	12.50	5	41.66	5	20.00
Total	46		112		12		25	

Note: N is number of patents

The notion of tech-knowledge firms is reasonable here, because these firms need a reasonable length of time to acquire the technical knowledge needed for industrial creativity. Although there is a modest relationship between the incidence of advanced technology use in small companies and their age (Baldwin and Diverty 1995), a notable relationship between the development of innovations in small Canadian firms and their age apparently exists (Table 15.2). Though many of the core's larger inventive firms were established much earlier than the region's SKT firms, there was an increased incidence among the larger firms to have been established during the 1970s (Table 15.2). Interestingly, many large companies disintegrated in Canada during the 1970s (MacPherson 1989). Yet, many of the large firms that came to patent new technology were established at this time along with a third of the SKT firms (Table 15.2). If some of the larger inventive firms started as small establishments, they would be the formidable "gazelles".

Of the larger technology firms that were established during the 1970s and 1980s, many had less than 400 employees[1] and inevitably started as smaller tech-

---

[1] The findings of this study are based on information gathered from the Patent Record (1975–76, 1981–82, 1989–90), PATDAT (1981–82, 1989–90), and the following industrial directories: Scott's, Canadian Trade Index, Canadian Inter-Corporate Ownership Manual, and Canadian Key Business (1975, 1976, 1981, 1982, 1989, 1990, 1991). This study's tables and figures are also based on these sources.

nology firms. It is useful to envision small technology firms as either fast or slow growing knowledge establishments, with neither necessarily being better than the other. They can also be thought of as distinct from other small firms in that they acquire (with time) technical knowledge to become innovative leaders.

Small technology-based companies that manage to become medium-sized innovative firms typically adopt a set of strategies that foster their quick growth (Isaiah 1992). Small technology firms can accelerate their growth if they pursue global markets, concentrate on competitive advantages, improve flexible production, incorporate product and process technology, obtain government R&D grants, file for patents in OECD countries, form strategic alliances, and raise capital by giving up some equity ownership (Isaiah 1992). Clearly, strategic innovative activity on many levels is central to the development of small technology firms. This is helped by the fact that small firms have fewer bureaucratic layers, which increases their flexibility for new, original ventures (Vossen 1998), and the motive of their shareholders for short-term profits is often less formidable (Dodgson and Rothwell 1994).

15.5 Location Tendencies of Small Key Tech-Knowledge Firms in Canada

In Canada, SKT firms have been dynamic in their location from 1975 to 1990 (Figs. 15.7–15.9). Small firm patent activity in Canada is also more spatially dispersed compared to large firm patent activity (Table 15.3). This situation reaffirms the important role small firms can play in helping to fill the regional-technological niches overlooked by other sizes of firms.

While major Canadian cities in all areas of the country had detectable numbers of small firm patents in 1975, this situation was unapparent in 1990 when several important cities, such as Quebec City and Winnipeg, had no leading small technology firms (Fig. 15.9). Toronto had, by far, the largest share of SKT firms from 1975 to 1990 and substantially more than Montreal (Figs. 15.7–15.9). In Montreal, where 8–10 percent of the inventions were patented by small firms, the same happened for 18–20 percent of Toronto's inventions in recent decades (Table 15.3).

The inventive growth of Mississauga's small firm sector during the 1980s (Table 15.4) likely complements the visible increase of corporate headquarters west of Toronto along the route 401 (technology) corridor. While the area has arguably become a corporate centre for Canada's electronics and pharmaceutical industries, the data reveals that these sectors did not pursue extensive technological linkages with nearby small firms (Table 15.4). Although the number of new technology partnerships between small and large Canadian firms has increased (Shipman 1993), it is not readily apparent in this situation. One explanation for this is that technological alliances can frequently develop between firms that are not in the same region, as typically happens in Canada (Manseau and Godin 2000).

Table 15.3. Number of Firm Inventions Patented in Canadian Cities, 1975–90

	1975			1981			1990		
	A	B	C	A	B	C	A	B	C
Toronto	172	31	18.02	218	33	15.13	103	27	26.21
Montreal	167	14	8.38	153	16	10.45	63	17	26.98
Vancouver	35	8	22.85	30	3	10	13	7	53.84
Hamilton	20	2	10	25	1	4	13	2	15.38
Mississauga	19	8	42.1	21	11	52.38	121	14	11.57
Sudbury	18	2	11.11	–	–	–	–	–	–
Calgary	11	3	27.27	21	7	33.33	18	4	22.22
London	9	0	Nil	4	1	25	4	0	Nil
Valcourt	8	0	Nil	–	–	–	0	–	–
Winnipeg	8	8	100	4	2	50	2	1	50
Kitchener	7	0	Nil	8	0	Nil	16	4	25
Quebec-City	7	4	57.14	1	1	100	–	–	–
Sarnia	7	1	14.28	18	0	Nil	6	0	Nil
Oshawa	5	2	40	3	2	66.66	3	2	66.66
Regina	4	2	50	2	1	50	2	1	50
Oakville	4	1	25	5	2	40	4	2	50
St. John's	3	3	100	1	0	Nil	–	–	–
Edmonton	2	2	100	13	5	38.46	11	6	54.54
North York	2	1	50	1	0	Nil	7	2	28.57
Saskatoon	2	2	100	1	0	Nil	6	4	66.66
Ottawa	2	0	Nil	16	0	Nil	12	2	16.66
Brooks	–	–	Nil	2	2	100	–	–	–

Note: *A* total number of firm patents; *B* total number of small firm patents; *C* percentage of firm patents developed in small companies

Table 15.4. Small Firm Patent Activity in Mississauga by Industry in 1990

Industry	Number of patents
Electronics	2
Chemical	2
Pharmaceutical	0
Machinery	6
Other Manufacturing	4
Services	0
N	14

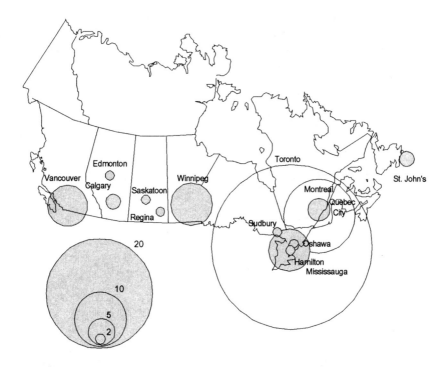

Fig. 15.7. Share of Small Firm Patents Developed in Canadian Cities in 1975

The incidence of small firm patent activity in places near Toronto, such as North York, Mississauga, Oakville, and Kitchener-Waterloo (places of around a quarter to half a million people), reflects a spatial dispersion of SKT firms within the greater Toronto region (Table 15.3). However, this movement has not benefited the cities of Windsor, Oshawa, and Hamilton, seemingly because they are specialised industrial centres of automobile or steel production. The inventive potential of small companies is influenced by what companies or sectors they serve. In the US, specialised industry-based cities, such as Detroit and Hartford, have also generated insufficient opportunities for growing small firms (Lyons 1995). Specialised centres are typically dominated by a few corporations that perpetuate a business environment that is not conducive to small firm entrepreneurship (Lyons 1995).

Although Canada's three largest cities had half the country's leading small technology firms in 1975, their share declined to 46 percent by 1990 (Table 15.5). Small firms in these cities inevitably endure higher cost structures, which can ultimately dampen new technological initiatives. To help overcome these costs and still benefit from being close to a highly urbanised centre, small inventive firms in Toronto are dispersing to places nearby. The greater Toronto area (based on a 100 km radius) had 43 small firm (key) patents in 1975 and 55 in 1990 (Table 15.3). The findings here partly support Lyons (1995) assertion that a locality's position within the high-technology production process can significantly influence small technology firm formation and growth. Also, population size and density, which is most noticeable within the greater Toronto area, continue to be important regional variables associated with the locale of SKT firms.

Table 15.5. Urban Size and Small Firm Patent Activity in Canada

	N 1975	%	N 1981	%	N 1990	%
Large Cities (N = 1,000,000 +)	53	51.97	52	50.98	51	45.95
Medium-Sized Cities (N = 100,000–999,999)	37	36.27	39	38.24	51	45.95
Small Cities or Towns (N = < 100,000)	12	11.76	11	10.78	9	8.10

Note: *N* is number of patents

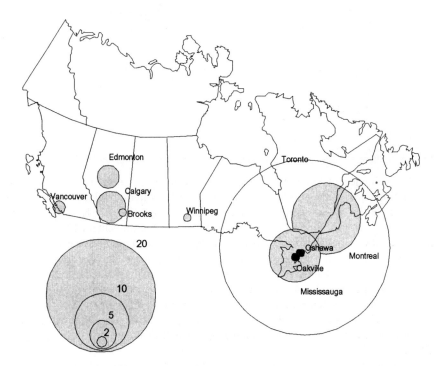

Fig. 15.8. Share of Small Firm Patents Developed in Canadian Cities in 1981

Lyons (1995) suggests that government sponsored growth zones, such as in Ottawa or the national capital region (Figs. 15.7–15.9), do not always provide a healthy environment for fast growing entrepreneurial firms. The situation here ultimately reflects the lower than average share of input-output linkages found in

Ottawa's high-technology sector (Bathelt 1989) and the infrequency of SKT firms in this important technology centre (Figs. 15.7–15.9).

Small technology firms located in peripheral centres largely invented for the regions primary industries. For example, the Delta Oil Tools, Colt Engineering, Geotech Resources, and Drill System companies were typical of the types of small firms patenting inventions in the Calgary area for the oil and gas industry (Note 1). Interestingly, the opportunity for small firms to develop new technology for nearby large firms is more apparent in periphery centres. This situation is likely strengthened by the fact that major cities in the periphery are located further apart compared to those in the core. These centres, compared to those in the core, arguably rely on localised knowledge to help benefit innovation to a greater extent, acting as "islands of innovation". In general, geographical proximity is important because knowledge spillovers can play a key role in the innovative capacity of small firms (Acs et al. 1994). Overall, the evidence points to a regional specialisation of SKT firms in Canada with an obvious core-periphery or advanced-primary manufacturing element.

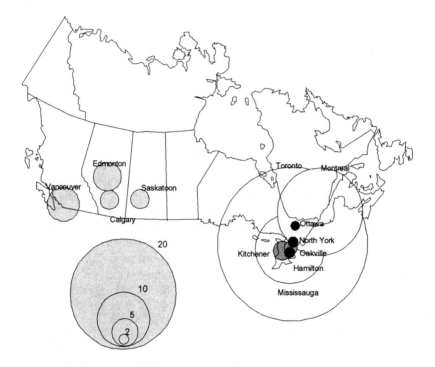

Fig. 15.9. Share of Small Firm Patents Developed in Canadian Cities in 1990

The Canadian urban-economic system has evolved to the extent that its largest cities are no longer the only viable places for SKT firms (Table 15.5). Medium-

sized Canadian cities collectively have become as important as their larger counterparts in harbouring such firms (Table 15.5). While small firm patent activity has
dispersed hierarchically within the Canadian urban system, this process has not
"trickled-down" to rural or small town Canada. These places surprisingly have become less inventive since 1975 (Table 15.5). Metropolitan or leading technology
regions in Canada still are the primary "seedbeds" for SKT firms in that these areas had 78 to 83 percent of the country's small firm (key) patents in recent decades (Table 15.6). A similar pattern of concentration in West Germany has led
Meyer-Krahmer (1985) to suggest that small firms in peripheral and rural areas
lack the same access to capital, large firm linkages, entrepreneurial leadership, superior management techniques, and skilled employees needed to invent compared
to their highly urbanised counterparts.

Table 15.6. Small Firm Patent Activity in Canadian Technology Centres

	1975		1981		1990	
	N	%	N	%	N	%
Ten most inventive cen- tres for small firms	83	81.37	83	81.37	87	78.38
Ten most inventive cen- tres by all firm size	76	74.50	77	75.49	85	76.57

Note: N is number of patents

15.6 Conclusion

Small firms have come under increasing study because of their ability to develop
new technology and elevate regional-technology conditions. This study confirms
that this recognition is warranted and that there is a distinct regionalisation among
small leading technology firms in Canada. These firms favour highly urbanised
areas, though somewhat less than that of large Canadian high-technology firms.
Also, when Canada experienced major industrial restructuring during the 1980s,
its SKT firms, unlike their larger counterparts, were not adversely affected by the
situation. The fact that the 1980s was a period of industrial turbulence and one of
adjustment from an older to "new" economy, has real consequences on the technology base of the country. During truly dominant periods of industrial turbulence, industries and economies arguably restructure in ways that are less favourable to the classical-sized inventive firms, those that are large.

Small key technology firms varied considerably in their location in Canada
from 1975 to 1990, thereby showing themselves to be a very dynamic spatial phenomena. While imperfect information and transaction costs inevitably exist for
small Canadian firms, this study suggests that it has impacted the incidence of
SKT firms in the country and has heightened their regional concentration to locations of learning and knowledge. This situation helped concentrate these firms
between the Montreal and Toronto areas. Within this concentration, some dispersion also took place. For example, Toronto's small firm sector became slightly

less inventive by 1990, but its urban field more than compensated. This situation complemented the growing importance of Canada's medium-sized cities as suitable places for SKT firms. In fact, such places recently held as many small firm patents as Canada's three largest cities. Unfortunately, this dual-spatial outgrowth of SKT firms did not benefit rural and small town Canada. Based on the regional findings, it is clear that patterns of concentration, dispersion, and specialisation describe the spatial arrangement of SKT firms in Canada, and that these patterns concur simultaneously.

Due to its apparent agglomeration advantages, the greater Toronto area prevails as Canada's pre-eminent region for SKT firms. Growing economic and corporate activities west of Toronto (along the route 401 technology corridor) has complemented the increased incidence of SKT firms in the area. It seems that large Canadian firms, however, particularly in the core, have been reluctant to readily form technical linkages with nearby small firms. This helps explain why the amount of inventing among small firms in the chemical, electronics, and services sector has not been substantial. It appears that large Canadian technology firms still prefer to source out knowledge activities inter-regionally or -nationally.

The possibility that there is a core-periphery element to Canada's spatial-inventive system is evident in that SKT firms in the core patented their inventions in a wider set of industries compared to their counterparts in the periphery. Unfortunately, those in the periphery patented fewer inventions in two key industries – chemical and electronics – and forfeited their advantage for product inventing shortly after 1975. Small key technology firms in peripheral locations also had a greater penchant for developing resource-based inventions compared to their counterparts in the core. There is a detectable pattern of industrial specialisation with respect to the country's SKT firms and that this pattern, respectively, has a core-periphery or advanced-primary industry component.

Small key technology firms in Canada did not expand their base of human capital in invention after 1981. It would seem that small firms need to seek external expertise to develop new technology and don't have the same resources that larger firms have for employing in-house inventors or R&D personnel.

Interestingly, many small Canadian key technology firms are older than expected. Therefore, the notion that small entrepreneurial firms can be thought of as "gazelle" type establishments does not adequately explain the situation for those that are truly innovative. Some level of maturity and stability in the life of many small firms, perhaps in the form of financial security and industry "know-how", seems necessary for them to be successful inventors and innovators. This study recommends that another classification of small firms, called knowledge firms, is warranted. Though these firms can be either fast or slow growing, they can have a substantive impact in industrial economies once they acquire the technical knowledge and/or resources needed to produce distinct technology.

References

Acs Z, Audretsch D (1988) Innovation in large and small firms: An empirical analysis. American Economic Review 78: 678–690

Acs Z, Audretsch D (1990) Innovation and small firms. MIT Press, Cambridge MA

Acs Z, Audretsch D, Feldman M. (1994) R&D spillovers and recipient firm size. Review of Economics and Statistics 76: 333–339

Antonelli C (1986) The determinants of the distribution of innovative activity in a metropolitan area. Regional Studies 21: 85–92

Audretsch D (1991) New firm survival and the technological regime. Review of Economics and Statistics November: 441–451

Audretsch D and Acs Z (1991) Innovation and size at the firm level. Southern Economic Journal 57: 739–745

Baldwin J (1995) Innovation: The key to success in small firms. Statistics Canada, Ottawa

Baldwin J, Diverty B (1995) Advanced technology use in Canadian manufacturing sector. Statistics Canada, Ottawa

Baldwin J, Johnson J (1995) Human capital development: The case of training in small and medium sized firms. Statistics Canada, Ottawa

Bathelt H (1989) The evolution of key technology centres in North America: A comparative analysis. Geographische Zeitschrift 77: 89–107

Breschi S (2000) The geography of innovation: A cross-sector analysis. Regional Studies 34: 213–229

Brouwer E, Budil-Nadvornikova H, Kleinknecht H (1999) Are urban agglomerations a better breeding place for product innovation? An analysis of new product announcements. Regional Studies 33: 541–549

Canadian Key Business Directory. (1975, 1976, 1981, 1982, 1989, 1990, 1993) Best Printing, Toronto

Canadian Trade Index. (1975, 1976, 1981, 1982, 1989, 1990) Canadian Manufacturers Association, Toronto

Camagni R (ed) (1991) Innovation networks: Spatial perspectives. Bellhaven, London.

Ceh B (2001) Regional innovation potential in the United States: Evidence of spatial transformation. Papers in Regional Science 80: 297–316

Ceh B (1997a) The recent evolution of Canadian inventive enterprises. Professional Geographer 49: 64–76

Ceh B (1997b) Technological progress and stability among small Canadian inventive firms. East Lakes Geographer 4: 65–74

Ceh B (1996) Temporal and spatial variability of Canadian inventive companies and their inventions: An issue of ownership. Canadian Geographer 40: 319–337

Ceh B, Hecht A (1990) A spatial examination of inventive activity in Canada: An urban and regional analysis between 1881–1986. Ontario Geography 35: 14–24

Dennis W, Phillips B, Starr E (1994) Small job creation: The findings and their critics. Business Economics 29: 23–24

Dodgson M, Rothwell R (1994) The handbook of industrial innovation. Edward Elgar, Aldershot Hants

Feldman M, Florida R (1994) The geographic sources of innovation: Technological infrastructure and product innovation in the United States. Annals of the Association of American Geographers 84: 210–229

Freeman C (1974) The economic of industrial innovations. Penguin, Harmondsworth

Firestone O (1971) Economic implication of patents. University of Ottawa, Ottawa

Intercorporate Ownership Manual (1975, 1976, 1981, 1982, 1989, 1990) Department of Consumer and Corporate Affairs, Ottawa

Isaiah L (1992) Winning strategies for small technology-based companies. Business Quarterly 57: 47–52

Jaffe A, Trajtenberg M, Fogarty M (2000) The meaning of patent citations: Report on the NBER/Case-Western reserve survey of patentees. National Bureau of Economic Research, DC, Working Paper W7631

Jaffe A (1993) Geographic localization of knowledge spillovers as evidence by patent citations. Quarterly Journal of Economics 108: 577–586.

Kleinknecht A, Poot, P (1992). Do regions matter for R&D? Regional Studies 26: 221–232

Lichtman D, Baker S, Kraus K (2000) Strategic disclosure in the patent system. Vanderbuilt Law Review 53: 2175–2217

Lyons D (1995) Changing business opportunities: The geography of rapidly growing small US private firms, 1982–1992. Professional Geographer 47: 388–398

MacPherson, A (1989) Small manufacturing firms and Canadian industrial development: Empirical and theoretical perspectives. Canadian Journal of Regional Science 22: 165–185

MacPherson A (1997) The contribution of external service inputs to the product development efforts of small manufacturing firms. R&D Management 27: 127–144

Manseau A, Godin B (2000) Canada's national system of innovation. McGill-Queen's University Press, Montreal.

Mitchelson R (1999) Spatial aspects of technology transfer: Evidence from Kentucky. Southeastern Geographer 39: 206–219

Meyer-Krahmer F (1985) Innovation behaviour and regional indigenous potential. Regional Studies 10: 523–535

Norcliffe G (1994) Regional labour market adjustments: The Canadian case. Canadian Geographer 38: 2–17

North D, Smallbone D (2000) The innovativeness and growth of rural SMEs during the 1990s. Regional Studies 34: 145–157

OECD (1996) Technology, productivity and job creation. OECD, Paris

PATDAT (1981, 1989) Ministry of Consumer and Corporate Affairs, Ottawa

Pred A (1966) The spatial implications of U.S. urban industrial growth. MIT Press, Massachusetts

Rothwell R, Zegveld W (1985). Reindustrialization and technology. Longmann, London

Schuetze H (1998) How do small firms innovate in British Columbia? In: De La Mothe J, Paquet G (eds) Local and regional systems of innovation. Kluwer Academic Publisher, Boston

Schumpeter J (1939) Business cycles: A theoretical, historical and statistical analysis of the capitalist process. McGraw Hill, New York

Scotts Directory of Atlantic Manufacturers (1982, 1990-1991) Scotts Directories, Oakville

Scotts Directory of Ontario Manufacturers (1975, 1976, 1981, 1982, 1989, 1990) Scotts Directories, Oakville

Scotts Directory of Quebec Manufacturers (1975, 1976, 1981, 1982, 1989, 1990) Scotts Directories, Oakville

Scotts Directory of Western Manufacturers (1975, 1976, 1981, 1982, 1989, 1990) Scotts Directories, Oakville

Shipman A. (1993) Inventors make out. International Management 48: 50–51

Stafford A (1952) Is the rate of inventing declining. American Journal of Sociology 52: 539–545

Statistics Canada (1981, 1986, 1991) Ministry of Supply and Services, Ottawa

The Patent Records (1975/76, 1981/82, 1989/90, 1990/91, 1999) Consumer and Corporate Affairs, Ottawa

Vossen R (1998) Relative strength and weakness of small firms in innovation. International Small Business Journal 16: 88–94

Wever E, Stam E (1999) Clusters of high technology SMEs: The Dutch case. Regional Studies 33: 391–400

Wheeler J (1990) The new corporate landscape: Americas fastest growing private companies. Professional Geographer 42: 433–444

16 The Location of Technological Innovations within the Japanese Semiconductor Industry

Tomokazu Arita[1] and Philip McCann[2]

[1] Institute of Policy and Planning Sciences, University of Tsukuba, Japan;
[2] Department of Economics, University of Reading, UK

16.1 Introduction

Much of the current literature on hi-tech developments within the electronics industry tends to focus on the spatial and organisational arrangements evident in innovative clusters such as Silicon Valley. There are, however, many very different forms of spatial organisation, which engender innovations within the semiconductor industry, and these variations depend on the particular sub-sector of the semiconductor industry. In this paper we discuss the case of Japanese vertically integrated semiconductor producers. The paper will analyse data from over 100 semiconductor plants operated by over 80 firms located within Japan. In particular, we will focus on the firms undertaking the wafer manufacturing processes. Our results indicate that the spatial arrangements here are very different from those evident in the US or Europe. As we will see in this paper, in order to discuss the geographical behaviour of many parts of the semiconductor industry, it is necessary to consider not only organisational issues, but also the different sub-sectors within the industry. From these perspectives, many of the generalisations made about the semiconductor industry based on observations of Silicon Valley are seen to be rather inappropriate.

The chapter is organised as follows. In Sect. 16.2 we review the types of arguments frequently associated with discussions about the spatial organisation of the semiconductor industry and spatial patterns of innovation. In Sect. 16.3, we describe the three different components of the semiconductor industry. As we will see, many of the issues raised in Sect. 16.2 really only relate to one sub-sector of the electronics industry, and the two other parts of the industry have been almost entirely ignored in the literature. In Sect. 16.4 we discuss our detailed indices of product innovations within the Japanese wafer-processing sub-sector of the industry, and in Sect. 16.5 we estimate relationships between geographical, firm and technological variables within a product-cycle framework. We find very little support for a product-cycle type model. In order to account for these findings, in Sect. 16.6 we explore the organisational issues governing the spatial patterns of product innovations within Japanese industry.

16.2 Geography and the Semiconductor Industry

Over the last decade there has been a significant growth in interest in the geographical behaviour of firms in the electronics and semiconductor industry (Oakey and Cooper 1989; Saxenian 1994; Almeida and Kogut 1997; Kittiprapas and McCann 1999). There are a variety of interrelated reasons for this recent research interest, which can broadly be grouped into three themes. The first theme is a general renewal of academic interest in geography and industrial location issues per se. This has been encouraged in part by the continuing process of economic integration in many parts of the world, such as the EU and NAFTA, as well as by the writings of certain influential commentators (Porter 1990; Krugman 1991). The second theme is a growth in interest in the particular characteristics of the electronics and semiconductor industry itself. The reason for this is partly that electronics, and in particular the semiconductor part of the electronics industry, is generally regarded as an industry which is both highly successful, and also at the forefront of human technological development (Piore and Sabel 1984; Best 1990). At the same time, innovations in this industry are often embodied into the production technology of other industries, thereby having induced productivity effects. Therefore, it is implicitly assumed that observation of the behaviour of the electronics and semiconductor sector may also provide clues as to the future trajectory of other industrial sectors in general. A third reason for the growth in interest in the electronics and semiconductor industry has been the apparent tendency of this industry to cluster in particular locations such as Silicon Valley (Scott 1988, 1991; Saxenian 1994; Angel 1991). The result of this behaviour is that certain areas appear to exhibit high growth performance in this sector, while other areas have been unable to develop any equivalent industry base (*The Economist* 1997). This has lead to concern among public policy planners in various countries and regions (Castells and Hall 1994) to understand the economic-environmental conditions under which such industrial clusters are fostered, in the hope of replicating these conditions elsewhere.

In order to generate such an array of new product developments, these combined features are assumed to imply that the semiconductor industry will also tend to be at the forefront of organisational developments (Eisenhardt and Schoonhaven 1990) and production process innovations (McCann and Fingleton 1996). Therefore, observation of the current organisational behaviour of the semiconductor industry may point towards the future behaviour of industry in general, as other industrial sectors attempt to imitate the successful organisation and production innovations exhibited by this sector. Indeed, much of the current thinking about the optimal relationship between industry organisation and geography has been developed on the basis of observations of the large numbers of small and medium sized semiconductor firms in locations such as Silicon Valley (Saxenian 1994; Scott 1988, 1991; Larsen and Rogers 1984). In many circles (Keeble and Wilkinson 1998) it has now become almost a matter of faith that many small and medium sized firms clustered at the same location will guarantee the maximum levels of product innovation (Aydalot and Keeble 1988; Saxenian 1994). The logic behind this argument is that such small firms are assumed to find it not only relatively easy to share information and to benefit from local information spillovers, but also to reconfigure their organisational and input-output linkages appropriately as new product developments occur. Empirical support for these arguments, which appears to confirm the local presence of industry-specific informal information spillovers, comes primarily from patent citation counts (Jaffe et al. 1993; Almeida and Kogut 1997). Meanwhile, these observations of the high growth performance of small firm clusters such as Silicon Valley (Saxenian 1994), Cambridge UK (Castells and Hall 1994) and Ile de France (Scott 1988) are contrasted with the relatively weaker growth performance of the large-firm parts of the electronics industry (Saxenian 1994). Explanations for the apparent difference in the growth performance of the small and large firm sectors are based on the assumptions that the organisational rigidity and well-defined boundaries of large hierarchical firms limit the ability of large firms to respond appropriately to the rapid market changes of these new industries (Saxenian 1994). Small firm clusters are therefore perceived to represent the future optimal spatial and organisational arrangements in industries with very short product life cycles (Piore and Sabel 1984; Porter 1990; Saxenian 1994).

Such arguments, however, are based on very strong assumptions about the relationship between information generation, information exchanges and geographical scales. Following Marshall (1920) and Vernon (1960), the clustering argument is based on the assumption that information spillovers are generated and realised specifically at the geographical scale of the local urban area. Urban clustering is therefore advantageous for industries which exhibit very short product life-cycles (Vernon 1966, 1979). Yet, recent research within the electronics and semiconductor industry (Suarez-Villa and Rama 1996; Suarez-Villa and Karlsson 1996; Wever and Stam 1988) suggests that agglomeration linkages, and the formal outcomes of any informal information spillovers (Audretsch and Feldman 1996; Suarez-Villa and Walrod 1997; Arita and McCann 2000) extend over much larger spatial scales than that of the individual urban metropolitan area. In the case of multi-plant multinational firms (Cantwell and Iammarino 2000), any such agglomeration effects may even operate over spatial scales larger than individual countries. These empirical observations therefore cast doubt on the assumed importance of specifically local inter-firm information spillovers as a source of competitive advantage (Porter 1990, 1998) within the electronics industry, and point rather more to the role of labour market hysteresis as a possible rationale for industrial clustering (Angel 1991; Arita and McCann 2000). More importantly, however, these observations also cast doubt on the whole hypothesis that small firm clusters represent something of an ideal spatial and organisational arrangement ensuring the maximisation of innovation, either for the semiconductor industry or any other innovative industry facing short product life-cycles.

Part of the problem here is that so much of the literature which purports to show a high correlation between spatial industrial clustering, small and medium sized firms and short product life-cycles has tended to focus on the spatial and organisational issues of only one particular part of the global electronics and semiconductor industry. The electronics industry as a whole is comprised of many sub-sectors ranging from the semiconductor industry to the consumer electronics sectors, and the semiconductor industry itself is comprised of three quite distinct subsectors, defined in terms of the nature of the activities and the transactions they undertake. Observations of Silicon Valley and the 'Cambridge Phenomenon' (Castells and Hall 1994) are actually primarily observations of groups of small firms whose activities correspond solely to only one of the three sub-sectors within the semiconductor industry, namely the Design sector. Yet, there are also many large vertically-integrated firms in this same sub-sector of the industry which are almost entirely ignored by the literature. Similarly, the other two parts of the semiconductor industry, the Wafer Process and the Wafer Manufacturing sectors, are characterised almost entirely by vertically-integrated wafer manufacturing and assembly firms. The spatial and organisational arrangements of the vertically-integrated parts of the semiconductor industry are completely different from the small semiconductor firms (Arita and McCann 2002a,b). The relationships between geography and technology within the semiconductor industry must therefore be considered individually for each of the three sub-sectors of the industry. Only in this way can we assess whether or not the types of spatial and organisational arrangements of Silicon Valley are more generally applicable to the parts of the industry.

Firm location behaviour within the semiconductor industry is often the result of different and sometimes conflicting objectives. Rarely is the geographical result in reality a Silicon Valley-style spatial clustering of highly innovative small firms generating very short product life-cycle outputs. This is partly why such high-technology clusters are of interest, but also it is why generalisations based on such observations should be avoided. In order to appreciate these points we must first discuss the nature and organisation of the semiconductor industry itself.

16.3 The Organisation of the Semiconductor Industry

In order to understand the organisation of the semiconductor industry it is first necessary to understand the different activities which take place within the industry (Nishimura 1995, 1999; EIAJ 1994). As we see in Fig. 16.1, the different activities in the semiconductor industry can be compared more or less directly with the different activities which take place in the book publishing industry.

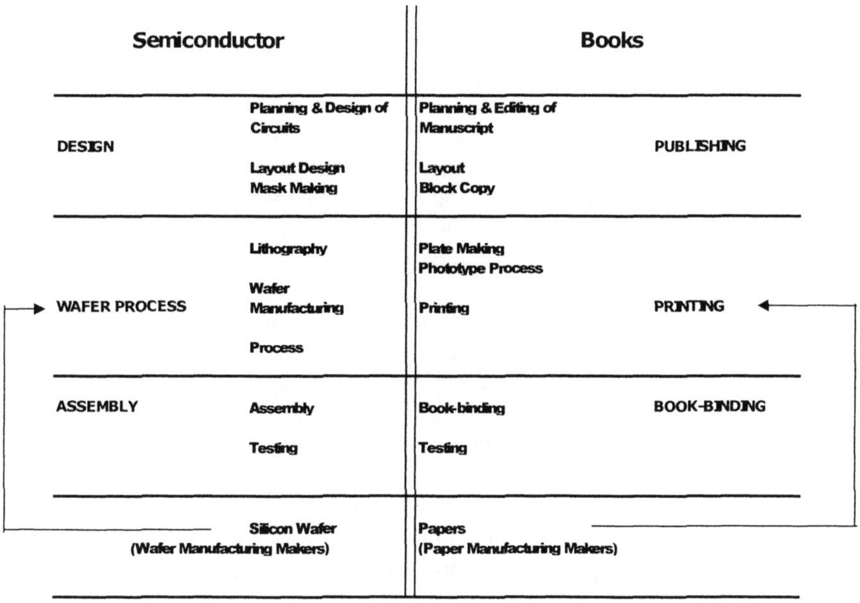

Semiconductor		Books	
DESIGN	Planning & Design of Circuits Layout Design Mask Making	Planning & Editing of Manuscript Layout Block Copy	**PUBLISHING**
WAFER PROCESS	Lithography Wafer Manufacturing Process	Plate Making Phototype Process Printing	**PRINTING**
ASSEMBLY	Assembly Testing	Book-binding Testing	**BOOK-BINDING**
	Silicon Wafer (Wafer Manufacturing Makers)	Papers (Paper Manufacturing Makers)	

Fig.16.1. Production Process of Semiconductor: Comparison with Book Publishing and Printing

The first stage of the production process is the silicon chip design stage, in which the functional logic of the chip and the three-dimensional circuit layout of transistors and capacitors within the silicon wafer are determined. This activity is carried out primarily using computer aided design (CAD) systems. This stage of the process can be compared with the planning, editing and layout stages of the book publishing process. The result of this stage is the production of masks, which are the three-dimensional templates of the chip. These Integrated Circuit (IC) design activities are undertaken both by the large number of small specialised IC design firms, and also by large vertically-integrated semiconductor producing firms. The activities are provided for by specialist CAD vendor firms which provide customised design software for the designers. At the same time, there has also emerged recently a sub-sector of the industry which is concerned only with the construction of intellectual property rights relating to IC designs. These firms design only logic functions without circuit layouts, and act in consultation with both small and large IC design firms in order to ensure patents are granted for the new chip protocol designs. The number of firms involved in this stage of the production process has grown enormously during the last two decades, with small design-oriented firms tending to be clustered in locations such as Silicon Valley. It is this part of the industry which has received so much academic attention. Yet, there are still many IC design activities which take place within vertically-integrated semiconductor producers both inside and outside of Silicon Valley.

The second stage of the process is the wafer process, the technology of which is determined by materials science. At this stage of the production process the circular silicon wafers, produced by specialist chemicals firms, are subjected to lithography. This is a process whereby ultra-violet light is used to illuminate certain parts of the wafer, according to the mask design, in order to bring about chemical changes within certain parts of the wafer. The wafers are then etched and treated, thereby removing the parts of the wafer subjected to the lithography. After as many as fifteen stages of lithography and treating, the result is a three-dimensional silicon structure. This stage of the semiconductor production process can be compared to the plate-making and phototype process which takes place in the book printing industry.

The final stage of the wafer production process is that of the wafer assembly process. Here, the circular wafers, which have been subjected to lithography and treating, are extracted and dissected into many small square chips, each of which is then framed in plastic or ceramics for insulation and protection. This stage of the chip production process is the equivalent of the book binding process within the book publishing industry.

The level of technology of the second and third stages of the wafer and assembly process is defined in terms of the minimum processing rule and the wafer size. The minimum processing rule is the definition of the level of miniaturisation of the technology, and the wafer size is the size of the individual silicon wafers which can be produced and then dissected to produce chips. The smaller the minimum processing rule and the greater the wafer size, the more advanced the technological generation. In terms of technology, the second and third stages of the semiconductor production process are just as important to the semiconductor industry as the first stage, and the product life-cycles are just as short. Different minimum processing rules and wafer sizes represent completely different generations of technology.

The majority of these second and third stage activities tend to be carried out by two groups of firms in more geographically dispersed locations outside of the US (Arita and McCann 2002a,b), and this may explain why these sectors have received relatively little academic interest. The first group of firms undertaking the wafer and assembly processes are the vertically-integrated semiconductor producers such as Intel and NEC, which undertake all of their own chip design and manufacturing activities. Firms such as NEC, Philips, Fujitsu and Motorola, which also manufacture finished goods, produce for internal demand as well as for other consumer firms, whereas firms such as Intel produce entirely for external customers. The common feature of the production of these firms is high volumes. The second group of firms undertaking the wafer and assembly processes are the specialist East Asian sub-contracting IC manufacturing firms. These are primarily Taiwanese, Japanese and Korean firms. They are comprised of a small number of specialist large firms, such as the Taiwan Semiconductor Manufacturing Company, which have both the capacity to produce ICs in large numbers, and also the technology to allow both the high degree production specificity and flexibility required to manufacture custom-designed ICs.

Having discussed the nature of the semiconductor industry, in the next section we will look at the relationship between technological change and spatial industrial organisation in the case of the semiconductor manufacturers who are located in Japan, in order to assess whether the spatial and organisational arrangements here mirror those often observed in the literature on the US industry. In particular we will focus on those firms which carry out the second and third-stage wafer process and assembly activities. The object of this exercise is to assess the extent to which orthodox product life-cycle approaches can broadly account for the technology-space relationship in the Japanese sector.

16.4 Data and Methodology

The data we employ comes from the 1999 Nikkei compendium of the semiconductor industry, and provides individual plant and production line data for every semiconductor firm located within Japan. The total number of such firms in Japan is 83, and these firms account for 123 individual plants. In terms of general establishment data, the Nikkei compendium provides us with the location details of each plant, the total employment levels of every plant, the actual floorspace of every production facility, and the total site area of a plant including areas external to the actual production activities. For technology indices, the Nikkei compendium provides us with information on the minimum processing rule and the wafer size of the products produced at each location. In the case of the minimum processing rule, a smaller size represents a newer vintage of technology, whereas in the case of the wafer size, a larger size represents a newer technology. Nikkei also provide us with details of the wafer processing capacity of the plant in terms of the total number of silicon wafers produced annually. As far as we are aware, such detailed semiconductor technology data has never before been employed statistically by applied economists. These general establishment level data and plant technology indices are then combined with regional spatial data. The local wage indices we use are the manufacturing wages for each of the forty-seven prefectures within Japan. These data come from the Japanese Office for Statistics. We also use a geographical information system to calculate the distance in kilometres between the location of the individual plant and the headquarters of its parent organisation, and also the distance between the location of the individual plant and Tokyo. The number of establishments for which all of the individual plant, technology and regional data are complete is 95, and the data summary statistics are given in Table 16.1.

Table 16.1. Data Definitions and Descriptive Statistics

	Mean	Standard Deviation
Distance from the plant to Tokyo (km)	335.53	275.59
Distance from the Plant to HQ (km)	269.69	293.12
Monthly Wage (Yen)	525693.51	124022.81
Plant Employees	1453.41	1567.71
Site Area (sq m)	138575.13	178250.30
Floorspace (sq m)	55732.99	58352.04
Minimum Processing Rule (um)	0.85	0.73
Wafer Size (mm)	150.00	41.10
Wafer Processing Capacity (per month)	21025.95	19720.02

Note. These are all the potential variables.   In order to treat every possible pair of variables, some missing data are omitted and the complete data set with the all above variables consists of 95 observations.

With our technology, plant and spatial data we can now begin to investigate the relationship between geography and the implementation of technology within the Japanese wafer processing component of the semiconductor industry. Following an orthodox product-cycle argument we can hypothesise that different generations of semiconductor technologies will be spatially differentiated within the Japanese semiconductor industry. In particular, we would expect that the most recently developed products requiring the most advanced, miniaturised and newer production technologies will tend to be implemented at more central locations. In terms of technology indices, more advanced generations of technology are represented by smaller minimum processing rules and larger wafer sizes. On the other hand, more mature vintages of product and process technologies would be expected to be implemented in more geographically peripheral locations exhibiting lower wage rates. The reason for this is that less advanced technology products will have become rather more standardised and easier to mass produce than more recent higher technology products. Moreover, increasing production quantities also imply the need for larger plants with larger land and labour requirements. This will provide an incentive for such plants to be located in lower wage and land price regions. Therefore, we ought to observe something of a positive correlation between increasingly mature vintages of a technology, the location of the product and process technology implementation, and the level of geographic peripherality of the establishment.

One issue which we need to consider is exactly what is meant by a 'central' location. In an orthodox product-cycle model we tend to think of a central location as being the dominant urban area (Vernon 1960, 1966) in which all of the major information-intensive activities of a particular sector or range of sectors are located. In the case of Japan, the urban area of Tokyo, known as the Kanto region, is very much the nationally-dominant region of the economy, and regional wages and land prices generally fall with increasing distance away from Tokyo. Tokyo is therefore used as the reference point for our calculations of the level of peripherality of an individual plant. At the same time, in order to allow for the fact that within corporate structures a plant's dominant information networks may not necessarily be linked to the Tokyo region, we also will consider notions of peripherality defined with respect to the parent company's Japanese headquarters.

In order to test for an association between the level of geographical peripherality and the vintage of technology implemented we set up a series of multiple regression models. In Model 1 we choose as our dependent variable the distance between the individual plant and Tokyo, and we regress this against seven potential independent explanatory variables. These variables are the local prefecture wage for manufacturing industry, the number of plant employees, the overall plant site area, the actual production floorspace of the plant, the minimum processing rule, the wafer size, and the wafer processing capacity. From the product-cycle argument we would expect that the estimated coefficients will be positive for the minimum processing rule, as well as the plant employment, site area and floorspace variables. Meanwhile, from the product-cycle argument we would expect that the estimated coefficients will be negative for the wafer size and local wage indices. The estimated coefficient for the wafer processing capacity might be expected to be positive, on the grounds that a larger wafer processing capacity will require generally larger facilities. On the other hand, this can also be interpreted as a partial index of production technology, in which case the expected sign may be negative. In Model 2 we repeat the exercise, but in this case the dependent variable is the distance between the individual plant and the location of its parent headquarters. In order to allow for the fact that the direction of causality in the product life-cycle model is ambiguous, in Model 3 we re-estimate our technology-location regressions by using the minimum processing rule as the dependent variable and including distance as an independent explanatory variable.

16.5 Results

Our first model, Model 1, uses Ordinary Least Squares to estimate the relationship between the distance of the plant from Tokyo as a function of all the other seven variables. The results are given in Table 16.2.1. As we see from Table 16.2.1, the results for Model 1 appear to be rather poor, with a low adjusted value of R^2. Only the local prefecture manufacturing wage appears to be significantly related to the level of geographic peripherality, although there is some evidence that the wafer processing capacity is also related to the location. Removing all the non-significant explanatory variables and re-estimating this relationship with only the wage variable provides us with results described in Table 16.2.2.

According to Akaike's Information Criteria (AIC)[1] the performance of the regression results reported in Table 16.2.1 is better than those reported in Table 16.2.2. In general, the results of Model 1 confirm the fact that for Japanese semiconductor plants, the distance from Tokyo is negatively and significantly related to the local manufacturing wage rate. There is also very tentative, but not significant, evidence that the plant's distance from Tokyo is related to the processing ca-

---

[1] See Appendix 16.A.

pacity of the plant. These are the types of general results we might expect to see in an economy with such a centre-periphery regional economic structure as Japan. However, crucially, there appears to be no relationship between the centre-periphery location of the plant and the level of technology employed or implemented.

Table 16.2.1. Results for Model 1. Dependent Variable: Distance from Plant to Tokyo

Parameter	Coefficient Estimate	t-statistic	Significance
Constant	796.766	6.363	0.000
Wage	−0.0009524	−4.492	0.000
Wafer Processing Capacity	0.001875	1.406	0.163
R^2	0.236	Adjusted R^2	0.219
RSS	5456545.8	AIC	5812285.383
White Test			
R^2	0.077		
nR^2	7.315		
Chi-squared with 5 degrees of freedom at the 5% level of significance	11.07		
VIF	1.096		

Notes. (i) White Test: The null hypothesis of homoskedasticity cannot be rejected at the 5% level. (ii) Observation of the Variance Inflation factor (VIF) indicates a low level of multi-collinearity.

Table 16.2.2. Results for Model 1: Reference. Dependent Variable: Distance from Plant to Tokyo

Parameter	Coefficient Estimate	t-statistic	Significance
Constant	882.486	8.027	0.000
Wage	−0.00104	−5.110	0.000
R^2	0.219	Adjusted R^2	0.211
RSS	5573794.0	AIC	5813490.902
White Test			
R^2	0.082		
nR^2	7.79		
Chi-squared with 5 degrees of freedom at the 5% level of significance	5.99		
Chi-squared with 5 degrees of freedom at the 1% level of significance	9.21		

Notes. (i) White Test: The null hypothesis of homoskedasticity would be rejected at the 5% level but not at the 1% level. (ii) The AIC of this table is larger than that of Table 16.2.1

As we have already mentioned, it may be argued that for plants within vertically-integrated corporate control and information networks, the reference point for notions of centrality will be the major decision-making centre of the corporate hierarchy. In order to account for this, in Model 2 we re-estimate the original model, but in the case of Model 2 we use the distance between the plant and its parent headquarters' location as the measure of peripherality.

Table 16.3.1. Results for Model 2. Dependent Variable: Distance from Plant to HQ

Parameter	Coefficient Estimate	t-statistic	Significance
Constant	842.356	7.036	0.000
Wage	−0.00122	−6.020	0.000
Wafer Processing Capacity	0.003274	2.568	0.012
R^2	0.382	Adjusted R^2	0.369
RSS	4988483.6	AIC	5313707.861
White Test			
R^2	0.109		
nR^2	10.355		
Chi-squared with 5 degrees of freedom at the 5% level of significance	11.07		
VIF	1.096		

Notes. (i) White Test: The null hypothesis of homoskedasticity cannot be rejected at the 5% level. (ii) Observation of the Variance Inflation factor (VIF) indicates a low level of multi-collinearity.

In Table 16.3.1 we see that the local prefecture manufacturing wage is still negatively associated with the distance from the plant to its headquarters, but this distance is also positively and significantly associated with the wafer processing capacity of the plant. The results of Model 2 are very similar, but much more robust, than those of Model 1. Once again, removing all of the variables in Model 2 and re-estimating the model with only the wage variables gives us the results reported in Table 16.3.2.

According to Akaike's Information Criteria (AIC) the performance of the regression results reported in Table 16.3.1 is better than those reported in Table 16.3.2. The results of Model 2 therefore indicate that the distance from the plant to its parent headquarters is negatively associated with the local manufacturing wage rate, as with Model 1, but also it is positively associated with the plant's wafer processing capacity. As with Model 1, however, there appears to be no relationship between the centre-periphery location of the plant and the level of technology employed or implemented.

Table 16.3.2. Results for Model 2: Reference. Dependent Variable Distance from Plant to HQ

Parameter	Coefficient Estimate	t-statistic	Significance
Constant	992.057	9.214	0.000
Wage	−0.001374	−6.892	0.000
R^2	0.338	Adjusted R^2	0.331
RSS	5346085.3	AIC	5575989.758
White Test			
R^2	0.081		
nR^2	7.695		
Chi-squared with 5 degrees of freedom at the 5% level of significance	5.99		
Chi-squared with 5 degrees of freedom at the 1% level of significance	9.21		

Notes. (i) White Test: The null hypothesis (homoskedasticity) would be rejected at the 5% level but not at the 1% level. (ii) The AIC of this table is larger than that of Table 16.3.1

Each of the models so far has confirmed that there appears to be a negative relationship between the geographic peripherality of the location of the plant and the local manufacturing wage rate, irrespective of whether location is defined with respect to Tokyo or the parent headquarters of the plant. At the same time, the processing capacity of the plant appears to be significantly related to the level of geographic peripherality, particularly when distance is defined with respect to the headquarters' location of the firm. However, for each of the models, there appears to be no significant relationship between the location of the production facility and either of the two indicators of plant-level technology. In part this may be because there is no systematic direction of causality in product-cycle models between the location of the activity and the level of technology implemented. Therefore in order to allow for this problem of a lack of causality in product-cycle models we re-estimate the model using the minimum processing rule as the dependent variable, and investigate the extent to which it is a function of all the other spatial and non-spatial variables. The results for Model 3 are given in Table 16.4.1.

Table 16.4.1. Results for Model 3. Dependent Variable: Minimum Processing Rule

Parameter	Coefficient Estimate	t-statistic	Significance
Constant	2.393	10.242	0.000
Wafer Size	–0.01026	–6.826	0.000
R^2	0.334	Adjusted R^2	0.327
RSS	33.334	AIC	34.7675041
White Test			
R^2	0.159		
nR^2	15.105		
Chi-squared with 5 degrees of freedom at the 5% level of significance	5.99		
Chi-squared with 5 degrees of freedom at the 1% level of significance	9.21		

Note. White Test: The null hypothesis of homoskedasticity would be rejected at the 1% level.

As we see, the minimum processing rule, which is one of the two technological indices, only appears to be related to the wafer size, which itself is the other index of technology. In other words, there appears to be no association between a plant's level of technology and any of the plant's geographical or production capacity variables. According to the White Test (White 1980), however, the regression results reported in Table 16.4.1 contain the problem of heteroskedasticity.

Unfortunately, if the wafer size variable is included in the dataset, it is not possible to rectify the problem of heteroskedasticity either by taking log transformations of the data, or by employing a two-step weighted least squares procedure.[2]

With the dataset available, the only system of estimated regression coefficients which passes the White Test is one in which the wafer size variable is omitted. These results are reported in Table 16.4.2. As we see in Table 16.4.2, under these conditions the single significant variable is the log of the plant employment size. To be specific, as the employment level of the plant increases, the minimum processing rule tends to fall.

---

[2] Although adopting either of these approaches increases the value of R^2 and reduces the value of AIC relative to Table 16.4.1.

Table 16.4.2. Results for Model 3: Reference. Dependent Variable: Minimum Processing Rule

Parameter	Coefficient Estimate	t-statistic	Significance
Constant	2.595	5.313	0.000
Ln No of employment	−0.255	−3.601	0.001
R^2	0.122	Adjusted R^2	0.113
RSS	43.911	AIC	45.79936
White Test			
R^2	0.056		
nR^2	5.32		
Chi-squared with 5 degrees of freedom at the 5% level of significance	5.99		
Chi-squared with 5 degrees of freedom at the 1% level of significance	9.21		

Notes. (i) White Test: The null hypothesis of homoskedasticity cannot be rejected at the 5% level. (ii) The AIC of this table is larger and the R^2 is much lower than that of Table 16.4.1

The results reported here appear find no support for the orthodox product-cycle argument. From Models 1 and 2, there is no evidence of any relationship between the location of a plant and the newness and sophistication of its production technology, nor is there any relationship between location and the employment size of a plant. Only the wafer processing capacity of the facility is positively associated with geographical peripherality of the plant from the parent headquarters. Although the wafer processing capacity of the facility is an index of a plant's size, the usual measure of plant size, which is the employment level, appears only to be related to the sophistication of the technology implemented, and not to the location of the plant. If anything, this result is completely counter to the simple product-cycle argument.

At face value, these general observations could possibly be interpreted in two quite different ways. The first argument is to assume that the levels of technology implemented are more or less the same for all plants in the sample, and that we would therefore expect to see no systematic differences in the locations of production technology. However, as we have already explained, different minimum processing rules and wafer sizes represent different generations of technology in an industry in which miniaturisation, and consequently increasing IC processing power, is the key defining feature of technological progress. This first argument is therefore unacceptable. The second argument is that the product-cycle model is not characteristic of the spatial patterns of technological implementation within the Japanese semiconductor industry. Evidence for this comes from the reported problems of heteroskedasticity which face all the logged or weighted versions of Model 3, along with the results of Table 16.4.2. Together, these findings suggest that we are probably dealing with a problem of omitted variables. The difficult question here, however, is exactly what the omitted variables might be. Unfortunately, the orthodox product-cycle argument provides no real clues. Therefore, it may be that the spatial patterns of technological implementation within the Japanese semiconductor industry are determined primarily by factors not included in product-cycle type specification. These are the issues to which we now turn.

16.6 Discussion

The alternative explanation for our lack of support for the product-cycle model within the Japanese semiconductor industry is that the spatial organisation of production within Japan is quite different from that of the US or other western economies. The Japanese semiconductor industry is comprised almost entirely of plants which are part of vertically-integrated hierarchical organisations, and the relationship between technology and geography in this industry depends on the spatial organisation of these vertically-integrated firm hierarchies. These are points we will now consider.

In terms of their spatial-organisational characteristics, the vertically-integrated Japanese semiconductor producers can be split into two groups. The first group, are the firms whose headquarters are based in the Kanto region and the second group are the firms from the Kansai region. Kanto and Kansai are the regions which contain the two largest urban concentrations in Japan, namely the Tokyo-Yokohama metropolitan area, and the Osaka-Kyoto-Kobe metropolitan area. All of the Japanese vertically-integrated semiconductor firms exhibit a similar, and very simple form of keiretsu organisational structure. The parent company generally has a series of plant locations at which high-level decision-making, research and product development take place. Within Japan, this first stage of the semiconductor production process, as described by Fig.16.1, tends to be situated geographically in the two major urban concentrations. Reporting directly to these plants is a second tier of plants, which consists of a series of wholly-owned subsidiary plants, almost all of which focus on the wafer process activity. Finally, there is a third tier of plants, which focus only on the wafer assembly process. The second and third stages of the semiconductor production process, which are the wafer processing and wafer assembly operations, take place in almost all central and peripheral areas of Japan. These affiliated wafer assembly plants, which may be either majority or wholly owned by the parent company, report directly to the second tier of plants, which themselves report directly to the top tier of plants. Only the higher level plants within the local groups generally report directly to the headquarters region, although there are a small number of geographically peripheral facilities which do report directly to the top level. Meanwhile, the overseas plants of these vertically-integrated firms all report directly to the headquarters locations. This is because there is no particular local hierarchical organisational network between plants located in the same global region, as there is between the plants within the same Japanese regions.

Examples of the spatial organisation of four semiconductor firms, Hitachi, Sony, Sharp and Rohm, are shown in Figs. 16.2–16.5. Each of these diagrams are compiled using data from *Sangyo Times* (1995) and the *Press Journal* (1995) which document all of the industry's plants by location, activity, and position within the corporate organisational hierarchy. All of the data for each of plants is 1995 data, which is the latest date for which complete information is available. The strict hierarchical organisational arrangements described above are largely replicated geographically. The higher level establishments are located in the two major urban concentrations, while the wafer plants and assembly plants are located in a variety of both central and peripheral locations. As we see, Hitachi and Sony are firms whose higher level establishments are located in the Kanto region around Tokyo, while Sharp and Rohm are firms whose higher level establishments are located in the Kansai region of Osaka-Kyoto-Kobe. In the cases of Sharp, Rohm and Sony, whose organisational structures are very simple, the wafer plants, which represent the local clusters of assembly plants, report directly to each of the higher-level establishments. The second and third tier plants are generally in more peripheral locations than the first tier plants. On the other hand, the organisational structure of Hitachi is much more complex, with second and third tier plants located in both central and peripheral areas. These patterns are typical in the Japanese semiconductor industry.

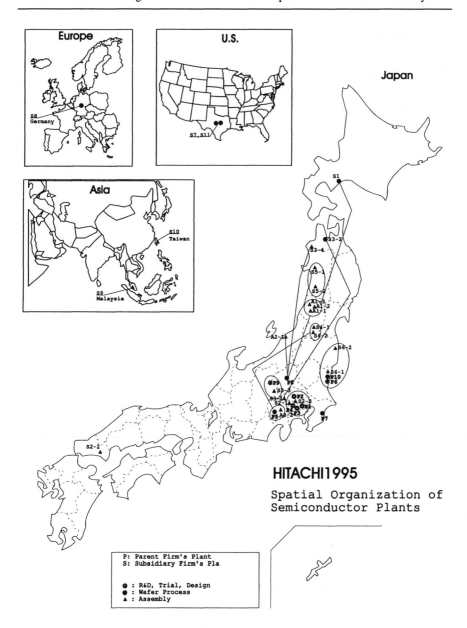

Fig. 16.2. The Spatial Organisation of Semiconductor Plants at Hitachi (1995)

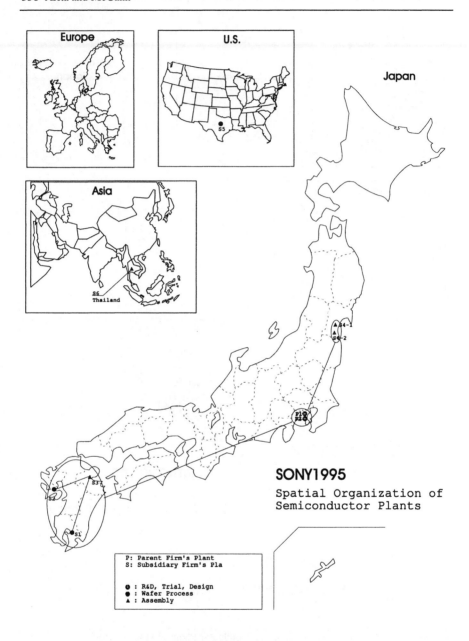

Fig. 16.3. The Spatial Organisation of Semiconductor Plants at Sony (1995)

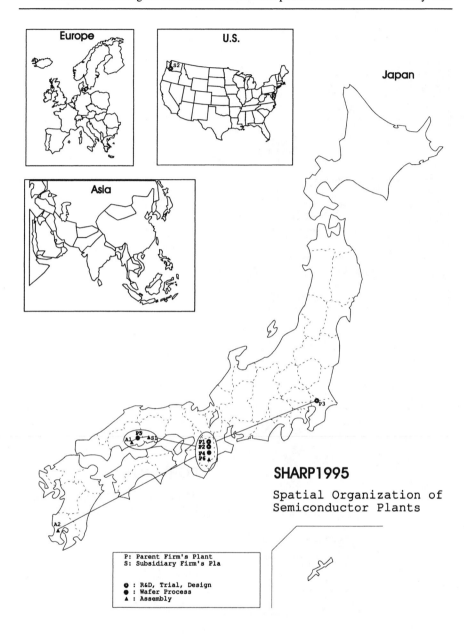

Fig. 16.4. The Spatial Organisation of Semiconductor Plants at Sharp (1995)

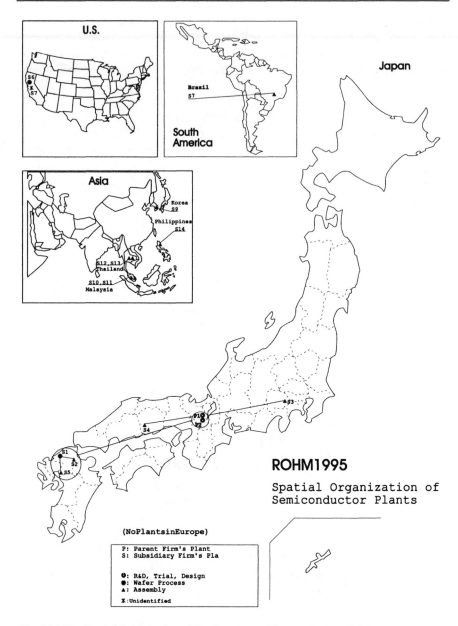

Fig. 16.5 The Spatial Organisation of Semiconductor Plants at Rohm (1995)

There is, however, a very particular logic to the spatial organisation of these plants. The plants are often arranged into local spatial clusters in which groups of assembly plants are located close to the particular wafer process plant that they report to. As we see in Arita and McCann (2002b), the firms often set up a networked cluster of adjacent plants in order *as a group* to produce a particular generation of products. Such organisational issues are determined within a multiproduct environment, in which corporate control is exercised with respect to the production of a range of different outputs for either intermediate or final consumption. As such, the spatial organisation of activities and the spatial implementation of technological innovations are determined primarily with respect to the organisational logic of the keiretsu systems. The resulting spatial patterns of plants are therefore primarily the result of the need for co-ordination between the plants within a well-defined system of formal inter-plant relations (Arita and McCann 2000). Descriptions of this particular industry based on a combination of standard western models, such as the local information spillovers-agglomeration model and product-cycle model, will be very misleading.

Similar caution must also be exercised when considering the issues governing the location of the higher-level establishments. The locations of the headquarters of each of these companies depend primarily on the initial location of the founding of the company. Although it may be tempting to attribute the reasons for these particular location patterns to agglomeration considerations of informal information spillovers, along the lines of the Silicon Valley descriptions above (Saxenian 1994), the argument cannot be sustained. This is because a great deal of internal secrecy surrounds the development of silicon wafers. Moreover, not only is internal secrecy a feature typical of many vertically-integrated firms (Simmie 1998), but also Japanese firms in general are notoriously secretive even in comparison to other hierarchical organisations. Therefore, any potential localisation effects could only be possibly associated with labour market hysteresis impacts (Simpson 1992), rather than any than issues relating to informal inter-firm information spillovers. The same argument also holds for the case of the wafer and assembly plants.

The results of these various organisational issues is that the spatial pattern of technological innovations and new-product implementations within the Japanese semiconductor industry in Japan cannot be accounted for either within a straightforward product-cycle framework, or by referring to Marshallian descriptions of agglomeration based on informal information spillovers. In Japanese industry, location issues are generally determined primarily with respect to organisational issues, which themselves are often quite different to the types of organisational arrangements typical in the US. As such, observations based simply on the Silicon Valley semiconductor industry, or even on comparisons with the electronics industry of New England (Saxenian 1994), are of little or no analytical use when discussing the spatial behaviour of the Japanese-based components of the global semiconductor industry. It remains to be seen from empirical work whether a more orthodox product-cycle relationship exists for the overseas investments of the Japanese semiconductor firms.

16.7 Conclusions

This paper has discussed the various sub-sectors of the semiconductor industry, and applied a simple product-cycle model to the case of the Japanese wafer-processing part of the industry based within Japan. The data we employ is some of the most detailed and disaggregated technological data available for such an industry. The models presented here find little or no association between the implementation of technological innovations and the location of the activity. There is some evidence for industrial clustering between local establishments, but this takes place within a tight organisational logic designed specifically to rule out information externalities (Arita and McCann 2002a,b). The only evidence we do find is that the larger capacity facilities will tend to be in the more geographically peripheral, lower wage and land-price regions, an observation consistent with orthodox location theory considerations. The explanation we offer for these observations is that the spatial patterns of production in the Japanese semiconductor industry are dominated by issues of decision-making and control within vertically-integrated hierarchical organisations. These particular types of hierarchical corporate relationships, and also these particular types of local wafer process-assembly plant organisational arrangements, only exist in Japan and within the individual keiretsu groupings. The arguments presented here suggest that the location behaviour of these vertically-integrated parts of the global semiconductor industry are governed primarily by traditional multiplant and multinational location considerations, in which different activities or groups of activities are located in different regions for different reasons, subject to the organisational arrangements of the firm. Observations contrasting the behaviour of Silicon Valley and other parts of the semiconductor industry (Saxenian 1994) are of very limited analytical use for more general industry-organisation discussions.

References

Akaike H (1973) Information theory and an extension of the maximum likelihood principle. In: Petrov B, Csake F (eds) Second international symposium on information theory. Akademiai Kiado, Budapest

Almeida P, Kogut B (1997) The exploration of technological diversity and the geographic localization of innovation. Small Business Economics 9: 21–31

Angel P (1991) High technology agglomeration and the labor market: the case of Silicon Valley. Environment and Planning A 23: 1501–1516

Arita T, McCann P (2000) Industrial alliances and firm location behaviour: some evidence from the US semiconductor industry. Applied Economics 32: 1391–1403

Arita, T, McCann P (2002a) The spatial and hierarchical organization of Japanese and US multinational semiconductor firms. Journal of International Management 8, forthcoming

Arita T, McCann P (2002b) The relationship between the spatial and hierarchical organization of multiplant firms: Observations from the global semiconductor industry. In:

McCann P (ed) Industrial location economics. Edward Elgar, Cheltenham, forthcoming

Audrestch D, Feldman MP (1996) R&D spillovers and the geography of innovation and production. American Economic Review 86: 630–640

Aydalot P, Keeble D (1988) High technology industry and innovative environments. Routledge, London

Best MH (1990) The new competition: institutions of industrial restructuring. Polity Press, Cambridge

Cantwell JA, Iammarino S (2000) Multinational corporations and the location of technological innovation in the UK regions. Regional Studies 34: 317–332

Castells M, Hall P (1994) Technopoles of the world: The making of the 21st century industrial complexes. Routledge, New York

Eisenhardt K, Schoonhaven CB (1990) Organizational growth: founding teams strategy and environment and growth among US semiconductor ventures 1978–88. Administrative Science Quarterly 35: 504–529

Electronic Industries Association of Japan EIAJ (1994) IC Guidebook 94. Tokyo (in Japanese)

Jaffe A, Trajtenberg M, Henderson R (1993) Geographic localization of knowledge spillovers as evidence by patent citations. Quarterly Journal of Economics 108: 577–598

Keeble D, Wilkinson F (1999) Collective learning and knowledge development in the evolution of high technology SMEs in Europe. Regional Studies 33: 295–303

Kittiprapas S, McCann P (1999) Industrial location behaviour and regional restructuring within the fifth 'tiger' economy: evidence from the Thai electronics industry. Applied Economics 31: 35–49

Krugman P (1991) Geography and trade. MIT Press, Cambridge MA

Larsen JK, Rogers EM (1984) Silicon Valley fever. George Allen and Unwin, London

Maddala GS (1992) Introduction to econometrics, second edition. Macmillan, London

Marshall A (1920) Principles of economics, eight edition. Macmillan, London

McCann P, Fingleton B (1996) The regional agglomeration impact of just-in-time input linkages: evidence from the Scottish electronics industry. Scottish Journal of Political Economy 43: 493–518

Nikkei Microevidence (1999) Nikkei Industries, Tokyo

Nishimura Y (1995) The future of the semiconductor industry. Maruzen, Tokyo

Nishimura Y (1999) The advance of the solution-business with the development of the System-LSI. In: Nikkei Micro Device. Tokyo, May, pp 54–63

Oakey RP, Cooper SY (1989) High-technology industry, agglomeration and the potential for peripherally sited small firms. Regional Studies 23: 347–360

Piore MJ, Sabel CF (1984) The second industrial divide: possibilities for prosperity. Basic Books, New York

Porter ME (1990) The competitive advantage of nations. Free Press, New York

Porter ME (1998) Clusters and the new economics of competition. Harvard Business Review (November-December): 77–90

Press Journal Inc. (1995) Japan semiconductor yearbook. Tokyo (in Japanese)

Sangyo Times Inc. (1995) The yearbook of the semiconductor industry in Japan. Tokyo (in Japanese)

Saxenian A (1994) Regional advantage: culture and competition in Silicon Valley and Route 128. Harvard University Press, Cambridge MA

Scott AJ (1988) New industrial spaces. Pion, London

Scott AJ (1991) Technopolis: High-technology industry and regional development in Southern California. University of California Press, Los Angeles

Simmie J (1998) Reasons for the development of 'islands of innovation': Evidence from Hertfordshire. Urban Studies 35: 1261–1289

Simpson W (1992) Urban structure and the labour market: workers' mobility, commuting and underemployment in cities. Clarendon Press, Oxford

Suarez-Villa L, Karlsson C (1996) The development of Sweden's R&D-intensive electronics industries: exports, out-sourcing, and territorial distribution. Environment and Planning A 28: 783–817

Suarez-Villa L, Rama R (1996) Outsourcing, R&D and the pattern of intrametropolitan location: the electronics industry of Madrid. Urban Studies 33: 1155–1197

Suarez-Villa L, Walrod W (1997) Operational strategy, R&D and intrametropolitan clustering in a polycentric structure: the advanced electronics industries of the Los Angeles Basin. Urban Studies 34: 1343–1380

The Economist (1997) Future perfect? A survey of Silicon Valley. March 29

Vernon R (1960) Metropolis 1985: An interpretation of the findings of the New York metropolitan region study. Harvard University Press, Cambridge MA

Vernon R (1966) International investment and international trade in the product cycle. Quarterly Journal of Economics 80: 190–207

Vernon R (1979) The product cycle hypothesis in a new international environment. Oxford Bulletin of Economics and Statistics 41: 255–267

Wever E, Stam E (1999) Clusters of high technology SMEs: The Dutch case. Regional Studies 33.4: 391–400

White H (1980) A heteroskedasticity-consistent covariance matrix estimator and a direct test for heteroskedasticity. Econometrica 48: 817–838

Appendix 16.A Selection of Regressors

For the approach to the problem of the selection of regressors, we use the Akaike Information Criterion (AIC). AIC suggests minimising $-2/n(\log L) + 2k/n$, where L is the likelihood function, n is the number of observations and k is the number of parameters in L. For the regression models this criterion implies minimising $RSS_j exp[2(k_j +1)/n]$, where k_j is the number of explanatory variables and RSS_j is the residual sum of squares for the jth model. Thus, for each model, we choose the model which minimises the AIC in each of the analyses.

17 Innovative Performance in the Capital Region of Norway[1]

Heidi Wiig Aslesen

STEP-group, Oslo, Norway

17.1 Introduction

The aim of this paper is to explore whether being located in a city has some effects on firms' innovation activity, and whether it has an effect on firms' collaboration for the purpose of innovation. The focus is especially on small and medium-sized enterprises (SMEs[2]) in the manufacturing industry. The paper empirically tests three hypotheses related to proximity and innovation. Firstly, do urbanisation economies have an effect on the extent of firms' innovation activity in the Oslo region?[3] Secondly, does city location have an effect on firms' use of external actors in the innovation process? Thirdly, does proximity to important tacit-knowledge providers (like the scientific community) enhance the use of formal innovation collaboration with these actors?

The paper explores whether geographical proximity to important actors in the innovation system is a sufficient condition for a regionalised innovation system. A common idea is that big urban agglomerations attract a large and differentiated variety of activities and thus become particularly suitable as breeding places for innovations. Along with this view, new and innovative firms and firms in new industries establish themselves very often in urban agglomerations; cities are therefore perceived to play a special role in technological change and innovation as compared to other locations.

Sect. 17.2 of the paper includes a literature survey, while Sect. 17.3 gives some background statistics on the Oslo region. Thereafter, the paper presents results from both quantitative and qualitative studies of innovation activity in the Oslo re-

---

[1] The paper is based on parts of the RITTS Oslo project (Regional Innovation Infrastructure and Technology Transfer Systems in the Oslo region, RITTS Oslo, Stage 1 report).

[2] In Norway small firms are defined as having between 0–19 employees, and medium sized firms have between 20 and 99 employees. Since the Norwegian Innovation Survey does not include firms with fewer than 10 employees, SMEs in this paper are defined as firms having between 10–99 employees.

[3] When in the article the Oslo region, Oslo area or Oslo is referred to, the two counties of Oslo and Akershus are meant.

gion, the capital region of Norway. The quantitative studies give insight into firms' innovation activity and firms' innovation collaboration with external partners by using data from the Norwegian Innovation Survey carried out in 1997.[4] By quantifying firms' innovation activity we are able to investigate if being located in a city has an effect on firms' performance. By mapping firms' innovation collaboration we are able to examine firms' interaction patterns (Aslesen 1999a).

In order to further explore and understand firms' choice of partners, focusing particularly on the links between SMEs and the scientific community, we carried out five qualitative industry studies[5] (Aslesen 1999b) in the Oslo region, presented in Sect. 17. 5 of the paper. The industries studied are graphics (printing and publishing), food, machinery and equipment, electronics and the electro-technical industry. Two of the industries, graphics and electronics, are defined as 'regional clusters'[6] (Isaksen and Spilling 1996). These studies were carried out in order to answer why proximity and density in a city-region were not a sufficient condition for firms' interaction with the scientific community, and to investigate the poten-

---

[4] In 1997 Statistics Norway carried out, for the second time, an innovation study in Norway based on the Community Innovation Survey (CIS). The first CIS data collection was carried out in 1993 after a joint initiative from EUROSTAT and DGXIII of the European Commission. Actual data collection and financing was left to national authorities. In the Norwegian case, Statistics Norway carried out both surveys. The survey gathered information from 3263 enterprises in Norway. It was based on a stratified random sample. It was stratified by enterprise size as measured by number of employees. A sample of enterprises between 10 and 99 employees was drawn, and there is a full count of enterprises with more than 100 employees. Enterprises with fewer than 10 employees are excluded altogether. In addition to size groups, strata have been defined by two-digit NACE codes. Random drawing has not been initiated unless there have been at least 15 observations in a cell (stratum) defined by size group and NACE code.

[5] The industry studies were all self contained and relatively independent analyses. The different studies were carried through in parallel, and the authors' ambition was to make studies that would be comparable in scope and which would be complementary with respect to choice of industry, but containing much common analytical substance. The industry analyses are based on three main sources: first, a range of in-depth interviews with people in the industries (managers, market directors, researchers and operators), in unions and other organisations working in the Oslo region, and from institutions in research and higher education in the area. Second, information has been gathered through the screening of research publications, annual reports, web sites, etc. Third, information on the industries, on employment, innovation patterns and technological collaboration, etc. has been obtained from a number of data-sets, some of which are maintained by STEP.

[6] The procedure used to identify potential regional clusters builds on the following three criteria: the identified regional clusters consist of labour-market regions, and Norway is divided into 103 such regions. The labour-market regions must be specialised in at least one of 39 industrial sectors, i.e., the location quotient for a sector is greater than 3.0. This means that an industry must have at least three times as many jobs in the region as 'expected', based on the industry's significance on a national scale. The 'specialised' sector must include at least 200 jobs and 10 firms in a region; we set this limit so as not to include many very small clusters.

tial barriers to the formation of a regionalised innovation system in the Oslo region. Finally, the last section of the paper gives some policy suggestions based on the findings presented.

17.2 Regional Learning and Innovation

Today it is acknowledged that technological change is one of the most important factors explaining economic development and growth. However, technological change is a complex process that is not yet fully understood. "This complexity stems partially from the diverse set of phenomena that are subsumed under the term innovation" (Fischer 2000). Innovation is looked upon as the core of technological change, and understood as the process that accumulates and develops knowledge of different types. The idea that innovation plays a key role in the dynamics of economic growth has become an integrated part of thinking around economic policy. Theoretical and political awareness of the effects of innovation has raised interest in how innovation actually takes place.

In innovation studies the emphasis on technological innovation has shifted from the single act philosophy of technological innovation to the social process underlying economically oriented technical novelty (OECD 1992). Innovation is recognised as a process of interactive learning, characterised by continuous internal and external feedbacks, which initiate steady changes to products, processes and services. Interactivity in the innovation process refers to internal collaboration between several departments of a company (R&D, production, marketing, distribution, etc.) as well as to external co-operation with other firms (especially with customers and suppliers), knowledge providers (like universities and technology centres), finance, training, and public administration. It is in this context that the concept of '*innovation systems*' has been introduced, in contrast to earlier research that based technological change on a narrow definition of R&D, thereby ignoring the importance of other types of innovation inputs.

The innovation system approach is not *one* formalised theory, but a conceptual framework in an early phase of its development. The idea behind this concept is that innovation is a socially and territorially embedded, interactive learning process, which cannot be understood independently of its institutional and cultural context (Lundvall 1992). Innovation and learning occur in various kinds of networks where different actors become involved, and where different kinds of knowledge are exchanged and exploited. Innovation is first and foremost a collective and social endeavour, a collaborative process in which the firm, especially the small firm, depends on the expertise of a wider social constituency than is often imagined (workforce, suppliers, customers, technical institutes, training bodies, etc.) (Cooke et al. 1994). These networks may extend from local/regional to international and global space. At this stage there is no agreement on which elements and relations are essential in relation to the conceptual core of this framework, or what is the precise content of it (Edquist 1997). This reflects a tendency to broaden the system to include any possible source of influence without dealing with the question where an innovation system starts or ends (Kaufmann and Tödling 2000).

Within system approaches to innovation different types of systems have been defined (Gregersen and Johnson 1997). Among these are the "localised systems" linking the importance of proximity on different geographical levels to innovation. The innovation systems could be local-, regional-, national-, or global systems of innovation. The first focus was on *national systems of innovation* (Lundvall 1992; Nelson 1993; Niosi el al. 1993; Edquist 1997). In this approach important research questions have been related to convergence or divergence between national innovation systems. The regional level has also become an important analytical level for research on innovation systems (Braczyk et al. 1998). The essential argument of these studies is that innovation is more frequent, and is more apt to be successful, when innovation and learning processes are locally embedded (Asheim 1994; Asheim and Isaksen 1996) and that regional agglomeration provides the best context for innovation-based learning (Hudson 1999). Geographical proximity is viewed as a necessary but not a sufficient factor for the existence of regionalised innovation systems. "A growing attention has been given to perspectives and strategies that can secure the innovative capability of regions in order to foster regional future of endogenous growth, making the learning capacity of the regional economy of strategic importance to its innovation and competitiveness" (Asheim 1999). The existence of (networks of) innovative, learning intensive firms at the regional level is perceived to secure and strengthen national competitiveness.

Specific forms of knowledge creation are localised and territorially specific, and this is tacit knowledge. The importance of tacit knowledge is often emphasised when discussing localised learning, "...tacit knowledge is still a key element in the appropriation and effective use of knowledge, especially when the whole innovation process is accelerating" (Lundvall and Borras 1999, p. 33). Tacit knowledge is highly personal, and is wedded to its human and social context (Morgan 1997, p. 495). For a receiver to understand tacit knowledge he or she must also understand its human and social context, which can only be done through face-to-face communication. Tacit knowledge, then, is only transferable through interpersonal contacts and verbal or non-verbal communication (Arnold and Thuriaux 1997; Foray and Lundvall 1996). As knowledge becomes more tacit it pays off to exchange it through proximity rather than distant relations (Rutten and Boekema 2000).

However, local production systems would face problems if only built on tacit knowledge, and lack strategic, goal oriented actions and strategies, which, basically, have to be supported by codified knowledge (e.g., formal R&D)(Amin and Cohendet 1999). Localised learning must build on the strategic use of codified, R&D-based knowledge in addition to tacit knowledge. Firms cannot rely only on 'tacit' localised learning in the long run. Codified knowledge, e.g., embedded in standardised technologies, can be transferred over long distances at low cost; spatial proximity between users and producers is not necessary, while spatial, social, and cultural proximity is a major precondition for the transfer of tacit knowledge. The firms that master knowledge that is not fully codifiable are thus connected to various kinds of networks with other firms and organisations through localised input-output relations, knowledge spillovers and their untraded interdependencies (Storper 1997).

Knowledge spillover occurs because knowledge created by one firm or another organisation is typically not contained within that organisation, and thereby creates value for other firms and other firms' customers. Three vehicles of such spillover may be distinguished (Fischer 2000); first, the scientific sector with its general scientific and technological knowledge pool; second, the firms-specific knowledge pool; and, third, the business-business and industry-university relations that make them possible. Untraded interdependencies derive from geographical clustering, both economic and sociocultural (developed routines, shared values, norms, rules, and trust). The combination of territorially embedded Marshallian agglomeration economies (mutual trust and 'industrial atmosphere'), knowledge creation and spillover and their untraded interdependencies (conventions, informal rules and habits) defines the importance of the regional scale in innovation systems (Fischer 2000).

Since innovation relies strongly on interaction and the ability to interact (Rothwell 1994), above average innovation activity not only depends on the number of co-operative relationships and learning capabilities, but is itself an indicator for utilising network interactions. Since the propensity for knowledge-spillovers and for finding network partners is higher in central metropolitan regions, innovative firms are not equally distributed geographically, but *expected to be located mostly in urban regions* (Isard 1956; Armstrong and Taylor 1993). Firms that are located in regions with high flows of both private and public or academic R&D are more likely to be innovative than firms located elsewhere. The reason is that there are tacit elements linked to this kind of knowledge, and physical proximity is then important in order to absorb the knowledge.

Hoover (1937) distinguishes between two types of external economies; localisation economies and urbanisation economies (Chinitz 1961; Hoover 1971; Isard et al. 1959). Localisation economies refer to externalities associated with the presence in one place of a mass of other producers in the same sector. Urbanisation economies, one the other hand, are found where there is a diverse industrial base, extensive infrastructure and services supporting it, and a concentration of institutions that generate new knowledge. The idea is that big urban agglomerations attract a large and differentiated variety of activities and thus become particularly suitable as breeding places for innovations (Glaeser et al. 1992). The notion is therefore that the city plays a special role in technological change and innovation as compared to other areas.

Breschi and Lissoni (2000) have made an overview of research trying to find evidence of localised knowledge spillover, and are critical of many of the studies carried out. They mean that the econometric evidence on the subject still lacks a firm enough theoretical background, and that what might appear as 'pure' knowledge externalities are externalities mediated by economic mechanisms, and that what appear to be knowledge externalities are actually well-regulated flows that are managed deliberated for appropriation purposes. We do find their thoughts challenging, and in this paper we will try to test whether there exist externalities that could have an effect on innovation. We will also see if formal innovation collaboration with firms and different actors in the innovation system has an effect on innovation.

Before we present our findings, we will give some background information on the Oslo region.

17.3 The Oslo Region: Employment and Business Activity

The Oslo region accounts for ¼ of all Norwegian employment, in all 440,000 employees. The region is the dominant centre of service industries. Private services represent almost half of all employment in the region, while almost 1/3 are employed in the public sector. In 1996, employment in public and private services represented as much as 80% of total employment in the region, which partly reflects a high share of part-time workers in service industries as compared to manufacturing industries. Nevertheless, large parts of important Norwegian manufacturing industries are also located in the region.

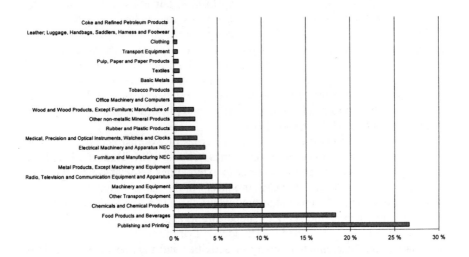

Fig. 17.1. Employment in Manufacturing Industries in the Oslo Region 1996: Share of Total Manufacturing Employment. Source: The Norwegian Firm and Enterprise Register

Employment in manufacturing industry represents about 10% of all employment in the region. The largest manufacturing industries are printing and publishing (27%), food and beverages (18%), and chemicals (10%).

The Oslo region represents 24% of national employment. There are five industries with a larger share of national employment than this 24% average. These industries are tobacco (76%), office machinery and computers (57%), printing and publishing (38%), radio and television (36%) and chemicals (26%).

In terms of work force competence, Oslo has a higher than proportional share in all higher education categories; 43% of all people with higher levels of education (more than four years, ISCED level 7[7]) work in Oslo. This is an expected consequence of being the capital and of housing the Central government, as well as county and municipal administration.

The high educational level in Oslo is also due to the concentration of a major 'knowledge infrastructure' in the form of research institutes, universities and science parks. We estimate that there are approximately 75 non-university research institutes in all fields, 3 science parks, and 20 higher education institutions with approximately 60,000 students. The technological and R&D capabilities of the research institute sector cover the whole range of relevant technologies for the region's production structure. Oslo Research Park currently has 49 firms, of which 60% are in the fields of IT and media, with the remainder spread between biotechnology, materials, pharmaceuticals and consultancy. The Science Park at Kjeller has major capabilities within energy and environmental technologies, aerospace, telecommunications, IT (especially satellite communications), and industrial mathematics applications. The Science Park at Ås specialises in agriculture, aquaculture, environmental sciences, and forestry and food sciences. Finally the region has a wide range of venture capital institutions, consultancy firms and technology-transfer institutions.

17.4 Innovation Activity and Innovation Collaboration

17.4.1 Innovation Activity

In this section we focus on the extent of innovative activity in firms located in the Oslo region as compared with the national average. We examine the proportion of firms that engage in innovation activity. Manufacturing firms were firstly asked if they had, during the period 1995–97, introduced technologically new or improved *products* and/or *processes*. Subsequently, they were asked if they had, during the period 1995–97, undertaken activity to develop or introduce technologically new or improved products or processes, but which had not produced any results in this period, either because the results were yet to come or because the attempts had failed. The firms that answered positively to any of these three alternatives are classified as innovative.

The question to be tested is if urbanisation economies seem to have an effect on firms' innovation activity i.e., are firms in the Oslo region more innovative than the average Norwegian firm? Do the proximity and density of a diverse industrial base, extensive infrastructure and services supporting it, and a concentration of in-

---

[7] International Standard Classification of Education (ISCED).

stitutions that generate new knowledge, create knowledge spillovers that have a positive effect on the innovation activity in this area?

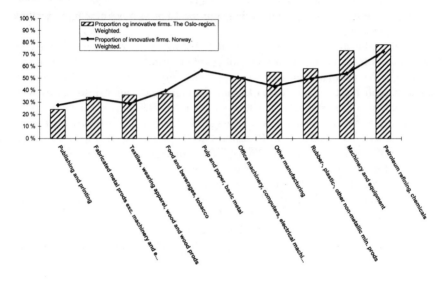

Fig. 17.2. Proportion of Innovative Firms in the Oslo Region and in Norway. Manufacturing Industry. Weighted Numbers. (*N*=312, 1976). Source: Norwegian Community Innovation Survey

Our sample is a stratified sample where strata have been defined by size groups and two-digit NACE codes. It is therefore necessary to use weighting procedures to recreate the proportions of the population. The weighted[8] proportion of innovative manufacturing firms in the Oslo region is 40%, the same as the average for Norway. Thus, we do not find evidence to support the hypothesis that being located in a city does have an effect on firms' innovation activity compared to other areas.

At the industry level, however, there are large differences between industries in terms of the proportion of firms participating in innovation activity. The 'petroleum-refining and chemical' industry has the highest proportion of innovative firms, followed by 'Machinery and equipment' and 'Rubber, plastics, other non-metallic min. products' (78%, 73% and 58%) (cf. Fig. 17.2). For these three in-

---

[8] That this will make a difference in our case should be evident from the fact that the main stratification variable, namely firm size (number of employees), also has a substantial effect on the probability of being innovative. Since the large firms are better represented in the sample than the small firms, the proportion of innovative firms will be higher in the sample than in the population. In the following we will therefore use the weighting procedures to be able to recreate the proportions of a given variable for the population. For the Oslo region regional weights are used, for Norway national weights are used.

dustries the Oslo region has a larger proportion of innovative firms than the average for Norway. This *may* suggest that these three industries are integrated into systems of innovation. Industries with low proportions of innovative firms are 'Publishing and printing', 'Fabricated metal products' and 'Food and beverages, tobacco' (24%, 34% and 39%). Important to note is that 'Publishing and printing' and 'Food and beverages, tobacco' are the dominant industries in the Oslo region, reducing the average innovation activity of the region. This underlines the fact that the innovation activity of a region is very dependent on the region's industrial structure. 'Publishing and printing' is also defined to be a 'cluster' in the Oslo area. Externalities associated with the presence of a mass of other producers in the same sector and area seem to have little effect on these industries' innovation activity, as innovation activity in the Oslo area is at the same level as the national average. This industry may then have an under-utilised innovation potential in Oslo.

Being located in a city seems to have different effects on different industries. Industries that are among the most innovative on a national scale seem to have an even larger proportion of innovative firms when located in a city. We now turn to look at the 'city effect' on the share of firms with innovation activity according to firm size.

By using the number of employees as measure of firm size, we have categorised the sample into 4 size groups: 10–49 employees, 50–99 employees, 100–249 employees, and 250 and more employees. The table below gives the proportion of innovative firms by size.

Table 17.1. Proportion of Innovative Firms by Size. Manufacturing Sector in the Oslo Region and in Norway. Weighted Proportions. (N=312, 1976).

Size groups	Number of firms in the sample. Oslo region	Share of innovative firms in the Oslo region. Weighted	Number of firms in the sample. Norway	Share of innovative firms in Norway. Weighted
10–49	175	31%	1188	33%
50–99	41	47%	317	54%
100–249	52	69%	306	65%
250+	44	82%	165	79%
Total	312	40%	1976	40%

Source: Norwegian Community Innovation Survey

The table shows a clear relationship between firm size and the share of innovative firms in the defined three-year period. In the largest size group (250+) 82% of the firms report innovation activity, while in the smallest size group (10–49) the proportion of innovative firms is only 31%. The Oslo region has a lower share of innovative SMEs (firms with less than 100 employees) than the average for Norway. Firms with more than 100 employees have a slightly higher proportion of innovators in Oslo than for Norway as a whole.

17.4.2 Innovation Collaboration

In this section we examine more closely possible knowledge flows between firms and external actors by looking at firms' innovation collaboration with other partners. The exercise gives insight into the actors or participants in the innovation system with which firms have formal contact.[9] The question is whether the Oslo region location has an effect on firms' use of external actors in the innovation process, since the propensity to find network partners is higher in central areas. Another question that derives from this is whether proximity to important tacit knowledge providers (like the scientific community) enhances the use of formal innovation collaboration with these actors.

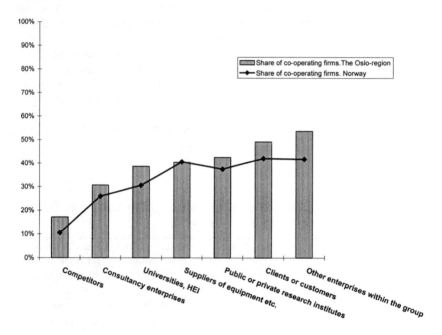

Fig. 17.3. Proportion of Firms with Different Domestic Collaboration Partners in the Oslo Region and in Norway. Manufacturing Industry. Weighted Shares. (N=82, 473). Source: 'Norwegian Community Innovation Survey'

Firms in the Oslo region have a higher proportion of firms engaging in innovation collaborate than the average Norwegian firms. This is true for almost all the innovation partners listed (besides suppliers of equipment) (Fig. 17.3). This might sug-

---

[9] The measure is simply a 'yes' or 'no' question of whether firms have engaged in innovation collaboration with any of the mentioned partners and will not take into account the number of co-operative actions. Further, we have no indication of how the firms value their collaborative partners, or of how successful the innovation collaboration project is.

gest that being located in an urban area, within close proximity of other producers, with the extensive infrastructure and the concentration of knowledge providers, does have an effect on firms' networks.

But, what kinds of external partners do firms use in the innovation process? 49% of innovative firms in the Oslo region have innovation collaboration with 'clients or customers', and close to 40% collaborate with suppliers. Partners within the value chain are thus important in the innovation process. In addition, a high proportion of firms collaborate with the scientific infrastructure, with as many as 43% having co-operated with research institutes and 39% with universities or higher education institutions (HEI). The proportion of firms in the Oslo region using the scientific community is slightly higher than the average for Norway. This supports the hypothesis that proximity to scientific institutions enhances a firm's linkage capabilities, suggesting further that location within an urban area has an effect on the level of interaction with the knowledge community.

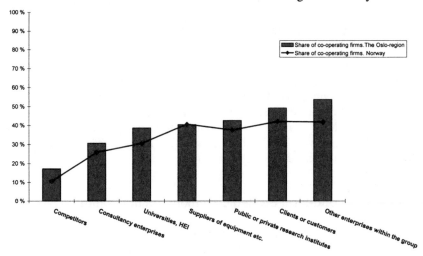

Fig. 17.4. Proportion of SMEs with Different Domestic Collaboration Partners in the Oslo Region and in Norway. Manufacturing Industry. Weighted Shares. (N=33, 240). Source: 'Norwegian Community Innovation Survey'

In general, there is a lower proportion of SMEs taking part in innovation collaboration with almost all categories of partners with the exception of 'Clients and customers' and 'Other enterprises within the enterprise group' (This is revealed by comparing Figs. 17.4 and 17.3). In other words, for SMEs, client- and customer-linkages seems to be more prevalent than any other form of linkage. It is in the use of 'Clients and customers' and 'Other enterprises within the enterprise group' that we find the greatest differences between SMEs located in the Oslo region and the averages for SMEs in the rest of the country. This suggests that location in a city area affects in particular the proportion of SMEs collaborating with partners within their vertical network.

Other categories of partners besides clients and customers are used less frequently by SMEs than by larger firms, indicating that SMEs networks are less complex than for larger firms. The proportion of SMEs engaging in innovation collaboration with the scientific community is approximately 10 percentage points lower than the average for all firm sizes (shown in Fig. 17.3). The Oslo region has the same proportion of SMEs collaborating with research institutions as the average for Norway, the share collaborating with Universities and/or HEI is slightly higher than the average. Fig. 17.4 also shows that consultancies are relevant partners for only a low proportion of SMEs.

These results suggests some innovation potentials in linking SMEs to more actors of the innovation system since there are clearly important actors in the innovation system that are partly missing as regards SMEs in the Oslo region. What then are the main barriers for SMEs in innovation collaboration?

17.5 Barriers to the Regional Innovation System

The main focus of this section is on the greatest barriers to the formation of an innovation system in the Oslo region, namely the apparent barriers between SMEs and the scientific community. The chapter will investigate the reasons for the insufficient interaction between SMEs and the scientific community in Oslo, and further examine SMEs' barriers to networking and to using external information and knowledge in general. The analysis is based on findings from five industrial studies performed for the RITTS Oslo project.

17.5.1 Lack of Long-term Strategic Thinking on Innovation in SMEs

Relatively few SMEs draw upon resources within the scientific infrastructure in their innovation process. One explanation for this uncovered in the industry studies is a lack of long-term strategic thinking on innovation activities in many SMEs. Innovation activities in SMEs often take place as an immediate response to customer demands, making the innovation process ad-hoc and unsystematic. There is an orientation towards "demand-pull" rather than "supply-push". In many ways this seems to hinder firms from having a more long-term approach to innovation, which might include incorporating horizontal partners into firms' networks. For example, the industrial activity of most printing and publishing companies in the Oslo region is based on customer contact and "making a living on a day-to-day basis". This is reflected by the fact that most of the companies interviewed could not see any obvious benefit in having contact with educational or research institutions.

Explanations for the inability to engage in long-term thinking on innovation are often related to SMEs' general lack of resources. For example, in the food industry (according to company interviews), small food companies are marked by such problems as: low levels of formal skills within the workforce, high work pressure ("few people get old in this industry", said one interviewee), low technological capability compared with the large companies, and low capital resources. Accordingly, few of these companies will find it fruitful – or even find the time – to participate in long-term strategic thinking on innovation with, for instance, a research institute. In the machinery and equipment industry, innovative firms have a need for long term R&D, and one of the factors hampering this is that firms have great problems obtaining finance for this kind of activity. These small independent actors have little power to 'lobby' for R&D schemes that are relevant to their industry.

Other factors preventing SMEs from strategic innovation projects might relate to the kind of SMEs dominating an industry. For example, family-owned companies, with a high degree of embedded tradition and routine that constrains their capacity for change, can be a hampering factor in attempts to raise the innovation activity in an industry. The graphics industry in the region is characterised by just such an owner-based structure. Companies in this industry are also very small. The strategic development of new products is not on the agenda, and is certainly not pursued systematically. As one interviewee said: "A company with 4–5 employees does not have time to develop an innovation. The companies that innovate are either large, or they have started up based on a good idea." This tends to make innovation an incremental process, which usually means finding new ways to coordinate and combine different skills in the production process.

17.5.2 The Mismatch Between 'Supply' and 'Demand'

The industry studies revealed that there are significant collaboration problems with the scientific infrastructure, as is also supported by other studies (e.g., Koschatzky 1998). The problems have their roots in apparent mismatches, both regarding culture and competence. As revealed in the innovation survey, these mismatches do not seem to be compensated for by geographical proximity.

In firms, as well as in research institutes, many highly competent people are defensive with respect to outsiders (the 'not-invented-here-syndrome'), and display what appears to be over-confidence with respect to the power of their own internal competence-base. They find it difficult to develop the mutual understanding, communication and the commitment that is necessary for fruitful collaboration. Their frame of reference and their motivations and values are disparate, and they operate in institutions and organisations that work differently and that are faced with divergent functional requirements. In many ways one can say that they operate in entirely "*different worlds*". Small firms often find that the cultural divide between themselves and researchers in institutes and universities is an insurmountable barrier to constructive collaboration. One symptom of this is that researchers tend not to understand how important specific research objectives can be for the future of a firm. For example, in the machinery and equipment sector in the Oslo region, the knowledge-supplying institutions that provide R&D often specialise in the most sophisticated techniques. R&D institutions are then often directed towards the technologically sophisticated and financially strong firms, and this network of relationships seems to function well. Small firms appear to be somewhat left out of these innovation networks, and feel that their *R&D needs are not taken seriously.*

Many firms focus on the importance of keeping within a project's budget and time-constraints in R&D collaborations. These are factors that are a *sine-qua-non* for the survival of firms. Among SMEs in the Oslo region, the university is considered a very difficult partner for industrial firms, including large firms. This is because administratively the university functions as a slow-moving, at times incomprehensible, bureaucracy. There is a perceived "lack of professionalism" within such institutions. SMEs need to relate to supply side actors who understand that *time is a scarce resource.*

The industry studies show that firms tend to find that neither higher-education institutions nor non-profit research institutes are easy to access or easy to build profitable partnerships with. Small firms find it very *hard to orient themselves in what is going on* in public institutions, and in the ways in which public institutions are engaged in efforts intended to be helpful for them. Furthermore, many companies are *unable to formulate their technological needs,* often due to lack of specialised knowledge or skills.

Business increasingly depends on specialised knowledge. It is often impossible to find the most advanced knowledge relevant for a specific business application within local research institutions. The quality of existing competence is also variable. A firm requiring the absolute best competence in a specific field in order to be competitive may find that the available Norwegian resources are inferior in quality to resources available abroad. This makes it important to link SMEs into national and international innovation systems. In the graphical industry, one reason why regional institutions with knowledge in the area of IT often do not play a role in the knowledge infrastructure of individual companies is that the Norwegian institutions cannot compete in the supply of information in these areas. For electronics firms, leading competence may be found in the US, and the cultural divides do not appear to represent serious problems. In this case however, geographical distance, time differences and travel costs do represent significant obstacles.

An analysis made of the R&D institutions in the Oslo region[10] concludes that the quality of research carried out in the Oslo region is of a high international standard. However, the *research institutes perceive themselves as national and not regional actors.* The consequence of this is that their location is often of little significance to them, and the notion of developing local and regional linkages in not perceived as important. In the food industry the experience is that the food research environments in the Oslo region are poorly adapted to the local food industry's activities. Most research is centred on raw materials handling, while the bulk of the region's actual industrial activity is in beverages and pastry/miscellaneous products.

---

[10] The 'supply side' analysis of the "RITTS Oslo-Stage 1 report" was carried out by three international consultants, Bruce Reed, Bob Hodgson and Michel Lacave.

Competence building does not only occur through networking with external actors. A prerequisite for the ability to network externally is having *sufficient competence internally*. The fundamental competence base developed over time by firms is at the core of successful operations, and the ongoing learning and development inside firms can never be substituted with *infusions* from external competence centres. The matching of education to business requirements for educated people appears to be a significant problem in the Oslo region. There are mismatches between what firms need in terms of educated people and what the educational institutions can offer. This is regarded as an important hindrance to firms' competitiveness. The graphical industry, for example, is undergoing a period of change in which traditional and digital processes are merging, but it is difficult to find people combining both of these skill-sets. IT is also increasingly important for producers of machinery, but the industry has problems in attracting skilled people.

The table below summarises SMEs main barriers to form a regional innovation system, as presented above.

Table 17.2. SMEs Barriers to Forming a Regional Innovation System

Main barriers to innovation:	
1. Lack of long-term strategic thinking on innovation in SMEs	- General lack of resources: • Low level of formal skills • Low technological capability • Low capital resources - High degree of embedded tradition and routine that constrains capacity for change - Problems with getting finance for R&D
2. The mismatch between 'supply' and 'demand'	- SMEs find it hard to orient themselves in what is going on in public institutions - SMEs are often unable to formulate their technological needs - SMEs find that their R&D needs are not taken seriously - Research institutes perceive themselves as national and not regional actors

17.6 Summing Up and Policy Suggestions

The paper started out with three hypotheses related to proximity and innovation. Our first hypothesis was whether urbanisation economies have an effect on firms' innovation activity in the Oslo region. The innovation survey demonstrates that on an aggregated level firms in the Oslo region are not more innovative than the average for the country. At an industry level, our findings suggest that some industries, especially those known to be highly innovative, seem to be even more innovative when located in Oslo, suggesting that some industries may be more able to make positive use of external economies than others. The innovation survey also showed that the Oslo region has a lower proportion of innovative SMEs than average for SMEs in the country as a whole, suggesting that city location does not necessarily have a positive effect on innovation.

Our second hypothesis was whether city location has an effect on firms' use of external actors in the innovation process. In terms of innovation collaboration, location in or near Oslo appears to have some effect on both the proportion of firms taking part in innovation collaboration and on the kinds of linkages they form. Our findings suggest that larger firms are better able to identify relevant partners (Kaufmann and Tödling 1999) than SMEs. Larger firms, to a greater degree than SMEs, take part in systemic innovation, and location in an urban area (as the Oslo region) seems to affect the proportion of firms taking part in the innovation system.

Localisation in Oslo also has an effect on SMEs' networks, but not on all types of networks. Clients and customer linkages (vertical linkages) seem to be more prevalent than any other form of linkage, a result that supports the idea of the important role played by producer-customer relationships in innovation processes within SMEs (Sternberg 1999). These kinds of collaboration are often related to more incremental, 'step-by-step' innovations (Håkansson 1992), as opposed to radical innovations. Studies point to less innovative firms as mainly engaged in intra-regional customer-oriented networks (Koschatzky 1999), meaning that customer-oriented networks are not sufficient for firms to be innovative. Innovative networks are localised, but linked to transaction intensive relationships, such as suppliers and customers.

Our third hypothesis was whether proximity to important tacit-knowledge providers (like the scientific community) enhances the use of formal innovation collaboration with these actors. For SMEs, localisation seems to have an effect on their vertical innovation linkages, but little effect on the horizontal innovation linkages (HEI, Research institutes, Consultancy firms, etc). Thus, in order for SMEs to improve their innovation activity, horizontal linkages in particular would need to be strengthened. Innovation collaboration with partners on a horizontal dimension is more likely to lead to major steps forward (i.e., radical innovations), and it has also been argued that "the upgrading of the partners increases the efficiency of the whole network" (Leborgne and Lipietz 1992, p. 399).

Our findings indicate that spatial agglomerations are not in and of themselves as supportive for innovation as so far been assumed. Further, we conclude that the presence of certain actors within a region is not a sufficient condition for generating interactions between them, particularly in the case of SMEs and their links with the scientific community, which are perceived as being particularly important for innovation. Using other definitions of innovation could modify our conclusion. The Community Innovation Survey (CIS) uses a broad definition of innovation. Subsequent studies using a more narrow definition could be of interest in order to test our results. Further, by looking at a broader sample, also including firms with fewer than 10 employees would be of interest. Micro firms are often perceived as the most dynamic group of firms with regard to innovation and networking.

What, then, are the challenges and barriers for SMEs in order to be able to join these innovation-collaborations that may lead to leap-wise changes? The challenges are complex, and the answers are diverse. This paper has shown that there are obstacles to the formation of a regional innovation system for SMEs in the Oslo region. There is a potential for increasing the average innovation activity in the region by integrating SMEs into the regional and national system of innovation. There is a need for both SMEs and the regional innovation system to take a more interactive approach. The knowledge infrastructure in the Oslo region must be made more accessible and responsive to the individual and collective needs of SMEs located in the region, in order for SMEs to acquire formally codified knowledge available through the regional or even the national innovation systems. Regional innovation strategies should aim towards supporting and exploiting the knowledge capacity of innovative firms for regional development through a stronger integration of these companies into regional networking and value chains (Koschatzky 1999). In this way these innovation systems would become more accessible and responsive to the individual and collective needs of internationally competitive SMEs.

It is clear that any integrated approach to knowledge infrastructure will require organisational innovation within the public sector itself (Smith 1997). Norway has developed a regional policy that supports the economic development of regions *outside* the Oslo region. The policies of the Ministry of Trade and Industry and the Research Council contain no special policies aimed at exploiting the knowledge bases of the Oslo region above others, and they appear unwilling to build on areas of comparative advantage in this region. This fact appears to have resulted in a failure to capitalise on the full potential of the Oslo region (Stage 1 report. RITTS Oslo).

In our analysis we find that SMEs in the Oslo region need assistance to become fully integrated into the regional innovation system. Policy suggestions as a result of the industry studies could be summarised in 5 points:

1. SMEs find that there is a lack of transparency in the scientific community in the region that makes it difficult for them to approach the scientific community with their needs. Efforts should be made to develop an organisation in the region with responsibility for generating and distributing full information on what the 'supply side' in the region actually can offer, i.e., a 'one stop shop'.
2. Technology transfer programmes between R&D institutions and firms should focus on firms' *needs* for problem solving. It is important to improve the manner, and the extent to which, institutions work with companies. SMEs collaborating with regional research institutions use the institutions in different ways compared to the larger firms. SMEs tend to have low profile contact, for instance, utilisation of equipment and laboratories as well as diploma theses (Sternberg 1999), as opposed to formal R&D projects. For research institutes to take part in these kinds of collaborations, the means must be given to researchers to make such collaboration feasible for the institutions.

3. Regional innovation policy should improve the information-base for establishments in central regions regarding potential collaboration partners located in the vicinity of the firm (Koschatzky 1999). The explicit formation of networks or meeting places would be an important way of making firms aware *of other firms in the region*, and of establishing personal networks. Case studies from urban regions demonstrate that innovative firms also lack this kind of information, and sometimes co-operate over longer distances even though the same qualifications could be accessed "around the corner". Linking together similar industries could give industries power to lobby for R&D schemes that are relevant to the industry. One of the greatest factors hindering SMEs from engaging in R&D activity is the lack of finance for this kind of activity.

4. Efforts should be made to make actors within similar sectors in the region come together to discuss their actual competence needs. Networks between the educational institutions in the region and manufacturing industry should be established. Competence building through relocating academically trained workers to SMEs is important for the formation of networks with universities and other knowledge institutions.

5. A very important activity for firms to engage in is employee training. Firms are constantly required to accommodate new information, new technology and enhanced quality requirements, and this leads to strong training needs. Employee training courses that are offered in the region must be short and reasonably priced. Institutions offering such courses should also have the ambition, autonomy and financial ability to quickly respond to firms' demands.

References

Amin A, Cohendet P. (1999) Learning and adaption in decentralised business networks. Environment and Planning D 17: 87–104

Armstrong H, Taylor J (1993) Regional economics and Policy. Harvester Wheatsheaf, New York

Arnold E, Thuriaux B (1997) Supporting companies' technological capabilities. Tecnopolis Ltd., Brighton

Asheim B (1994) Regionale innovasjonssystem: Teknologipolitikk som regionalpolitikk. STEP-report 1994/18. Step Group, Oslo

Asheim B, Isaksen A (1996) Location, agglomeration and innovation: Towards regional innovation systems in Norway? STEP report 1996/13. Step Group, Oslo

Asheim B (1999) Innovation, social capital and regional clusters: on the importance of co-operation, interactive learning and localised knowledge in learning economies. Paper presented at the Regional Studies Association International Conference on Regional Potentials for an intergrating Europe, University of the Basque Country, Bilbao, Spain, September 18–21 1999

Aslesen HW, Braadland TE, Ekeland A, Orstavik F (1999a) Performance and co-operation in the Oslo-region business sector. Step-report 5/99. Step Group, Oslo

Aslesen, HW, Braadland TE, Hvidjensen L, Isaksen A, Orstavik F (1999b) Innovation, knowledge bases and clustering in selected industries in the Oslo-region. Step-report 4/99. Step Group, Oslo

Braczyk H-J, Cooke P, Heidenreich M (eds) (1998) Regional innovation systems. UCL Press, London

Breschi S, Lissoni F (2000) Knowledge spillovers and local innovation systems: A critical survey. Paper presented at the 40th European Congress of the Regional Science Association, Barcelona, Spain

Chinitz B (1961) Contrasts in agglomeration: New York and Pittsburg. American Economic Review 51: 12–27

Cooke P, Morgan K (1994). The creative Milieu: A regional perspective on innovation. In: Dodgson M, Rothwell R (ed) The handbook of industrial innovation. Edgar Elgar, Cheltenham

Edquist C (1997) Systems of innovation approaches: Their emergence and characteristics. In: Edquist C (ed) Systems of innovation: Technologies, institutions and organisations. Pinter, London

Fischer MM (2000) Innovation, knowledge creation and systems of innovation. Paper presented at the 40th European Congress of the Regional Science Association, Barcelona, Spain

Forray D, Lundvall B-A (1996) The knowledge-based economy: from the economics of knowledge from the learning economy. In: OECD (ed) Employment and growth in the knowledge based-based economy. OECD, Paris, pp 11–32

Glaeser E, Kallal H, Scheinkman J, Shleifer A (1992). Growth of cities. Journal of Political Economy 100: 1126–1152

Gregersen B, Johnson B (1997). Learning economics, innovation systems and European integration. Regional Studies 31: 479–490

Hoover EM (1937). The measurement of industrial location. Review of Economics and Statistics 17: 162–171

Hoover EM (1971) An introduction to regional economics. Knopf, New York

Hudson R (1999) The learning economy, the learning firm and the learning region: A sympathetic critique of the limits to learning. European Urban and Regional Studies 6: 59–72

Håkansson H (1992) Corporate technological behaviour. Co-operation and networks. Routledge, London

Halvorsen K (2000) RITTS-Oslo Stage 1 Report. Oslo Business Region.

Isaksen A, Spilling (1996) Regional utvikling og små bedrifter. HøyskoleForlaget, Kristiansand

Isard W (1956) Location and space-economy. A general theory relating to industrial location, market areas, land use, trade and urban structure. MIT Press, Cambridge

Isard W, Schooler EW, Vietorisz T (1959). Industrial complex analysis and regional development. Wiley, New York

Kaufmann A, Tödling F (1999) Innovation systems in regions of Europe – A comparative perspective. European Planning Studies 7: 699–717

Kaufmann A, Tödling F (2000) Systems of innovation in traditional industrial regions. The case of Styria in a comparative perspective. Regional Studies 34: 29–40

Koschatzky K (1998) Firms innovation and region: The role of space in innovation processes. International Journal of Innovation Management 2: 383–408

Koschatzky K (1999) Innovation networks of industry and business-related services-Relations between innovation intensity of firms and regional inter-firm cooperation. European Planning Studies 7: pp 737–759

Leborgne D, Lipietz A (1992) Conceptual fallacies and open questions on Post-Fordism. In: Storper M, Scott AJ (eds) Pathways to industrialisation and regional development. Routledge, London, pp 332–348

Lundvall B-Å (1992) Introduction. In: Lundvall B-Å (ed) Systems of innovations. Pinter Publishers, London, pp 1–19

Lundvall B-Å, Borras S (1999) The globalising learning economy: Implications for innovation policy. Office for Official Publications of the European Communities, Luxembourg

Morgan K (1997). The learning region: Institutions, innovation and regional renewal. Regional Studies 31: 491–503

Nelson RR (Ed.). (1993). National innovation systems: A comparative analysis. Oxford University Press, Oxford

Noisi J, Saviotti P, Bellon B, Crow M (1993) National systems of innovation: In search of a workable concept. Technology in Society 15: 207–227

OECD (1992) Technology and the economy; the key relationships. Report of the group of experts of the Technology/Economy Programme, OECD, Paris

Rothwell R (1994) Issues in user-producer relations in the innovation process: the role of the government. International Journal of Technology Management 9: 629–649

Rutten R, Boekema F (2000) Developments in learning regions: Theory and practice from a Dutch case. Paper presented at the 40th European Congress of the Regional Science Association, Barcelona, Spain

Smith K (1997) Economic infrastructure and innovation systems. In: Edquist C (ed) Systems of innovation: Technologies, institutions and organizations. Pinter, London, pp 86–106

Sternberg R (1999) Innovative linkages and proximity: Empirical results from recent surveys of small and medium sized firms in German regions. Regional Studies 33: 529-541

Storper M (1997) The regional world; Territorial development in a global world. The Guilford Press, London

18 Innovation and Firm Location in the Spanish Medical Instruments Industry

Manuela P. Pérez and Angel M. Sánchez

Centro Politécnico Superior, University of Zaragoza, Spain

18.1 Introduction

Over the past twenty years a considerable amount of empirical evidence of one sort or another has been amassed which demonstrates that the processes of innovation and technological change are spatially differentiated, both regionally within states and internationally between nations (Harris 1988). Similarly, empirical evidence around the world has demonstrated the interrelation between economic growth and technological change on a national scale and even at regional level. In that sense it can be argued that activities related to technological innovation are a key factor in regional development (Stohr 1988). Economic growth and prosperity are materialised through the creation of new activities originated in firms by innovative managers. If the firm creates its own technology, or incorporates it exogeneously, this will result in an increase in its competitiveness. When this happens simultaneously in a group of firms located in a particular area the combined effects may contribute to a spatial dynamism and development of the area.

High technology industries are one of a region's assets in achieving desired economic growth. During the 1970s and 1980s several agglomerations of 'hi-tech' companies – software, telecommunications, biotechnology, etc. – developed in many 'Silicon Valleys' around the world. At the same time, regional governments from industrialised countries supported the exogenous and endogenous regional development of these companies within Technology Parks and Innovation Centres (Castells and Hall 1994). Some of these 'hi-tech' companies have exhibited spectacular rates of growth in employment, sales, exports and assets. At the same time, the geographical areas in which 'hi-tech' firms are important have also exhibited in some countries major indirect employment creation in the business and consumer service sectors. For example, the experience of some Japanese Technopolis in prefectures away from Tokyo indicates that the development of 'hi-tech' companies in peripheral regions has reduced the regional differences in production and employment (Stohr and Ponighaus 1992). There is also the role of 'hi-tech' firms in industrial networks, in which they are thought to contribute to the transfer of technologies and to strengthen the technology level of other companies (Autio 1997).

'Hi-tech' industries are usually defined as those which simultaneously invest more resources in research and development (R&D), employ higher percentages of qualified personnel, and produce goods and services which are more innovative and with a shorter life cycle than the average industry. One of the industries with these characteristics in the US and Europe is the medical equipment industry. This industry develops and manufactures the instruments and equipment used by physicians and nurses in hospitals, clinics and primary care centres. Besides being a key technological element in the Health Care system, the medical equipment industry also exhibits high growth rates because the population of industrialised countries is rapidly ageing and demanding better health care. Medical equipment companies are also attracted towards medical complexes than can function as a growth pole for some urban economies (Van den Berg and Van Klink 1996).

The largest medical equipment industry is in the United States. In the European Union there are about some 5,000 manufacturers, employing some 240,000 persons; Germany is the largest European supplier and accounts for 40% of the production and 54% of the value added. Other important European manufacturers are located in France, the United Kingdom and Sweden. The medical equipment industry shows a high degree of spatial concentration. For example, agglomerations of medical equipment companies are found in the south-east of England, the surroundings of Paris, or near the scientific universities of Lund in Sweden.

In spite of the importance of the medical equipment industry, there are almost no studies that analyse the factors determining the spatial concentration of innovative activities within this industry. This paper wants to contribute to the research area of regional development and technological change, and studies the degree of spatial concentration of economic and patenting activities in the Spanish medical equipment industry. The paper is structured in the following way. The second section shows the spatial distribution of economic and patenting activities in the 1979–95 period. The third section offers an approach to the factors determining the spatial distribution of medical equipment's patenting activities, and discusses the results from an empirical study. Finally, some conclusions are included.

18.2 Distribution and Degree of Spatial Concentration of Economic and Patenting Activities in the Spanish Medical Equipment Industry

The Spanish economy has traditionally been characterised by a concentration of economic activity in the two large metropolitan areas (Madrid and Barcelona), which in 1995 accounted for 35% of the total Gross Domestic Product. The rest of the Mediterranean area is of secondary importance with a few exceptions, mainly Valencia and Alicante, as is the Basque Country. One might add a few other provinces which have also maintained a high level of growth (Zaragoza, Navarra and Seville) but the rest of the country, with a few rare exceptions, does not possess a sufficiently high level of economic activity to be worth mentioning.

'Hi-tech' activities are concentrated in a few Spanish regions. In 1998, three out of seventeen regions accounted for 63.6% of total Spanish R&D expenditures (Madrid 30.9%, Catalonia 22.8%, and Andalucia 9.9%). The industrial innovative activities are also spatially concentrated because three regions accounted for 58% of innovative expenditures in the Spanish industry in 1997: Catalonia (25.3%), Madrid (22.4%) and the Basque Country (10.3%). Regarding to the Spanish 'hi-tech' industries, all studies show that the medical equipment industry has been one of them for the last fifteen years (e.g., Giraldez 1988; Crespo and Velazquez 1999).

The Spanish share of the European medical equipment market in 1997 was 10.9% of consumption, but only 5% of production and 3% of value added. The Spanish market relies heavily on imports from Europe and the US because only half of the Spanish market is supplied by firms located in Spain. A study of the Spanish foreign trade revealed that Spanish imports of medical equipment exceeded exports in each singular product in the period 1985–95 (Martínez and Urbina 1998). Table 18.1 shows some descriptive statistics of the Spanish medical equipment industry in the 1993–98 period and its comparison to the whole Spanish industry.

This section of the paper deals with the degree of spatial concentration of economic and innovative activities in the Spanish medical equipment industry. One straightforward measure of economic concentration is the regional or local distribution of firms and employment. Therefore, Table 18.2 indicates the provincial location of Spanish medical equipment manufacturers in 1998, and as can be observed, two provinces – Barcelona and Madrid – concentrated 76.7% of manufacturing firms and 79.5% of manufacturing employment in the medical equipment industry. The rest of Spanish manufacturing companies are relatively evenly distributed among other provinces. The concentration of medical equipment companies and employment is much higher than the total employment industry concentration as the last column shows in Table 18.2.

Table 18.1. The Spanish Medical Equipment Industry

	1993		1995		1998	
	MED	IND	MED	IND	MED	IND
Sales per employee	8,059	15,680	8,972	19,829	10,830	22,825
Investment per employee	317	759	353	870	473	1,089
Employees per company	7.0	14.9	7.5	15.6	7.7	15.7
% of firms with less than 20 employees	n.a.	n.a.	93.1	87.4	94.8	86.6
Hourly employee cost	1,409	1,897	1,477	1,983	1,564	2,116
Cost by employee	2,492	3,312	2,611	3,467	2,790	3,721
% employees in total industry	0.38	100	0.36	100	0.42	100
% sales in total industry	0.19	100	0.16	100	0.20	100

Notes: MED: Medical equipment industry; IND:= Total Spanish Industry. Economic figures in national currency (thousand). n.a: not available. Source: Spanish Industrial Survey. National Institute of Statistics.

Table 18.2. Province Distribution of Companies and Employment in the Spanish Medical Equipment Industry

Spanish province	Number of manufacturers	% in total	Employees	% in total	% total industry employment
Barcelona	231	48.7	6,804	53.8	16.1
Madrid	133	28.0	3,258	25.7	10.8
Valencia	26	5.5	542	4.3	6.6
Asturias	8	1.6	120	0.9	2.2
Alicante	7	1.5	227	1.8	4.8
Navarra	7	1.5	174	1.3	2.5
Guipuzcoa	6	1.2	268	2.1	3.9
Sevilla	6	1.2	152	1.2	2.9
Gerona	5	1.1	273	2.2	2.5
Vizcaya	5	1.1	100	0.8	3.1
Other provinces	40	8.6	730	7.1	44.6
Total	474	100.0	12,648	100.0	100.0

Source: Own elaboration

However the degree of spatial concentration of medical equipment manufacturers is even greater when only the 'hi-tech' products are considered (Table 18.3) because all were located in Madrid or Barcelona. Even when the analysis includes the main and most used medical equipment such as monitoring or diagnosis, the degree of spatial concentration of manufacturers in Madrid is over 50% in most equipment and more than 30% in Barcelona. With the exception of the Community of Valencia, the other provinces must rely on distributors and sales representatives to buy medical equipment.

Table 18.3. Province Distribution of Manufacturers and Commercial Firms of 'High Tech' Medical Equipment

	Manufacturers	Distributors	Importers	Services
Madrid	6	8	10	1
Barcelona	3	8	11	2
Valencia	–	1	–	–
Other provinces	–	6	–	–
Total	9	23	21	3

Notes: Other provinces are Las Palmas with two companies, and La Coruña, Navarra, Toledo and San Sebastian with one company each. Source: Own elaboration

The second spatial dimension analysed in this paper is the distribution of technological activities. However, although the question of how to measure technological change has concerned economists for a long time, no widely accepted procedure has been developed so far. Much of the technological change is the product of R&D activities and one of the few direct reflections of the output of R&D activities is the number and kind of patents applied for or granted to different firms (Griliches 1990). The number of inventions that have been patented is probably the most widely used proxy measure of innovative activity though patents are a flawed measure of innovative activity. The major problems with patents are that not all inventions are patented and that not all patented inventions will become innovations and successful products. In addition, patents differ in their economic impact. The quantity and quality of patenting may depend on chance, how readily a technology leads itself to patent protection and business decision-makers' varying perceptions of how much advantage they will derive from patent rights. Surveys of firms in the US and in Europe give evidence that the percentage of innovations that are patented vary by sector (Arundel and Kabla 1998).

In spite of the previous considerations, many authors have used patent data as an output indicator of the technological activities that are converted in products and process innovations (i.e., Ernst 1997). Similarly we have used the CIBEPAT database of the Spanish Patent Office to assess the degree of spatial concentration of the technological activities in the Spanish medical equipment industry. The study includes all patents and utility models granted to Spanish residents in the 1979–1995 period. Both patents and utility models have been included in the analysis because both are results of technological activities carried out at a firm or R&D centre. The difference between a patent and a utility model lies in the period granted to the applicant, which is 20 years to a patent but only 10 years to a utility model, and in the innovativeness degree which it is smaller in an utility model than in a patent. The period of study begins in 1979 because the CIBEPAT database did not include information on the province of residence of the applicants before that year. The study ends in 1995 because there is a few years' time lag between a patent or a utility model application and when it is later granted, and we wanted to make sure that at least all patents granted in 1995 were included in the study.

Table 18.4 shows that 38.8% of patents and utility models of medical equipment inventions have been granted to residents of Catalonia, 24.3% to residents of Madrid and 11.5% to residents of the Community of Valencia. These three regions concentrated 75% of the protected innovations developed during the 1979–95 period, a higher degree of concentration than all the industrial patents in Spain (Coronado and Acosta 1997). But if we take into account only the patents granted to firms – and we exclude patents granted to individuals or institutions – the degree of spatial concentration is even higher because Madrid, Catalonia and the Community of Valencia account for 84.3% of patents and 86.6% of utility models granted to firms in the 1979–95 period.

This high degree of spatial concentration in the number of patents and utility models is similar to the concentration of the R&D expenditures in medical and health related activities in Spain. Table 18.5 shows that these three regions – Catalonia (basically the province of Barcelona), Madrid and the Community of Valencia (mainly the province of Valencia) – concentrated 86.4% of firms and 85.7% of employment in the medical equipment industry, and 69.1% of the R&D expenditures in medical and health activities.

Table 18.4. Regional Distribution of Patents and Utility Models Granted to Spanish Residents in the 1979–95 Period for Medical Equipment Inventions

Spanish region	Number of patents	% in total	Number of utility models	% in total	Number of firm patents	Number of firm utility models
Andalucia	36	5.0	68	3.7	6	12
Aragón	24	3.3	67	3.7	10	17
Asturias	7	1.0	38	2.1	0	9
Baleares	8	1.1	17	0.9	2	4
Canarias	14	1.9	23	1.3	1	0
Cantabria	1	0.1	6	0.3	0	0
Castilla-La Mancha	7	1.0	5	0.3	0	1
Castilla-León	2	0.3	37	2.0	1	3
Catalonia	280	40.0	697	38.7	107	267
Extremadura	5	0.7	14	0.8	0	2
Galicia	17	2.3	25	1.4	1	1
Madrid	152	21.1	461	25.6	35	168
Murcia	9	1.2	25	1.4	0	4
Navarra	24	3.3	16	0.9	6	6
Basque Country	25	3.4	109	6.1	5	17
La Rioja	3	0.4	5	0.3	0	0
Valencia	104	14.4	185	10.2	30	57
Total	718	100.0	1798	100.0	204	568

Notes: The codes of the International Classification of Patents included in the study are: A61B, A61C, A61D, A61F, A61G, A61H, A61J, A61K, A61L, A61M, A61N, H04R25/00, H01J35/00, H05G2/00, and G02C.

Table 18.5. Spatial Concentration of Production and Technology in the Spanish Medical Equipment

Spanish region	% Manufacturers	% Employment	% R&D in Medical Sciences	% Patents	% Utility Models
Catalonia	51.2	53.8	27.1	40.0	38.7
Madrid	28.0	25.7	34.3	21.1	25.6
Com. of Valencia	7.2	6.2	7.7	14.4	10.2
Total 3 regions	86.4	85.7	69.1	74.6	74.7

Notes and sources: The percentages are of the national total for each variable. The R&D data in medical sciences are from the period 1983–95 and come from the Annual Reports of the National Health and Pharmacy Plans. The data on patents and utility models are from the period 1979–95.

Table 18.6 shows the Patenting Index (PI) and the Relative Technological Advantage (RTA) of each Spanish region in medical equipment products. The Patenting Index is defined as the number of patents granted by million of inhabitants. Two Patenting ratios have been calculated: the first ratio (PI1) only includes patent data while the second ratio (PI2) also includes utility model data. For the first index Navarra has the largest value (46.1 patent per million of inhabitants), followed by Catalonia (45.9) and Madrid (30.2), and the lowest values are for Cantabria (1.9) and Castilla-León (0.8). The second Index gives the largest value to Catalonia (160.4 patent and models by million of inhabitants), followed by Madrid (122) and Navarra (76.9), while the lowest values are for Cantabria (13.2) and Castilla-La Mancha (7.2).

Table 18.6. Patenting Index (PI) and the Relative Technological Advantage (RTA)

Spanish region	% total patents	PI1	PI2	RTA1	RTA2
Andalucia	3.3	4.9	14.4	1.08	1.24
Aragón	3.4	20.2	76.6	1.11	1.05
Asturias	2.6	6.4	41.3	0.86	0.42
Baleares	4.5	10.5	32.9	1.49	1.46
Canarias	8.1	8.7	23.0	2.66	1.67
Cantabria	0.7	1.9	13.2	0.22	0
Castilla-La Mancha	2.5	4.1	7.0	0.82	0
Castilla-León	0.5	0.8	15.5	0.17	0.39
Catalonia	3.1	45.9	160.4	0.98	1.21
Extremadura	6.4	4.6	17.7	2.10	0
Galicia	5.0	6.2	15.3	1.64	2.96
Madrid	2.6	30.2	122.0	0.85	0.63
Murcia	3.5	8.2	31.0	1.16	3.71
Navarra	4.2	46.1	76.9	1.37	1.04
Basque Country	1.5	11.9	63.8	0.48	0.23
La Rioja	2.7	11.3	30.3	0.89	0
Com. of Valencia	4.9	25.9	72.0	1.61	1.74
Spain	100.0	18.1	63.4	0.87	0.79

Notes: The percentage of patents means the ratio of medical equipment patents on the total patents granted to residents in that region. Two Patenting ratios have been considered. PI1 has been calculated as the number of patents granted in the 1979–1995 period to Spanish residents in the medical equipment sector per million of inhabitants. PI2 also includes the utility models. The Relative Technological Advantage RTA is the ratio between the national and regional percentage of the patents granted to medical equipment and the total number of patents in each region. There are two RTA ratios: RTA1 includes all patents while RTA2 only includes patents granted to companies and institutions. Source: Own production

Table 18.6 also shows the percentage of medical equipment patents on the total patents granted to residents in each region. The national average is 3%, which means that 3% of the patents granted to Spanish residents between 1979 and 1995 were for inventions related to medical equipment. Ten out of seventeen Spanish regions have higher percentages than national average, which indicates that those regions have some degree of patenting specialisation in medical equipment in comparison to patenting in other activities.

18.3 Factors Determining the Spatial Distribution of Medical Equipment Patenting Activities

Any explanation of the patenting activities of industrial firms has to be based on an understanding of the determinants influencing this behaviour (Fischer et al. 1994). In this section elements from different theoretical contributions and empirical studies will be drawn into a conceptual framework for analysing determinants that may explain the spatial patenting in the medical equipment industry. Four factors have been analysed: firm size, proximity to medical activities, agglomeration, and networking.

18.3.1 Firm Size

The relationship between firm size and invention/innovation has been a matter of long-standing debate (Rothwell and Dodgson 1994; Dijk et al. 1997). Some scholars argue that large size favours invention because larger firms have a greater capacity to raise capital, manage information, maintain large R&D facilities and attract the best technical specialists. However, other scholars (i.e., Rothwell and Zegveld 1982) stress the importance of smaller firms, especially of 'hi-tech' firms, in the process of technological change due to their greater flexibility to adapt to changes in external environments (Nooteboom 1994; Rothwell 1991). Besides, small firms explore more technological areas by innovation in less 'crowded' areas, and are tied into regional knowledge networks to a greater extent than large firms (Almeida and Kogut 1997).

The development of medical equipment requires different technical capabilities. While it is possible to develop and manufacture surgical instruments in a very small 'hi-tech' firm, other medical equipment such as a magnetic resonance equipment demands large technical resources which are only available at large firms. Nevertheless an analysis of the Spanish foreign trade of medical equipment revealed that the deficit is greater in the 'hi-tech' small instruments than in the larger and more traditional equipment (Martínez and Urbina 1998). Therefore we establish the following hypothesis:

> H1 – Patent intensity at regional (province) level is positively correlated with average firm size in the medical equipment industry.

18.3.2 Proximity to Medical Activities

The second determinant of regional (province) patenting activities included in this analysis is the local proximity to medical equipment users. The development of medical equipment requires a close user-manufacturer interaction between scientists and engineers in the medical equipment companies and physicians and nurses in the hospitals and clinics (Mitchell 1991). For example, Lotz (1991) found that, in the Danish medical equipment industry, science appears predominantly in the user-environment and as a result, invention is fuelled by specific requirements from physicians and by new medical knowledge. Shaw (1998) also found in a study of new product development in the UK medical equipment industry that there was a continuous interaction during all the 10 stages in the innovation cycle identified, resulting in 65% of these innovations being commercially successful. This interaction occurred in part because one major element in the innovation process for medical equipment which tends to make this process unique is the requirement that any equipment that is to be potentially introduced into clinical use first needs extensive clinical assessment and trial because human life may be at risk.

The scientists and engineers then work together with the user in an attempt to test out the conceptual basis of their solution to the need normally in the form of a hand-built prototype. Dependent upon the perceived degree of output-embodied benefit arising from being involved in the further process of innovation, the user could then be involved in the development, testing and evaluation of the prototypes and final products, making marketing assessments, joint specifications, involvement in the market launch, marketing, and the diffusion of the innovation. Therefore we expect that:

> H2 – Local proximity to medical activities is positively correlated with patenting intensity at the regional level.

18.3.3 Agglomeration of Technological Activities

The third determinant of patenting is the agglomeration of economic and technical activities. The advantages of agglomeration for 'hi-tech' companies have traditionally been claimed by supporters of the location theory on the basis of external economies of scale, i.e., access to R&D facilities, skilled labour force, research universities, and high levels of information (Kleinknecht and Poot 1992; Mustar 1997). The experience indicates that agglomeration and technological externalities are important factors in the early years of a 'hi-tech' complex. For example, in the Technopolis of Cambridge (United Kingdom) Segal et al. (1985) estimated that 12% of the early 'hi-tech' companies were spin-offs from the University of Cambridge and that most of the other companies were spin-offs from the university spin-offs.

However, once this early stage of agglomeration is over, the closeness to the university or to the initial agglomeration of 'hi-tech' companies becomes less important. For example, in Cambridge currently only 10% of the 'hi-tech' companies are located in the Technology Park that was the nucleus of the early agglomeration. This and other evidence suggests that we must think at least in regional terms if we want to analyse technological complexes (Vedovello 1997; Westhead 1997). Besides, since urban agglomeration is an indicator of economic and technological concentration we would expect to find a positive relationship at the regional level between patenting and technological agglomeration.

H3 – Patenting in the medical equipment industry is positively correlated to the agglomeration of technological activities.

18.3.4 Information and Communication Technologies for Networking

Scientific research increasingly depends on network linkages and information diffusion. The emergence of institutional or informal networks, formed by clusters,
groups or vertical associations of firms, appears to be one major feature of the
contemporary industrial economy indicated by the application of Information and
Communication Technologies (ICT). These resources are needed for investing co-
operatively in the creation of new knowledge (R&D, design, engineering), and for
the external introduction of new knowledge through innovation acquisition, adaptation, and implementation (Belussi and Arcangeli 1998). Brouwer and Kleinknecht (1999) found that R&D collaborators have a much higher propensity to patent their innovations, since they want to protect their most precious findings
before they lay them open for their collaboration partners. This result would suggest that networking promotes patenting and we should include a measure of networking as an explanatory variable on our study. However, even though much
networking goes via personal and informal contacts, we believe that easy communication is a condition for keeping up those informal contacts by phone and e-
mail.

The major bottlenecks for small firms in peripheral regions, which are poor in
terms of the infrastructure and other factors needed for innovation projects, are
found in the areas of human capital, information provision and risk capital. However, 'hi-tech' regions sustain their competitive advantage in their capacity for
continuous learning and innovation (Lawson and Lorenz 1999). Larger firms and
particularly multi-site establishments may overcome those barriers more easily,
but small firms in peripheral regions may be at a great disadvantage to innovate
due to the underdevelopment of information resources. Therefore we would expect to find a positive correlation between the use of ICT and medical equipment
patenting at a regional (province) level.

Although the use of ICT in medical equipment industries themselves could be
analysed, the hypothesis is established between patenting and the use of ICT at the
regional (province) level. The intensity of use of information technologies is rather
high in agglomerations and therefore patenting in any industry may perform more
efficiently because companies and other agents may have access to patent databases. This relationship has not been tested before and it could be a weak one but
empirical evidence shows that technological activities may benefit from the use of
information technologies. Therefore we establish the following hypothesis:

H4 – Patenting in the medical equipment industry is positively correlated at the regional (province) level with the use of Information
and Communication Technologies.

18.4 Empirical Results and Discussion

To explain the spatial distribution of innovative activities in the medical equipment industry we have carried out a regression analysis by OLS using regional patents and utility models granted to Spanish residents. The dependent variables used for the study have been two: the number of patents and utility models by employee granted to Spanish firms (PTMEH), and the number of patents and utility models by inhabitant granted to firms, institutions and individuals in that region (PI2). Both variables are for the 1979–95 period and are related to patenting by industrial companies (PTMEH) and patenting by all economic agents (PI2). Two analyses have been made for each variable at both the province and the regional level. The independent variables used have been:

- SIZE: average number of employees per firm in the regional (province) medical equipment industry.
- BEDS: number of beds in regional (province) hospitals and clinics. A large number of beds is an indicator of a greater demand for medical equipment but also of a greater specialisation and qualification of physicians than at regions with smaller hospitals.
- CONC: regional (province) distribution of total R&D and technological expenditures.
- INFOR: regional (province) number of telephone lines.

Table 18.7 indicates the descriptive statistics and correlations of the independent variables. The values of the independent variables are the average for years 1990 and 1995 which were the data available for this study during the period 1979–95 of patenting activities. There is no colinearity among these variables. Then, Tables 18.8 and 18.9 show the results of the regression analysis for each dependent variable. Both are explained at 70% by the model which indicates that the approach developed in this paper is valid for both firms' and total patenting at regional and province level. Durbin-Watson statistics in all models are around 2 which means that residuals are not correlated and neither are the observations.

Table 18.7. Descriptive Statistics and Correlations Matrix

	Mean	SD	1	2	3
1. SIZE	24.3	30.9			
2. BEDS	4246.3	598.0	−0.018		
3. CONC	5.5	8.1	−0.008	0.125	
4. INFOR	37.1	5.4	−0.009	0.324	0.378

Source: Own production

At the regional level (Table 18.8), the variable CONC is statistically significant at the 99% level and the variable INFOR at the 95% level. The variables SIZE and BEDS behave as expected but they are not statistically significant. The region as a unit of analysis may be a rough level of aggregation. The results of the model at the province level (Table 18.9) indicate that INFOR is the most explanatory variable for both PTMEH and PI2 at the 99.9 level, and that CONC is also significant but at a lower level. Both results from Tables 18.8 and 18.9 support the third and fourth hypotheses of the paper. But now, the variable BEDS also becomes significant at the 99% level for the total number of patents and utility models. This result supports the second hypothesis of the paper: the propensity to patenting in medical equipment is higher in those provinces with a higher ratio of the number of beds in hospitals per inhabitant. Nevertheless patenting by manufacturing companies is not explained by the agglomeration of medical activities. This suggests limits in the role that agglomeration plays in this industry's innovation activities.

Table 18.8. Explanatory Model of Regional Patenting of Medical Equipment by Manufacturing Firms (PTMEH) and by Firms, Individuals and Institutions (PI2)

	PTMEH	PI2
Constant	-50.5^{**}	-129.9^{**}
	(2.38)	(2.49)
CONC	1.12^{***}	2.82^{***}
	(3.65)	(3.86)
INFOR	0.92^{*}	2.73^{**}
	(1.79)	(2.31)
SIZE	0.11	0.22
	(1.01)	(1.18)
BEDS	0.005	0.01
	(0.98)	(1.15)
	$R = 0.845$; $R^2 = 0.719$; $\Delta R^2 = 0.623$; $F=8.045$; $p=0.002$; $n=17$; Durbin-Watson = 2.15	$R = 0.864$; $R^2 = 0.759$; $\Delta R^2 = 0.673$; $F=9.623$; $p=0.001$; $n=17$; Durbin-Watson = 1.95

Notes: PTMEH – Number of regional patents and utility models granted to Spanish firms per million of employees. PI2 – Number of regional patents and utility models granted to firms, individuals and institutions per million of inhabitants. INFOR – Number of phone lines per inhabitant. BEDS – Number of beds in clinics and hospitals. SIZE – Average number of employees by medical equipment manufacturing firm. CONC – Regional distribution of R&D and technological expenditures. t-values are between brackets; * $p<0.1$, ** $p<0.05$, *** $p<0.01$. Source: Own production

Both models at the regional and province level indicate that CONC and INFOR are the most explanatory variables. This result enables us to explore a further argument within this paper, concerning the spatial distribution of medical equipment activities. Market and technological information are the main inputs of any 'hi-tech' activity, which are not always restricted within any specific region. Many 'hi-tech' companies have networks with companies and R&D centres around the world. Similarly, a few studies have evidenced that a 'hi-tech' company may locate in regions with no labour or raw materials agglomeration, as long as the already existing infrastructure – universities, telecommunications, etc. – does not prevent the new 'hi-tech' company from surviving after its initial location (Oakey and Cooper 1989; Martínez 1992). Some studies (i.e., Karlsson and Olsson 1998) even show that peripheral regions are able to provide an innovative environment for small firms, whereas large firms need the richer environment offered by the core regions. Therefore smaller firms may be early adopters of new technologies even if they are located away from large urban agglomerations.

However, patenting activities are concentrated in large urban agglomerations. The paper's results indicate that patenting in the medical equipment industry is strongly located in Spanish core regions. Therefore new companies should be hard to find outside these core regions. But a few studies (Oakey and Cooper 1989; Martinez 1992) show that peripheral regions may develop small 'hi-tech' sectors when the two following conditions are, at least, fulfilled: that the company's entrepreneur has strong personal links within that region and assumes its lack of industrial services; and that the type of production of the company is economically feasible in that region. Even if there are few industrial services available, as long as the type of product or production are not in need of agglomeration economies with other 'hi-tech' companies, it is possible for a 'hi-tech' company to locate in a peripheral region when the distance to its markets is not an economic disadvantage. While such firms may encounter greater environmental constraints as they grow than their counterparts in core regions, these very constraints may in fact stimulate greater pro-active entrepreneurial behaviour that in turns renders the firm more competitive in wider markets. Although fewer small firms may be successful in peripheral environments, those that are may prove to be even more competitive than the average small firm in core regions which has not had to overcome environmental and resource constraints to the same degree (Vaessen and Keeble 1995).

Table 18.9. Explanatory Model of Province Patenting of Medical Equipment by Manufacturing Firms (PTMEH) and by Firms, Individuals and Institutions (PI2)

	PTMEH	PI2
Constant	-0.033^{****}	-0.14^{****}
	(5.34)	(6.09)
INFOR	0.019^{****}	0.045^{****}
	(6.29)	(7.17)
CONC	0.001^{****}	0.001^{*}
	(4.45)	(1.96)
BEDS	-0.001	0.002^{***}
	(0.98)	(3.28)
SIZE	-0.004	0.013
	(0.27)	(0.21)
	$R=0.835$; $R^2 = 0.692$; $\Delta R^2 = 0.665$; $F = 25.08$; $p=0.000$; $n=50$; Durbin-Watson = 1.78	$R=0.829$; $R^2=0.681$; $\Delta R^2=0.652$; $F=23.71$; $p=0.000$; $n=50$; Durbin-Watson = 1.50

Notes: PTMEH – Number of province patents and utility models granted to Spanish firms per million of inhabitants. PI2 – Number of province patents and utility models granted to firms, individuals and institutions per million of inhabitants. INFOR – Number of phone lines per inhabitant. BEDS – Number of beds in clinics and hospitals. SIZE – Average number of employees by medical equipment manufacturing firm. CONC – Province distribution of R&D and technological expenditures. t-values are between brackets; * $p<0.1$, *** $p<0.01$, **** $p<0.001$. Source: Own production

This is the case for many medical equipment products because they have high value added but low weight per unit. Therefore it would be feasible that a new medical equipment company may locate out of the agglomeration zones. Table 18.10 shows the regional distribution of the new medical equipment companies located in Spanish Technology Parks and Business Innovation Centres.

Table 18.10. Regional Distribution of Spanish Medical Equipment Companies Located at Technology Parks and Business Innovation Centres

Andalucia	5
Aragón	2
Basque Country	2
Catalonia	3
Community of Valencia	1
Galicia	2
Navarra	1
Total firms	17

Source: Own production

These companies are developing medical equipment of high technological content and many of them are spin-offs from companies and universities. For example, the two companies located in the Business Innovation Centre of Aragon are spin-offs from research projects, one from a university department and the other from a medical instruments company. The degree of spatial concentration indicated in Table 18.10 is very low in comparison with the distribution of medical equipment manufacturers (Table 18.2), which had 80% of firms and employment located in only two provinces. These companies have used the regional services available at the Business Innovation Centres to patent these technological developments. Access to internal services greatly simplifies the administrative process of patenting. It is not possible to forecast future decentralisation of new Spanish medical equipment companies and therefore data from Table 18.10 do not imply any changes in the previous conclusions. Even though a few new medical equipment companies have been established away from core regions, patenting is still strongly concentrated in a few central regions. Then this argument about patenting, location and peripheral regions shall be further analysed in future studies when more data are already available.

18.5 Conclusion

In this paper we have carried out an analysis of the spatial distribution of innovative technology in the medical equipment industry using patents granted as an indicator. The spatial distribution of the results of the technological process (patent grants per region or province of residence of the first applicant) shows a polarisation towards the two large urban agglomerations of Barcelona and Madrid, while the rest is shared by the Community of Valencia and the Basque Country.

The spatial distribution of patenting has been found to be positively correlated with the concentration of technological activities and medical facilities. However, at the province level the analysis has found that use of information technologies and proximity to medical facilities are more important for patenting than the concentration of technological activities, which allows for the possibility that small 'hi-tech' medical equipment firms may develop and locate in peripheral provinces. Due to low transportation costs of most of medical instruments to their markets, some industrial and university spin-offs have developed and located in Innovation Centres and Technology Parks around the country.

References

Almeida P, Kogut B (1997) The exploration of technological diversity and the geographic localization of innovation. Small Business Economics 9: 21–31

Arundel A, Kabla I (1998) What percentage of innovations are patented? Empirical estimates for European firms. Research Policy 27: 127–141

Autio E (1997) New, technology-based firms in innovation networks symplectic and generative impacts. Research Policy 26: 263–281

Belussi F, Arcangeli F (1998) A typology of networks: flexible and evolutionary firms. Research Policy 27: 415–428

Brouwer E, Kleinknecht A (1999) Innovative output, and a firm's propensity to patent: An exploration of CIS micro data. Research Policy 28: 615–624

Castells M, Hall P (1994) Technopoles of the world – The making of 21st century industrial complexes. Routledge Publishers, London

Coronado D, Acosta M (1997) Spatial distribution of patents in Spain: Determining factors and consequences on regional development. Regional Studies 31: 381–390

Crespo J, Velazquez F (1999) Principales rasgos de los sectores innovadores en España. Papeles de Economía Española 81: 104–113

Dijk B, Fröhlich J, Gassler H (1997) Some new evidence on the determinants of large and small firm innovation. Small Business Economics 9: 335–343

Ernst (1997) The use of patent data for technological forecasting: the diffusion of CNC-technology in the machine tool industry. Small Business Economics 9: 361–381

Fischer MM, den Hertog R, Menkveld B, Thuzik R (1994) An exploration into the determinants of patent activities: some empirical evidence for Austria. Regional Studies 28: 1–12

Furio E (1996) Desarrollo territorial y procesos de innovación: Los milieux innovateurs. Estudios Territoriales 28: 639–649

Giraldez E (1988) Comportamiento inversor de los sectores de alta tecnología, 1975–1985. Papeles de Economía Española 34: 431–353

Griliches Z (1990) Patent statistics as economic indicators: A survey. Journal of Economic Literature 28: 1661–1707

Harris R (1988) Technological change and regional development in the UK: Evidence from the SPRU database on innovation. Regional Studies 22: 361–374

Karlsson C, Olsson O (1998) Product innovation in small and large enterprises. Small Business Economics 10: 31–46

Kleinknecht A, Poot T (1992) Do regions matter for R&D? Regional Studies 26: 221–232

Lawson C, Lorenz E (1999) Collective learning, tacit knowledge and regional innovative capacity. Regional Studies 33: 305–317

Lotz P (1991) Demand side effects on product innovation: The case of medical devices. Copenhagen Business School, Institute of Industrial Research

Martínez A (1992) Regional innovation and small high technology firms in peripheral regions. Small Business Economics 4: 153–168

Martínez A, Urbina O (1998) Estructura y competitividad exterior del sector de productos médico-quirúrgicos en España. Boletin Económico de Información Comercial Española 2580: 25–36

Mitchell W (1991) Using academic technology: Transfer methods and licensing incidence in the commercialization of American diagnostic imaging equipment research: 1954–1988. Research Policy 20: 203–216

Mustar P (1997) How French academics create hi-tech companies: The conditions for success or failure. Science and Public Policy 24: 37–43

Nooteboom B (1994) Innovation and diffusion in small firms: Theory and evidence. Small Business Economics 6: 327–347

Oakey R, Cooper S (1989) High technology industry, agglomeration and the potential for peripherally sited small firms. Regional Studies 23: 347–360

Rothwell R (1991) External networking and innovation in small and medium sized manufacturing firms in Europe. Technovation 11: 93–112

Rothwell R, Zegveld W (1982) Innovation and the small and medium sized firms: Their role in employment and in economic change. Frances Pinter, London

Rothwell R Dodgson M (1994) Innovation and size of firm. In: Dodgson M, Rothwell R (eds) The Handbook of industrial innovation. Edward Elgar, Cheltenham, pp 310–324

Segal N, Quince R, Wicksteed P (1985) The Cambridge phenomenon: The growth of a high-technology industry in a university town. Brand Brothers, Cambridge UK

Shaw B (1998) Innovation and new product development in the UK medical equipment industry. International Journal of Technology Management 15: 433–445

Stohr W (1988) La dimensión espacial de la política tecnológica. Papeles de Economía Española 35: 132–152

Stohr W, Ponighaus R (1992) Towards a data-based evaluation of the Japanese technopolis policy. Regional Studies 26: 605–618

Vaessen P, Keeble D (1995) Growth-oriented SMEs in unfavourable regional environments. Regional Studies 29: 489–505

Van den Berg L, Van Klink A (1996) Health care and the urban economy: The medical complex of Rotterdam as a growth pole? Regional Studies 30: 741–747

Vedovello C (1997) Science parks and university-industry interaction: Geographical proximity between the agents as a driving force. Technovation 17: 491–502

Westhead P (1997) R&D inputs and outputs of technology-based firms located on and off Science Parks. R&D Management 27: 45–62

Index

List of Contributors

Acs, Zoltan J.
University of Baltimore
Baltimore, MD 21201, USA

Alanen, Aku
Statistics Finland
Työpajakatu 13, Helsinki, 00022 Tilastokeskus, Finland

Arita, Tomokazu
Institute of Policy and Planning Sciences, University of Tsukuba
1-1-1, Tennodai, Tsukuba, Ibaraki, 305-8573, Japan

Aslesen, Heidi Wiig
STEP-group
Hammersborg Torg 3, 0179 Oslo, Norway

Camagni, Roberto
Department of Management, Economics and Industrial Engineering, Politecnico di Milano
Piazza Leonardo da Vinci 32, 20133 Milan, Italy

Capello, Roberta
Department of Management, Economics and Industrial Engineering, Politecnico di Milano
Piazza Leonardo da Vinci 32, 20133 Milan, Italy

Ceh, Brian
Department of Geography, Indiana State University
Terre Haute, IN 47409, USA

Fischer, Manfred M.
Department of Economic Geography & Geoinformatics, Vienna University
Rossauer Lände 23/1, A-1090 Vienna, Austria

FitzRoy, Felix
University of St. Andrews
St. Andrews, Fife, KY 169AL, Scotland, UK

Fromhold-Eisebith, Martina
Division Systems Research Technology-Economy-Environment
ARC Seibersdorf Research GmbH, A-2444, Seibersdorf, Austria

Fuchs, Gerhard
Center for Technology Assessment
Industriestr. 5, 70565 Stuttgart, Germany

Groot, Henri L.F. de
Department of Spatial Economics, Free University
De Boelelaan 1105, 1081 HV Amsterdam, The Netherlands

Huovari, Janne
Pellervo Economic Research Institute
Eerikinkatu 28 A, 00180 Helsinki, Finland

Kangasharju, Aki
Government Institute for Economic Research
Hämeentie 3, 00531 Helsinki, Finland

Karlsson, Charlie
Jönköping International Business School, Jönköping University
Gjuterigatan 5, P.O. Box 1026, SE-551 11 Jönköping, Sweden

Klaesson, Johan
Jönköping International Business School, Jönköping University
Gjuterigatan 5, P.O. Box 1026, SE-551 11 Jönköping, Sweden

Kleinknecht, Alfred
Department of Economics, Delft University of Technology
Kanaalweg 2b, 2628 EB Delft, The Netherlands

Kulkarni, Rajendra
School of Public Policy, George Mason University
Fairfax, VA 22030-4444, USA

Lever, William F.
Department of Urban Studies, University of Glasgow
25 Bute Gardens, Glasgow, G12 8RS, Scotland, UK

Masurel, Enno
Economic and Social Institute, Free University
De Boelelaan 1105, 1081 HV Amsterdam, The Netherlands

McCann, Philip
Department of Economics, University of Reading
RG6 6AW, Reading, United Kingdom

Montfort, Kees van
Department of Econometrics, Free University
De Boelelaan 1105, 1081 HV Amsterdam, The Netherlands

Nijkamp, Peter
Department of Spatial Economics, Free University
De Boelelaan 1105, 1081 HV Amsterdam, The Netherlands

Norton, Pat
Movieu.net
2 Guernsey Street, Marblehead, Massachusetts, 01945, USA

Paelinck, Jean
School of Public Policy, George Mason University
Fairfax, VA 22030-4444, USA

Pérez, Manuela P.
Departamento de Economía y Dirección de Empresas, University of Zaragoza
María de Luna 3, 50018 Zaragoza, Spain

Ridder, Geert
Department of Economics, University of Southern California
Kaprielian Hall, Los Angeles, CA 90089, USA

Sánchez, Angel M.
Departamento de Economía y Dirección de Empresas, University of Zaragoza
María de Luna 3, 50018 Zaragoza, Spain

Schartinger, Doris
Division Systems Research Technology-Economy-Environment
ARC Seibersdorf Research GmbH, A-2444, Seibersdorf, Austria

Smith, Ian
University of St. Andrews
St. Andrews, Fife, KY 169AL, Scotland, UK

Stough, Roger
School of Public Policy, George Mason University
Fairfax, VA 22030-4444, USA

Suarez-Villa, Luis
School of Social Ecology, University of California at Irvine
Irvine, California 92697-7075, USA

Varga, Attila
Department of Economic Geography & Geoinformatics, Vienna University
Rossauer Lände 23/1, A-1090 Vienna, Austria

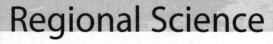

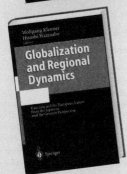